JANE AUSTEN'S REMARKABLE AUNT

PHILADELPHIA HANCOCK

For my dear children,
Timothy, Nicholas and Clare

JANE AUSTEN'S REMARKABLE AUNT

PHILADELPHIA HANCOCK

'A Girl of Genius and Feeling'

JAN MERRIMAN

PEN & SWORD HISTORY

AN IMPRINT OF PEN & SWORD BOOKS LTD.
YORKSHIRE – PHILADELPHIA

First published in Great Britain in 2024 by
PEN AND SWORD HISTORY
An imprint of
Pen & Sword Books Ltd
Yorkshire – Philadelphia

Copyright © Jan Merriman, 2024

ISBN 978 1 03611 185 4

The right of Jan Merriman to be identified as Author of this work has been asserted by her in accordance with the Copyright, Designs and Patents Act 1988.

A CIP catalogue record for this book is available from the British Library.

All rights reserved. No part of this book may be reproduced or transmitted in any form or by any means, electronic or mechanical including photocopying, recording or by any information storage and retrieval system, without permission from the Publisher in writing.

Typeset in Times New Roman 10.5/13 by
SJmagic DESIGN SERVICES, India.
Printed and bound in the UK by CPI Group (UK) Ltd.

Pen & Sword Books Limited incorporates the imprints of Atlas, Archaeology, Aviation, Discovery, Family History, Fiction, History, Maritime, Military, Military Classics, Politics, Select, Transport, True Crime, Air World, Frontline Publishing, Leo Cooper, Remember When, Seaforth Publishing, The Praetorian Press, Wharncliffe Local History, Wharncliffe Transport, Wharncliffe True Crime and White Owl.

For a complete list of Pen & Sword titles please contact
PEN & SWORD BOOKS LIMITED
George House, Units 12 & 13, Beevor Street, Off Pontefract Road,
Barnsley, South Yorkshire, S71 1HN, England
E-mail: enquiries@pen-and-sword.co.uk
Website: www.pen-and-sword.co.uk

or

PEN AND SWORD BOOKS
1950 Lawrence Rd, Havertown, PA 19083, USA
E-mail: uspen-and-sword@casematepublishers.com
Website: www.penandswordbooks.com

Contents

Acknowledgements vi
Introduction vii

Chapter 1	Family and Childhood: 1730–1745 1
Chapter 2	The Milliner's Apprentice: 1745–1751 7
Chapter 3	Off to India: 1751–1752 13
Chapter 4	Marriage and Early Years in India: 1752–1756 25
Chapter 5	Life in Fort St David: 1756–1758 38
Chapter 6	A Meeting in Kasimbazaar: 1759–1761 49
Chapter 7	Motherhood in Calcutta: 1762–1764 62
Chapter 8	Going Home: 1764–1765 70
Chapter 9	Home in England: 1765–1768 77
Chapter 10	Hancock and Hastings Return to India: 1768–1770 ... 93
Chapter 11	'Grass Widow' in London: 1770–1772 108
Chapter 12	Philadelphia, Her Husband and 'The Waistcoat Wars': 1772–1774 118
Chapter 13	Warren Hastings Makes a Gift: 1772–1774 130
Chapter 14	The Death of Mr Hancock: 1775–1776 141
Chapter 15	Off to Europe: 1776–1780 150
Chapter 16	Philadelphia and Eliza's Friend The Comtesse de Tournon: 1780–1782 164
Chapter 17	A Daughter Married: 1782–1784 175
Chapter 18	Off to Guyenne: 1784–1786 181
Chapter 19	Return to England: 1786–1788 195
Chapter 20	Paris, Revolution and Return to England: 1788–1791 ... 206
Chapter 21	Final Days: 1791–1792 212

Endnotes 223
Selected Bibliography 244
Index 251

Acknowledgements

I WOULD LIKE to thank a number of people whose encouragement and assistance have helped me write this biography of Philadelphia Hancock. They include the esteemed Austen family scholar, the late Deirdre Le Faye, the President of the Jane Austen Society of Australia, Susannah Fullerton, researcher Dr Charlotte Mitchell who discovered the true identity of the Reynold's portrait of Philadelphia and her family, Hoare's bank archivist Pamela Hunter, French scholar and friend Beverly Clark who assisted me with translations, my fellow Austen enthusiasts from the Southern Highlands Jane Austen Group, Austen scholar Professor Jocelyn Harris, all my friends and family who had to endure seven years of my obsession with Philadelphia's story, and in particular Amy Jordan, of Pen & Sword Books. Most of all, I must thank my dear Philip for his generous support through it all.

Introduction

ON A COLD February morning in 1752, twenty-three years before Jane Austen was born, her father's sister Philadelphia, or 'Phila' as she was known in the family, left the southern English port of Deal in a small dinghy to go aboard the *Bombay Castle,* a stout East Indiaman anchored in the Downs. She was setting out on a long sea-journey to the Coromandel Coast of India in search of her future. She was 21, single and poor, not unlike a Jane Austen heroine, but it was a much longer and riskier journey than any of her future niece's fictional heroines would undertake. For Philadelphia, though, the chance was worth it.

Her aunt's history had later impressed the young Jane Austen, for in 1792, a few months after Philadelphia's death, the 16-year-old Jane wrote of Cecilia Wynne, a character in her short fiction, *Catharine, or the Bower*, whose experience as an orphaned 'girl of genius and feeling' being 'sent in quest of a husband to Bengal', precisely mirrored that of her recently deceased aunt.[1] Such a connection between author and aunt interested me. Other critics also have noticed this strong reflection of Philadelphia's life in *Catharine, or the Bower* and have commented how 'her heroine voices a bold social critique, the uncharacteristic (for Austen) frankness of which can be attributed to.... [the] family connection to the Anglo-Indian marriage mart through her paternal aunt... and the pervasive negative stereotyping of so-called "speculators" and "adventuresses" like Philadelphia Austen'.[2] Other echoes of her aunt's younger and older life can be seen in such Austen characters as Fanny Price, Mrs Jennings and Mrs Dashwood.

How did this aunt who had provided inspiration for the young Jane manage to make her way in the world? How did the course of her life reflect the lives of other women of her times? What worlds did she move in? What people did she meet? What was her connection to the life and work of her inimitable niece? Little was known about Philadelphia, yet her daughter Eliza, was said to be 'a central figure in Jane Austen's life'.[3] I set myself the task to find out all I could about Philadelphia Austen, her life, her times, the people she knew, and the trajectory of her life.

Jane Austen had two paternal aunts, her father George's two surviving sisters, with Philadelphia older than him by just over a year and a younger sister named Leonora. Not much is known of Leonora, and while she was supported by both brother and sister later in life, it appears Jane Austen's family had little to do with her. Philadelphia's life, however, took a very different turn to either that of her brother or sister; a rather unusual life for a young woman of her class and time. She was not famous, she did not set the world on fire, and in many ways she was unexceptionable, yet her life is worth examining from a distance of almost 300 years for what it tells us about the lives of such women; the kind of young women her niece fictionalised and brought to life in her novels.

Philadelphia Austen was born into a well-established West Kentish family, of the 'middling sort' but she soon found herself orphaned and poor. The plight of the orphan, bereft of the loving comfort and financial provision of parents is a venerable literary trope of eighteenth- and nineteenth-century fiction. Jane Austen's works are no exception. Some of her characters, like Jane Fairfax in *Emma* are genuinely orphaned, others such as Fanny Price in *Mansfield Park* or Harriet Smith in *Emma*, may be only orphan-like, but they all share an impoverished dependence upon others, usually, but not always, relatives, kind or otherwise, and the necessity of these friends and relations to help them find a means of independence; perhaps through appropriate employment, perhaps through marriage.

The grim paragraphs that open Chapter 2 of Volume Two of *Emma*, introducing the background of the enigmatic Jane Fairfax, establish the orphan's predicament.

Jane Fairfax was an orphan, the only child of Mrs Bates' youngest daughter.

> The marriage of Lieut. Fairfax, of the -------- regiment of infantry, and Miss Jane Bates, had had its day of fame and pleasure, hope and interest; but nothing now remained of it, save the melancholy remembrance of him dying in action abroad – of his widow sinking under consumption and grief soon afterwards – and this girl.[4]

The final words, 'and this girl', invite the thought of what is to be done with 'this girl'. It suggests that even from the tenderest age she is a burden, an expense, an inconvenience to someone. Jane Fairfax is fortunate. She is raised by her fond but poor widowed grandmother Mrs Bates and her maiden aunt Miss Bates until, by the age of 9, an opportunity comes for Jane to be taken

Introduction

up by Colonel Campbell, a well-to-do army friend of her late father, and she is taken to a world of status and comfort, and all the material and educational benefits it can supply, as a much-loved companion to the colonel's daughter. Jane Fairfax comes to be almost a second daughter to the Campbells. But there is no dowry for Jane, no fortunate marriage prospect in sight and when the daughter is married and Jane comes of age, it is time for her to make her own way in the world and find a 'means of respectable subsistence hereafter'.[5] Colonel Campbell hopes that Jane's excellent education will fit her to become a governess.

The orphaned Philadelphia had to pursue a life away from the protective ties of parents and later also of a husband, and to find those elusive goals of eighteenth-century womanhood as portrayed in Austen's fiction: respect, independence and financial security. Hers, is an untypical story of eighteenth-century womankind, framed by the confines of women's lives of that time and it gives an opportunity to explore those times from the locus of one particular woman.

In his memoir of Jane Austen, written over fifty years after her death, her nephew James Edward Austen-Leigh, 'the youngest of the mourners [who] attended the funeral of my dear Aunt Jane in Winchester Cathedral' wrote that 'of events her life was singularly barren'.[6] It is not clear what he actually meant by 'events', but the notion that there was something uniquely empty about Jane Austen's life is overstated. But if we take Austen-Leigh's notion of a life of 'events' as being one of major personal difficulties being overcome, challenging journeys undertaken, or of connections to the great public affairs and personalities of the time, then Jane Austen's Aunt Philadelphia would certainly fit the bill for a life strikingly less 'barren' of events.

To try and tell the story of Philadelphia Austen's life, and to construct a frame of wider contemporary reference around the experiences of her life, has been an interesting but challenging task. Exploring what little records there are of both Philadelphia's life and the story of women's lives at all of that period recalls Anne Elliot's words to Captain Harville in *Persuasion*. Anne tells him that 'men have every advantage of us [women] in telling their own story. Education has been theirs in so much higher degree; the pen has been in their hands'.[7]

While teasing out the salient facts of Philadelphia's life, I have been struck by the neglect of the story of women's lives, the implicit denigration of the validity of their experiences and of how little their lives mattered in recorded history. Her story has not been easy to construct. Most biographies of women who were neither queen nor courtesan at this time, struggle to draw upon official documents, so personal letters, diaries and journals are the usual source for women's histories. But very few of Philadelphia's letters have come down to us. She gets a mention here and there in the correspondence of others, but they are scant. The major sources of information are the copies of her husband's letters to her from India, preserved in his letter book held among the Hastings Papers in the British Library, published in part in R.A. Austen-Leigh's *Austen Papers* in 1904 and the letters of her daughter Eliza to her cousin Phylly Walter, documented in full in Deirdre Le Faye's 2002 work *Jane Austen's 'Outlandish Cousin': The Life and Letters of Eliza de Feuillide*.

But telling Philadelphia's story is worth the effort, as it throws significant light on how a woman like Philadelphia Austen, given her circumstances, sought to more than just survive, but to prosper. It also exemplifies how little agency such women had in the control of their destinies. This too is a theme threaded throughout Jane Austen's fiction. One thinks of the Bennet sisters in *Pride and Prejudice*, caught in a legal patriarchal trap that essentially disinherits them from any real prospect of a comfortable marriage within their society, or of Mrs Dashwood in *Sense and Sensibility* whose capacity to provide a home and income sufficient to sustain her family is swept away with the untimely death of her husband. Or an intelligent, sensible young woman of seven-and-twenty, like Charlotte Lucas in *Pride and Prejudice* who sees nothing but marriage to the appalling Mr Collins, Elizabeth Bennet's rejected suitor, as offering the possibility of some purposeful life. Again the words of Anne Elliot resonate here when she talks of the way women's capacity to act is so circumscribed.

> We cannot help ourselves. We live at home, quiet, confined, and our feelings prey upon us. You are forced on exertion. You have always a profession, pursuits, business of some sort or other to take you back into the world.[8]

The traces left of Philadelphia's life may be small but they are spread large across England, India and France. She appears modest in her aspirations, yet was prepared to take great risks to move far out of that provincial milieu which must have seemed her birthright. There are aspects of her life that challenge conventional ideas of eighteenth-century respectable middle-class women. She also met some exceptional people in her life, whose stories in themselves are of lively interest.

Of particular fascination is the intriguing connection she had with Warren Hastings, orphaned and poor, but a brilliant scholar who had gone out to India as an East India Company (EIC) 'servant', as they were called, at 17, and became the first governor general of Bengal and chief of all the company's Indian settlements. Philadelphia and Hastings' close connection began in Bengal in 1759 and continued over the decades, until Philadelphia's death. The closeness of their relationship has often been either ignored or dismissed as merely an example of Hastings' characteristic loyalty and generosity to the

Introduction

wife of an old friend and business partner. But to look into it deeply, is to reveal that there is clearly much more to it than that. Were they once lovers? Was her daughter actually Hastings' child? His only surviving child, in fact. Much of the persuasive evidence I have assembled and examine here, explores the extent of Philadelphia's deep affection for Hastings and his abiding loyalty to her, whom he called, 'my dear and ever-valued friend'.[9]

Philadelphia's story shows the progress of her life from her provincial childhood, then orphaned little girl, her milliner's apprenticeship in Covent Garden, the East India Company 'bride', and then wife to an absent husband and mother to a much-loved child, the more famous Eliza de Feuillide whom, when Philadelphia is widowed, she takes to France where they live for many years mixing with the great and perhaps not so good. We journey from the small town of Tonbridge in Kent, to London, to India, to France and finally back to London. Along the way, Philadelphia's journey takes in exotic places and interesting people. It is a journey through an eighteenth-century world rather different from her novelist niece's world, but nevertheless a world Philadelphia and her daughter brought to Jane. This book aims to find a place for the neglected story of Philadelphia Hancock, described in her young niece's tale, *Catharine, or the Bower*, as 'a girl of genius and feeling', in Jane Austen's wider family story.

Chapter 1

Family and Childhood
1730–1745

Catharine had the misfortune, as many heroines have had before her, of losing her parents when she was very young...
Catharine, or The Bower, p. 203

PHILADELPHIA WAS BORN on 9 May 1730 and baptised on 15 May 1730 in Tonbridge in Kent.[1] She was the second child born to William Austen and his wife, Rebecca Walter (née Hampson). William was a surgeon practising in Tonbridge, a market town on the Medway River about 28 miles south-east of London in the heart of West Kent. Philadelphia's parents were married in 1728 when he was 26 and his wife a young widow of similar age with a 6-year-old son. An unusual aspect of Philadelphia's parents' marriage was that it did not take place in their local parish church in Tonbridge, but in London in the 'Liberty of The Fleet', the term referred to marriages performed both in and near the London debtor's prison, called The Fleet, by clerics who had the misfortune to find themselves confined to The Fleet as debtors.[2]

One wonders why a respectable surgeon and a widow's marriage did not take place in the local Tonbridge Parish Church of St Peter and St Paul, where they ultimately came to be buried. The reasons for the popularity of Fleet marriages were that they could be done quickly, did not disrupt the everyday activities of the participants, and the marriage could be kept secret from family and friends. Fleet marriages were said to be popular with couples from Kent and Surrey. The motive may have been to do with Rebecca's financial status. Although she was the daughter of a baronet, she had little to contribute financially to the marriage. William's aunt, Mary Tilden, thought that her nephew could have made a more fortuitous marriage.[3] Another more obvious reason for the Fleet marriage might be found in the date of their first child's baptism, 14 September 1728, a scant eight months after their marriage.

Philadelphia's mother was the eldest of four daughters of Sir George Hampson Bt., MD, a physician.[4] The widowed Rebecca's first husband was William Walter, also a 'doctor of physik', who had died at the age of 29, leaving Rebecca with one surviving child, a son, William Hampson Walter.[5]

Of the children born to Rebecca and William Austen, the first was a girl called Hampson who died just before her 2nd birthday. Philadelphia was next, then George, Jane Austen's father, born one year later on 1 May 1731. The last child was Leonora, born in February of 1733. Rebecca had previously had three children by her first husband, but only one had survived. Rebecca herself died just a few weeks after the birth of Leonora. Three years after Rebecca's death, Philadelphia's father married Susanna Kelk, then aged 49. Alas, less than two years after their marriage, William Austen also died. The children were left orphaned in the care of their stepmother. But not for long.

Susannah Kelk has something of a poor reputation in the Austen family history. Described in Austen-Leigh's memoir as being someone of whom little was known, and in Deirdre Le Faye's account, *A Family Record*, an enlarged and revised edition of William and Richard Arthur Austen-Leigh's original 1918 book, Susannah was one who had no legal responsibility nor felt any moral obligation to look after her late husband's children.

A walk up Tonbridge High Street today reveals a handsome porticoed three-storied building known as Ferox Hall. It plays a significant role in the story of Susannah Kelk and casts another perspective on this depiction of the negligent stepmother.

Susannah was born in 1687, one of thirteen children of a cloth-maker, James Kelk, and his wife Anne Duke, in Cornhill in London. At some point three of their daughters, including Susannah, were sent from London to live with their mother's sister Sarah in Tonbridge.[6] The girls' aunt Sarah had married well to Mr John Danvers, the owner of Ferox Hall and the significant estate attached to it. The elder sisters, Anne and Mary, married but Susannah remained single. Anne married a reverend, Mr Elton, and lived in Tunbridge Wells, while Mary married George Hooper, whose son, another George Hooper, married Elizabeth Austen, William Austen's sister. With her aunt's death, Susannah married the now widowed William Austen, her neighbour of many years, and her relative by marriage. Susannah then was widowed herself after she had been married to William Austen a mere eighteen months. She brought some property but no children to the marriage, and she was a woman over 50 at the time of her husband's death. She had no children of her own, and little opportunity to have developed much attachment to these children, aged 7, 6 and 5, one supposes. Furthermore, what means would she have had to maintain and educate them? In their marriage settlement, William had given her a life interest in his house and lands till her death, when they would pass to his children. She herself had brought into the marriage eleven acres of land in Tonbridge that eventually went to George Austen.

In their father's will, the children were to be given up to the care of their uncles, Francis and Stephen. Francis, was a lawyer and a bachelor and lived in Sevenoaks and Stephen was married, with one child and lived in London. Stephen Austen was in business as a bookseller and stationer with premises by St Paul's Churchyard in London, dealing in bibles and medical books at the sign of the 'Angel and Bible'.[7]

At the age of 10, and assisted financially by Uncle Francis, George returned to Tonbridge to live with his aunt Betty Hooper to attend Tonbridge Grammar School. The youngest child, Leonora, remained with Stephen and his wife, and continued to live with that family for the rest of her life, even when her uncle died and her aunt remarried. But what happened to Philadelphia in her childhood years after the death of her father? That proves difficult to ascertain with any certainty, but she may not have stayed long in Uncle Stephen's household but was sent to live with relatives of her mother's until she turned 15. Certainly, the degree to which Philadelphia remained close throughout her life to these maternal cousins strongly indicates that she did. These were the Freeman, Cure and Payne families; all well-to-do and well-connected. They come up regularly in Philadelphia's story.

Philadelphia's mother, Rebecca Hampson, had a brother and three younger sisters. Her brother was Sir George Hampson and her sisters were, Elizabeth, Jane and Catherine Margaret. They all married well.

Elizabeth's husband was George Cure, an upholsterer and furniture maker in the Haymarket in London. His entry in the *Dictionary of English Furniture Makers* declares 'he operated a very substantial business… and that his commissions were almost exclusively with Frederick Louis, Prince of Wales'.[8] Elizabeth Cure died childless in the same year as Philadelphia's mother died. Her widowed husband married again, this time to Catherine Payne, a relative of the husband of Philadelphia's mother's youngest sister Jane. They had two sons, George Cure and Capel Cure.

Jane Hampson had married a Gloucester alderman and mercer, Capel Payne and had two children, a son George and a daughter Catherine. The family were prosperous and well-connected. Their daughter Catherine had sufficient court associations, to become one of the Women of the Bedchamber to the then Princess of Wales.

Philadelphia's Payne cousin George was educated at Oxford and was a barrister-at-law of the Inner Temple and rose to become a 'bencher' i.e. a judge, with a fine house at Brooklands near Weybridge in Surrey. He married and had five children. At one point he was appointed ambassador to the Emperor of Morocco. He was also a friend of Warren Hastings and one of his daughters, Maria, with whom Philadelphia's daughter Eliza was very friendly, lived in later life as companion to Hastings' wife Marian.

The youngest of Rebecca's sisters, Catherine Margaret, married Cope Freeman, a wealthy gentleman with plantations in the West Indies, like Sir Thomas Bertram of *Mansfield Park*. They had five children, one surviving son, John Cope, and three daughters close in age to Philadelphia. The girls were Mary Clementina, known as 'Molly', Stella Frances and Catherine Margaretta. Molly never married, Stella married an elderly admiral later in life, and is mentioned by Jane Austen in a letter to Cassandra in February 1813.[9] The youngest sister, Catherine Margaretta married twice, once at 16 to Charles Stanhope of Westminster and when widowed to the Rev. Mr John Price-Jones, who had been the vicar of Yateley in Hampshire. We hear more of her only child, Philip Dormer Stanhope, who turned out a bad lot and came later to plague Philadelphia's husband in India.

Philadelphia's four Freeman cousins were orphaned when their parents died at sea while returning from the West Indies, leaving the daughters to the charge of Jane Payne and his son's guardianship to George Cure. So it is possible to say that if the young Philadelphia did go to live with her maternal relatives, then it was her cousins she lived with.

A well-to-do West Indies plantation and slave owning family, the Freemans were not unlike the Bertrams of *Mansfield Park*. Philadelphia's cousin, John Cope, was a wealthy young man. He was 'listed in the Jamaican Quit Rent books for 1754 as the owner of 1194 acres of land in St Catharine, 1000 acres in St James's and 2511 acres in St John, total 4705 acres'.[10] There is similarity between the young Philadelphia's fate and that of the fictional Fanny Price and her Bertram cousins. If Philadelphia did go to live with her Freeman cousins, this would have brought her in close contact with her Payne family cousins as well.

So perhaps living with her cousins not dissimilar in age and personal circumstances but significantly better off, may not have been such a bad option for the orphaned Philadelphia. In later life, Philadelphia's husband writes, in a letter to her from Calcutta on 6 December 1771, that 'he held himself under great obligation to Mr Freeman, the younger, for the kindness he had shown Philadelphia in the former part of her life', and that his regard for her cousin 'Molly' Freeman 'took its origin from what you had told me of her kind Behaviour to you when your Situations were different'.[11]

Philadelphia's brother George had some privilege, as the only son, in gaining a good education that fitted him out for a life that promised a possible living in the church and of making a home for himself and a family of his own. Leonora stayed on as a dependent for the rest of her life with Uncle Stephen's family in London. But Philadelphia's became a peripatetic life and she never really had a permanent home of her own; a place where she belonged. So it is comforting to know that the young Philadelphia, separated from her brother and sister, at least had some 'kindness' shown to her. One is reminded again of lonely little Fanny Price in *Mansfield Park* and the kindness shown to her when she was found one morning by her cousin Edmund, the youngest of the sons, sitting crying on the stairs.

'My dear little cousin', said he with all the gentleness of an excellent nature, 'what can be the matter?' And sitting down by her was at great pains to overcome her shame in being so surprised and persuade her to speak openly.[12]

That Philadelphia received an adequate education is evident from the two letters written by her that still exist. They are well written. She writes fluently and correctly in a formal but quite personal and natural style. Her education was most likely to have been with her Freeman female cousins when she lived with them in their home, under a governess and probably a tutor or two.

The kind of education available to girls of Philadelphia's social class and financial circumstances was limited and, most commonly, home-based. While there was some basic schooling, mostly of the '3 Rs' kind, girls' education on the whole emphasised the moral and social attributes and accomplishments that would fit them as appropriate wives to men similarly socially positioned.[13] It also included needlework and the practical aspects of organising domestic arrangements such as supervising food provision, managing servants, and caring for the health and well-being of family members.

Philadelphia's education also would have included the acquisition of accomplishments. But probably not too many. We have some insight into how Jane Austen herself might have viewed the importance of 'accomplishments' in a young woman's education from the Netherfield drawing room encounter in *Pride and Prejudice* when Elizabeth Bennet is required to stay on at the Bingley household to care for her ill sister, Jane. It is an early episode in the novel that is critical to the development of Darcy's attraction to Elizabeth, which clearly has nothing to do with the level of Elizabeth's 'accomplishments'.

Miss Bingley launches into ecstasies over Mr Darcy's sister's 'accomplishments' and the rather dim Mr Bingley joins in, marvelling over the way all young ladies are so accomplished. 'They all paint tables, cover screens and net purses.... and I am sure I never heard of a lady being spoken of for the first time, without being informed that she was very accomplished'.[14] Darcy begs to differ, maintaining that he knows very few really accomplished women. His too-eager acolyte Miss Bingley jumps in with a list of required accomplishments to add to Mr Bingley's list.

> A woman must have a thorough knowledge of music, singing, drawing, dancing and the modern languages ... she must possess a certain something in her air and her manner of walking, the tone of her voice, her address and expression ...[15]

But Darcy claims that a truly accomplished woman must not only 'possess' all these conventional attributes of accomplishment but also demonstrate a mind of considerable 'improvement' formed by 'extensive reading'. Elizabeth counters mockingly that if that is his definition of an accomplished woman, she rather wonders that he knows any at all. Is this then an argument from Austen that you cannot have both; develop an educated, cultivated mind and also acquire, or even want to acquire, the artifices of a young woman well-prepared for the marriage market?

In the eighteenth century, accomplishments were seen as critical to a girl's success in attracting the interest of a future husband. Accomplishments were a set of elements of performance that allowed a young woman to display herself in an alluring way to a young man, to invite his admiration. Accomplishments could also embrace knowledge that was considered polite and appropriate to a gently-born female to allow her to take her place in the conversation of an elegant drawing room. Note that Mr Darcy maintains that serious improvement of the mind for a young woman could only be acquired through 'extensive reading', not through any higher level of formal schooling. This acceptable knowledge could have included the study of French or Italian but it was not the kind of learning that was the province of men: 'classical and Biblical languages, analytical and scientific discourse, controversial writing, theology and Mathematics'.[16] Such learning, it was feared, would coarsen a young woman, masculinise her and put her completely out of the marriage market. In the later eighteenth century Mary Wollstonecraft would argue in *A Vindication of the Rights of Woman* that denying women the right to a more substantial education infantilised them and left them unnecessarily dependent on men. As was often the case, however, as with Philadelphia in her adulthood, or the fictional Mrs Dashwood in *Sense and Sensibility*, despite achieving the imposed and formalised dependence of marriage, women were nevertheless often left high and dry, through widowhood or desertion, and had to draw on their own resources as best they could to attempt to build a decent life for themselves and their children despite the limitations of their education.

For Philadelphia, though, whatever her education had been, and the childhood that she had shared with her maternal relatives, it was to end when she turned 15. It was time for her to receive another 'education', to move to London, to an apprenticeship in a trade, appropriate to a young woman and one that might allow her an opportunity to earn her own living and perhaps ultimately improve her marriage prospects. A very different life for Philadelphia was now before her: the world of work. And that place of work would be in the thriving, bustling and disreputable area on the edge of the emerging West End of London, Covent Garden.

Chapter 2

The Milliner's Apprentice
1745–1751

By giving her an education, he hoped to be supplying the means of a respectable subsistence thereafter.

Emma, p. 154

BY THE MID eighteenth century, the rapid expansion of the fresh fruit and vegetable market in Covent Garden and the arrival of theatres, coffee houses and other houses of lesser repute had been enough to drive the former aristocratic occupants of the area west to more salubrious domains. By day it was a thriving centre of commerce, by night it was thronged with theatre-goers and pleasure-seekers. The former houses of the upper classes were now bookshops, milliners, tailors, haberdashers, taverns and coffee houses, as well as gambling houses, drinking dens and, inevitably, brothels. Young people flocked to London from the countryside in search of work and some ended up in Covent Garden where there was work aplenty, respectable or otherwise.

In May of 1745 Philadelphia turned 15, old enough to be apprenticed, and whoever was making the decisions on her future, it was clear she now had to make her own way in the world. Her brother George at 14 was still at school in Tonbridge and proving himself a scholar and on his way to a scholarship to Oxford. Their sister Leonora was 12 and still living with Uncle Stephen, the bookseller's family in London. She was later called 'poor' Leonora by Philadelphia's husband and one wonders why she deserved that epithet. And while Philadelphia and George remained close to each other and gave financial support to their younger sister, it seems the rest of George Austen's family had little to do with their Aunt Leonora. Philadelphia's husband's letters from India, however, show that Philadelphia kept in contact with her sister and continued to take an interest in her well-being.

It may be that the Austen side of the family took charge of Philadelphia's immediate future now, because there are echoes of the way in which her father William and her four uncles were provided for by their widowed mother, in Philadelphia's treatment. Influential relatives of her grandfather, John Austen IV, were important in assisting these fatherless young boys with the connections needed to be well-apprenticed when they reached the eligible age. Philadelphia's father William was apprenticed to the surgeon William Ellis, a close friend of his mother's brother, Robert Weller. While the profession of surgeon did not have the status of a physician, Ellis, whose practice was in Woolwich, was surgeon to the household of the then Prince of Wales. The fee paid was substantial, over £115. Philadelphia's Uncle Francis became a wealthy lawyer, an agent to the aristocratic Sackville family of Knole, and enhanced his fortune by marrying two wealthy widows. He had been apprenticed to an attorney, George Tilden of St Clements Inn, who was related to the aforementioned aunt, Mary Tilden.[1] A millinery apprenticeship would not have been considered a step down socially within the family, but a means by which Philadelphia could earn a living.

So at 15, Philadelphia was found a position that could provide for her needs now and for a future beyond penury and dependence. Her options were limited. From the miniature we have of her, it is clear that she was an attractive young woman and she seems to have shared the intelligence, vivacity and drive that characterised her brother George. But whatever her personal charms, without a significant dowry, a marriage of fortune was unlikely.

As with the fictional Jane Fairfax, there was hope, I surmise, that her male relatives could provide Philadelphia with the 'means of respectable subsistence hereafter'.[2] Either her Freeman cousin or her Uncle Francis, who had been charged, along with Uncle Stephen, in her father's will with the education of his brother's orphaned children (or perhaps it involved both cousin and uncle), did what Philadelphia's grandmother, the widowed Elizabeth Austen had done for her four sons, and paid a premium for an apprenticeship for Philadelphia. One of the few established apprenticeships for women was as a milliner. Her apprenticeship cost £45 and was paid to a milliner, Mrs Hester Cole, of Russell Street, Covent Garden, for the term of five years. Mrs Cole had inherited the business from her husband Christopher Cole. We know these details because researcher, Robin Vick, Claire Tomalin tells us, found the very entry in the Apprentices Register in the Public Record Office.[3]

The choice of master or mistress was an important one, involving handing over a substantial sum of money and while in essence a business contract, it was nevertheless giving over the care and provision of a 15-year-old female family member to an adult outside the family. As in most matters of importance in those times, the decision usually involved some family connection where possible. Was there a family link here? Probably. As we have already seen, this was the case with her uncles' apprenticeships. I conjecture the connection may have been the prosperous upholsterer and furniture maker to the Prince of Wales, George Cure who had been married to one of Philadelphia's maternal aunts. His upholstery premises were also in the West End, in the Haymarket not far from Covent Garden.

The Cure family relationship was kept up in the next generation of Austens. In a letter from Jane to her sister Cassandra in 1811, we read of a 'Mr Cure' being one of the guests attending a large evening party held by Philadelphia's daughter Eliza at the time when she was married to her cousin, Henry Austen and living in fine style in Sloane Street, Chelsea.[4]

Tomalin calls Philadelphia's position as a milliner's apprentice as 'only on the border of respectability' and 'To be described as a little milliner carried a suggestion of something altogether more dubious.'[5] The idea that Philadelphia's millinery apprenticeship was some kind of demeaning secret, never to be mentioned in the family is worth exploring, as is the view that eighteenth-century millinery shops were fronts for bawdy houses.

Research done by Robin Vick, mentioned by Tomalin, draws attention to a peculiar coincidence in that the name and location of Philadelphia's new mistress are the same as a fictional millinery shop that is the cover for a brothel in the infamous pornographic work by John Cleland, *Fanny Hill*.[6] It was published in 1748–49, during the period of Philadelphia's apprenticeship. To set the illicit premises in Covent Garden at that time was to be expected. It was a well-established area of prostitution throughout the eighteenth century. But prostitution was essentially Covent Garden's night-time business, centred on the theatres and taverns in and around Drury Lane but by day Covent Garden was a booming retail centre. The choice of the name of a real milliner for his fiction was either Cleland's idea of a joke or to give verisimilitude to his work. It does not give any credence to the premises of Philadelphia's mistress, Hester Cole being anything more than a well-situated milliners. That Hester Cole continued to carry on the successful business of her late husband suggests that her flourishing business was just that: a milliners, and one of hundreds of such businesses run by women in eighteenth-century London.

Philadelphia, really little more than a child, was now sent to London to live a life in an area of some notoriety. It may have been a struggle to maintain her respectability in such an environment, but there was nothing inherently 'unrespectable' about a millinery apprenticeship. However, the eighteenth-century female apprenticeship story is a complex one, and like much of women's work history has been little told until recently.

Research undertaken by Amy Louise Erikson, examining the City of London livery company records in order to throw light on the role of women in the trades of these companies in the first half of the eighteenth century, shows that while women were not numerous in the trades in general, they had a significant presence in the millinery trade, which embraced many more aspects of making apparel items than just hats.[7] There were good livings to be made by respectable women, either married, widowed or single, who ran businesses of sufficient profit to warrant employing three or four apprentices and command substantial premiums. 'At the top end of the business a milliner might run her own shop with many employees and a prestigious clientele'.[8]

There is no mention in any of the early Austen family histories of Philadelphia's millinery apprenticeship, but the profile of the average apprentice Erikson provides fits closely to Philadelphia's circumstances in life. A large number of girls from gentry and professional families throughout England were apprenticed as milliners as a means for a young woman to acquire a skilled occupation and also increase her chances of marriage.

> the hallmarks of millinery apprenticeships, that is: girls of gentry, clerical, professional or prosperous trade paternity, often from outside London, apprenticed with relatively high premiums to a married master and mistress or to a mistress alone.[9]

While there were risks in surrendering country-raised daughters to a city apprenticeship, many parents clearly considered it a worthwhile option. The evidence suggests a parental dual strategy for daughters: occupational training followed by marriage. Employment was likely to be a more continuous part of their life than marriage, sustaining them whenever marriage failed, for whatever reason.

The term millinery in the eighteenth century was derived from 'Millaners, merchants from the Italian city of Milan, who travelled to northern Europe trading in silks, ribbons, braids, ornaments, and general finery'.[10] An interesting example provided by Erikson of what milliners made and sold comes from the sisters of the artist/engraver William Hogarth:

> Milliners Mary and Anne Hogarth had a business card engraved in 1730 by their brother William Hogarth, which illustrated a wider range of products than that envisaged by the OED, including children's as well as women's clothing, men's waistcoats, and fabrics for both clothing and upholstery: ye best and most fashionable ready-made frocks, sutes of fustian, ticken and holland, stript dimmity and flannel wastcoats, blue and canvas frocks, and bluecoat boys dra/rs, likewise fustians, tickens, hollands, white stript dimmitys, white & stript flannels in the piece. By Wholesale or retale at reasonable rates.[11]

The Milliner's Apprentice: 1745–1751

That the male gaze sexualised so-called 'little milliners', both in words and image, such as in *Fanny Hill* and the engraving called *The Morning Ramble or The Milliner's Shop* where amongst the items illustrated are 'love' and 'coxcombe', is not surprising given that millinery was a trade dominated by women in the world of men; a place where women were to be found in numbers was always going to be a target for male sexual predations and fantasies.

Philadelphia's life as a millinery apprentice was obviously not one of leisure or independence. An apprentice lived and worked on the premises and was entirely reliant on their mistress. But Covent Garden must at least have been a lively place in which to live and Philadelphia, as far as we know, remained at Mrs Cole's in Russell Street for at least her full five-year term, and fulfilled her obligations to her mistress. She may have remained there until she reached her majority in 1751.

What did those years mean to Philadelphia? Was it all drudgery, as Deirdre Le Faye suggests 'crouched over... work-tables for excessively long hours in cramped air-less back rooms'?[12] All women did needlework, just called 'work' at that time and it certainly wasn't the 'maid-of-all-work' kind of drudgery of scrubbing floors and fireplaces. It was part of the world of fashion and fine fabrics, which must have had some appeal. While the back-rooms were cramped, the shops themselves were usually well-presented, as were the milliners who served the customers. If her mistress was kind enough, considerate and fair, then for an orphaned girl who could not have even remembered her own mother, that may have been a comfort. There were also other young women who shared Philadelphia's life at Mrs Coles. They may have offered her friendship and help in difficult times. Much later in her only surviving letter to Warren Hastings, from Paris in March 1780, Philadelphia wrote of the 'many mortifying and disagreeable Events in my Life' but I think it is unlikely that becoming a millinery apprentice was one of them.[13] Many years on, the mature Philadelphia demonstrates a keen desire to be out and about, and in the bustling West End there were plenty of diversions close at hand for the young Philadelphia. But perhaps I am putting too much sparkle on her life as a milliner's apprentice, though she at least gained skills in needlecraft that were not without application and perhaps even enjoyment in later life. And they could well have given her the 'means of respectable subsistence', while also as Erikson points out, improve her marriage prospects.

But whatever the delights or miseries or future prospects, the life of a milliner in Covent Garden might have held for Philadelphia, she came to the end of her apprenticeship in 1750. In May of that year Philadelphia turned 20. On completion of her apprenticeship she may have continued on in employment with Mrs Cole or elsewhere at another establishment in London, or she may have lived with relatives either in London or Kent. Under the terms of her father's will when all of his children reached the age of 20, they were entitled to a one-third share of his estate, and perhaps a share went to Philadelphia at this time.

After reaching her majority in May 1751, however, she soon embarked on a very different future for herself. Philadelphia took her chances on a long sea-voyage to seek another viable prospect in the mid-eighteenth century for an attractive young British woman from a respectable family; to travel to India and find a suitable husband in the employ of the Honourable East India Company. This was to lead to a remarkably different, though much riskier future for Philadelphia from that of her scholarly brother George, now safely ensconced in Oxford with a scholarship place from his Tonbridge School. Austens always had a culture, it appears, of pushing on to gain a foothold in the world. George was doing it his way through his capacity for scholarship, Philadelphia had to find another way. She was off to India.

Chapter 3

Off to India
1751–1752

---

to a girl of any delicacy, the voyage in itself since the object of it is so universally known, is a punishment that needs no other to make it very severe.

Catharine, or The Bower, p. 218

BY THE LATE nineteenth century, a single woman travelling out to India seeking marriage had become derogatively known as part of 'the fishing fleet', but in Philadelphia's time, it was still a fairly rare undertaking. The young women who made this challenging journey, according to Ann de Courcy in her book *The Fishing Fleet: Husband-Hunting in the Raj* (2012) were:

> Sometimes adventuresses, sometimes they were sent out by the East India Company (EIC), sometimes they were gently born but without family or financial support at home, and with little possibility of that elusive prospect, the advantageous marriage.[1]

Most of the young women who went out to India had connections there through family and friends. Some young women had been sent back to England as children to stay with relatives while their parents continued in India serving the Company. On reaching marriageable age, they returned to India, even when their parents were no longer there. Many had brothers and cousins serving the EIC, or female relatives married to EIC 'servants'. And some of these young women were very young indeed, 15 and 16, as was the case of two young women we shall hear more of later: Margaret Maskelyne, who became Lady Clive, and her cousin, Jenny Kelsall.

But in 1751, Philadelphia, at 21, was no child. Permission, though, was needed from the East India Company Court of Directors. It would have been virtually impossible for a single young woman even to have been admitted on board an EIC ship by the captain without Company permission, and under the protection of a responsible older woman.

The records of the East India Company show that in November 1751, Philadelphia, along with another young lady with the same sureties, a Mary Elliot, petitioned the Court of Directors for leave to travel to India on the *Bombay Castle* to join 'friends' in Fort St David on the Coramandel Coast in the Madras presidency of the EIC.[2] Philadelphia's and Mary Elliot's sureties were London merchants James Adams and John Lardner. Her co-petitioner, Mary Elliot, is assumed to have already been a friend of Philadelphia's and they were going out to India together. It would be an adventure!

So what happened to Philadelphia's co-petitioner, Mary Elliot? It is difficult to tell. She seems to have sailed with Philadelphia on the *Bombay Castle,* if we are to accept the evidence of a letter to Robert Clive, written by his friend back in London, Charles Boddam, giving him the news on the travellers who were going out on the latest East Indiaman. He draws particular attention to the women who were going out and gives some details including their names:

> There are eleven young ladies coming out, viz. Mrs Keene and Mrs Edwards, two young ladies to Mrs Ackell, Miss Eliot [sic] and Miss Austin [sic], Miss Roots, a Scotch lady, and a prodigious fine girl it's said, and Miss Maskelyne, your friend's sister. The others I have not heard the names of, but however I would advise you to guard your heart well against them … these beauties will have a wonderful effect on you.[3]

This letter was dated May 1752, some months after the *Bombay Castle* had set out. But there is no further record of what happened to Mary Elliot. Did Mary in fact not sail on the ship, but decided to remain in London? It is unlikely, given that Boddam writes his letter four months after the *Bombay Castle*'s departure and lists Mary Elliot's name specifically along with Philadelphia's as 'two young ladies to Mrs Ackell'. Mrs Ackell was presumably to be their host on arrival in India, but anything more about her I have been unable to discover. If Philadelphia was travelling out with a definite marriage prospect in mind, was Mary Elliot in a similar situation? Perhaps, but we simply do not know.

In the early twentieth-century, an alternative life for Mary Elliot was constructed. It stemmed initially from doubt amongst early biographers as to just who Warren Hastings' first wife was. Sydney C. Grier, the nom de plume of the nineteenth-century novelist Hilda Caroline Gregg, conjectured in an appendix to her book, *The Letters of Warren Hastings to his Wife*, that his first wife, Mrs Mary Buchanan, widow of a Captain John Buchanan, whom Hastings had known, and who died in the so-called 'Black Hole of Calcutta', was in fact Philadelphia Austen's fellow petitioner and friend Mary Elliot. There is more to say about this conjecture of Grier's later, but it is unconvincing and requires an elaborate imagining of unknown events in Mary Elliot's life, for which there is no evidence.

But back in England in 1751, travel to India was not even then an unknown path for a young woman to take in search of a husband. As early as 1668 the Court of Directors of the EIC had advertised for 'single women and maids, related to the soldiers or others … shall be willing to go to Bombay' and in that early period 'the company paid the passage to India of willing women'.[4] In 1671 the company paid for twenty British women to go out to Bombay. They were paid a considerable allowance for a year, during which time it was anticipated that they married with the approval of the company. If they didn't marry they were expected to return to Britain.

The Company policy of paying young single women to go out to India had died out by the end of the eighteenth century. It is impossible to know what other rationale than family interest or pressure to find a suitable husband drove Philadelphia's decision to leave England and travel alone to India to stay with 'friends'. Or was there too, a sense of adventure?

It is not clear who paid for Philadelphia's passage. Her Uncle Francis, by the 1750s a wealthy and well-connected lawyer, must have had some role arranging for Philadelphia a possible marriage to one of his clients now in India, Tysoe Saul Hancock, a surgeon of the East India Company, who in 1751 had just been appointed as a surgeon in Fort St David. He was single, respectable and from a Kent family background, like the Austens. Although his income as a surgeon would have been modest, he would have had prospects of wealth as a trader, and at 30 and having lived in India for some years already, was understandably in want of a wife.

Other marriage prospects would have eluded Philadelphia despite her personal appeal. In England in the mid-eighteenth century, women outnumbered men of marriageable age, but in India, European women were very few and far between. So the opportunity for a reasonably appealing young woman, though without any kind of fortune, was an excellent one. Amongst the single young women arriving in India at that time, Philadelphia would have been marked out as attractive, vivacious and elegant, I think. We have a number of personal descriptions of Philadelphia's character and qualities from a variety of sources beyond just the family. But what other connections did she have in Fort St David except for this client of her uncle? None it seems. Philadelphia most likely went out to Fort St David with the matter settled and the choice of husband made.

A single woman going out to India without any connections could challenge her respectability. Among the letters of Philadelphia's friend Margaret

Maskelyne (later Margaret Clive) when she was back in England, there are some relating to a request from an old school friend of hers, Elizabeth Sellen, to provide a recommendation for her to go out to India in search of a husband. In correspondence in 1761 between Margaret, her friend Major John Carnac, Amelia Vansittart (the then governor's wife in Calcutta) and Elizabeth Sellen herself, we find that Margaret has doubts about her friend's idea of going out to India for a husband as the young woman does not know anything about India, nor has any connections there. Except of course she does know the very well-connected Margaret Clive. Furthermore, Margaret considers it is not quite the best form to be going out to India without any established connections in order to seek a husband. Margaret tries to talk her friend out of it, but without success.

Margaret certainly does very well by her friend, writing requests to Governor Vansittart and his wife, to Major Carnac, and also to Philadelphia to offer assistance to Miss Sellen. The young woman heads off to India with letters of recommendation in which Margaret hopes will see her well-treated. After Elizabeth Sellen's arrival in India, Margaret has letters from John Carnac and Amelia Vansittart telling of how her old school friend is getting on. She has some problems, though is well looked after by them all, including Philadelphia. Margaret is told the young woman is an unlikely prospect for marriage, even with the benefit of a recommendation from Margaret Clive, and all the enticing connections it implied, as she was having recurring 'fits'. 'As to Miss Sellen (poor girl)' Carnac writes on 19 November 1761, 'She has in addition to her many other Disadvantages, the misfortune of being violently troubled with fits'.[5] All is not lost, however, for Margaret receives a letter from her old school friend, written on 17 December 1761, probably about six months after her arrival in Calcutta, with the good news of a recovery from her 'Malady & [is] ... now on the verge of Matrimony, the Gent's name is Reed, a factor'.[6]

She also writes of how welcoming both Philadelphia and the Vansittarts were upon her arrival and also of her health problems. Her fits were probably brought on by heatstroke, rather than some more insidious cause, and ceased when her body and behaviour adjusted to the climate and the hot season abated.

Philadelphia would have known about the fortuitous marriage prospects in India, compared to what was available to her in England. It was a choice that she accepted, as a matter of honour and with respect for those who made it possible. The fact that the gentleman in Fort St David awaiting her arrival was a surgeon, like her father, a son of a vicar, came from a similar rural Kentish background as herself and was known to her uncle, as well as his being able to give her a home, a family and hopefully considerable financial stability, must have been much in his favour. Weighing against the proposition would have been the long and dangerous voyage out, the strangeness and challenges of life in India and that she had no personal knowledge of him beforehand.

She must have decided that the advantages outweighed the not inconsiderable drawbacks.

In *Pride and Prejudice*, when Charlotte Lucas shocks her friend Elizabeth Bennet by accepting the proposal of the obnoxious Mr Collins, Austen brings out two very different views of marriage. Charlotte's view is more the conventional eighteenth-century position; Elizabeth's is a more romantic, even sentimental position that was beginning to become more accepted. Novels popular with female readers in the second half of the eighteenth century, like Fanny Burney's 1778 novel *Evelina*, promoted the idea of choice and love and the freedom of young people to choose whom they would marry. In Philadelphia's time this was an unconventional notion for middle and upper class young women without a substantial independent income. Despite Austen's heroines marrying for love and freedom of choice, in life, her own view may have been more pragmatic, as in her letter to her niece Fanny Knight of 13 March 1817, where Austen proffers some advice about a suitor of Fanny's. 'Single women have a dreadful propensity for being poor, which is one very strong argument for matrimony'.[7] But there was clearly also a place even in the late eighteenth century for a marriage such as Charlotte Lucas's who essentially connives at and accepts Mr Collins's proposal in order to gain a home of her own, some independence and a substantial rise in status and income. It is clearly Charlotte's decision to make; calculated albeit. While Elizabeth is stunned when Charlotte tells her she is marrying Mr Collins, Charlotte counters with an elegant argument of reproach.

> When you have time to think it over, I hope you will be satisfied with what I have done. I am not romantic, you know; I never was. I ask only for a comfortable home; and considering Mr Collin's character, connections and situation in life, I am convinced that my chance of happiness with him is as fair as most people can boast on entering the marriage state.[8]

And indeed, later when Elizabeth visits the Collins' married household, she does admit to herself that Charlotte has been able to construct an acceptable life with her foolish husband. It may be a repulsive basis for a marriage to Elizabeth, but there is validity in Charlotte's argument, and one readily accepted by many women of her time and in her position, though Austen herself could not do it when at the age of 26, she was proposed to by a well-off younger man, and old family friend, Harris Bigg-Wither, whom she initially accepted and then withdrew the next morning.

In *The Watsons,* Jane Austen's c.1804 abandoned novel, the author dwells on themes of penniless young women and their ruined marriage prospects in pertinent discussions of marriage that are relative to Philadelphia's situation. Two of the Watson sisters, Emma and Elizabeth, canvas the arguments of the merits of marriage versus the single life for poor young women. While there is always an argument for marriage as provision against a single woman becoming old and poor and an object of mockery, there is the usual counter argument against marrying *just anyone*. Emma Watson feels that:

> To be so bent on marriage, to pursue a man merely for the sake of a situation, is a sort of thing that shocks me; I cannot understand it. Poverty is a great evil; but to a woman of education and feeling it ought not, it cannot be the greatest. I would rather be a teacher at a school (and I can think of nothing worse) than marry a man I did not like.[9]

Her more pragmatic sister, Elizabeth, puts her argument for being less fussy about whom one might marry. 'I should not like marrying a disagreeable man any more than yourself; but I do not think there *are* many very disagreeable men; I think I could like a good-humoured man, with a comfortable income' she tells her sister. The latter argument is fair enough, and while Philadelphia may not be as calculating as a Charlotte Lucas, she would have set off to India with a view of her chances similar to Charlotte's.

When, on 18 January 1752, Philadelphia set sail for Fort St David, she sailed on an East Indiaman, the name given to those ships purpose-built for the trade to India. They were merchant ships with a formidable capacity to carry huge amounts of cargo, plus a few passengers and with the fighting features required by a man-of-war. It was a lucrative trade. East Indiamen needed to be capacious to store the cargo; they needed to be strong and well-armed to fight off pirates or even the ships of rival companies; and they needed to be comfortable for their captains and for important passengers busy making fortunes in the east. Paying passengers were happily taken on board, and the ships were well-fitted for the aspiring officers of the Company. The fares paid went straight to the captain.

The ship set sail from the Downs, in the Channel near Deal in Kent. As a young woman of that time in her circumstance she would have had few personal possessions. She would not have taken the great amount of luggage the wealthy with their large families took out. A small chest perhaps that could have fitted on the back of the coach containing some clothes, a few books, paper and pens for letter writing, items considered essential to take out to India and some personal possessions. Items of value needed to be well secured.

As described in her memoir, *Original Letters from India (1779-1815)*, Mrs Eliza Fay, in 1779, travelling both by sea and land with her husband had a number of trunks stored in the steerage section of the ship. She had 'books, wearing apparel, beds, with laces, buckles, rings etc.' which were all ruined by water or stolen during the very difficult period of her journey out of their imprisonment in Calicut.[10] She also had her own tea kettle. Wise woman. Able to make a 'cuppa' even in the most rat-infested hole. Valuables such as money and watches she and her husband carried about their person, the watches concealed in Mrs Fay's hair.

Most women certainly had a piece of needlework to be going on with, and Philadelphia's skills would have been put to good use. When Margaret Maskelyne, now the married Mrs Clive, came back to England on the *Royal George* in 1760 with her husband, his senior officers and their families, she became very friendly with little Louisa Forde, daughter of Clive's right-hand man Francis Forde, and during the long voyage was kept busy making the little girl clothes to wear when she got back to England.

During the voyage, Philadelphia would have had, for the first time in many years, leisure hours a-plenty. Some women would take a few extra small luxuries for the journey, so perhaps Philadelphia packed a basket of food or wine for herself. Some family mementos? What might her brother George have felt about losing his sister to such a journey? He probably accepted that it was an appropriate option for her. At only 20 himself and still at Oxford, though now having taken his degree, and won an exhibition, he would remain there for further studies in divinity, George was unlikely to ever be in a position to provide for Philadelphia.

From Deal, she would have been rowed out in a small boat to the ship lying at anchor. On these East Indiamen voyages there was usually but one stop between England and India. After leaving the Downs, the *Bombay Castle* did not arrive at its first landfall until 18 June, when it came into the port of Benkulen in Sumatra. This was the East India Company's trading factory of Fort Marlborough, centre of its pepper trade. Then it was up to Fort St David on the Coromandel Coast, arriving on 31 July 1752.

The voyage out would not have been without its discomforts and dangers. While there is no account from Philadelphia of either of her journeys, we can glean some shared experiences from other first-hand accounts of shipboard life for a woman in the eighteenth century, such as from Mrs Eliza Fay's record. After travelling out to India with her husband, she was later left with only her clothes as possessions after being deserted in Calcutta by a husband who had made enemies of all the establishment figures there, and who had conceived a child by another woman. Eliza Fay went back to England on her own to start again. But she had no luck, and like many other expatriates, decided that India offered better opportunities for her, where she 'had met such friendship and generosity, and where so much general encouragement was given to the efforts of respectable individuals'.[11] Eliza Fay, like many of the Englishwomen who spent time in India, had prized the life and the friendships there.

Despite the horrendous voyage back to England undergone just a year before, Eliza Fay set off again, India-bound in 1779, having engaged a young single woman, Miss Hicks, who was 'of the strictest integrity, and who possessed many valuable qualifications' to be her assistant in a school she intended to open in Calcutta. Mrs Fay received a special deal from the captain, who had been the commander on her voyage home, for a reduced fare, by taking charge of 'four ladies, who wished to have a protectress during the voyage.'[12] One can assume the eleven young women sailing out with Philadelphia, a generation earlier, also had a similar 'protectress'. The four ladies under Mrs Fay's protection, her assistant Miss Hicks and herself occupied only a small section of the ship's roundhouse, and in these cramped living quarters, they remained confined for almost the whole voyage, as Mrs Fay comments:

> we were only five times on deck during the passage, which was owing to a previous arrangement between the Captain and me to guard against imprudent attachments, which are more easily formed than broken.[13]

The young women under her protection would have left their cabins for their meals, taken with other passengers of similar status, most likely in the cuddy, a cabin in the aft of the ship used as a saloon or dining room. Perhaps occasionally the young women stole out from under Mrs Fay's beady-eyed supervision for a breath of fresh air and to take in the star-laden southern night sky; with the danger of an 'imprudent attachment' or not, as may be.

Fresh food was not plentiful and it required the captain to ration it carefully. At the beginning of the voyage Philadelphia and her companions would have had a degree of fresh meat from the live animals taken on board, and limited fresh fruit and vegetables. But considering the ship did not set down in another port until five months later that must have well and truly run out. It was then mostly salted beef and pork, cheese and biscuits, and with the drinking water turning foul.

In the confined and cramped conditions, it must not have been easy for even a healthy young woman like Philadelphia to have stayed fit and well and in good spirits. There was always a threat from diseases such as typhoid spreading rapidly with devastating consequences. But Philadelphia no longer had to work, and she must have been entertained by what happened on board. She also had the companionship of young women bound by a common purpose, and the captain also had some responsibility for organising entertainments for his passengers. Celebrations on board included special dinners, such as Eliza

Fay tells of on board her ship when the captain 'celebrates in high style' the birthday of his fiancée, a Miss Ludlow.

With eleven young women on board there must have been a possibility of dancing for Philadelphia on the *Bombay Castle*. Mrs Fay gives a vivid account of a dance on board her ship when 'going at the rate of eight knots an hour off the Cape, with a heavy swell':

> ...the young folks, nevertheless so earnestly solicited for a dance, that the Captain could not refuse; so all the furniture being removed out of the cuddy, I led off by particular request; but had only gone down one couple when a tremendous *lee lurch* put us all in confusion. I declined standing up again, but the rest during three or four hours, tumbled about in the prettiest manner possible, and when no longer able to dance, made themselves amends by singing and laughing; no serious accident happened to any one, and the evening concluded very agreeably.[14]

Sounds like tremendous fun. But not all of one's companions on board could be as agreeable as these young people seem to have been. Confined in close quarters with few opportunities to get away from them, Philadelphia would have been at the mercy of her companions, amusing and agreeable, or not.

Lone women, in particular could find their position difficult. On Mrs Fay's return voyage to England, as she wrote in a letter to her sister from St Helena in 1782, she had to endure quite offensive behaviour from the 'gentlemen' on board. On that voyage, there seems to have been only one other adult female fellow-passenger, a Mrs Tottingham, who is travelling with her husband, the colonel and their children, along with seven 'military gentlemen', two returning EIC civil servants and thirteen children, 'under the captain's care'. These two ladies had a hard time of it enduring the drunken, boorish behaviour of their male fellow passengers.

> Who became so very rude and boisterous that Mrs Tottingham withdrew entirely from the table, and never left her cabin for the last thirteen weeks: but the Colonel took care to send her whatever was necessary; I had no one to perform the like kind office to me, and was therefore forced to venture up among them, or risk starvation below.[15]

Hopefully, Philadelphia and the other 'young beauties' were spared such obnoxious circumstances. Philadelphia, in fact, had unanticipated good luck in having the presence of the 16-year-old Margaret Maskelyne, previously mentioned, also orphaned, and brought up by maiden aunts in Wiltshire, going out to join her brother Edmund Maskelyne who was an officer in the EIC army, stationed in Madras. Like Philadelphia, she was also making the journey with a marriage prospect in mind.

In Bence-Jones' biography of Robert Clive he describes Margaret as 'just the sort of girl who would have gone to India in search of a husband, having neither parents nor money'.[16] Just like Philadelphia Austen. Unlike Philadelphia, though, Margaret had other family connections in India. As well as her brother, she had a cousin, Eliza Walsh, who had followed her own officer brother out to Madras in the late 1740s. Margaret had been living with aunts but had also attended a girls' school, St Christopher's in Cirencester. She came from a family where education was important, and her older brother Nevil, became the Astronomer Royal. Margaret was well-educated for a young girl at that time with more intellectual interests than was common.

Like Philadelphia, Margaret was lively and engaging and to her family was worthy of a good marriage; something superior to what might have been possible to her at home living with the aunts in Wiltshire. Her wider family took a keen interest in her future. In early 1751 Margaret's cousin Eliza Walsh, now married to merchant Joseph Fowke in India, writes to her aunts that cousin Edmund had 'laid out a husband for Peggy [Margaret] if she chooses to take so long a voyage for one, that I approve of extremely'.[17] That 'husband' was to be Robert Clive, who was to become famous as 'Clive of India', the soldier-conqueror of Bengal, responsible for so much of the richest part of India falling under the authority of the Company. So clearly there were fortunate matches to be made in India for young women prepared to take a risk.

Among those risks for Philadelphia and her fellow passengers were the terrible perils inherent in the sea itself. The South Atlantic and Indian oceans were notorious for the violent storms against which the wooden crafts of the eighteenth century had few means of combat. Nothing but the sky could tell the sailors what was coming, and they had little means of avoiding it. In the account of a return voyage to India from England on board a Portuguese ship, the attorney and man-about-town William Hickey, whose eponymous *Memoirs* give a vivid, if slightly dubious testimony of life in late eighteenth-century India, writes of seeing a great cyclonic storm brewing in the sky to the west of Ceylon.

The horizon, he describes, was 'blackish purple, above which rolled great masses of cloud of deep copper colour moving in every direction with uncommon rapidity ... enough to appal the bravest man on board'.[18] Hickey's description of the sailors' reaction to what they saw is chillingly authentic: 'not a syllable [was] uttered by anyone, all looking in stupid amazement'. Impossible to avoid the advancing cyclone, all on board, did what they could below decks to prepare for the disaster that was coming. The sea was a foaming mass of huge waves breaking over the tossing ship. Incredibly the ship stayed afloat although almost torn to pieces and many of the crew were lost.

It is now the point to return to the young Jane Austen's story *Catharine, or The Bower*. From an early age, Austen wrote prolifically with the manuscripts later copied out by her and collected into three notebooks, entitled *Volume the First*, *Volume the Second* and *Volume the Third*, now held in the Bodleian Library and the British Library. *Catharine, or the Bower* is from Volume the Third, with the date given as 1792, when Jane was 16. Her aunt Philadelphia had died in the February of that year and Philadelphia's daughter Eliza stayed with the family in Steventon for most of the second half of that year, recovering from the ill-health and depressed spirits that plagued her after her mother's long illness and death.

Many scholars point out a number of aspects of similarity between the fate of the character of the eldest Miss Wynne, Cecilia, in the story, and that of Philadelphia.

> It was now two years since the death of Mr Wynne, and the consequent dispersion of his family, who had been left by it in great distress. They had been reduced to a state of absolute dependence on some relations, who, though very opulent and very nearly connected with them, had with difficulty been prevailed on to contribute anything to their support.... The elder daughter had been obliged to accept the offer of one of her cousins to equip her for the East Indies and though infinitely against her inclinations, had been necessitated to embrace the only possibility that was offered to her of a maintenance; yet it was one so opposite to all her ideas of propriety, so contrary to her wishes, so repugnant to her feelings, that she would have almost preferred servitude to it, had choice been allowed her. Her personal attractions had gained her a husband as soon as she had arrived at Bengal.[19]

There are unmistakeable echoes here of Philadelphia's real life experiences in the young Jane's telling of the tale of orphaned children reluctantly taken in by relatives and of 'one of her cousins' who arranges for Cecilia to travel to Bengal. No choice is offered to Cecilia. Does this accurately reflect Philadelphia's position?

There is a degree of licence perhaps taken with Catharine's repugnance at the whole idea of the transactional nature of what Cecilia undertook. From Catharine's perspective, a voyage to India to secure a husband was seen as a distasteful exploit, and she is clear in her mind that Cecilia was coerced into going to the East Indies. It does not, however, seem to have been the actual situation with Philadelphia.

But whatever the imperatives of Philadelphia's journey, she survived all the vicissitudes of the long sea voyage; no doubt an experience she held with her throughout her life. An insight into Philadelphia's character and the impact of her life experience is gained from a letter written by her sister-in-law, Mrs George Austen, mother of Jane, to Philadelphia's half-brother William's wife, Mrs Walter, dated 26 August 1770. Mrs Austen recounts a visit by Philadelphia, whom she calls 'Sister Hancock', and her 8-year-old daughter Eliza to Steventon in the summer of 1770.

Leaving Steventon, Philadelphia and her daughter set out by carriage to return to London across the isolated and notoriously robbery-prone Bagshot Heath. Mrs Austen writes that compared to Mrs Walter:

> … she [Philadelphia] showed more Courage than you had and set out in a Post Chaise with only her little Bessy, for she brought neither Clarinda or Peter with her, but believe she sincerely repented, before she got to her Journey's end, for in the middle of Bagshot Heath the Postilion discover'd She had dropped the Trunk from off the Chaise. She immediately sent him back with the Horses to find it, intending to sit in the Chaise until he return'd, but was soon out of patience and began to be pretty much frighted so began her Walk to the Golden Farmer about two miles off, where she arrived half dead with fatigue, it being in the middle of a very hot day.[20]

After a few more mishaps, Philadelphia and Eliza arrive safely back in London.

I am not sure that Philadelphia's view of the journey would have necessarily been the same as Mrs Austen's. Having undertaken a perilous sea-journey by herself halfway across the world, one doubts that Philadelphia would have felt she needed special courage to undertake a trip by post-chaise from Hampshire to London, even if it meant travelling without servants and across Bagshot Heath.

When she reached the choppy waters off the Coromandel Coast of India, Philadelphia must have felt the relief of safe arrival, albeit there was still the very tricky journey by masulah (a small shallow-drafted open row-boat) used to shoot the waves and carry passengers and cargo ashore to the European settlements on the Madras coastline. Many a traveller was washed overboard and drowned either on setting out from, or on first arriving in India. Philadelphia, however, successfully made the beckoning safety of dry land. She had made it to India and was ready to welcome whatever Fate had arranged for her.

Chapter 4

Marriage and Early Years in India
1752–1756

Her personal attractions had gained her a husband as soon as she had arrived in Bengal, and she had now been married nearly a twelve month.

Catharine, or The Bower, p. 205

THE *BOMBAY CASTLE* arrived at Fort St David, the East India Company stronghold on the Coromandel Coast in the Madras 'Presidency', on 31 July 1752. In her petition to the East India Company, Philadelphia refers to the 'friends' she would join in Fort St David. The EIC settlement was near the town of Cuddalore and was now the Company's main settlement and headquarters in the Madras Presidency. The other Indian presidencies were in Bengal to the north and Bombay on the west coast. The settlements had grown from original EIC trading posts, known as 'factories', where the local merchants and skilled artisans, such as silk weavers, moved in to conduct their trade with both the British who lived there and the Company.

Who were these 'friends' of Philadelphia in Fort St David? One would assume there was some female connection to welcome Philadelphia; most likely the 'Mrs Ackell' mentioned in Robert Clive's friend's letter to him informing him of the 'beauties' sailing out to India on the *Bombay Castle*. Six months after her arrival, Philadelphia marries Tysoe Saul Hancock, a client of her Uncle Francis. He is 30 years old, a surgeon employed by the Company who had already been there for four years, and had recently been promoted to the post of surgeon. He was clearly prepared to marry the young woman, parentless, though of good family, without any kind of dowry, but recommended by his English agent, her uncle, Francis Austen. That Philadelphia was pretty is without doubt, as we can see from both a miniature portrait, by the renowned miniaturist John Smart and a recently identified family portrait painted by Sir Joshua Reynolds.

Returning to *Catharine, or the Bower*, the youthful Jane Austen has her heroine Catharine, or Kitty as she is more often called, and was the original title the author gave to the work, express further views on Cecilia's journey to Bengal and matrimony, in a conversation with her friend Miss Stanley:

> do you call it lucky for a girl of genius and feeling to be sent in quest of a husband to Bengal, to be married there to a man of whose disposition she has no opportunity judging till her judgement is of no use to her, who may be a tyrant, or a fool, or both for what she knows to the contrary? Do you call that fortunate?[1]

This viewpoint is familiar ground in the adult Austen's subsequent novels. As well as Elizabeth's view of Charlotte Lucas's marriage to Mr Collins, there is Maria Bertram's marriage to Mr Rushworth in *Mansfield Park*. It is clear that some of this story of Cecilia Wynne is close to Philadelphia's. It is both an opportunity and a risk.

Miss Stanley has a more favourable view than her friend Catharine of such an arrangement and puts quite the gloss on it:

> Well I do think there never was so lucky a family. Sir George Fitzgibbon, you know, sent the elder girl to India entirely at his own expense, where they say she is most nobly married, and the happiest creature in the world… I cannot conceive the hardship of going out in a very agreeable manner with two or three sweet girls for companions, having a delightful voyage to Bengal … and being married soon after one's arrival to a very charming man immensely rich. I see no hardship in that.[2]

For Catharine, though, it is a much chancier prospect as 'it was by no means certain that she would be so fortunate, either in her voyage, her companions or her husband'. Miss Stanley begs to differ: 'I do not see that at all. She is not the first girl who has gone to the East Indies for a husband, and I declare, I should think it very good fun if I were as poor'.

So poverty is the driver; a way out of its clutches. Philadelphia herself, some years later as a married woman with a child and living in Calcutta was to assist other young women coming out to India to seek suitable husbands. Apart from the previously mentioned Miss Sellen, she assisted Mary Ironside, who had a brother already in India.

While Tysoe Hancock may not have been the man of her dreams or the love of her life, and a surgeon's pay of £30 per annum was modest, he did have, like most Company men, the potential to make money from private trade. He proved a loyal, caring husband to Philadelphia and one who gave her social opportunities in India, which she would have never found in her previous situation in England.

From the extant letters of Hancock to his wife, he presents as an intelligent, generous and kind man. He was a fond husband who took on the responsibilities of that role devotedly, despite the many difficulties of their married life, including long physical separation, poor health, financial worries and years of childlessness. His letters show a conventional admiration for Philadelphia, and this pretty, slim, vivacious young wife, seven years his junior, filled a need he had for a companion in an otherwise personally lonely expatriate life for a single man of the less sociable disposition possessed by Surgeon Hancock; and a surgeon's life was never an easy one, wherever he may have been practising.

Medicine was one of the traditional 'learned professions', the others being the church and the law, which developed in the latter half of the eighteenth century, as 'liberal professions', i.e. professions regarded as 'suitable occupations, both socially and financially, for the sons of gentlemen'.[3] The medical field, however, was divided into three: physicians, surgeons and apothecaries. Only medical men with a university degree, and entitled to be Fellows of the Royal College of Physicians could have the status of gentlemen. Surgeons were indentured as apprentices, as were apothecaries.

Tysoe Saul Hancock was born on Christmas Day, 1723, the eldest son of the Reverend Thomas Saul Hancock, rector of the parish of Wormshill and vicar of Hollingbourne in Kent and his wife Elizabeth. Here implies some Austen Kentish connection. Thomas Saul Hancock and Elizabeth Colborne had married in 1717, another Fleet marriage, in London, where they are listed in the register of clandestine marriages as resident in the parish of St Martin-in-the-Fields for Thomas Saul, and in St Andrews, Holborn for Elizabeth. The groom was 21 and the bride 22. The groom was on his way to becoming a student at Trinity College Cambridge, having matriculated from Christ's Hospital school in 1716. His father, also Thomas, was a harness-maker and citizen of London in St-Martin-in-the-Fields. Thomas Saul graduated with his M.A. from Cambridge in 1723, the year that their son Tysoe was born, at which time Thomas Saul was rector at Wormshill. He continued to hold that position even while becoming vicar of Hollingborne in 1727 until his death at age 45 in 1741.[4] Tysoe was the eldest son.

At the time of his father's death, Tysoe Hancock was already apprenticed to the surgeon Samuel Liege in St Marylebone.[5] Had he gone to Christ's Hospital like his father? Perhaps. Christ's Hospital, also known as The Bluecoat School because of the colour of the children's uniform, was founded in the mid-1550s as a charity boarding school for the orphaned and the poor of London tradesmen. It had an emphasis on education and by the time Thomas Saul Hancock attended in 1716 there were opportunities now available for the clever boys to study the classics and be prepared for matriculation to university, mostly to Cambridge.

A younger brother of Tysoe, Thomas, was admitted to Christ's Hospital school in 1742, the year after their father's death. Records show he matriculated to Pembroke College, Cambridge in 1744 and took his degree in 1748–49, but it is not clear what happened to him thereafter and he is not mentioned in his brother's correspondence.

Tysoe Hancock was apprenticed as a surgeon in 1738 with the usual apprenticeship from five to seven years, until a majority was reached. The training included regular anatomy and surgery classes, attendance at dissections and the study of texts as well as the general dogsbody work that any apprentice was obliged to perform for their master.[6]

By the time Hancock qualified as a surgeon, the London surgeons had broken with the Barber-Surgeons' Company to become the Surgeons' Company. There was fierce competition between the three branches of medicine, with the physicians, as graduates of a university, a selective group with only a few hundred members and able to charge high fees. Physicians were, in theory, exclusively permitted to deal with the interior of the body: examine, diagnose, and advise and direct surgeons and apothecaries. Surgeons, on the other hand, were expected to take instructions from physicians and to deal only with the external body. Apothecaries were supposed to only prescribe and sell potions and cures. But there was a good deal of overlapping between the three branches. Apothecaries could also attend lectures with the surgeons and gain further expertise.

There were so few physicians and their fees were so high that most people, including the better-off, turned to surgeon-apothecaries for day-to-day medical advice and treatment. This was especially so in the country. In *Emma*, the medical man in Highbury, and a frequent visitor to Hartfield, is the much valued, particularly by Emma's father, Mr Perry, an apothecary.

Being a surgeon challenged practitioners' aspirations to be considered gentleman, concerned as the practice was with intimate attendance to the body itself. It also exposed its practitioners to dangerous and distressing circumstances. A famous surgeon of the day, Percival Potts, a clinical surgeon at St Bartholomew's Hospital, wrote of surgeons whose only real interest in an operation was in beating the clock and described amputation as 'terrible to bare and horrible to see'.[7] It would not have been an occupation to everybody's taste, though of course surgeons administered to patients for conditions not requiring surgery. Surgery was usually a matter of last resort.

There was not a lot of money to be made as a young surgeon just out of his apprenticeship in eighteenth-century England and there was a great deal of competition among the surgeons and from the apothecaries and an oversupply of both.[8] The work could be taxing and dangerous. Medical practitioners must have exposed themselves to contagious patients and unhealthy environments. Perhaps life expectancy for medical men was not high, as I note that Philadelphia's surgeon father was only 37 when he died, and her mother's first husband, also a surgeon, died in his twenties.

While Hancock's prospects may not have been all that encouraging, he would have worked as a qualified surgeon for a few years in London before he took passage to India for the Honourable East India Company as a surgeon's mate. Acting as a surgeon's mate on an EIC ship going out to India would have allowed him to earn his way out, and not have had to pay the high cost of passage. There were four options available for a position with the Company at that time, and you had to have referees to successfully petition the Board of Directors to be either a writer, which was an administrative or clerical position, a factor, working in one of the company's trading posts, known as factories, a cadet to serve in the Company's increasingly significant military arm or as a surgeon stationed in one of the major centres.

The 25-year-old Hancock went to India to make his fortune, like most of the other young adventurers of the Company, not so much in the pursuit of their occupation, but with the intention to trade in the Indian goods much desired in Britain, as well as in the lucrative trade to China. Initially, Hancock took up a position first as surgeon's mate in the town of Cuddalore, near Fort St David, in 1749, and then, in April of 1751, was promoted to head surgeon at Devikottai, a settlement about 100 miles further south and recently captured by the EIC.

An official record of 30 April 1751 supports Hancock's Devikottai appointment:

> It being extreamly [sic] necessary to have an Able Surgeon at Devecotah [sic] and Mr Hencock [sic] who was upwards of Three Years a Mate in the Company's service and assisted in the King's Hospital in Cuddalore during the time of the Sea and Land Forces were here, being Esteem'd [sic] very skilful in that Profession. As we have but few Opportunitys [sic] of meeting with Persons so well Qualified It's Agreed to Entertain him to be Head Surgeon at Devecotah [sic] at the same Salary and Allowances as our Head Surgeons here.[9]

Though he had his surgeon's duties to perform for the Company, he could also undertake private practice and engage in trade and undertake surgeon's duties to the army garrisons during periods of warfare.

His impending promotion and increased salary may have given him the confidence to contemplate marriage. He was a competent and conscientious surgeon, though he expresses his distaste for the profession in a letter written to Philadelphia from Calcutta on 23 November 1769 where he claims that 'You know how much I hate the Practice of Physick, yet I am obliged to take it up again: nothing could have induced me to do so, but the Hopes of thereby providing for my family'.[10]

We have further evidence he was held in high regard by his compatriots in India. In a letter written by fellow Calcutta resident the Rev Samuel Staveley to their mutual friend Warren Hastings written in April 1762, he writes of the recovery of a friend due to Hancock's 'Skill' in the devoted treatment and attention he gave to a mutual friend Lyon whom Hancock had been looking after 'Night and Day' in long absence 'from his Wife and Daughter'.[11]

The most significant person Hancock treated was the young Robert Clive, for wounds he received in April of 1752 in battle during the Carnatic Wars. These were decades-long conflicts between the French and the British in the Carnatic region along the east coast and inland of the Indian peninsula. Clive gained his injuries at the village of Samiaveram, up-river from Devikottai, where his forces were surprised by a raid by the French. Clive rushed out of his tent in his nightshirt in the darkness after the alarm was sounded. He was set upon and received sword blows to his head and chest. While he lost a considerable amount of blood, he escaped serious injury and went on to lead the successful defence of his force's position. Surgeon Hancock's treatment of Clive's wounds must have been efficacious, and Clive did not forget Hancock's ministrations when Clive was later in a powerful position to help him.

Hancock must have been still serving as a surgeon at Devikottai and through the first years of their marriage, when Philadelphia arrived on the *Bombay Castle*, as he did not take up his Fort St David surgeon's appointment until 1754, two years after their marriage. Philadelphia may have stayed on in Fort St David for a time after her marriage, till her husband could join her, as she was to do in Bengal later, or she may have spent those first years in Devikottai.

The town nearest Fort St David was Cuddalore, where Hancock had worked at the military hospital during the time of the first Carnatic War. While Philadelphia lived comfortably in India for eleven years and in a very real sense prospered there as a married woman, it was however, a volatile time for the country, which also had its impact on her. There was considerable disquiet on the sub-continent. Colonial rivals, the French and British were locked in a struggle for dominance, with both using Indian rulers and their armies against each other. This was the period of the Seven Years' War, a truly global conflict fought between the French and the British across four continents.

What do we know of Philadelphia's life after her marriage in Cuddalore for the next six years? Very little, but we can speculate from the few specifics and some of the generalities available from letters and diaries of the period.

Marriage and Early Years in India: 1752–1756

We have a description of Fort St David in 1754 from a surgeon of the East India Company, Edward Ives, who came out to India as a military surgeon to establish a military hospital in Fort St David. Ives' ship anchored in the 'roads' off the fort at the mouth of the estuary of the Gaddilam River. There was no harbour or wharf, so tenders had to come out to the ship to carry cargo and passengers ashore. While that particular trip to Fort St David was not as spectacularly dangerous as the ride ashore through the surf at Madras, it was challenging enough.

The settlement of Fort St David is described by Ives as Philadelphia would have seen it:

> Fort St David is a strong but small and regular fortification built on a rising ground about a mile from the Black-Town which is called Cuddalore ... In it reside the greatest part of the native Indian inhabitants of Fort St David's boundaries. Both the town and the fort are situated near the seaside.... The country within the boundaries is very pleasant and the air fine.[12]

Philadelphia's first impressions of India must have been like many other British new arrivals after their long ocean voyage. On the one hand relief to be on land again, but such a strange and exotic place to be in, finding her senses assailed by the sights, the vibrant colours, the smells and the strange sounds of such a place. As a seamstress, perhaps Philadelphia would have been struck by the fabulous colours of the women's clothing, as other visitors reported their amazement at the brilliant clothing the Indian women wore. A visitor to Bombay noted with admiration of Parsee women 'walking about in ... skirts of the most brilliant hues-an exquisite pale cherry and an emerald green appeared to be their favourite colours.'[13]

The bustle and noise of the London of her Covent Garden days would have little prepared Philadelphia for the vibrancy of tightly-packed Indian town life. The markets burst with the colour of tropical fruits and flowers and the smell of spices and pungent cooking odours, as well as the odours of human and animal waste and an all-pervading smell of burning dung. There were masses of people packed into the crowded towns; people who must have looked and sounded so different from the people she left behind in England. There were exotic sites to see, even in the Fort St David settlement, but Philadelphia was probably also pleased to see some more conventional sights, as described by Ives.

> In the neighbourhood of the agreeable retreats... are many pleasant rows of the ever-green tulip tree, which are planted through great part of the boundaries, in the same manner as the elms in

> St. James's Park. At some little distance from one of these walks, is a building, belonging to the company, and designed for the governor, and called 'the garden-house.' It is roomy, handsome and well built; and has a very good and large garden belonging to it, with long and pleasant avenues of trees in the back and front.[14]

Philadelphia would have soon retreated to one of the houses within the settlement boundaries, well away from the areas of native populations and where the British had built themselves the comfortable garden houses Ives described;

> In the district are many neat houses with gardens. The latter were laid out with much good taste by the company's gentlemen who either had been or were in the company's service. These gardens produce fruits of different sorts, such as pine-apple, oranges, limes, pomegranates… and many others. At the end of each gentleman's garden there is generally a grove of shady coco-nut trees.[15]

Obtaining leave from his post in Devikottai and after travelling up the coast north, Hancock and Philadelphia married in Cuddalore on 22 February 1753. Most likely it took place in Christ Church, Old Town, the former Catholic Church under the Portuguese, which had been handed over to the Protestant Swedish missionary, Rev John Keirnander (who became a great friend of Margaret Clive's) when the EIC took over the settlement in 1744. Philadelphia would remain in the Madras Presidency, mostly in Fort St David, for the next five years.

As the wife of a civil surgeon in the service of the EIC in India in the 1750s, Philadelphia would have had little to do with her husband's professional duties or with his business dealings, but as the wife of a 'gentleman' of the Company, and in a small British community, she would have taken her place among the very few European women and the men who were her social equals, and carried out the domestic and social duties expected of her gender and class. She would have been busy with many of those domestic chores of household management typical of eighteenth-century middle-class women of modest means, but the Indian environment was so very different to England and allowed her to have many more servants than she could ever have contemplated in England. Philadelphia's life must have been one primarily of leisure, in contrast to the labour required of a milliner.

As a married man now, Surgeon Hancock would have had to provide a house for himself and his wife more suitable than his previous shared bachelor's accommodation. Most single EIC officers lower down the hierarchy usually lived with fellow officers. Presumably, her husband provided Philadelphia with one of those 'neat houses with gardens...laid out with much good taste', as described by Edward Ives. An anonymous account held in the British Library, of the siege of Fort St David by the French from 28 April to 2 June 1758, refers to Hancock's house as being on an island outside the Fort. The now abandoned house is occupied by the French early in the siege, with a huge fire being lit in its garden.

The houses of Europeans in India were quite sparsely furnished with 'a few chairs, a few black-wood and marble-topped tables ... *almiras* or wardrobes and 'cots'", as Clive's house in Calcutta was described in 1759.[16] With shutters closed against the morning's heat, Philadelphia might have acquired her own cool and comfortable 'boudoir' to relax in, with an airy wicker chair in which to sit and give her servants their instructions for the day, such as is depicted in a painting of Lady Impey, wife of the first chief judge of the Calcutta court, done in around 1775–78, most likely by the Indian painter Shaikh Zain ud-Din.

Mary Impey had married the barrister Elijah Impey, bore him four children and went to Calcutta in 1772, when he was appointed Chief Justice in the newly created Supreme Court in Bengal. The painting, done in the traditional Moghul style, shows her seated in her 'boudoir' surrounded by various servants including a young boy with a fan, her interpreter, a tailor bringing her a new hat, her steward or *banyan* with his list of purchases and various others, such as a door keeper, usher, gardener and embroiderers.[17]

As a surgeon's wife, Philadelphia would have not had the status or the income available to Mary Impey to have supported such a household as depicted in the painting, but she would have certainly had a *banyan* who procured all the household requirements, a *mali,* or gardener, to look after the grounds and to bring her fresh produce; at least a cook or two, and various male and female house servants who would undertake a great variety of tasks.

Philadelphia's upbringing in the middle-class homes of her wealthier relatives, her education at home with masters shared with her cousins, and her training as a milliner, placed her as reasonably accomplished, while perhaps more practical than many of her peers in that very small world of the British women in India in the mid-eighteenth century. It may have been a lonely life in Fort St David, with her surgeon husband away from home a good deal attending to the Company's officers and families.

The resident deputy governor at that time was the young and unmarried Richard Starke, so his residence is unlikely to have been the centre of much social life for Philadelphia. Perhaps she turned to her servants for companionship, as Philadelphia later showed considerable fondness for her Indian women servants. Her husband's letters to her from India later have references to her enquiries about the well-being and whereabouts of her Indian servants left behind after her return to London. She would have occupied her time purposefully, and appears to have enjoyed her life in India. The references to her later in letters when the

Hancocks moved to Calcutta, present her as a lively, helpful and eager person, fond of her Indian servants, happy in company and enjoying travelling about.

Moving beyond and between the EIC settlements could be a challenge. Ives states that only a few EIC officers, such as the deputy governor for example had carriages, most went on horseback; though they also employed umbrella carriers to shield them from the sun and a traditional form of local carriage by palanquin, a kind of sedan-chair, which had become more and more popular. As Ives describes it:

> Almost all the residents in India keep their Palanquin, which is a covered machine with cushions in it arched in the middle, to give more room and air, and is carried on the shoulder of four or six men.[18]

As a Company surgeon in Fort St David of some year's standing, Hancock certainly would have required at least a horse to get around, while he was young enough and fit enough, to tend to his patients around and beyond the settlements. Now, with a wife as well to transport, he may have reluctantly acquired a carriage, even if it was an expense he could ill-afford. Later, when Hancock comes back to Calcutta after the family's earlier return to England, he laments in his letter of 15 March 1775 to Philadelphia that:

> I am obliged to keep a Carriage by the Necessity to which my Appointment reduces me of attending Families who now constantly reside at their Country Houses and only come to Town on Business.[19]

Philadelphia's means to get around for short distances was walking with a hired 'Roundel boy' carrying a large roundel or umbrella shielding her from the heat of the sun. Perhaps she enjoyed the occasional use of a palanquin for longer distances or even a hired carriage or shared carriage with a friend for evening events. Margaret Clive's friend Elizabeth Sellen was provided with transport by palanquin by the governor of Bengal, Henry Vansittart when she first arrived in the settlement.

Fort St David, like all major EIC settlements sat near a river-bank, as well as close to the sea, and carriage by water was a very common method of going longer distances to settlements such as Madras and Calcutta, though it had its perils, with rivers liable to flood in monsoonal rains and with notorious sections of rivers full of treacherous eddies and shoals, and the boats perhaps no more than, such as Mrs Eliza Fay describes:

> When we came to the water side what should this mighty boat prove but a narrow Canoe, with paddles, scarcely big enough

to contain us and our four rowers.... As we proceeded the Waves gradually rose higher, and began to break over us: one man was continually employed in baling out the water, though his only utensil was a bamboo, which hardly held a quart.... I sat at first with my face to the storm, but afterwards moved to the front, and when I saw a wave coming, bowed my head to receive it.[20]

These were not journeys to be lightly undertaken.

The cool of the evening in the gardens that ran down to the river was the time to meet with friends and socialise, even with a somewhat reluctant socialiser for a husband. For when he returns to India, he writes from Calcutta on 3 September 1773 in response to a letter from Philadelphia where she refers to a lady she has met in London who had got to know her husband in Madras, and he bridles:

Who the lady from India is I cannot guess: I am not acquainted with more than five or six, and these I very seldom see; I never breakfast, dine or sup from home; I never go to any publick or private Diversion.[21]

One hopes for Philadelphia's sake, in the early 1750s, as a younger man with a new wife, he may have been more prepared to enjoy himself in company.

There is no evidence that Philadelphia was ever unhappy or found life in Fort St David difficult. She comments in a letter to her husband that she is not of a melancholy disposition. She made the best of whatever situation she found herself in. She warmed to life in India, much as Margaret Clive did when she expressed herself as regretful, when writing to her friend John Carnac that she would never again return to India where she had been so happy.

Philadelphia may have felt much the same. Her marriage would have been in a general sense, a comfort to her and no doubt to her family. She had secured a home, some financial security, enhanced her status and relieved her male family members from responsibility for her. While Philadelphia's apparent warm and affectionate nature was far from the chilly pragmatism of Charlotte Lucas, it was enough to accept what Hancock could offer her. She was able to find happiness in her situation and gained ready acceptance in that small community of British expatriates. Her status as a respectable married woman made good any fall from status that came from being orphaned, penniless and reduced to earning her own living as a milliner. That could be well and truly left behind in that company, and Philadelphia was certainly not alone in her modest background amongst the society out there in India.

Her shipboard friend Margaret Maskelyne's husband, the 'hero' Robert Clive himself was a poor young man from the provincial town of Styche in Shropshire whose father was a lawyer struggling to bring up a family of thirteen children. The stories from his childhood indicate Clive was a troubled, difficult youth, sent to live with relatives, expelled from grammar school, and for whom, at the age of 18, a position as a writer with the Honourable East India Company was an opportunity to better himself financially and to get him out of his family's hair, so to say. In India he found his chance, not as a clerk but as a soldier in the conflicts the Company engaged in. In this role, his mettle was tested and what counted as problematic in a small provincial English town becomes the stuff of legendary battlefield boldness and military flair.

In India, Philadelphia was situated comfortably within her own class of poor but well-bred young women and the impecunious younger sons of the lower gentry and the professional classes, and recalling that, after all, her mother, Rebecca Hampson, was the daughter of a baronet, so Philadelphia did have some connection to a degree of rank.

When Philadelphia arrived in Fort St David in July of 1752, the political situation in southern India was highly charged. The economic rivalry between the French and the British for profitable possessions had been continuing all the previous decade, with the British slowly gaining the upper hand. Both allied themselves with different Indian leaders who were striving to take the place of the declining Mughal Emperor. The Madras Presidency, not Bengal was then the centre of British power under the EIC. Madras itself had been attacked by the French in early 1752 and Clive, in a famous battle had beaten them off and by June, just before Philadelphia and his future wife Margaret arrived, he and his commander Major 'Stringer' Lawrence had accepted the surrender of the French. Clive had returned to Madras, the conquering hero. A few months later he married Margaret and the couple returned to England on the *Bombay Castle*'s return voyage. Margaret had been in India for less than a year. It seemed that Clive was to enjoy the fruits of his victory back home in England. But that was not to be.

In 1754 when Edward Ives gave his observations on the EIC settlement of Fort St David, Philadelphia had been settled in India for almost two years. She must have felt comfortable and familiar with her surroundings, her friends and her way of life. The great political disturbances in the country however continued, as the power of the Mughal Emperors crumbled and the European powers competed with each other and the other Indian power groupings for control of the bulk of southern India.

Though Fort St David was not threatened at that point, the British government was concerned at the French build-up in the region and decided that the EIC needed the support of the Royal Navy, and they needed Robert Clive again. His attempts to enter parliament in England and build a significant political career for himself at home had not been that successful. Speed and bold surprise did not work quite so well on the Machiavellian political battlefield of aristocratic wealth and power in eighteenth-century Britain. Money had been lavishly spent, and with the intention of returning to India, Clive accepted the EIC post of deputy governor of Fort St David for five years with the right to succeed as governor of Madras, as well as a military commission as lieutenant colonel of the Foot in the 'East Indies only' as 'part of a ... plan for further striking a blow at French power in India'.[22]

Clive and Margaret set sail from England for Fort St David in April 1755. Margaret had to leave back home two infant sons, but took with her Jane (Jenny) Kelsall, her 16-year-old cousin. Philadelphia's reunion with her shipboard friend Margaret, now the deputy governor's lady, would be a significant enhancement to her life in India.

Chapter 5

Life in Fort St David
1756–1758

I flatter myself your Opinion of my friends Mr and Mrs Hancock is the same as mine. I have indeed a great Regard for her & am pleased by Her letter that you were so much attached to her Family ...

Letter from Margaret Clive to Major
John Carnac, 16 September 1761

IT MUST HAVE been a delighted Philadelphia when in June 1756 her friend Margaret from the *Bombay Castle* days, arrived in Fort St David as the wife of the new deputy governor of the Madras Presidency. For Hancock too, his medical attention to Clive when he was injured in battle four years earlier would have stood him in good stead with the new deputy governor, the chief of the Company in that settlement and second only to Governor Pigot in Madras. While Fort St David was something of a backwater, nevertheless their welcome was impressive. A welcome Philadelphia must have witnessed:

> On June 22, 1756, Clive made his formal entry into Fort St David as Deputy-Governor, the guns booming a salute...He now had the title 'Worshipful', rode in a state palanquin and lived in the Garden House, with its portico, its grounds shaded by tulip trees.[1]

Edward Ives had described the deputy governor's Garden House as 'roomy, handsome and well built; and has a very good and large garden belonging to it, with long and pleasant avenues of trees in the back and front'.[2]

The friendship between the then 16-year-old Margaret Maskelyne and 21-year-old Philadelphia, which had begun in 1752 on the *Bombay Castle* was sustained throughout their time in India and for some time when they were both back home in England. Margaret Clive's letters imply a close friendship and admiration for Philadelphia over this period of time. Margaret now:

> At the age of twenty, [had become] the first lady of the settlement... [and] was henceforth to occupy a station far above that in which she had been brought up-rising from Fort St David to be the undoubted Queen of Calcutta, and then, with scarcely a break, being metamorphosed into a very rich peeress in England-she never seems to have been in the least conceited.[3]

The governor's lady and the Company surgeon's wife, if we can judge from Margaret's later letters, appear to have very much enjoyed themselves and each other's company. Margaret was intelligent and spirited and I think we can assume Philadelphia shared those qualities. Margaret's young cousin Jenny Kelsall, who had come back to India with her, was now married to an older naval officer, Captain Thomas Lathan, whose ship HMS *Tyger* had brought the first contingent of British government troops to India. While Margaret still had Jenny's companionship to some extent, the first lady must have looked to Philadelphia for the open and warm companionship she enjoyed during the many absences of her husband Clive.

After the Clives' return to England, four years later, Margaret writes to her friend Major Carnac, on 16 September 1761, of her esteem for Philadelphia:

> I flatter myself your Opinion of my friends Mr & Mrs Hancock is the same as mine. I have indeed a great Regard for her & I am pleased to find by her Letter that you were so much attached to her Family, & thought my Voyage worth relating to her.[4]

At the time of this letter, Major Carnac was commander-in-chief of the Company's army, and based in Calcutta, after Clive had returned to England. Philadelphia was then living in Calcutta, and while no letters between Philadelphia and Margaret have been found, from references in other letters to and from Margaret, they clearly kept up a correspondence

When Margaret arrived in Fort St David she was pregnant with her third child, but Philadelphia had not yet enjoyed the same expected blessing of marriage. As a married woman with a busy husband away attending patients and having no children of her own, Philadelphia would have been free to join Margaret at the governor's Garden House on many occasions and have shared in the social life then available. Fort St David had its share of outings in carriages, dinners, balls, musical evenings and parties in the gardens. It was a small society and her intimate friendship with the governor's wife would have ensured Philadelphia a regular round of invitations. And while Philadelphia enjoyed many aspects of her Indian life, something was missing. The main occupation of young married women of that time was the bringing-up of their children. However, for the entire period of their six years' of marriage in Fort St David there were no children for Tysoe and Philadelphia, as far as we know, and there are no 'Hancocks' buried in the cemetery of Christ Church in Cuddalore. So there must have been some empty hours and regretful thoughts for Philadelphia which a busy domestic and social life could not quite replace.

Philadelphia's close connection to Robert Clive's wife, as well as Hancock's earlier acquaintance with Clive in Fort St David, not to mention his treatment of Clive's wounds in Samiaveram was helpful to Hancock's career. Clive's role from 1756 on further increasing the strength of the EIC's hold on the riches of Bengal was to directly benefit the Hancocks.

When the EIC's Fort William in Calcutta fell to Siraj ud-Daulah on the 20 June 1756, the scene of the infamous 'Black Hole', the Clives were making their formal entry into Fort St David, over 1,000 miles and many weeks of travel south. It would be some time before the news reached Fort St David of the destruction of the EIC's Bengal stronghold and the loss of the Company's most profitable trading centre. It was a disaster for the Company's bottom line and sent shivers through all the EIC 'Gentlemen', as a surviving military officer of the siege who escaped down river to Fulta, William Lindsey, wrote in a letter a month later to Robert Orme, then a member of the EIC Madras Council:

> [It] makes me tremble when I think of the consequences that it will be attended with, not only to every private Gentleman in India but to the English nation in General. I hardly think all the force we have in India will be sufficient to resettle us here into any footing of security, we now being almost as much in want of everything as when we first settled here.[5]

Lindsey's pessimism appears justified, however it did not take into account the extraordinary military capacity and drive of Robert Clive. So while Philadelphia was enjoying the newly arrived company of Margaret Clive and the more lively social opportunities it offered, she would have been quite unaware that far to the north the carnage being delivered to the Company's foothold in the richest of provinces was threatening all the Company's servants' livelihoods and well-being.

In August 1756, two months after the siege of Calcutta, news of it reached Clive. He was not only deputy governor of Madras, but also, held a military leadership position as the lieutenant colonel of the EIC's infantry. He was immediately ordered back to Fort St George in Madras to attend the inner council meetings to decide how to proceed in the face of the loss of Calcutta. When the decision was finally made to retake Calcutta, Clive was put in charge as 'the capablest [sic] person in India for an undertaking of this nature'.[6] Cometh the hour; cometh the man.

While Clive's expedition headed north from Madras in October, the pregnant Margaret remained in Fort St David. With her husband once again on active military duty, and while she was a woman of strength and spirit herself, it was another anxious time for her. She sought comfort among her closest confreres, which included her cousin, Jenny Latham, her priest, the Swedish missionary pastor the Reverend John Kiernander and Philadelphia. During these early days in Fort St David, Margaret had received news that one of her infant boys she had left behind in England had died. The warm companionship that we know Philadelphia was able to give must have been a source of distraction, at least.

In their daily lives, most Company wives took up the established routine of Europeans in India, and Philadelphia would have been no exception. The early morning was the time for domestic work to be done inside the shuttered rooms of the house: letters home, household management tasks, orders to the *banyan* and packages dispatched down to a boat to be sent out to an England-bound ship. While we have very few letters surviving from Philadelphia at all, she must have kept up her correspondence with family at home, especially with her brother George, now at Oxford. It is clear from her husband's later correspondence that she was a conscientious letter writer and eleven years in India did not dim her connection to her family, as on her return she maintained close relations with the Austen, Walter, Freeman, Payne and Hampson families.

The main meal was taken in the early afternoon, prepared by the household cooks, perhaps two or three. Like many British who lived in India, Philadelphia acquired a real taste for the curries, pickles, chutneys and spices of that country, as well as the fresh fruit so plentiful there. Later, back in England, Philadelphia's husband mentions in his letters that he has dispatched to her the pickles and chutneys she so liked. Wine was the favoured libation in the Indian heat, with EIC gentlemen bringing out with them crates of hock and claret from London vintners, Constantia wine from the Cape and the ever-popular Madeira. When in Fort St David as deputy governor, Clive ordered 'eight chests of claret and two of hock [to be] sent out every year by his father.'[7] When Warren Hastings returned to India in 1769, as second to Governor Du Pré, he left a 'standing order to send him annually three chests of claret and one of hock' to his London wine merchants.[8] Eating and drinking were the great diversions of British life in India, and corpulence often prevailed amongst many of the EIC gentleman; including Clive and Hancock.

Mrs Eliza Fay gives an account of one dinner party in her time in Calcutta in the late 1770s, probably little different from those of Philadelphia's day.

> The dinner hour as I mentioned before is two, and it is customary to sit a long while at table; particularly during the cold season; for people here are mighty fond of grills and stews, which they season themselves, and generally make very hot. The Burdwan stew takes a deal of time; it is composed of everything at table fish, flesh and fowl'.[9]

After dinner, at the hottest time of the day, Philadelphia would have happily adopted the custom of retiring, lightly dressed, into the shady confines of her 'boudoir', 'sleeping away the hottest hours in the day [thought] necessary even to the strongest constitution'.[10]

In the cool of the evening, Philadelphia accompanied by friends socialised in the gardens of the various Company garden houses or perhaps on the verandah of her own. Some musical entertainments by talented amateurs might have been on offer and the occasional ball. In a later letter to Major Carnac in early June of 1759, when in Calcutta, Margaret looks forward to her husband and all the other friends with him, whom she calls 'heroes', being back down in Calcutta in time for a ball organised for 23 June to celebrate the second anniversary of Clive's great victory at Plassey. She promises Carnac a number of dances, of a less strenuous kind. Apparently, because of the shortage of young women, older women kept up the dancing in India much longer than they did back in England.

As Margaret's confinement drew near, a close female relative, or an older friend like Philadelphia was an important support. The way Philadelphia was called upon a number of times by her sister-in-law Cassandra Austen to assist her in her confinements, suggests Philadelphia had gained some experience in India. She may have been with Margaret at this time, and if we can judge from Eliza Fay's account of being with one of the Calcutta judge's wives, Lady Chambers, during the birth of one her children, the relationship did not need to be especially close or of long-standing.[11] Caring, competent female friends were valued by the British gentlemen's wives when giving birth far from home and family.

Margaret's baby was a daughter called Jane and she remained in Fort St David for the outcome of her husband's northern march to retake Calcutta and waited for the call to join him. The EIC wanted much from the action in Bengal, nothing less than their factories and settlements in Bengal recovered, their rights and privileges fully restored, reparations made and the future of all their possessions and trading rights secured.[12] As it turned out, Clive secured far more than the Company could have dreamed of.

In December of 1756 Clive finally headed up the Hughli River from the coast. His forces stopped at the island of Fulta, the Dutch East India Company settlement down-river from Calcutta and where the EIC evacuees had taken sanctuary in squalid conditions. In the eight months since the fall of Calcutta, half of these survivors had perished. Among the survivors was Mary Buchanan, the widow of Captain John Buchanan, and her two infant daughters. Also now on Fulta, since October, after escaping from Kasimbazaar, was the 24-year-old Warren Hastings, still a junior administrator for the EIC and trying to do what he could to assist the refugees. Captain John Buchanan had been known to Hastings in his early days as a young writer when he had been sent up to the IEC's factory in Kasimbazaar in 1752 to learn the Company's trade.[13] Within weeks of his arrival in Fulta, Hastings married Buchanan's impoverished widow Mary. It is perhaps not that surprising, as passion, compassion and a certain impetuousness were notable traits of Hastings' character. Hastings did not spend much time with his new wife, as he soon joined-up as a volunteer with Clive's forces to re-take Calcutta. It was the first of his only two times in arms, as he recalled in old age: 'I carried a soldier's musket and served in the ranks in the character of a volunteer'.[14]

Did Philadelphia know anything of the young Warren Hastings at this point? Most likely not, despite there being family connections, originating with her sister-in-law, George Austen's wife Cassandra's family, the Leighs of Adlestrop, Gloucestershire, who were neighbours of the Hastings family in nearby Churchill. A cousin of Cassandra's, Mary Leigh, in a letter to Hastings written on 24 January 1790, refers to Hastings' sister Anne as, 'my old friend'.[15] The marriage of Philadelphia's brother George to Cassandra Leigh, however, is still some time in the future, and Philadelphia is yet to set foot in Bengal.

Clive's forces re-took all the former EIC possessions in Bengal, capturing a ruined Calcutta by 2 January 1757. Then it was on deeper into Bengal to defeat the Nawab, secure the Company in Bengal for now and in the future, and as the war in Europe against the French threatened, to also again take on the old enemy in India.

Clive continued the struggle on the Company's behalf, and by April there was a scheme to overthrow the Nawab of Bengal. The Battle of Plasesy was fought and won by Clive in June 1757, and his troops poured into Kasimbazaar. The Nawab Siraj ud-Daulah was betrayed and murdered by the son of the new Nawab, and the new leader of Bengal, Mir Jaffir,

> was seated on the throne at Murshidabad by Clive in person, to whom he made a gift of some £240,000…(with) two hundred boats, with flags flying and music blaring, carried treasure to Calcutta.[16]

Clive had taken the authority of Bengal from the Nawab and had placed it in the hands of the EIC, for better or worse. The centre of EIC power in India moved to Calcutta, and Clive as the head of the only capable military force in the country, at the age of 32 became virtually the dictator, though without any particular formal position, of a country almost the size of France.[17]

Reports of Clive's successes soon reached Margaret in Fort St David and she made her way north with her baby daughter and by 12 July 1757 was in Calcutta. Clive was still up in the old capital, Murshidabad, when Margaret arrived in Calcutta, but in August he came down for a brief reunion. A little later, in the autumn of that year her baby daughter 'Jenny' died. Another heartbreaking wrench for Margaret no doubt. Philadelphia, her friend, was left behind in Fort St David, but that was soon to change.

During the time of all the tumult in the north, Fort St David continued its quiet backwater ways, but trouble was brewing. The renewed 'Seven Years' War' between the British and French brought a French naval fleet to the Coromandel Coast in March of 1758 which took on the EIC possessions within the Madras Presidency. Cuddalore surrendered to the French after a short siege on 6 May 1758 and then Fort St David was itself put under siege, with the first battery of French guns opening on the fort on 16 May. It offered little resistance and even without the fort being breached, the garrison surrendered to the French on 2 June as prisoners of war.

And what of Surgeon Hancock and Philadelphia amidst all this turmoil? Although there is no direct account of their fate, they most likely fled north to Madras after the fall of Cuddalore and before the siege of Fort St David had begun, as *The Medical Register of India* has him appointed as a surgeon at Fort St George in Madras in June of 1758.[18]

It may have been a hasty escape for Philadelphia and her husband, leaving their possessions and most of their servants behind. Hancock had lost his surgeon's position and income, and Philadelphia her home. Her husband, if he had been trading, lost perhaps much more. Hancock wrote later of having being 'ruined' three times, and this would have been one of those times. A traumatic event too for Philadelphia, as she too writes many years later to Hastings from Paris of having faced many 'mortifying and disagreeable events in her life'.[19] This may well have been one of them. While arriving destitute in Madras, the Hancocks were fortunate to have the support of Clive who saw that Hancock gained a Madras appointment and for Philadelphia to come up to Bengal and stay with the Clives in Calcutta, where he was now governor.

A letter from Clive in April 1759 suggests his 'friend Mrs Hancock' has already been staying with Margaret in their house for some time. It suited both of the women. There are delightful intimate glimpses into Philadelphia's life at this time in Margaret Clive's letters to her friend and confidante, Major John Carnac, who often stayed in the Clive household. He knew Philadelphia well.

Margaret remained in Calcutta for two and a half years in a house bought by Clive, as there was no longer an official governors' house in Calcutta after the turmoil of the previous years. The devastation of the EIC fort, factory and grand houses had been almost complete when Calcutta had been retaken in January two years earlier. William Dalrymple in his book *Anarchy*, on the history of the EIC sums it up exactly:

> All burned-out shells rising jagged from the lott-littered riverfront.... The wharves were derelict; inside the mansions, the gorgeous Georgian furniture, family paintings and even harpsichords had been burnt as firewood where they stood in the middle of what had once been drawing rooms.[20]

It took some time to restore Calcutta to anything like its former glory. Margaret preferred to spend her time with her small circle of close friends, which now once again included Philadelphia. The Clive household was described as 'full of guests' and the companionable Philadelphia was a very welcome one of these.[21] In a letter to Carnac dated 30 May 1759 Margaret describes drinking to the health of her absent friends with a glass of Madeira for their safe return from the fighting in the north, along with 'Mrs Hancock [who] is squeezing mangoes down her throat to your health and safe return, and if she be not sincere, she wishes they may choke her. Amen say I'.[22]

So, we have this vivid image of Philadelphia suggesting an open, unrestrained quality to Philadelphia which clearly appealed to Margaret and others in her circle. While she was apparently always elegant and observed the expected polite norms of her society, there is a streak of inhibition and a kind of freedom there in Philadelphia's character which shows up elsewhere too.

Also, the social mores that operated in British India were somewhat different. When it came to social status or 'rank', it did not count in India in quite the same way as back home. The family connections in England may have been useful for men in order to advance their careers within the Company, but out in India itself, those connections related to EIC service were more significant in securing advantageous positions. Even those in the highest positions within the Company in India usually came from the 'younger sons', lower gentry and professional and middling classes. The two spectacular examples are Robert Clive and Warren Hastings themselves, both from provincial families, one whose father was a solicitor and the other a clergyman. Neither were in any sense wealthy or influential. India was indeed the land of the self-made person and how you prospered there was very much up to you, and of course your luck. For Europeans, to just survive, physically, was challenge enough.

For Philadelphia, the surgeon's wife, it was her connections to people of power like the Clives that gave her the social advantage. Furthermore, there were so few European women in India at that time, and few women had their closest female family members there with them, such as mothers or sisters, that when you found a compatible female friend you tried to keep them close. Family life was very limited; infants were left behind in England when married women came out with their husbands and other infants left behind in India when they returned home. The few families there were among the EIC's more senior ranks were much favoured by their friends. The big, connected families of brothers and sisters, cousins, nieces and nephews, grandparents, aunts and uncles that young officers left back in Britain were clearly missed.

The devastating effects of the climate and diseases on Europeans in India led to a certain sense of urgency to make hay while the sun shone, to succeed quickly in building wealth and to get out before you succumbed to fearful illness and death, as so many did. Over half of young EIC officers did not survive their appointment after five years. For women, while not subjected to having to be out in the heat and dangers ever present in the outside environment and also not drinking alcohol anything like as much as their menfolk did, it may have been slightly less dangerous, but they had the usual dangers of childbirth to confront. It can be assumed that the tenuousness of life in India resulted in the heightened and even brittle quality to how life was lived. The formalities of etiquette at home were more relaxed in India. Women received mixed male and female company at home visits and the ubiquitous morning visits at home in England were replaced by much later afternoon visits in India.

In another letter to Major Carnac Margaret writes of Philadelphia and the Calcutta physician Dr Fullerton going out with her in the cool of the evening for a ride in the chaise and in another of how they are all plagued by various insects: 'swarms of flies, mosquitoes, cockroaches and dumbledores' and that Philadelphia has been bitten by centapieds'.[23] She comments further in her letter that they are being so much attacked by mosquitoes, despite the nets over their beds that she says of herself and Philadelphia that 'One would think we were young ladies just come out of Europe, they bite so, I thought I was too ancient to attract them'. The young women of 21 and 17 who had arrived in India six years earlier are now quite the old India hands.

By the end of June 1759 Clive's battles in the north are over, temporarily, and he returns to Calcutta at the end of July. On 28 June, Hancock has been given a surgeon's position in Bengal by Clive, and now takes up his appointment in Kasimbazaar, over a hundred miles north up the Hughli River, and takes Philadelphia with him. Clive has referred to Philadelphia as soon 'running away from us' to join her 'little husband'.[24] Margaret gives birth to another child in India, a boy whom she names Robert. Perhaps before she left for Kasimbazaar, Philadelphia was there to assist, along with Margaret's own doctor, William Fullerton.

So it was goodbye again for Philadelphia and Margaret Clive, for by the time of Philadelphia's return to Calcutta, the Clives had departed for England and it would be five years before Philadelphia was back in London and their friendship, to some extent resumed. But by then, Margaret was now 'Lady Clive', wife of the immensely wealthy and famous, Lord Clive, and the old relaxed intimacy of the friends' Calcutta days could not be recaptured even though Margaret, 'never showed the slightest inclination to drop the friends and acquaintances of her humbler days'.[25]

But for now, it is 100 miles up the Hughli River to Kasimbazaar for Philadelphia, and the elegant leisured life as a guest in the governor's residence in Calcutta must be exchanged for no doubt less salubrious accommodation in Kasimbazaar in the great silk-producing region of Bengal, and renewed attention to her husband's wants and needs.

The EIC settlement in Kasimbazaar had its usual fort to defend it from marauders, with hundreds of silk winders at work, drawn to the burgeoning trade of the European companies and in the 'godowns' (the name given to the warehouses in India where the finished products were stored) and where the locally-made gorgeous coloured taffetas were kept ready for export. There was the counting house and the Treasury, the hall where the EIC gentlemen met each week to consult on business and discuss the politics of the Nawab's palace nearby at Murshidabad, upon whose tolerance of and financial benefit from, the EIC was so dependent.

The small EIC community had their terraced, verandahed houses with shaded gardens which looked out onto the river below. On the nights of the many Muslim festivals the river would be an enchanting sight for Philadelphia, having come up from the Hindu region of Fort St David, with the river here being: 'alight with floating lamps, while a mosque … (could be) heard at prayer each day through the trees of their garden'.[26]

Kasimbazaar must have been like starting all over again, as when Philadelphia first came to Fort St David. She may have brought some personal possessions with her, but as they had escaped the French siege of Fort St David they may have had little opportunity to bring much up to Madras. Clive described Hancock as 'destitute'. There would have been new servants to employ and new people to meet.

The most significant of these people was the young Company chief, Warren Hastings, just 28, two years younger than Philadelphia, with a dying wife, whose young daughters by her first husband would soon be sent home to their maternal grandmother in Ireland, and a 2-year old son, George. More than any other critical incident in her life, this was the encounter that forged the trajectory of Philadelphia's life thereafter; though perhaps not always altogether happily.

As her husband took up his position of surgeon, Philadelphia adapted to a new place. It is likely that she arrived in Kasimbazaar when Hastings' wife was either *in extremis* or had already died. She may have been able to offer comfort to her, if Mary Hastings was in fact still alive, and to Hastings and his little boy. Hastings was not only the factory chief in Kasimbazaar but also the resident (a kind of EIC ambassador to the Nawab), in the capital Murshidabad.

Mary Hastings died on 11 July 1759, when Hastings was away from Kasimbazaar on business; which was a source of great distress to him, as he wrote to both Clive and his friend Holwell. To Clive, he requested that he be excused from attending the 'durbar' (a formal meeting with the Nawab's court) as the blow he had received from the death of his wife was 'too severe to recollect myself in an instant' and to Holwell he stated that he felt cruelly punished by such an end to his happiness as 'it has fallen to the lot of very few men so early in life to be forced to so cruel a trial'.[27] Hastings was a youngish man in distress, with his wife's death a cruel blow and a little son wanting his mother's love. At this moment Philadelphia came into his life, and it was the beginning of a special connection between them, one which would be sustained for over thirty years.

Chapter 6

A Meeting in Kasimbazaar
1759–1761

Before I close my letter let me gratify my present feeling by telling you that great as my obligations have been to you, you have increased them by a recent & disinterested instance of your friendship for me in your last letter.
Letter from Warren Hastings to Philadelphia,
31 January 1772

THE CONNECTION BETWEEN Philadelphia and her family and Warren Hastings is a complex web. When Philadelphia first arrives in Kasimbazaar, the pretty, vivacious and relatively young wife of the newly-appointed Surgeon Hancock, Hastings' wife Mary is either dying or recently deceased. There has been much speculation about the background of Hastings' first wife Mary, but it is certain that she was the widow of Captain John Buchanan who died in the siege of Calcutta in 1756.

Captain Buchanan of Craigieven and his wife Mary sailed to India in 1753 when he transferred from the British Army to the army of the East India Company, stationed at Fort William in Calcutta.[1] The only evidence of Mary Buchanan's maiden name comes from documents related to Hastings who refers to his wife's mother's name as 'Jones'. It is not hard then to believe that Mary Buchanan's maiden name was Jones. John Buchanan had been known to Hastings in Kasimbazaar, in his early days there when Buchanan was 'in command of the escort bringing bullion to the royal mint'.[2]

Mary Buchanan had two infant daughters, Catherine and Elizabeth, by her first husband when they were caught up in the siege of Calcutta's Fort William garrison. By August, the now-widowed Mary Buchanan and her daughters were with other refugees on the island of Fulta under the Dutch East India Company, down river from Calcutta. They were all in a desperate situation, dying from disease, lack of shelter and starvation. The young Warren Hastings, had first been imprisoned by the Nawab's forces in Kasimbazaar, then obtained his release, and in early October 1756, six months after the siege, escaped Kasimbazaar and made his way down to Fulta to assist the refugees. Within weeks of arriving, Hastings, at the age of 24, married Mary Buchanan, and almost immediately volunteered with Clive's forces to go back up to Calcutta to re-take the fort.[3]

After the takeover of Bengal by Clive's EIC forces, Hastings resumed his position at Kasimbazaar, and by late 1757 he was chief of the factory and had settled there with his wife and his new-born son George. But while his prestige rose with the EIC in mid-1758, privately his life began to unravel. He had told his guardian back in England that his marriage, though seeming perhaps imprudent, had made him very happy, but his wife was ailing. Another baby, a girl, born in the autumn of 1758 died a few weeks later and his wife never fully recovered her health after her daughter's birth.

It is possible, as was not uncommon, for accommodation for Europeans was always hard to come-by and expensive, that when they arrived in Kasimbazaar, the Hancocks stayed in Hastings' house, Philadelphia helping out, with his wife seriously ill, a little son needing care and Hastings often away. It was a very small European community, with even fewer women than in Calcutta. Some sort of connection developed between Hastings and Philadelphia. Hancock was himself only 36, but his letters show him to be something of an 'old-before-his-time' sort of person. Whether this was an affectation, or he really did feel that the years of living in India, with its debilitating heat and disease, had made his body age. Without children of her own and a husband busy with his official work as surgeon and even busier perhaps with his new trading partnership with Hastings, called 'Hastings and Hancock', which was set up at this time, there would have been time for Philadelphia to spend with little 2-year-old George Hastings and become close to Hastings.

As in Fort St David and Calcutta, most of Philadelphia's life was domestic: supervising the household management, doing needlework, some reading, writing letters home and making her husband's life comfortable. From Hancock's later letters when they were thousands of miles apart, we can infer that Philadelphia went to some effort to accommodate her quite demanding husband, even from the distance of thousands of miles away. She endeavoured to oblige him in many ways: financially, in news-giving and reassurance about family, sending parcels of newspapers and magazines and things that were not available in India but designed to give comfort to his life out there.

Her social life in Kasimbazaar would have been a contrast to the one she so recently shared with Margaret Clive back in Calcutta; bolstered as it was by the amenities available to the governor's lady. It is not difficult to see how

Philadelphia and Hastings may have been drawn to each other by their regular contact during this lonely and trying time for him. The friendship of married women and single men in the British Indian community of the eighteenth century was viewed more liberally than it was in later centuries. In describing Margaret Clive's close friendship with Major John Carnac, Bence-Jones points out that:

> Relationships of this sort were more understandable to the eighteenth-century ... where it made no difference to Margaret's great love of Clive; nor did it lead to any jealousy between Clive and Carnac. On the contrary, they were to be lifelong friends.[4]

Once this friendship between Philadelphia and Hastings was established, it remained a very warm one. The warmth of the tone of the one surviving letter of Hastings to Philadelphia is striking. It was written to Philadelphia on 31 January 1772 from Fort St George in Madras, thirteen years after she first came to Kasimbazaar. Hastings had gone back to India from England in 1769 and was about to leave Madras for Calcutta to take up his appointment as governor of Bengal. He begins quite properly but distinctly affectionately, with: 'My dear Madam- I reserve myself the pleasure of replying at large to your letters'.[5]

Philadelphia had written to him many times since he left London three years earlier, though many of those letters have not necessarily been immediately replied to, it appears. Hastings writes of his going to Bengal and doubts: 'whether I shall really profit by the change, but either my pride or partial attachment to Bengal makes me much pleased with it'. He tells Philadelphia that he has sent her gifts: 'a pipe of old Madeira, which was spared to me as a favour... [and] three pieces of chintz, being the first trial made of painting on dooruars'. He writes of the closeness of Philadelphia and his sister's family, the Woodmans, as 'two families united'. He shares personal information with Philadelphia regarding his finances and his health as well as assuring her that her husband, of whom he states that: 'I hear he is thoroughly well, though he sometimes talks of his old fever, the gout'.

The letter concludes with reference to her daughter and very tenderly, albeit cryptically, and with a marked degree of emotion:

> Kiss my dear Bessy for me, and assure her of my tenderest affection. May the God of goodness bless you both! ... Adieu, my dear and ever-valued friend. Remember me and make my Bessy remember and love her godfather & and her mother's sincere & faithful friend.[6]

The tone of this letter to Philadelphia makes an interesting contrast to another letter he writes a few weeks later to Mrs Henry Vansittart, whose husband's journey back to India from England as the proposed new governor in Calcutta ended disastrously. His ship was never heard of again after it left the Cape of Good Hope in December of 1769.

Hastings had become close to the Vansittart family in Calcutta at the same time the Hancocks were there, when Henry Vansittart was first appointed governor. Hastings' biographer Feiling states that while Hastings' acquaintance with the Hancocks was a significant friendship, in his circle, an 'infinitely more vital and lasting was the affectionate friendship he achieved with the new Governor (Henry Vansittart) and his family'.[7] Not sure that is correct.

Mrs Vansittart was Amelia Morse, who had been the daughter of Nicholas Morse, a former governor of Madras. Hastings writes in response to Mrs Vansittart's letter given to him by her son who is just about to leave Calcutta for Madras. Gleig, in his 1841 publication *Memoirs of the Life of the Right Honourable Warren Hastings*, includes both letters, the Vansittart letter 'because of the tone of good feeling which it breathes' but makes no comment about the letter to Philadelphia, yet it is so much more full of personal feeling.[8]

Hastings opens his letter to Amelia Vansittart with 'Dear Madam', not the 'My dear Madam' of his letter to Philadelphia. He gives a complimentary account of her son and then moves on to express his condolences on the assumed loss of her husband. There is the true indication of the warmth of his affection for her husband, but there is little of anything like the expression of feeling towards her that he shows for Philadelphia in his letter to her. His concluding expression to Amilia Vansittart is warm, but is conventionally restrained and formal: '[I] assure you that I am, with the greatest esteem and respect, dear Madam, your most obedient and humble servant'.[9]

There are many regular letters noted in Hastings' Indian letter files to have been written to Philadelphia Hancock, but the contents of those letters were not recorded. But clearly, this comparison of his letter to Philadelphia to one written to another wife of a close friend indicates an intensity in his friendship with Philadelphia quite on another level to that of his friendship with Amelia Vansittart.

The position of factory chief at Kasimbazaar was a significant position within the Company and 'always entrusted to one of the Company's rising men'.[10] Warren Hastings, brilliant scholar at Westminster School but orphaned and poor, had gone out as a 'writer' for the Company at 17 and by the time of Philadelphia's arrival, was EIC chief in Kasimbazaar, as well as the resident, similar to an ambassador for the EIC, in nearby Murshidabad. It was a demanding appointment requiring him to spend time in both places 'pricing silks' in Kasimbazaar and keeping close watch on the various factions at the Nawab's court in Murshidabad.

Philadelphia would have also met at this time, Hastings' friends Francis Sykes and Randall Marriott, both of whom retain friendships with the Hancocks later in life. These men had been with Hastings since his earliest days in Kasimbazaar and on whom he had now to rely for the day-to-day running of the factory. Francis Sykes was a young Yorkshireman who had come out to India as a writer in 1750 and eventually amassed a great fortune and became one of the original, much envied 'nabobs' as they were characterised when they returned to England, very rich and seeking influence.

The Hancocks' stay in Kasimbazaar did not continue for long. Hancock's posting there lasted from 23 June 1759 until 16 September 1760, when at Clive's insistence Hancock was appointed to Calcutta as second surgeon. Hastings opposed the appointment. The reason often given was that he wanted it for his personal doctor, but perhaps he may have wanted the Hancocks to remain with him in Kasimbazaar for other reasons. Clive, however in a letter he writes to Hastings on 14 August 1759 is adamant that Hancock have the position:

> My Intention of Getting Dr. Hancock appointed Surgeon on Mr. Forth's Resignation. I have that Gentleman's Interest much at heart, there has been a long Friendship subsisting between Us, his Merit & Distress'd Situation entitle him to every Service in my Power'.[11]

Like many EIC wives, Philadelphia had to be prepared to be on the move at any time and her life was highly mobile compared to the sedentary lives of her relatives back home. Brother George had moved between Tonbridge and Oxford in his youth, and then settled in Hampshire for the next forty years. Sister Leonora lived in her uncle and aunt's house in the City of London for virtually all of her life. Later, when Philadelphia returned to England she continued to move often; perhaps a reflection of a restless spirit or a seeking of other places, other chances. India changed her and set her apart from the other Austen folk. As Margaret Macmillan points out in her book *Women of the Raj* it could be a peripatetic life for EIC wives:

> Few... spent all their time in India in one spot. Men were moved about by their regiments, their firms, their departments; and the wives packed up the household and followed them...The frequent moves left their mark on all the British in India. They were rarely in any place long enough to establish a sense of belonging... It was hardest of all on the women who had to dismantle their carefully constructed nests and build them again miles away.[12]

From the glimpses we have of her life in Bengal, Philadelphia had made a home and felt at home there. In a later letter sent to her from Calcutta on 14 August 1772 from her husband, he writes of: 'the friendly hospitality which was formerly so remarkable here'.[13] When Philadelphia is mentioned in the letters of others, detailed later, of her life in India, they indicate she enjoyed a pleasant life and a wide acceptance in the small community.

Leaving Kasimbazaar and Warren Hastings behind in September of 1760, the Hancocks now settle in Calcutta, their home for the next four and a half years. How would returning to Calcutta after Kasimbazaar have been different for Philadelphia? Busier, one assumes, as it was a livelier, more gregarious kind of place, and while much of the old splendour had gone there was an eager restoration taking place. Her old friend Margaret Clive, however, was no longer there and her new friend Warren Hastings was left behind in Kasimbazaar.

Robert and Margaret Clive and had returned to England in the February of 1760. Margaret had again left behind an infant son, little Bob, the only survivor of the two children born while she was living in India, in the care of Dr William Fullerton because the baby was not well enough to travel back to England.[14] It must have been another heartbreaking wrench. Eliza Fay in her account describes the distress of her friend Mary Hosea leaving on the ship *The Grosvenor* on her return to England from Calcutta having to leave behind her baby:

> Poor Mrs H- was dreadfully affected at parting with her infant; it seemed cruel for a mother to abandon her child only twenty-five days old; but it must in all probability have fallen a sacrifice.[15]

Well might Mrs Hosea have been suffering, for their ship, the *Grosvenor* was driven ashore on the east coast of Africa in the middle of the night. The survivors set out to walk to the Cape, but only three seamen made it. It was one of many sad losses, for Margaret Clive was never to see again her little boy she left behind, as he died within the year.

While the Clives were no longer in Calcutta, Philadelphia's former close friendship with Margaret must have helped her re-establish her associations there. Dr Fullerton was still there. Margaret's great friend and correspondent, Major John Carnac had left with the Clives in February, but when they reached the Cape he received his appointment to be in charge of Company troops in Bengal and returned to Calcutta. He was to provide a continuing link between Philadelphia and Margaret. There is a small circle of EIC people and their families to whom Philadelphia and Tysoe Hancock remained close.

So there is no reason to think Philadelphia was unhappy to leave Kasimbazaar, but her new friend Hastings remained in Kasimbazaar despite efforts by the EIC to encourage him to come down to Calcutta. Even while Clive was governor, Hastings had been offered promotion to Calcutta on a number of occasions but he had always refused them. While his current position was difficult, caught as he was between the intrigue of the Nawab's court and rampant corruption amongst EIC 'servants'. Though he was privately confessing to friends that he hated it, he was reluctant to leave. Perhaps he thought it would be 'out of the frying pan into the fire', or as some admission of failure on his part.[16]

In Calcutta, Surgeon Hancock was spending more and more of his time as a merchant, in the business of 'Hastings and Hancock' and probably less as a doctor, though he clearly still practised. But for not for much longer as an official EIC surgeon. While not enjoying an establishment like the Clive's had occupied in Calcutta, Philadelphia now had a house of her own, perhaps the one described later, below, by her husband, when after his return to India, Hancock mentions in a letter written to Philadelphia in March 1770 a house in Calcutta where Philadelphia had lived previously.

> You must remember the House which belonged to Mr Butler, and which you lived in formerly: this I have bought cheap, & thereby lessened the enormous expense of house-rent... I fear it is very hot, since so many houses have been built at the back of it.[17]

The 'Mr Butler' is 'Padre' Butler, one of Margaret Clive's two clergymen friends whom she mentions in a letter to Carnac as 'Dr Butler'. A description of the EIC better quality housing is given by a contemporary visitor:

> In all good apartments the houses are upstairs and all on one floor; ... most of the houses are built with a verandar which is a terrace on a level with the rooms in the front ... the rooms are few but mostly large and lofty.[18]

The new governor (or president) was Henry Vansittart (known to all as 'Van'). He and Hastings had first met in July 1760 and found much in common and so become friends. Van was warm and mild-mannered, and like Hastings a keen scholar of Persian, comfortable in India and happy to put his trust in the Indian people. With Van in the chair, Hastings was finally persuaded to come down to Calcutta in February 1761 to take up a position as the President's assistant.[19]

Hastings' twentieth-century biographer, Keith Feiling says of this time that 'We know little of his personal life at this stage'.[20] But we do know he was now alone, a widower for over three years, with his little son now sent back to England with his then closest friend Francis Sykes. This was the common practice. Boys were sent home very young, girls a little later.

Many of the small children sent home for their own benefit did not survive the voyage. Eliza Fay describes how she sent back to England, 'for education', a little boy who was the abandoned natural child of her errant husband. The boy was under the care of the former Miss Hicks, whom Mrs Fay had brought with her when she had come back out to Calcutta, was now married and become Mrs Lacey, and returning to England.

But alas, four days into the voyage:

> Owing to the rapidity of the current, the vessel struck on a sand… and every European on board unhappily perished, except the second officer in whose arms the poor little boy expired.[21]

Miss Hicks did not survive the waves either. So many of the women who made that voyage on the prospect of bettering themselves, ended-up with a great deal of sadness and heartbreak: from children lost, being beset by ill-health and husbands dying. The widows of EIC officers found themselves in a very parlous state; unless they were young enough, and not encumbered by too many children, to marry again.

Sykes was 31 and unmarried when he and little George Hastings made the journey back to England, arriving in the late summer of 1760. And what happened to little George? Not much is known for certain, but he may have remained in some way in Francis Sykes's care, although there is an Austen family tradition that he ended up in the care of Philadelphia's soon to be sister-in-law's family, the Leighs of Adlestrop, in Gloucestershire, neighbours from Hastings' childhood years. But it is also clear that Francis Sykes still held significant responsibility for young George, for on 23 May 1763 there is the first of a number of entries among the Hastings papers of a record of expenses incurred by Francis Sykes on behalf of young George, now 5-and-a-half: 'To going to Oxford on George's Acct. and returning' for £4.12.0.[22]

The family tradition has it that George Hastings was in the care of Philadelphia's brother, George Austen and his wife Cassandra Leigh, when they were newly-married in 1764.[23] But the little boy may well have come into George Austen's care before he married. After an unpromising start to life George Austen had done well. By 1763, when he most likely received the 5-year-old George Hastings into his care for his education, George Austen was 31, had taken his two degrees at Oxford, and been admitted as a Fellow of St John's. He had also previously lived back in Tonbridge, as an 'usher' or junior master at his old school, Tonbridge Grammar School, where he had boarded and tutored students. Returning to Oxford, to be ordained as a priest, he now had the position of a Junior Proctor of the university, and with the living of Steventon in Hampshire presented to him by his second cousin, Thomas Knight I. Not financially spectacular, but a very substantial basis for a career in the church and/or the university.

So by 1763 George Austen certainly had the experience and the credentials for his sister Philadelphia, now a close friend of Warren Hastings to recommend him for the task of tutoring little George Hastings and to take responsibility for the education and board of the child, and have been able to make suitable arrangements for looking after the child in Oxford. In May of 1763 when Francis Sykes makes his visit to Oxford, George Austen was not yet married to Cassandra Leigh, though it is likely that they were engaged.

The next entry in Sykes's record of accounts for young George, is for: 2 December 1763: 'Paid Mr Austin on Acct. of George's expences' £50'.[24] That sounds like six months' worth of expenses for the little boy.

A further entry in Sykes' accounts on young George's behalf is on 28 December 1763 for: 'Postage of letters from Oxford', a cost of six shillings. It is an odd expense, just to be itemised separately, but sounds like some important information regarding little George was conveyed in those 'letters'. Letters to Hastings, still in India, and also to his attorney in London, brother-in-law, John Woodman perhaps?

Then a month later on 20 January 1764 the entry reads: 'Paid Mr Austin his salary due ye 14th Inst.' £100; and 'Advanced Mr Austin Acct. George's Expences', £20. Was this money for the tuition George Austen had already undertaken or for the upcoming six months? In other words, was Francis Sykes 'settling up' on all that was owed George Austen regarding his care of the little boy? It is so, for the last entry in Sykes's record of expenditure on Hastings' behalf is an ominous one, just ten days later on 30 January 1764. It is for the substantial sum of £41: 'To a Handsome Marble Tomb Stone, Expenses of Shipping it & other small Expense'.[25] It suggests the little boy, whose sixth birthday was in December, was now dead. The sad fate of his child was not known by Hastings until a year and a half later, upon his return to England.

To have Hastings in Calcutta must have been pleasing to his friend Philadelphia, and perhaps a relief also to her husband, juggling his surgeon's work with the 'Hastings and Hancock' trading partnership, to have Hastings close at hand. Hastings' rising star was to be of benefit to them all, it would be hoped, for the next month, on 23 March 1761, Hancock resigns his position as surgeon with the EIC, having held his post in Fort William for less than a year. He now is free to become a full-time merchant in the 'Hastings and Hancock' partnership.

Hastings had not lived in Calcutta before and with perhaps few/any close friends there except the Hancocks. Other old friends, had either returned home or were far away. Hastings tells in his letters of having to travel around a great deal. These letters Feiling says show him to be 'the same likeable human being'. Interestingly, Feiling points out that at this time his nearest friends:

> Now seem to be the surgeon Tysoe Saul Hancock, whom Clive had brought from the coast, and his wife Philadelphia, who was born an Austen and the aunt of the immortal Jane.[26]

What strikes me about this comment regarding Philadelphia is that Hastings' friendship with Philadelphia is positioned in this context as of equal importance to his partnership with Hancock.

Warren Hastings is an exceptional person, and would be in any time and place. He is, as Claire Tomalin points out in her biography of Jane Austen, a true 'meritocrat'; one who got to his position almost entirely on his own merits.[27] His scholarship, his immersion in the language, culture and customs of India singled him out amongst his fellow EIC servants. He was highly respectful of the best values and traditions of the Indians, often taking their side in disputes with the EIC councillors. He also believed in fairness and somehow managed to pass 'through the annals of the East India Company with credit and integrity'.[28]

Unlike other EIC contemporaries, Hastings was personally quite abstemious; slim and slightly built, and good looking, despite his prematurely receding hairline. He dressed soberly, exercised regularly, drank and ate moderately. At this time in his life he 'kept his health by an hour's ride at dawn and then a cold shower, in some idle hours strummed the guitar'.[29]

One can speculate what the nature of the relationship was between Hastings, Hancock and Philadelphia. While Hastings by 1763 had acquired a town house in Calcutta and a country house outside in Alipore, as was the fashion for senior EIC servants, it might have suited them all for Hastings to have stayed at the Hancocks's house in Calcutta in that February of 1761 when he first came down to live in Calcutta. Was it something of a *menage a trois*?

Major John Carnac thought so. In a letter to Margaret Clive, written from Calcutta on November 1761, he writes of 'the extraordinary familiarity in which she lives with a man [Hastings] with whom I can't conceive how she ever came to have any connection'.[30] At the same time to a close male friend, Captain Caleb Powell, also a friend of Hancock's, he writes of 'the rather close intimacy between the Lady and Hastings' and of 'their [Hastings and Philadelphia] being almost constantly together'.[31]

We know that ten years later, after falling in love with a beautiful young married woman on the ship back to India, Hastings lived in a *menage a trois* situation in Madras, as deputy governor, with the lady and the husband. Did Hastings enjoy the company of Philadelphia when her husband was busy with his surgeon's practice and trading? In the letter quoted earlier, Hastings writes of his 'great obligation' to Philadelphia. One wonders what that was. Her discretion? Her tender affection shared with him at some lonely point in his life?

Tysoe Saul Hancock was no great mover or shaker. In his later letters to Philadelphia, he sees himself as essentially a failure. Yet he gained the respect and friendship of Hastings, though Clive's comments on him are more ambiguous. In his explanation to Hastings as to why Hancock deserves the Calcutta supernumerary surgeon's appointment Clive writes, in August of 1759, that 'there has been a long Friendship' between them and that Hancock deserves the assistance Clive gives him out of 'Merit' as well as because of his 'Distress'd Situation'.[32] From Philadelphia we have no word of disparagement about him. She maintained her position of loyal and caring wife throughout and kept her duty to marry him, whatever she may have thought, when she arrived in Fort St David eight years earlier and throughout their married life he was dedicated to maintaining her.

Philadelphia's teenaged niece Jane, many years later, in 1792 writes critically of a prospective husband in India in *Catharine, or The Bower.* She herself never knew the Hancock uncle, but cared much for her father's sister. Jane was 17 when 'Aunt Phila' died. Marriage and the shared values upon which it rests is Jane Austen's territory, so perhaps the family view was that Philadelphia had a kind of 'forced' marriage to someone not quite as deserving of her virtues as he should have been. Clearly, whatever she may have thought of Surgeon Hancock, once she was in India, for Philadelphia there was really no turning back. Some of Hancock's later letters to Philadelphia in the last years of his life in India are quite bullying. He may have been, of course, by then, unwell and unhappy and reconciled to never seeing his wife again, and no longer cared for her kind ministrations and attempts to make his life better, even from so far a distance.

While Philadelphia fulfilled her obligations of marriage, as Hancock did his, there is, at this point, a yawning gap in the matrimonial 'contract' between her and Mr Hancock; the absence of children. They marry in the February of 1753, and it is now February 1761; a very long time in the eighteenth century for a young healthy married woman to remain childless. Tellingly in his 19 November 1761 letter to his male friend Caleb Powell, Major Carnac is more forthcoming in his gossip about Hancock's situation than he is to Margaret Clive. He writes thus:

> The scandalous chronicle gives the credit thereof to Mr Hastings, and indeed, her being so long without children, the impotency with which Hancock has been always charged, and the rather close intimacy between the Lady and Hastings.[33]

It must have therefore been a struggle for Philadelphia by this time to accept that she was to have no children, and to find a purposeful life. Her husband was away frequently, attending to patients either living in their garden houses out of town, as well as trading in distant places which were the source of the manufactured goods and raw materials that 'Hastings and Hancock' traded.

Hastings' position on the council brought financial advantages, such as gaining the contract to supply bullocks for transport. Hastings, himself, looked to his Indian banyan (trader) to manage most of his business and disapproved of the corrupt and ruthless practices whereby other EIC servants made their fortunes. His biographer, Feiling makes the point:

> In the private papers of 'Hastings and Hancock'… their instructions forbade the use of sepoys (Indian soldiers in the Company's employ) the beatings, and the usual oppressions, 'many so scandalous', he wrote of one agent whom they dismissed, 'that I can no longer put up with them without injury to my own character'.[34]

Hastings takes up his post in Calcutta in mid-February 1761, with his friends the Hancocks now well established there. In Carnac's letter to Margaret Clive on 19 November 1761, he refers to Philadelphia's 'extraordinary familiarity in which she lives with a man [Hastings]'.[35] Does he literally mean they live together in the same house? It suggests that is the situation, and by the end of May 1761, Philadelphia would have known she was pregnant, with the baby being conceived sometime in mid-March. The rumour mills of Calcutta would soon be grinding to some conclusions not favourable to Philadelphia.

By late 1761 Philadelphia was now preparing for the birth of her child, and felt the combination of joy at the prospect of a long wished for child and the dangers and terrors of childbirth. And if she knew the child was not her husband's but Hastings', what were her thoughts about that? There is no doubt in my mind that from the extent of their contact even later in their lives, from the financial and other support he gave her and the expression of her only surviving letter to him, that she cared deeply for Hastings.

Philadelphia had written to her friend Margaret with news of her impending confinement and had asked to nominate her as the child's godmother. So one can assume Margaret knew of Philadelphia's impending confinement, and from all that we know of Margaret's warm and open nature she would have been happy for her friend.

And did anyone in Calcutta at that time really care that Philadelphia's child might have been Hastings'? Seemingly not. That Philadelphia's friends were happy for her is shown by a letter to Margaret Clive from Amilia Vansittart, the governor's wife who also writes from Calcutta on 11 November 1761 stating, 'Your friend Mrs Hancock is at last happy in the hopes of being a Mother which I am sure will give you great Satisfaction as it does all her Friends'.[36] And even John Carnac preserves his admiration and respect for Philadelphia, despite the gossip.

Philadelphia could look forward to basking in the success any new mother feels with her gift of a child, Surgeon Hancock at 38 could take the role of proud father and the close-knit EIC Calcutta group, where children living among them were scarce and highly prized, got a new plaything to enjoy. Everyone was happy.

Chapter 7

Motherhood in Calcutta
1762–1764

Her own Natural Understanding & Disposition improved by the Precepts of such a Mother as few Children are blest with ...
Warren Hastings letter to Tysoe Saul Hancock,
5 November 1769

PHILADELPHIA'S ONLY CHILD was born on 22 December 1761. A baby daughter, she was christened on 23 January 1762 and given the name Elizabeth.[1] Warren Hastings was her godfather and the absent Margaret Clive, was one of two godmothers, the other being a Calcutta friend Mrs Elizabeth Cockell, 'whose name has been given to the child', writes Carnac to Margaret Clive on 2 February 1762.[2] Mrs Cockell was also godmother to George Austen's second son. The connection between Mrs Cockell, the Hancocks and Austens is not revealed, but she was the wife of an EIC agent William Cockell. Yet another woman whose history is difficult to determine. It is worth noting that Hancock's mother was also called Elizabeth. The baptism would not have been held in a church, as the old Anglican church of St Anne's within Fort William had been destroyed after the siege in 1756 and 'a large room near the gateway of the old Fort was fitted up as a Chapel, which served as the Presidency Church for twenty-seven years, until the building of St. John's'.[3]

Throughout her life, Elizabeth was rarely known as 'Elizabeth'. The infant daughter was either 'Bessy' or 'Betsy' and by the time she became a young lady of 16, preferred the more sophisticated name 'Eliza'; and it is as Eliza she is generally known these days when Jane Austen scholars turn their spotlight on Jane's favourite cousin, and later sister-in-law. We will call her in this work by her later choice, 'Eliza'.

So Philadelphia's ninth year in India starts very differently for her with an infant daughter now to care for and her husband a full-time merchant, though still maintaining a private medical practice. Some increased prosperity was coming through his efforts in trading full-time and through the close connection to the new councillor and close aid to Governor Vansittart, Warren Hastings.

When Philadelphia briefly lived with Margaret Clive in Calcutta two years earlier, we had glimpses of her personal life thorough Margaret's letters. Now other Calcutta friends mention her and her child and husband in their letters, to Hastings in particular, on the many occasions he is away from Calcutta, or when the correspondent is away. The child appears the centre of attention. This extract from a letter by the Reverend Samuel Staveley in April of 1762 to Hastings when Betsy is just 4 months old, sets the tone:

> Greet Ironside. Tell him his amiable Sister & my Dear Friend our Dear Friend Mrs Hancock sup'd last night at ye Gardens & sup with Us again to Night there all snug … Our Friends are all well…& Miss Betsy Hancock ... Little Betsy is very fond of Miss Ironside & her Guitar, she is a sweet little Girl … tis a fine little Girl, they are very well.[4]

Ironside was Colonel Gilbert Ironside who was travelling north with Hastings under Vansittart's orders to the Nawab's temporary capital, Monghyr. Ironside's sister, Mary, had been assisted in going out to India into Philadelphia's care by Margaret Clive. Miss Ironside found Philadelphia pleasant company and is living with her at this time. As an accomplished young woman, now impoverished, with a brother in India in the army, no doubt Margaret thought Mary Ironside's best option for a secure financial future would be marriage. Hopefully her pretty playing on her guitar in the gardens in the evenings attracted the right kind of attention.

While Staveley's tone may be cloying, it is interesting to note that Hastings, the man leading the council's dangerous foray into the Nawab's centre of power to examine EIC abuses would be seen to be pleased to hear this gossipy news from Calcutta about his friends' children.

Clive was well and truly gone, and Hastings was by now a significant figure in Bengal, the close associate of the new governor (virtually his deputy) and member of the governing council. He was really the only one on the council whom Vansittart could trust to take a less hawkish position against the Nawab. Hastings had enemies who would have been happy no doubt to throw mud on his character. But Calcutta was not England and society there was much less hide-bound and probably sexual morality was more laissez-faire. Hastings' later relationship with the woman who became his second wife was really more scandalous than what might have been his connection to Philadelphia, but it had no impact on his status or reputation, even when he became governor of

Bengal. But for a woman, it could be different outcome, and for an unmarried woman, a fatal fall. Married women, were, however, somewhat protected and if indeed Eliza was conceived by Philadelphia within the passionate embrace of another man who was not her husband, the truth of it was kept secret.

Hastings, Hancock, and Philadelphia had nothing to gain from any acknowledgement of Eliza's paternity other than that Hancock was her father. Perhaps Hancock was indeed Eliza's father. But while there is no direct acknowledgement from any of the main players that Hastings is Eliza's natural father, the comments from elsewhere that suggest otherwise include one from the pen of her yet to be born niece, Jane. In a letter to her sister Cassandra on 15–16 September 1713, a few months after Eliza's death, Jane Austen writes of a visit to Warren Hastings by their brother Henry who had married his cousin Eliza late in her life. Jane comments cryptically that: 'Mr Hastings never hinted at Eliza in the smallest degree'.[5] What might she have meant?

As Henry was fairly recently bereaved, and certainly knew of Eliza's lifelong connection to her godfather, he expected Hastings to at least express his condolences. Jane Austen too appears surprised by this silence of Hastings. But he is now an old man of 81, and all that part of his life is so long ago. Hancock has been dead for nearly forty years, Philadelphia for over twenty years, and now Eliza is too. He says nothing.

Whatever apprehensions Philadelphia might have had with the birth of her child, they must have been soon overtaken by the delight of a healthy baby girl, and the happy acceptance of Hastings to be her godfather and with Margaret Clive as a godmother, meant Eliza started life bathed in the reflected glory of two of the most famous names in British India. It was an auspicious start for little Elizabeth Hancock, though for Philadelphia, it was once again a challenge to her reputation. Maintaining her reputation and that of her daughter's in the face of such assumptions as those Major Carnac professed, must have required effort and *sangfroid* on her part. But both Hastings and Hancock played their part in protecting Philadelphia.

Having a young child meant that Philadelphia would have needed an 'ayah', or Indian maid/nanny to help with Eliza's care. Perhaps she already had her maid with her, brought up from her time in Fort St David. The maid may have been with Philadelphia even from the earliest period, a young woman called Clarinda, of apparently South Indian origin. We have a portrait of Clarinda and many references to her in Hancock's, Philadelphia's, Eliza's and even Hastings' letters.

Whenever and however Clarinda came to Philadelphia, she remained with Philadelphia the rest of her life and was an integral and much-loved part of the Hancock family, and known personally to the wider Austen family. Many years later, in a letter from Philadelphia's sister-in-law, Mrs George Austen to another sister-in-law, Mrs William Walter, recounting a visit by Philadelphia and Eliza to Steventon, Mrs Austen refers in a very familiar way to 'Clarinda'.[6]

Ayahs were often responsible for all aspects of care for the children, morning, noon and night, but from the closeness of Philadelphia and Eliza's relationship, it looks more like Clarinda shared in Philadelphia's care for Eliza and long after Eliza was a grown woman, Clarinda remained an important member of the family. She was probably a young girl when she came to Philadelphia, and may have never married, nor had any children of her own.

Clarinda remains part of the Hancock household in Calcutta and travels with the family when they leave India to return to England. It was not uncommon, even in the mid-eighteenth century, for Indian servants to be brought back to Britain with returning families. Records show it was mostly women servants brought back, usually to assist in the care of small children on the long voyage and that they were brought back 'entirely for the convenience of their masters and mistresses as cheap labour', or more compassionate reasons as such as a 'reluctance to leave behind a favourite, a faithful servant'.[7] There are virtually no accounts by these Indian servants of their feelings and experiences of the lengthy voyage and their lives in England during this period.

Once they left India, these servants were entirely at the mercy or otherwise of their British masters and mistresses. While some of them were abandoned when they reached Britain, others were unhappy in the life in Britain and were returned home to India. Hastings and his second wife brought back to Britain two young male servants and four Indian maid servants from India when they returned. The maids were unhappy and went back home to India. It is hardly surprising.

But Clarinda did not return to India, nor was she abandoned by Philadelphia, though she may not have been all that happy. She must have left behind family, but perhaps they had been left behind in Fort St David long before.

In a later letter, Hancock writes to Philadelphia of the 'friendly hospitality' of Calcutta of those days. The *tête-a-tête* that Philadelphia has regularly with the Reverend Staveley indicates that she was a more than welcome member of that group. Even if the others saw what Carnac saw in her 'extraordinary familiarity' with Hastings, it appears not to have affected her standing among them. That Philadelphia was very happy to be out and about and perhaps not be too concerned about what others may think, can be shown in a reference to her in a letter from Margaret Clive to John Carnac in March of 1763 regarding a recent journey Philadelphia had made with Governor Vansittart's party.

Henry Vansittart was known to be brilliant, charming and good-natured, and with something of a disregard for convention, and he causes a scandal when he goes to visit the Nawab and takes his wife and Philadelphia with him.[8] Muslim society kept women in strict purdah and it was seen as an affront to have taken these

English women with him in this open way. It shows Philadelphia as quite happy to go along on such an excursion, and also not caring too much about the purdah convention. Can one detect a certain free-spiritedness there? Having already lived in Bengal for four years, she certainly must have known of the convention.

So by mid-1763 Philadelphia is nicely settled into Calcutta life and her daughter now toddling about healthily in Clarinda's care. Knowing how high the death rate among infants was, and having seen her friend Margaret lose her little daughter at just over twelve months, it must have been some relief to see her daughter thriving. Whatever the distressful circumstances were that came with their flight from Fort St David five years before, Philadelphia could hopefully now leave them well behind. Her husband is beginning to accumulate some wealth from his investments for Hastings and Hancock, and she is clearly Hastings' favourite among the ladies of Calcutta.

Philadelphia was more secure in her life, enclosed in a community of people who were fond of her and welcomed her with 'friendly hospitality'. She had a family of her own now with a child and a husband providing social and financial stability. She also had the extra solace that came from her 'extraordinary familiarity' with an exceptional man, Warren Hastings. But there had been from the time of Eliza's birth, an apparent desire to return to England and then to live in France, for Carnac tells Margaret Clive that as soon as Philadelphia is recovered from the birth of her child, 'she embarks with her husband on board one of our ships & they both intend paying their compliments to you before they take their passage to France'.[9] But that implies Hancock would have had enough money to return. He clearly did not at that point, and was striving to get rich with his trading partner Hastings.

Over the next two years Hastings was stepping into high office with the Company as a well-established member of the council, and although these times after Clive had departed Bengal were tumultuous, there were some positives for the British. The army had seen off the French in Pondicherry in the Madras Presidency, the Moghul Emperor had been defeated and the Mahrattas (the Hindu self-ruling group from the north-west Deccan plateau who had long challenged the Moghul Empire's authority) had been defeated by a Moslem army and could be ignored for a while at least by the British in Bengal. Although at 32, still young, as were many of the leaders of the EIC in Bengal at that time, Hastings was becoming a man of influence and financial substance. The old Nawab of Bengal, Mir Jaffir, who had been deposed by the British in 1760 was then allowed to live under EIC protection in Calcutta. In July 1763 the council declared war on his successor, Mir Kasim and when Mir Jaffir was reinstated as Nawab and moved back to his capital, he gifted his lands and buildings at Alipore, within the EIC settlement area of Calcutta but then outside of the main town, to Hastings in gratitude for his reinstatement.

Motherhood in Calcutta: 1762–1764

The Calcutta gentlemen all liked to enjoy their country houses and Hastings had a passion for gardening. He also had by now a town house in Calcutta. Later he was to expand one of the houses on his Alipore estate to become Belvedere, where he later lived as governor general. The much extended building survives to this day as the National Library of India.

His original house in Alipore was described as:

> opposite the paddock gate consisting of hall, a large verandah to the southward, and six rooms. Two small bungalows, large tank of excellent water, and above 63 biggas of land, partly lawn, but chiefly garden ground in high cultivation, and well stocked with a great variety of fruit trees.[10]

Bengal, from 1763 to late 1764, however, was still a place of great confusion and bloodshed. Hastings and Vansittart had urged the council in Calcutta to pull back on the excesses of the Company's servants in Bengal, to keep to the commitment of shared power with the Nawab and to have the Company's servants respect the rights of the sovereign prince.[11] But from his new capital of Monghyr, Mir Kasim began to take matters into his own hands, recruiting European mercenaries to lead and train his army to challenge the Company's position in Bengal.

Governor Vansittart and Hastings were a minority of 'doves' on the council, with the 'hawks' determined to put the Nawab in his place. There were furious debates in the council with Vansittart's and Hastings' support for the Nawab's rights bringing about abuse on their heads from other council members. At one point Hastings' arguments caused such fury in one of the councillors that he rose and struck Hastings across the face and called him and Vansittart the 'hired solicitors' of the Nawab.[12] In October 1763, when an attempt to take the city of Patna by an EIC army lead by the most hawkish chief factor, William Ellis, failed and the Company survivors taken prisoner and later executed, including Ellis, any peaceful alternative to dealing with the crisis was lost. Hastings' and Vansittart's position looked hopeless.

The warfare against the British raged across Bengal, until it ended finally with the Battle of Buxar in October 1764. A huge 150,000 strong combined Mughal army had moved against the Company. The EIC were vastly outnumbered, but under the leadership of some EIC officers, including Margaret Clive's friend, Major Carnac and with the usual mix of superior fire power and organisation, luck, determination and the Mughal army's disorder, the British finally won. British supremacy over Bengal was established to a degree undreamt of twenty years before.

By the end of 1764, however, this was all too late for Hastings. His personal standing in the Company appeared quite undone and the Company's position looked fragile. 'Making war against the Nawab they had personally installed only five years earlier, was not only a political embarrassment for the Company; it was a financial disaster'.[13]

Back in England these reports of bloodshed and confusion sent EIC shares sharply downwards. The peaceful, powerful, highly profitable situation that Clive had apparently left had been an illusion, and had been totally undermined within a few years, primarily through greed, aggrandisement and folly. Although Vansittart recommended Hastings to the Directors of the EIC as being the 'one person here that I recommend as for the charge of this government', there was now no chance of that eventuating.[14]

As 1764 closed, the news of her brother's marriage to Cassandra Leigh in the April would have reached Philadelphia and have given her cheer. And while Calcutta itself had not been threatened by the warfare elsewhere in Bengal, nevertheless it must have been a worrying time for Philadelphia, and by the end of 1764 the pleasant life established for her in Calcutta may have seemed over. Her friend Margaret Clive was now long gone, Hastings' stellar advancement in the Company and rising wealth had stalled and her husband struggled to consolidate their wealth for a future beyond India. Her daughter was now three and a long held desire to return to England and then possibly France, had been put on hold for many years. All in all, it must have seemed the time to go home.

In late 1764, Vansittart's position as governor came to an end. He was to be replaced by the only man the Company saw capable of rescuing its position, Robert Clive, now Lord Clive, and a Knight of the Bath. He may have been pleased to return. Life in England, and the English climate had not really suited him, and even with his wife Margaret's company, an expanding brood of children, and such honours has had been bestowed on him, he had written to Major Carnac earlier in the year that, 'We are not so happy in England as you imagine, and many of us envy you your way of life in India'.[15]

Hastings resigned his position with the Company in December 1764, a month after Vansittart left. Hastings' decision to leave was a bitter pill, for it meant his enemies were in the ascendant. He had been gone from England for fourteen years, but at 32, was still a young man, had made a modest fortune but had anticipated a much brighter future in India.

Hancock's trading partnership with Hastings would have been difficult to continue without Hastings' money and influence. Hancock had some private practice as a doctor, but he was no longer a Company servant, and his capital would have been limited. With their very close connection to Warren Hastings in terms of living, business and friendship, for them to return when he returned must have been the obvious choice for the Hancocks. Since mid-1759 when they first moved to Kasimbazaar, the Hancocks had established a life so closely connected to Hastings, that staying on without him must have appeared unconscionable. Hastings still had not re-married, and with the likelihood that Philadelphia's only child was his and with their continued closeness, he too may have been more than happy for them to come back with him.

Most Anglo-Indians who returned to Britain with trading interests kept their investments going in India. It was the best chance to continue to make the profits that were possible there, as opposed to getting out what they could of their capital, trying then to actually turn it into cash to invest in the comfortable and secure but very limited home investments of the time. That was not the Indian way. As Hastings' biographer Feiling states: the business papers of 'Hastings and Hancock' show that they 'were winding up their opium transactions, for any price they could get.... leaving behind most of [their] trading capital... to be looked after by [their] friends.'[16]

Hastings thought he had substantial capital to continue to trade profitably, Hancock probably less so. With a wife and daughter and servants to relocate, Hancock would struggle financially with the costs of removal and maintaining a lifestyle in London commensurate with his expectations. But Tysoe Hancock, Philadelphia's 'little husband', as Clive called him privately and somewhat derisively, must have felt obliged to go, whatever anxieties and uncertainties he felt.

Philadelphia would have had all the usual mixed emotions about leaving what was a secure and happy home in Calcutta and taking that challenging sea-voyage back to England. It was now thirteen years since she had left England. Her family must have been distant in her memory, but not forgotten nor lost contact with. George's wife Cassandra was expecting their first child in that February, sister Leonora was still residing with their aunt and her second husband Mr Hinton in London. Philadelphia had taken her chances on the voyage to India, and it had worked out well. She had married Hancock and been a dutiful wife, up to a point, and had a precious child. She had moved in the most elite Anglo-Indian circles, where she had been welcomed, admired and respected. She had formed a close relationship with the wife of Robert Clive and become an intimate of Warren Hastings.

She had survived the voyage out to India, its climate, its diseases and the perils of childbirth; all of which had taken many a young woman before her. She had a husband who would now provide for her and a daughter who was growing up fine and healthy. The chance for Philadelphia had been worth it. At 34, she still had plenty of life ahead of her, but like many other returning Anglo-Indians, would she be satisfied with the old life at home or would she find that she too had acquired the wanderlust of change?

Chapter 8

Going Home
1764–1765

'And I do assure you ma'am', pursued Mrs Croft, 'that nothing can exceed the accommodations of a man of war; I speak you know of the higher rates... and I can safely say, that the happiest part of my life has been spent on board a ship.'

Persuasion, pp. 94–95

'GOING HOME' WITH WEALTH established was the prize of success in India for EIC servants and their families. The old life left behind: the families, friends and places, often took on a particularly rosy glow when viewed from the steamy intensity of Indian life. But India had changed them. Most had been young when they first went out. Hastings was just 18, Margaret Maskelyne 17, Philadelphia 21 and Hancock 22. For some, 'going home' was not the permanent return they had intended and women like Margaret Clive, Eliza Fay and others returned to India out of necessity or inclination. Then there were those born in India of British parents who grew up in India, lived there, married, were employed by the EIC or if they were female, brought their children up there, such as the famous 'Begum Johnson', and when they went back to Britain as adults never felt happy there and returned to India.

'Begum Johnson', a title of reverence for a widow, was born Frances Croke, around 1725, daughter of the governor of Madras and his Portuguese wife. She married four times. She accompanied her third husband, William Watts, a senior EIC official, and their children back to England in 1758. She hated living in England but endured it till her husband died, and with her children grown up, returned to her beloved India. She married again, this time to the Reverend Johnson, but when he decided to retire to England, she stayed on, living in comfort in Calcutta as a rich woman until a great age and died in 1812, greatly revered by the community. Her tomb still stands today in the churchyard of St John's Calcutta.

Margaret Clive had wanted to return with her husband when he went out to India for the third time in 1764. She wrote to her old friend John Carnac in May of that year that she was prepared to: 'Follow the fortune of my first and best friend, my husband … contributing towards making my Lord's stay in India less afflicting to him'.[1] Margaret was pregnant again, however, with a child due in October, and it was decided she was not well enough to travel.

For Philadelphia, there would be no journeying a second time to India, but did she too never quite feel at home in England again? Packing up and transporting the possessions acquired in India when undertaking a long sea voyage, would not have been a problem for Philadelphia, with no doubt a fair supply of servants to assist, but the expense of transporting the goods was considerable. Even so, many well-to-do returning Anglo-Indians took enormous amounts of baggage home with them. Mrs Fay describes some of these departures:

> It is almost incredible what quantities of baggage, people of consequence invariably take with them; I myself counted twenty-nine trunks that were sent on board, for Mr and Mrs H (Hosea).[2]

Obviously, if you had valuable items, and plenty of money, you might well wish to go to the trouble and risk and take them with you. When Hastings' second wife, Marian von Imhoff, left India alone ahead of him, near the end of his appointment as governor in 1784, he happily indulged her passion for splendour and comfort with a journey which cost him £5,000. This purchased two staterooms and a ship's hold that 'bulged with her treasures... over all of which her Majesty's Customs later-on held serious debate'.[3]

But there was no Marian around twenty years earlier, and Hastings was known then for his abstemious lifestyle, though always generous with those he cared for. Philadelphia and her husband would have taken a modest amount of baggage, by Indian standards, for their personal use on the voyage, their future life in London and as gifts for family. Both Hastings and Hancock, when they return to India, frequently send valuable and useful gifts back to Philadelphia in England, such as fabrics, perfumes, spices, pearls, diamonds and wine, so one assumes she took back some such items with her.

While Hancock did not make the fortune he had hoped from his seventeen years in India, he might have trusted that the capital he had accrued and the investments left behind in India in his partnership with Hastings would produce an income sufficient to provide a comfortable living for his family in London. But expenses proved high, at around £1,500 a year. It was a lot of money. He must have been hoping to maintain a very substantial income from investments in India. When he returned to India he comments in a letter to Philadelphia on 17 January 1770 that she:

> Used to be Surprized at our Expences considering our Mode of living, you must now be convinced that it was (not) possible for us to have Spent less even on our frugal plan.[4]

It is pretty clear early on that they were going to run out of the money to support their lifestyle. There was social pressure to live up to your apparent station in life. This was what Hancock wanted for himself and his family. One assumes keeping up appearances in London, even if living quietly would have required a washerwoman, maid of all work, kitchen maid and cook at least. Mr Bennet, in his modest estate in *Pride and Prejudice* has an income of £2,000 a year and keeps a wife, a carriage, five daughters and a fair number of servants, including a manservant and a cook and at least one lady's maid. And that was in the country, not expensive London.

Hancock was now still relatively young, at 41, but seventeen years in India had taken its toll. Regular bouts of gastric infections and possibly malaria and other feverish conditions were highly debilitating, and the heavy diet and solid drinking of alcohol did not help. When back in London, Hancock saw his working life as over and a return to England with a wife and daughter a demonstration of his success.

Philadelphia had been keen to leave, and she had her chance secured with Hastings' resignation. Perhaps life without the 'extraordinary familiarity' of her life there with Hastings was a difficult prospect before her. Also her daughter was now just over the age of 3; seen then as a suitable age for young children to travel safely home to Britain. Furthermore, Philadelphia's attachment to her daughter meant she would never have given up Eliza to travel back to England without her mother. Nevertheless, however the decision was arrived at, Hancock and Philadelphia accompanied Hastings on his return to England, travelling on the same ship with at least one servant, Clarinda. Philadelphia left behind other female servants who apparently mattered to her, as she enquires after them when her husband returns to Calcutta. In a letter to her six years after leaving them behind in Calcutta, he gives an account to Philadelphia of 'your two girls'. The sentiments he expresses may have been upsetting for Philadelphia to read, though her feelings did not cause him to soften his news in any way:

> I can now finish the history of your two girls, as far as I believe you will concern yourself about them. Salima has two children, is

very seldom sober, & is quite common in the barracks at Madras. I am told that Diana instead of being married to a Portuguese, is in keeping with a young fellow who will probably leave her in the town very soon.[5]

Another significant person Philadelphia farewelled was the occasionally mentioned Mrs Bowers. She was more than just a friend to the Hancocks. In the Reverend Staveley's April 1762 letter to Hastings telling of the doings of his Calcutta friends, Staveley writes of the health of a mutual friend Thomas Lyon. Staveley also accords Lyon's recovery in some part to Mrs Bowers.

> Lyon thank God is so well that by the Skill of our excellent Friend & Physician Hancock & as good a woman as I wish to meet with Mrs Bowers he is able to get off his Cot, be dressed and set in a great Chair.[6]

Was Mrs Bowers assisting Hancock in a nursing role? 'Mrs Bowers' is Mary Bowers, a survivor of the Calcutta siege of 1756. The list of women survivors published in an account recorded in *The London Magazine: Or, Gentleman's Intelligencer* of June 1757 included Hastings' wife-to-be, Mrs Buchanan and one child and the name 'Bowers'. Mary Bowers's gravestone still exists in the old South Park Street Cemetery in Calcutta, and has her age on her death in 1781 as being 55, so she would have been 25 at the time of the Calcutta siege. Was she a widow? Widows had a tough time of it surviving in India after the death of their husband, but she never returned to England.

Mary Bowers must have been close to the family during Philadelphia's years in Calcutta, and later when Hancock returns to India. In a letter to his daughter Eliza written in December 1770, he mentions Mrs Bowers's interest in hearing about how Clarinda is going. Mary Bowers continues her generous and caring ways towards the Hancocks, obviously keeping an eye on Hancock as his health declined. The Reverend Staveley's estimation of Mrs Bowers as being 'as good a woman as I wish to meet with' was quite correct.

The Hancock and Hastings party left India in January 1765 on the Royal Navy ship the *Medway*, a fourth rate ship of the line that had come out to the East Indies in 1760 to take part in action against the French. She was returning home to England to be paid off, surveyed and eventually undergo what was called 'a grand refit'. Was it unusual for a group of passengers to be taken home on a warship from India? It may have been uncommon but not unheard of. Hastings' prominent position on the council probably gave him some cache to obtain the passages for himself and the Hancocks. The accommodations on a man of war were probably not that much different from an Indiaman, though it carried many more guns.

In Jane Austen's naval novel *Persuasion*, Captain Wentworth opposes women being on board a fighting ship and, with excessive gallantry defends himself by:

> professing he would never willingly admit any ladies on board a ship of his; excepting for a ball or a visit....from feeling how impossible it is... to make the accommodations on board such as women ought to have.[7]

His sister, the admiral's admirable wife Mrs Croft has been a frequent passenger on board her husband's fighting ships and gives praise of the life of a captain's wife on board a man-of-war:

> And I do assure you...that nothing can exceed the accommodations of a man of war... any reasonable woman may be perfectly happy in one of them; and I can safely say, that the happiest part of my life has been spent on board a ship.[8]

So comfort may have perhaps been assured for Philadelphia. Passage arranged, belongings packed up, sold or given away, farewells made, Hastings and the Hancocks with their maidservant Clarinda and perhaps a male servant called Peter, were going back to what everyone considered 'home', though it had not been home for any of them for many years, and even to begin that journey was not easy. In Calcutta the shore was steep and the water deep. They would have taken a 'budgerow' or barge, till the tidal waters began at Culpee and then boarded their ship at Kedgeree. Hastings would have had any superior accommodation available to himself on board, no doubt at some cost. Twenty years later, the chief officer's cabin on the Indiaman, the *Atlas*, cost him £1,000 just to accommodate his wife's companion Mrs Motte on the return voyage to England.[9]

Hancock had the passage of four or five people to pay for on the *Medway*, and probably their accommodation would have been more modest. Apart from a very few separate cabins on the quarterdeck, below decks were 'cabins' where canvas partitions separated them and kept neither people nor furniture secure when bad weather sent everything flying about. Privacy was virtually non-existent, with every sound audible to those nearby. Nevertheless, Hancock paid a considerable sum of money for this journey. He states in a later letter that the journey home cost him £1,500.

The pilot would take the ship out onto one of the 'roads', i.e. the shipping lanes off the coast of Bengal. When the pilot quit the ship he would take some precious letters with him, written by the passengers to be put on the next vessel for England, in the hope it would reach 'home' before they did, with news of their departure, the name of their ship and impending arrival back in England. The only stop on the voyage would most likely have been either the Cape, or St Helena.

Amongst the scholarly Hastings' possessions would be some serious reading. When he left on his next voyage to India he purchased from his bookseller in London, Hume's *History and Essays,* Robertson's *Charles V,* two volumes of Diderot, James Macpherson's *Fingal* and Dow's *Hindustan*.[10] While the tedium of a long sea voyage could be relieved by some good books, Philadelphia would have had her needlework to occupy her, the care of her daughter and the companionship of her husband, her great friend Hastings, and Clarinda. Cramped in close quarters for a long time with total strangers could be trying. During a particularly long journey back to India on the *Kent* via Rio de Janeiro, the irascible Robert Clive complained about the wife of his second in committee, Mrs Sumner who: 'Seemed possessed of every disagreeable quality which ever belonged to the female sex'.[11]

Other features of shipboard life on a naval warship would have been less pleasant for Philadelphia to have witnessed: flogging and prostitution. It was a not uncommon practice of the royal navy to allow prostitutes to come on board when a ship was in or near a port. Sheila Kindred in her book, *Jane Austen's Transatlantic Sister: The Life and Letters of Fanny Palmer Austen* refers to a passage in an anonymous pamphlet published in 1828 opposing 'certain immoral practices in His Majesty's navy' which describes the arrival of prostitutes on board ship when, 'the captain and his wife were actually on the quarterdeck on a Sunday morning while seventy-eight prostitutes were undergoing an inspection'.[12]

As for flogging, there would have been the usual cruel punishments carried out on board but while the seamen would have been mustered to witness any flogging as a salutatory lesson, any women and children on board would have been kept out of the sight of it, though not perhaps the sound. Kindred refers to the testimony of one naval captain's wife of the period, Mrs Betsy Fremantle, living on board her husband's ship, where she records that she could, 'distinctly hear the poor wretches cry out for mercy ... which broke my heart'.[13]

The year of 1765 was a year of peace, with the Seven Years' War now over, so there was little danger of the *Medway* encountering any action except against pirates along the African coast. A fourth rate British warship with 60 guns should have guaranteed a passage safe from attack by pirates. The other great source of discomfort and danger was inevitably the weather. Of travel by sea Hastings records his view of the perils of the weather on the long sea passage:

> The Want of Rest, the Violent Agitation of the ship, the Vexation of seeing and hearing all the Moveables of your cabin tumble about you, the Pain in your Back, Days of Unquiet and Apprehension, and above all the dreadful Fall of the Globe Lanterns.[14]

But the *Medway* made good time, and having left Calcutta in early February, by June the party were sailing into the Channel. There must have been great excitement at reaching English shores and anticipating the gentle pleasures of life at 'home', often perhaps yearned for in the steaming hot days in Calcutta. And yet, there would be challenges ahead of them.

Chapter 9

Home in England
1765–1768

I shall not often see her [Philadelphia], she is going to retire to the country with her husband and with one of the prettiest sensible children in the world...

Letter from Margaret Clive to John Carnac,
8 May 1766

PHILADELPHIA NEVER DID 'retire to the country', even though it was from time to time an expressed wish of hers. More of a dream than a reality, though much later she did live in rural France for two years. In the end, it may not have suited her. Once in London the Hancocks had to find a new home; as did Hastings, but they lived not far from each other. Hastings had left India disconsolate and embittered, as one biographer has pointed out:

> Due to moderation, a feeling for the people he was called upon to administer, honesty and freedom from the get-rich-quick virus, he was returning, to all intents and purposes a failure.[1]

His fortune was limited. He had made the modest profit by Indian standards from trade in Bengal of around £30,000, most of which had been left behind invested under 'Hastings and Hancock', with Francis Sykes overseeing his interests.[2] His grief at finding on his arrival that there was no young son alive for him to meet again must have added greatly to his disconsolation. He and the Hancock family did not entirely go their separate ways though and remained close geographically in London, still bound by ties of business, friendship and something more than mere friendship between Hastings and Philadelphia. There was obligation there.

Philadelphia lived in London for the next twelve years, with regular visits out of town to relatives and friends. Her home for the next year or so was in

Norfolk Street, on the 'left hand' side just off The Strand leading down to The Embankment.[3] It was not a particularly fashionable area, so rents would have been more affordable than the centres of society, focused on the newly-developed terraces and squares of St James and Westminster. Perhaps it was an area Philadelphia was familiar with, being not very far from Covent Garden; her old haunt when she was the millinery apprentice. Did she visit her former mistress Mrs Cole's establishment in Russell Street, Covent Garden, I wonder? Perhaps she did, as she was a warm, caring person without pretensions or snobbery. Hancock's younger brother Colbron's glass-making business was located in The Strand.

What do we know of Philadelphia's life for these next few years? There is the usual scattering mention of her in the letters of family and friends as our main source of information. Limited as they are, they do give the flavour of the life of a quietly-living woman, not part of the fashionable world but to whom her extended family was important and her daughter's well-being of paramount importance. Making her new home comfortable, introducing her husband to her relatives and maintaining her link to Hastings occupied her. Her rented houses would have had perhaps some furniture in them already. She receives gifts of chintz later from Hastings when he is back in India to use decoratively. Her portraits show her elegantly but simply dressed and her practical experience in the millinery trade probably gave her an eye for cloth and colour. As an Austen, like her niece, she had no taste for ostentation, even if she did move in the circles in India that eighteenth-century English society held as representatives of the most blatant displays of ostentation. She certainly acquired some Indian tastes, but they were of the modest kind, such as spicy pickles, Attar of Roses perfume, good quality fabrics and perhaps just a few diamonds and pearls. Norfolk Street, does not exist anymore, but Essex Street, in Temple, just four blocks away and parallel to it does still exist and was where Warren Hastings lived when the Hancocks were in Norfolk Street. East India House, the London Headquarters of the EIC was located not far away up Ludgate Hill into the City in Leadenhall Street. If Hastings was considering a return to India and resuming his career there, he would need to maintain his contacts at the Company.

What would have been Philadelphia's style of living in those years? She was used to London life, its dirt and bustle, and unlike Mrs George Austen, her sister-in-law who found a visit to London a noisy, dirty and confusing trial to be endured for a very short time, Philadelphia was not much bothered by it. The crowds, the noise, the bustle and dirt would not be an issue for someone who had lived in Calcutta for five years.

The Strand had been a busy shopping centre since the seventeenth century, when the New Exchange had been built on the south side, as Pepys described it, with rows of shops filled with luxury goods, and many seamstresses and milliners. Tempting no doubt for the likes of Pepys, and Philadelphia may have felt quite at home. We know from the letters of Jane Austen that she herself enjoyed the novel opportunities that London offered for shopping, exhibitions and entertainments. But Philadelphia may not have enjoyed such to the same degree, for we have a brief account of her from Margaret Clive, who sees her from time to time in those months after her return.

It may have been an awkward friendship to resume, with Philadelphia now the mother of a child for whom Margaret is godmother and finds delightful, but knows is rumoured to be Hastings'. The easy familiarity of Fort St David and Calcutta could not be so readily recaptured in Georgian London, and while Philadelphia and Margaret in India came to occupy very different stations in life, it was still India in the 1750s, and at that time a very small expatriate society. Theirs had been a long and close friendship, and while Margaret was known to be not much interested in the connections of fashionable society and happy to keep up her India friendships, she was now Lady Clive, with her husband recently invested with the Order of the Bath by the king. She was a markedly devoted wife to someone who must not always have been an easy husband to love, and her reputation was also his reputation.

She visited Philadelphia upon her return. In a letter to her friend Major Carnac in December 1765, she says that she has seen the Hancocks a number of times. The friendship was re-established between her and Philadelphia, though not quite on the easy terms as before. It seems Hancock's 'indisposition makes them dislike meeting much company' and that nowadays Philadelphia is 'so reserved that she seldom chuses [sic] to see her acquaintance but in the utmost privacy', she tells Carnac in a letter on 8 May 1766.[4] Margaret Clive is now living in a very fine town house in Berkeley Square, but the Clives too are something of outsiders in that world. They gave no 'balls, routs or similar entertainments'.[5] Margaret preferred the country, where they had taken a house near Clive's native Shrewsbury. Bence-Jones, Clive's biographer, states that: 'The Clives' circle was ... mainly limited to relatives and friends from India'.[6]

Margaret speaks fondly of Philadelphia in letters in those first few years of the Hancocks's return to England. In late 1765 and 1766 Margaret writes in praise of Philadelphia and her daughter to both Carnac and her husband. She tells Carnac in her December 1765 letter that she finds her 'little god-daughter a wonderful fine child, & am much pleased with her'.[7] To her husband, a week later she writes that she has seen the Hancocks and finds Eliza, now 4, 'one of the prettiest children I ever saw'.[8] But there is a cautious tone adopted here that seems to be a defence of Philadelphia's reputation and an indication that Margaret does not have very much to do with Philadelphia, though she remains someone Margaret holds in great regard and she 'sees nothing but the utmost propriety' and 'just the same she was to all appearance… without reserve, and agreeable as usual'.[9]

But Clive, now back in India, has already written Margaret a long letter, begun in September 1765 which ultimately brings an end to Philadelphia and Margaret's friendship.

Clive writes that his wife must:

> In no circumstances whatever keep company with Mrs Hancock for it is beyond a doubt that she abandoned herself to Mr Hastings, indeed, I would rather you had no acquaintance with the ladies who have been in India, they stand in such little esteem in England that their company cannot be of credit to lady Clive.[10]

As Margaret had already been told by Carnac four years previously of the scandalous rumour abroad in Calcutta that Hastings was the father of Philadelphia's child, and that Carnac had been shocked to find that Philadelphia and Hastings lived in such 'extraordinary familiarity' that it gave rise to the rumours, Clive's claims of Philadelphia's 'abandonment', were hardly new to Margaret. What would have likely shocked her would have been the strength of his instructions to her. Few eighteenth-century wives would have defied such orders by their husbands.

On receipt of Clive's explicit instructions, it was inevitable that Margaret could not maintain her close ties with Philadelphia. She was trying to manage the situation.

Concerning this letter, Clive's biographer, Bence-Jones notes that:

> These lines though still legible, have been crossed out, almost certainly by Margaret who wished to preserve Philadelphia's good name, while knowing already that her child was rumoured to be by Warren Hastings. The fact that she also crossed out the sentiments that follow would suggest that she was ashamed of Clive's censorious outburst.[11]

The world of Clive is the world of the patriarchy and the great division of women into two: those who are above reproach and sexually available only to their husbands and the rest, essentially whores in his mind, who are available to all and any men. Margaret is however sensitive to other shades of female identification and there is a kind of female solidarity evident here in her response to Clive's admonishments. Her friend cannot be so readily categorised and dismissed,

On 8 May 1766, Margaret writes to Carnac and tells her old confidante, that she continues to find Philadelphia's 'deportment' completely appropriate and has no wish to shun or condemn her. Margaret is happy to give Philadelphia the benefit of the doubt and points out that other mutual friends and acquaintances find no fault with her. She gently puts it that 'if anything is amiss, she [Philadelphia] has only the punishment of remembering it'.[12] The word 'amiss' is so mild a term compared to Clive's 'abandoned herself', or Carnac's 'extraordinary familiarity' that we can only admire Margaret Clive's loyalty, kindness and generosity to her friend. But faced with her husband's stricture, a break is inevitable. Margaret explains to Carnac that she hopes to manage it without giving much hurt or offence:

> I shall not often see her, she is going to retire to the country with her husband... My Lord's injunctions are so positive not to keep up the acquaintance that I shall not seek for occasions of meeting... she may never know that his Lordship has any idea prejudicial to her, & she knowing that my application to my very particular amusements & studies, music and Italian, have for some time spoiled me as a letter writer, will not wonder I am silent.[13]

The hope that somehow the friendship would just wither on the vine and save Philadelphia from shame or embarrassment, does not come to pass. While the plan of the Hancocks in mid-1766 is to live quietly in the country, that never happened and they remained in London. Clive came back to England in July of 1767, just over a year after Margaret had confided to John Carnac that she hoped Philadelphia's move to the country would allow the friendship to lapse in a way that gave no offence. But there came a time when Margaret would have to rebuff her friend.

Six years later, after his return to India, in November 1773, Philadelphia's husband wrote to her, of 'Lady Clive's most extraordinary Coolness' towards Philadelphia.[14] So sometime after June 1766 and before mid-1773 Margaret brought her friendship with Philadelphia to an end. It must have been a hurtful moment for Philadelphia and perhaps for Margaret too. We know how protective Philadelphia was of her daughter and the implied blow to Philadelphia's reputation, albeit a private one, must have intensified the worries she may have had over her daughter's future marriage prospects. With virtually no fortune and the possible rumour of illegitimacy attached to her, Eliza's future could be grim.

The friendship with Margaret Clive, begun on the voyage to India on the *Bombay Castle* over fifteen years before, came to an end, but Margaret Clive was no malicious gossiper and Philadelphia was fortunate to have other close friends and family. They saw no reason to treat her in any way but fondly and generously and did not see their reputations threatened by acquaintance with her, whatever they may have heard or suspected. We can assume most had never even heard the rumours, some who had and refused to entertain them and perhaps a few others, in this mid-eighteenth-century world, had come to their own conclusions and saw the close connection with Hastings and the serendipitous birth of her only child after nine years of childless marriage, as no bad thing for everybody. Certainly, hers and Hastings' closest family embraced Philadelphia and Eliza most handsomely.

Philadelphia's first reunions on arrival home after her thirteen years away were with her Austen and Hampson extended family. To see her brother and sister again, to meet her sister-in-law, the no-nonsense Cassandra Leigh, and their new baby, James, her half-brother William Walter and his burgeoning family, as well as her Freeman and Payne cousins was obviously important for Philadelphia. She had left on her great and risky adventure to India as a young, single woman with few prospects and connections, and now returned as a married woman with a respectable husband with sufficient fortune to maintain her comfortably and with some status in the world. Added to this she had a particularly delightful little daughter and an exotic Indian servant. She must have had a touch of glamour about her, living in a fashionable part of London and with friends like the wife of the great Lord Clive and the important EIC administrator, Warren Hastings. Her intimate connection to Hastings drew her into his family too, especially his sister Anne's family, the Woodmans, who became like a second family to Philadelphia.

Introducing her husband to her family, who mostly lived in the country, meant visits out of town. But the one close member who lived in London was her sister Leonora, the youngest of the three orphaned Austen children. Hancock clearly met Leonora at this time, as he refers to her a number of times in his letters. He calls her 'poor Leonora', as though she is to be in some way pitied. Quite why is not clear.

Leonora is still living with her uncle Stephen's widow and her second husband, John Hinton. The Hinton household at 24 Paternoster Row, is within walking distance of the Hancock's residence in Norfolk Street, so there were opportunities for Philadelphia to take Eliza and her husband to visit her sister in the neighbourhood she knew from her earlier years. A household in the printing/publishing/bookselling business in those days was usually located above and behind the premises of serious, noisy and messy production, so there may have been limits for visitors. Whatever the extent of the contact, Leonora was never forgotten and when the time came for further provision for her maintenance, neither George (though probably less able with his ever-increasing family) nor Philadelphia, shirked their responsibility to their sister.

Seeing her brother George again and meeting his wife and child for the first time must have been a priority when Philadelphia landed back in England. Her daughter, still called Betsy or Bessy by everyone, became a great favourite with the family and remained so throughout her life. Philadelphia's husband was welcomed into the family, and was godfather to George and Cassandra Austen's second child, George, born in August 1766.

The first indication of Philadelphia's seeing her brother again comes from an entry in her brother's account at Hoare's bank in Fleet Street in London for July 1765 suggesting that he is in London just a few weeks after Philadelphia has taken up residence in Norfolk Street.[15] George Austen most likely also met Warren Hastings at that time.

One can speculate on that first meeting, probably in the Norfolk Street drawing room, with Philadelphia's reunion with the much-loved brother; he of the bright eyes and gentle manner, the renowned 'tenderness' and 'sweet benevolence of his smile' as his daughter Jane described him many years later. Philadelphia would have already undergone the slightly anxious meeting of her brother with her husband for the first time. It would have been all politeness, of course but their characters were quite a contrast: the somewhat bluff old India-hand surgeon and the gentle, charming clergyman. Apart from the extreme awkwardness of his child having died under the Reverend Austen's care, the intellectual Warren Hastings and George Austen perhaps had more in common. Little Betsy must have been a distraction to them all; and George would have been no doubt pleased that Philadelphia had such good connections, and he either never suspected or chose not to suspect that the little girl was anything but Philadelphia's legitimate daughter. He would have seen how much joy her child gave to Philadelphia and probably that would have been enough for him.

By the time Philadelphia was reunited with her brother and sister, she would have already met Hastings' family, his sister Anne, her husband John and their son Thomas (Tommy). Anne Hastings had been, like her younger sibling, brought up in their grandfather's household in Churchill, Worcestershire with their unmarried aunt, Elizabeth Hastings caring for them. Anne remained with her aunt, who at some point moved to London, to Kensington, and Anne lived there with her aunt until she was married to the lawyer John Woodman, in 1758 when she was about 27 and the groom, 34.

Anne Hastings and John Woodman were married in the fashionable church of St George's Hanover Square in May 1758, where Mr Woodman was a parishioner. Woodman was an attorney employed as steward for the Earl of Bridgewater, whose London house was located in St James's. The Woodmans were living at number 1 Cleveland Row, St James's. Hastings' goddaughter, Eliza and his dear friend Philadelphia became almost part of the Woodman family, and Hastings' later letters from India were often written to include both of the families, which he considered as united as one. So this relationship with Hastings' family, which begins within days, of her arrival in London, endures for Philadelphia, throughout the rest of her life.

What the Woodman's knew of a particular relationship between Hastings and Philadelphia and the rumours about Eliza's parentage, we do not know. Mr and Mrs Woodman esteemed Philadelphia enough to give their daughter, born in 1770 and yet another Elizabeth, as her second name, 'Philadelphia'. Though perhaps a hint is given in the idea that has been suggested that at some point Tommy Woodman and Eliza Hancock might be a match. It never eventuates. Eliza and her mother take off for France. They were probably never too well-suited. The Westminster and Trinity educated Thomas Woodman eventually became Rector of Hastings' ancestral parish of Daylesford and at the fine age of 51 married Hastings' wife Marian's German niece, Louise Chapuset.

Hastings apparently enjoyed little other company in those London years. He sought out few old acquaintances, had no particular employment, pursuits or lady companions. He appears somewhat at a loose end, perhaps in grief for his dead son and possibly lonely, with his passion and dedication to India seemingly now a hopelessly lost cause. While he had not made much of a fortune, perhaps to fill the void, he spent money like there was no tomorrow, going through his capital at a great rate, hoping those back in India looking after the 'Hastings and Hancock' trading business would bring in the promised profits.

Hancock, preferring to stay home, probably did not keep a carriage. Hastings, however, kept an elegant post-chaise, a small enclosed carriage with windows seating two or three people, which was the favoured town transport for a well-to-do young gentleman. Hastings' post-chaise was said to be, 'chaste and expensive, its body being painted a pleasant pompadour while the Hastings crest and arms were embraced within green and gold wreaths'.[16] I like to think of Philadelphia and Eliza being whirled about London by Hastings from time to time.

That first year in London must have been an exciting and heartening time for Philadelphia. Hancock and Hastings were both prepared to spend money liberally and in the way people of fashion and fortune spent it. They were not at all the wealthy 'nabobs' who they might have been characterised as, but still, there was an expectation to live a little like they were. Nothing shows this more than having their portraits painted by Sir Joshua Reynolds.

Reynolds was England's leading portrait painter of the second half of the eighteenth century. Amongst the increasingly wealthy aristocracy and gentry, the commissioning of a portrait symbolised status and wealth. Reynolds's style of portraiture was noted as 'the grand style', celebrated for the way it gave an air of refinement to his subjects. They wore their best clothes and were posed gracefully. People commissioned these portraits as either adornments to their homes or as gifts to others close to them.

Hastings' portrait is a well-known work in the National Portrait Gallery in London, taking its place among other Georgian period portraits in the Gallery.

Hastings, the first governor general of Bengal is now a famous historical figure, but that future appeared remote at the time the portrait was painted. Reynolds' records show it was done from March 1766 over a number of sittings. It is described on the National Portrait Gallery's website as a 'magnificent portrait by Reynolds with a pile of papers, a pot of ink with a quill and a seal with Persian script' and 'wearing semi-formal attire, his clothes of different colours and fabrics: the blue silk and woollen coat with a velvet collar, the black velvet breeches, and the printed cotton (probably Indian) waistcoat'.[17]

It is indeed a striking portrait of the slim, handsome, still youngish man. Hastings was 34 at the time of the first sitting for the portrait. His pose is elegant and languid, dressed plainly but wearing the essential embroidered waistcoat and the blue coat of a servant of the East India Company. When completed, the portrait did not travel with him out to India but remained behind in England in someone else's possession; perhaps it was even painted as a gift. It must have come into Philadelphia's possession, for it was hanging in the dining room of Eliza's London home when Jane Austen was a regular visitor there many years later.

Prior to Hastings having his portrait painted, the Hancock family had their portraits painted by Reynolds. Hancock always emphasised in his letters to Philadelphia that he wanted 'the best'. It was certainly an extravagance, but one in that first six months or so of their London life, he felt was warranted. The existence of this portrait of the Hancock family, unknown until very recently, is due to the scholarship of Charlotte and Gwendolyn Mitchell, who published their findings in 2017. The Reynolds portrait has been the property of the Gemaldegalerie in Berlin since 1976 and was described in the catalogue as being of *George Clive and his family with an Indian maid*. The Mitchells' research revealed beyond doubt that the true identification of the portrait by Reynolds is: *Tysoe Saul Hancock, his wife Philadelphia, their daughter Elizabeth and their Indian maid, Clarinda.*[18]

The family at this moment in their lives, newly arrived in London, leaps out of the canvas from the shadowy world of letter fragments and rent book records, into a visceral, physical reality. There they are: plain-featured pudgy-faced husband, lovely Clarinda, their Indian maid, eyes cast down, exquisite bright-eyed daughter in her Indostan dress with its veil, and Philadelphia herself, slim and elegant, cupping her daughter gently by the chin and looking out on the world. The three female figures are bound together, maid and mother seemingly bent on keeping the little girl still, while the man is an onlooker. Reynolds has no trouble enhancing the appearance of the women, while even the master of 'the grand style' cannot do much to make Surgeon Hancock look anything more than what he is. And while his eye line looks a little beyond the others in the painting, and his dark blue coat looks dull against the glorious pale silks worn by the female figures, there is perhaps a slight look of pride on the face of Hancock.

Mitchell & Mitchell's research reveals that between August 1765 and February 1766, there were a number of sittings recorded by Reynolds for Mr and Mrs Hancock and that the painting started out as two separate portraits, one of Hancock and one of Philadelphia and Eliza. They were later combined and with Clarinda added to become a landscaped shape group portrait. It may have ended up as a single painting as an economy measure.

The portraits began on 12 August 1765, barely two months after the Hancock family's arrival in London. But it was a long time before the final payment was made; not till 27 August 1767 when Hancock paid £75.[19] Perhaps that included the gilt framing. By that time, it must have seemed an extravagance. For a vanity project, £75 was a great deal of money.

It is probable that the Hancocks made their visits to Philadelphia's extended family in the September of 1765. Her stepmother Susannah was still alive, living in their father's house in Tonbridge in West Kent. She was now aged 78, but there appears to have been no contact by Philadelphia with her stepmother and when Susannah Austen dies, three years later in 1768, there is nothing in her will for these children of her long dead husband. In their father's will they were all entitled to a third of a share in their father's estate after the death of their stepmother, and indeed the house was sold in 1768 in the November of that year.

While Philadelphia may not have introduced her husband and daughter to her Tonbridge stepmother, her Hampson family cousins were quite a different matter. We know from Hancock's later correspondence with Philadelphia from India that he had met and got to know Philadelphia's mother's family quite well; in particular the Freeman, Payne and Walter families.

The rich, plantation-owning Freeman family home was in Salisbury in Wiltshire, where the sisters were born, but by at the time of her return, in 1765, her two single cousins, Molly and Stella were living in London. Their brother, John Cope Freeman was well-established at Abbots Langley in Hertfordshire; he had married in 1756, had a son, Henry-Thomas and had been appointed in 1763 as Sheriff of Hertfordshire. Their married sister, Catherine-Margaretta had married young, to Charles Stanhope of Westminster in 1746.

On reaching their majority, or upon marriage, the Freeman sisters were left a modest inheritance in their father's will. In one letter to Philadelphia, Hancock sends his 'love to Miss Freeman', evidently meaning Molly. He liked Molly in particular, but he did not much approve of Stella, as he tells Philadelphia that his opinion of Molly 'is as great as it is mean of her relation', meaning Stella.[20]

Stella, was, however, a real survivor. She outlived all her siblings and became the inheritor of the family's West Indian wealth and her brother's Hertfordshire estate in Abbot's Langley. At the age of 68, Stella married Admiral John Carter

Home in England: 1765–1768

Allen, at his home in Devonshire Place, Marylebone. Stella was soon widowed and lived in Devonshire Place and later at Langley House, where she died in 1821. Her estate went to the only surviving great-grandchild of Catherine Hampson and Cope Freeman, the daughter of Philip Dormer Stanhope, called Stella Eloise Stanhope. The estate was granted substantial compensation when its slaves in the West Indies were emancipated.[21]

Re-connecting with her half-brother William Hampson Walter and his family and introducing her husband and daughter to them, must also have been a priority to Philadelphia in that first year back from India. William Hampson Walter was living in Kent, where he remained all his life, though in a number of different locations. In 1735, at the age of 14, when Philadelphia was four and George was three, William Hampson had been apprenticed to a Tonbridge mercer, Samuel Vanderlure. At this time his half-brother George began as a pupil at Tonbridge School and lived in Tonbridge with his aunt and uncle Hooper. In 1745 William marries Susannah Weaver of Maidstone in Kent. This is the year that Philadelphia begins her apprenticeship in Covent Garden.

So in the year of her return from India, her half-brother William Hampson has been married for twenty years to wife Susannah, and is now 44 years old with a family of two girls, Sarah (Sally) and Philadelphia (Phylly) and four sons. He had means enough to see the boys well educated. Phylly, named after her aunt, is the youngest, born in the same year as Eliza, and it was a connection that was encouraged. Mrs George Austen has also remained in close contact with her Walter sister-in-law and the three families share letters, news and visits.

Philadelphia also keeps up the bonds with her Payne cousins; a relationship her husband is particularly interested in encouraging. Overall, Hancock seems impressed by Philadelphia's family connections, though he has his grumbles about her aged uncle, Francis Austen, his attorney and agent. He is convinced Uncle Francis keeps him in the dark about the state of his financial affairs and is anxious when Philadelphia has to approach her uncle for funds. Did they make the trip down to Sevenoaks to see Uncle Francis in his grand 'Red House'? Perhaps not. George Austen seems to have seen it important to make a visit from time to time, and for Uncle Francis to be godson to his first born child, James. Though any hopes George may have had of becoming his uncle's heir disappear when Francis Austen, at 50, marries a wealthy widow who bears him a son in short order. Philadelphia and George's cousin, Francis Motely Austen goes on to inherit a very handsome fortune. Even though Hancock complains about Philadelphia's uncle's handling of his affairs, he does in his early letters following his return to India, request that she passes on his remembrances to Mr Austen.

Hancock also makes the point to his daughter in a letter from India urging her to keep-up her friendship with the Payne cousins. George Payne's mother

Jane Hampson, was allotted the care of the three Freeman cousins upon the death at sea of their parents in 1734 by the terms of their father's will. It is likely that Philadelphia spent time in her childhood also in the care of the Payne household and kept the connection throughout her life. Philadelphia's cousin, barrister George Payne had five children, with four daughters close in age to Eliza who certainly continued the friendship into adulthood.

Philadelphia was quite busy keeping up with all these family connections in 1765 and 1766, but she also established other new friendships outside the family that remained important to her, apart from the Woodmans. These friendships of interest included the Misses Hinchliffes. Deirdre Le Faye wonders how Philadelphia became such a close friend of, as her daughter Eliza later describes them, the 'virtuous spinsters', sisters of Dr John Hinchliffe, Master of Trinity College Cambridge and Archbishop of Durham and Peterborough. Their names were Martha and Elizabeth Hinchliffe, and while they became important to Philadelphia later, the friendship was most likely forged from connections made in these first few years back in London. So what was this connection, so secure that Miss Elizabeth Hinchliffe's Woodstock Street Mayfair address could be used to reliably ensure that Philadelphia's and Eliza's correspondence could reach them in Paris, and one to whom small amounts of money were paid regularly by Philadelphia when she was living with Eliza in France? Presumably to recompense Miss Hinchliffe for her efforts on their behalf.

Their brother, John Hinchliffe was a contemporary of Warren Hastings at Westminster School, who, in the same year Hastings went to India, went up to Cambridge. He formed ties with the aristocratic Crewe family, and married the sister of his Crewe patron. He rose through the ranks of the clergy, after being usher at Hastings' old school, Westminster and briefly succeeding the Headmaster there in 1764. John Hinchliffe's origins were remarkably humble. His father Joseph was a livery stable-keeper, whose business was in Swallow Street, Mayfair, just off Piccadilly on the north side. Joseph Hinchliffe's wife predeceased him in 1771 and when he died in 1775, he was living in Woodstock Street in Mayfair. He left various properties to his son and two daughters who were all in their early forties, though only his son was married. John Hinchliffe was then Bishop of Peterborough. Philadelphia's connection to these ladies is most likely to have come through her connections to Hastings and the Woodmans and living near Woodstock Street in Mayfair. Hastings was famously devoted to his school and old Westminster fellows.

Throughout 1766, life is rather good for Philadelphia. She and Eliza have that connection with the old Indian way of life through their Indian servant Clarinda, and the friendship of their family and of some old India friends. She is living in a fashionable part of London, enjoying the comforts of that life. There are welcoming visits to and from her extended family and people write fondly of her. In a letter to Hastings in August 1765, his old friend Randall Marriott requests that he pass on his best wishes to their Indian friends now returned home, and specifically mentions Philadelphia, her husband and their daughter:

> I shall now conclude my Friend, with requesting You kindly to remember me to Mr & Mrs Hancock, Mr Van ... and all my old Friends- Greet little, Great I believe I should say, Betsey Hancock with many Kisses and my Salaams & George [Vansittart]give a good hearty shake by ye hand .... Write me particularly how these little ones do.[22]

The Vansittart family were living in Burlington Street Mayfair, near to Hastings and not far from the Hancock's new Bolton Street address. In another letter on 2 September 1766 Marriott again asks that his 'best wishes' be passed on to the Hancocks as he has not time to write to them personally.[23]

But life also had its problems for Philadelphia. There was her husband's health. Margaret Clive mentions Hancock's looking very overweight and unhealthy and in his letters on his return to India he refers to his 'old' problem of 'the gravel' and 'gout' recurring. Hancock in 1766 is not an old man, just 42, but conditions such as 'the gravel' (kidney stones), and 'gout' indicate chronic disorders that can be painful and debilitating.

The profits of the partnership of 'Hastings and Hancock', left in the hands of others back in India were going seriously downwards, while the debts of the partners were mounting in London. Both Hastings and Hancock began to borrow to keep themselves afloat. On 15 April 1766, George Austen sells some South Sea Annuities and receives £217.12.9 for them. This amount, less four shillings, he passes on to Hancock five days later.[24] This may have been either a loan or repayment. Money now seems short, as by November 1766, only eighteen months after arriving in London, Hancock gives a £1,000 bond to William Summer. This is basically a loan from Summer to Hancock. It must have allowed Hancock to keep his head above water for a time.

Hancock was not alone in struggling with lack of income from his Indian investments. His business partner Warren Hastings was in financial difficulties too. He was supposedly not extravagant, but 'he hated poverty' and liked to live well.[25] While he had no immediate family for whom he was responsible, he was generous and did enjoy living in a certain comfort and style. We have already seen that in those first years in London he kept a fine-looking carriage, lived in a fashionable part of town and followed the Hancock's lead in having his portrait painted by Reynolds. He also settled an annuity of £200 a year on his aunt Elizabeth and gifted an inheritance to his sister Anne Woodman, as well as continuing provision for his deceased wife's two daughters from her first marriage. Perhaps their maternal grandmother in Ireland, Mrs Jones, to whom their care had been entrusted almost a decade ago had died, for before he left again for India he allocated £20 a year to Mrs Forde, the wife of his old Indian friend, Colonel Forde, to be responsible for the welfare of his stepdaughters, now in their mid-teens. These long-orphaned sisters were somewhat cast adrift in their lives, though Hastings maintained financial support to them well into their adulthood.

Hastings also borrowed money to keep him afloat, including a £6,000 bond from the same William Summer. Hastings had also been very unwell during 1767, though the cause of his illness is not clear; probably a legacy of his time in India, such as recurrent malarial fevers or dysentery.[26] Whatever the illness, it caused him to lose a great deal of weight and run up a substantial apothecary's bill. At this point in his life he was bedevilled by bitterness over his failure to attain in India what he had seemed on track to achieve, grief at the loss of his son and now financial worries. His grief and illness and may have also been of concern to Philadelphia.

By 1768, things were looking difficult for Philadelphia. Living in a fashionable part of London and moving in well-heeled circles came at a substantial price. Their costs were well beyond Hancock's income. Neither his individual Indian investments, nor his trading partnership, were going at all well. In Hastings' friend Sykes's correspondence he points out that Hastings' accounts were in total confusion. Sykes also makes the same point to Clive, urging both men, who held significant influence in EIC appointments, to support Hastings' desired return to India. Perhaps exaggerating somewhat the extent of his money problems, Sykes claimed 'He is almost literally worth nothing'.[27]

Hancock, with a wife and child to support was in an even worse position. There was also the difficulty of remitting back to London any profits in India available to him. It was succinctly put that 'The problem of remitting home a fortune made in India caused eighteenth-century Company servants almost as much anxiety as the problem of making one'.[28] Hancock opens an account at Goslings Bank in Fleet Street, where Hastings also banked, in March of 1768 with a deposit of £500, and over the next four months steadily withdrew regular and substantial amounts to pay to various gentlemen.[29]

A name in Hancock's ledger that catches one's interest is the payment to George Berg of 8 guineas on 19 May 1768. This is undoubtedly the same 'Mr Berg', Eliza's music master, of whom Philadelphia later complains to Hancock, as not being very kind to Eliza. Hancock writes in reply in his characteristic blunt style:

> It has never been in my power to know what Mr Berg's temper is, I chose him for his skill in the Fundamentals of Musick. I am

not surprized at his never praising the child: he sees her not with either a mother or father's eye.[30]

Hancock engages George Berg to teach Eliza the harpsichord when she is six and a half, and at the age of 11, she is still under his instruction. Hancock often reiterates that he wants the best education for Eliza, and tends to want 'the best' in many things. George Berg was a well-known figure among the musicians of mid-eighteenth-century London, as this entry from *HH Music Publishers* on-line notes indicates that:

> George Berg (1730–1775), was a London organist and harpsichord teacher who during a quite brief period (1755–70) was a highly productive composer, whose works ranged from operas in Italian to short glees and catches.[31]

There were also payments by Hancock to his brother Colbron in support of his glass-making business, payments to goldsmiths, perhaps more borrowings or payments of interest, and other major regular payments amounting to almost £400 to London tradesmen and providores in 1768. He is trying to settle and consolidate his debts.

In 1768, the family moved to Bolton Street, just off Piccadilly, a fashionable area of London's West End but in a modest house. The Woodman family are close by in Cleveland Row, and Hastings is also now living in Piccadilly. No doubt there would have been the usual end of year birthday celebration for Hastings' thirty-fifth birthday in December of 1767. These regular December birthday celebrations, initially at Hastings' aunt Elizabeth's Kensington house, now included the Hancocks, with Eliza's sixth birthday also celebrated at the same party by both families. The December joint birthday parties for godfather and goddaughter continued to take place with both families for many years, later at the Woodman's and then at Philadelphia's home, and show a marked intimacy between the two families.

While the Hancocks moved to Mayfair, George and Cassandra Austen and their little boys were finally able to leave the rented Deane parsonage and settle in the modestly renovated Rectory at Steventon in the summer of 1768. The home where Philadelphia's niece Jane is born and spends the first twenty years of her life, becomes also a special place of refuge, first for Philadelphia and then Eliza when life delivers them some difficult blows. They both found good company, comfort and an affectionate welcome for them from their Steventon relations.

Restrict their spending as he might, there was no ignoring the fact that Hancock's Indian investments were returning very little in the way of readily remittable profits to him in England; debts must have been mounting and anxiety increasing. Where was the money to come from to provide the basics for himself and his family, let alone 'the best'? Would he have been forced to become a surgeon again, setting himself up in London, perhaps with some of his old India connections? It may have been difficult and expensive to do so, besides being to him entirely unappealing. No question of Philadelphia, clearly, of returning to her old trade of millinery.

The only option plausible to Hancock to create an income was to return to India. There he would be in a position to take charge of the running of his partnership with Hastings and revive his own position as a full-time merchant. Fortunes were still being made in India, by those who knew how to make them. He had the experience and contacts. He had originally resigned his surgeon's position with the EIC in mid-1761 to pursue the career of merchant, and he had done sufficiently well to return to England with his family with a sense he had made enough for 'a competency'. If he were to go back, by himself, incurring only the expenses of a single man out there, he obviously thought he could make enough in a few years to return with sufficient capital to see him and his family to live adequately on the interest. The sum of £44,000 would do it, he thought. And there was his friend and business partner, Hastings, the 'trump card' in Hancock's life.

So her husband made the decision by autumn of 1768 to leave his wife and daughter behind and go back to Calcutta to try and secure the family's fortune. Philadelphia could not have been sanguine about this, but obviously had no choice but to acquiesce. She may have had fears for her financial capacity to live alone and care for her daughter, and fears for the health and well-being of her 45-year-old husband out in India once again. The next seven years of 'grass' widowhood would challenge Philadelphia yet again and the India she had left only three years before must have been often in her mind.

Chapter 10

Hancock and Hastings Return to India
1768–1770

Mr Hastings was very kind in leaving you money. I am greatly in his debt.

Letter from Hancock to Philadelphia,
Calcutta, 23 November 1769

HANCOCK MOST PROBABLY left on the *Lioness*, an East Indiaman of 499 tons under the command of Captain William Larkins which sailed from Portsmouth on 8 December 1768 bound for the coast of India and the Bay of Bengal. Hancock shows in his letters that he knew Captain Larkins well, a connection most likely forged on board the *Lioness* sailing out, because he sends back goods to Philadelphia by Captain Larkins, including Constantia wine from the Cape. William Larkins was a seafaring man of similar age to Hancock, who prospered as captain of the *Lioness* and went on to own his own eponymous East Indiaman, the *Larkins*, captained by his son Thomas. He had two other seafaring sons in the EIC maritime service and one other who became a writer with the Company and rose to be in Hastings' service as accomptant general.

The *Lioness* arrived in Culpee, the main stopping off point for Calcutta on the Hughli River on 30 May 1769. Both Hancock and Larkins soon made their way up to Calcutta; Hancock in hope of resuming his merchant business and Larkins to take the EIC Directors' package of letters to the governor. The governor at that time was Clive's successor Henry Verelst and the instructions Larkins brought sent a chill through the traders of Bengal, as Hancock writes to Philadelphia from Calcutta on 23 November 1769:

> Unfortunately for me the Lioness brought positive orders that no man should on any consideration be indulged with a Dustuck [a licence to trade free of duty] except those who were of the Rank

of Factors. This order put it entirely out of the Governor's Power to serve me in the only Article which had the least probability of being Serviceable to me.[1]

Verelst resigned in December and sailed back to England with Larkins on the *Lioness* on the 8 January 1770. Hancock was left to struggle as best he could in the increasing heat of that summer in Bengal, when the monsoon never came, the crops failed and a great famine overtook the people.

In late 1768, Hancock had not been alone in considering a return to India. Many EIC servants did the same and indeed Hastings and Hancock may have come to the agreement that they would both return. Hastings was keen to return. Hastings was also being urged to return for financial, if no other reason by friends such as Francis Sykes, who came back to England in 1768 shocked by his friend's dire financial circumstances.[2] Hastings was being seen favourably once again by the discordant and faction-riven EIC Court of Directors. He had more-or-less 'hung around' London doing little more than marking time; spending money and earning very little, enduring the lassitude that came over him when not driven by high-pressured employment. India was where his future lay, he became convinced. He applied himself to writing up proposals for reform of the Company that gained some circulation.[3]

Hastings was applying to go as a Company servant befitting his former position as second in the council in Calcutta. His first approach to the EIC Directors for re-instatement was ignored, but finally late in 1768, looking for an able lieutenant in the strife-torn Madras Presidency, Hastings received his position. He was to be deputy governor in Fort St George in Madras with the assurance the governorship would be his by succession.

So both Hancock and Hastings were returning to India but Philadelphia was not to be one of the party this time. She would be saying goodbye to both her husband and her most 'dear and ever-valued friend'. She might well see neither of them ever again. By the time of Hastings' posting to Madras, Hancock had already left for Calcutta. Perhaps both men had been expecting to be in Bengal together, but Clive was no friend of Hastings and may have been initially strongly against Hastings' appointment. The Madras position kept Hastings out of Bengal to some satisfaction for Clive.[4]

The return of Hancock to India was expected by Philadelphia to be a temporary expediency, to save them financially. But having borrowed money from William Summer to fund his fare and the expenses for setting up a new home in Calcutta, there must have been very little left for Philadelphia to live by after her husband's departure. Hancock's last ledger entry in his Goslings account was for 8 October 1768, and shows nothing left. What did Philadelphia have to live on? Enough cash and credit to see her through till the promised prompt and ample remittances from her husband in the form of exchangeable bills and diamonds, came to her through his agent, her uncle Francis Austen. She had no bank account. Hancock was optimistic that his health and energy would hold out and the tie with Hastings remained important for both. For Philadelphia, a great fondness for him, and for Hancock an even more influential friend in the future; one who could perhaps guarantee a prosperous position for him and his family. There was some kind of assumed pact between the erstwhile lover, Hastings, and the husband Hancock, that Hastings would always financially assist Philadelphia and Betsy when he was in a position to do so. Whatever it was, Hastings generously came to the party. And it was soon needed.

While her husband sailed the seas on the perilous voyage east, Philadelphia would have been anxious about her situation and probably embarrassed at the reason for her husband's going back to India without her. Clearly he could not afford the expense of taking them all back to India. He must go alone and try to recover their finances. The fare to India was around £250, which he borrowed. There is no mention in the Austen family records or letters about their reaction to Hancock's departure, but Philadelphia would have been assured of her family's moral and emotional support, at least, and she also had the Woodman family close by and of course Hastings was still there, living round the corner in Piccadilly for a few months more.

As soon as Hancock left England for India, Philadelphia began writing to him. She wrote regularly and frequently for six years, but none of her letters have survived. There is, however, preserved among the Hastings Papers in the British Library her husband's letter book. In the main these are copies of his letters to her and the record runs for almost six years: from November 1769 to August 1775. The content of her letters to him, the earlier ones numbered, though not always consistently, are referred to in his responses and so her letters are revealed as a kind of palimpsest: a shadow of what she has written to him, preserved in the text of his replies.

Hancock's letter book was discovered by Sydney C. Grier, the nom de plume of the late nineteenth-/early twentieth-century novelist Hilda Caroline Gregg. The first of her many novels, *In Furthest Ind*, published in 1894, was 'a fictional memoir of a seventeenth-century Englishman's adventures in India'.[5] Grier found Tysoe Hancock's letter book among the Hastings Papers when researching Hastings' life for a subsequent publication, *The Letters of Warren Hastings*. This led to her 1904 article in *Blackwood's Magazine*, about the Hancock family called, 'A Friend of Warren Hastings'.

In letter books, private and personal letters were often recorded as having been sent but not always copied. An EIC servant such as Hancock recognised the importance of the letter book to keep track of correspondence due to the enormous time disparity between letters sent and responses received. In Hastings' letter books, while deputy governor of Madras and governor of Bengal he would have had clerks to keep them. These are also among the Hastings Papers in the British Library. Hastings sent many letters to Philadelphia from the time of his return to India in 1769 to around the time of his marriage in 1777, but the contents of the letters are not recorded, just the note when they were sent. Only one of his letters to Philadelphia appears preserved.

The letters of her husband tell us more about Philadelphia's life at this time, and hints about her earlier life, than any other source. They are more than just glimpses of what she said and thought, of whom she met and where she might have journeyed, but a multi-dimensional picture of her. It is primarily her husband's presentation of her, but it transcends merely his view of her too. For a time, Philadelphia's life comes more vividly before us.

The letters are personal and frank. There is little ornamentation, but they do show Hancock to be a well-read man. He is not at all pompous, or self-important and is in many ways caring and kindly. Above all, he is a realist, almost a cynic, even. Throughout the letters, as the years go by and financial success eludes him, any prospect of return to his family disappears and his health begins to fail. His is an increasingly jaundiced view of the world; perhaps depressingly so for his wife. As a surgeon, he has no doubt seen a lot of the worst of the human condition, of people *in extremis*, of life 'here one day and gone the next', to give himself any illusions about what life holds. He makes few references to anything in any way concerned with religion, despite the fact he was a son of the cloth, except as a standard ending to his letters to Philadelphia, such as that 'That God may bless you with health & happiness is the constant prayer of My dear Phila Your most affectionate ...'.[6] There is, though, a telling reference to religion in a request to Philadelphia to send him no more books on religion, for which he has neither the time nor the inclination to read.

His letters show him focused on the practicalities of life: his obligations to his family, his efforts to make money to support them in England as well as himself in India. He understands very well how the system operates, and where his obligations are due. He knows the way to wealth is through trade and influence but lacks the luck, energy and guile to pursue it successfully.

He also shows affection, not just to Philadelphia but to his daughter Eliza, and also to their Indian servant Clarinda and to other members of Philadelphia's family. He asks to be remembered to Philadelphia's uncle Francis Austen, her brother George, and her cousins. He says that he has a great regard for Clarinda and to keep his daughter's remembrance of him alive. He despairs that Eliza will forget all about him. Hancock's letters to his wife, and her letters to him have persistent recurrent and significant themes over the years.

Money matters predominate. From the first to almost the last, he addresses his concerns about making money, remitting it to Philadelphia and its management in England. She responds with her anxieties over money. Next, are the various transactions relating to packages of goods between them; what he can obtain in India of use and value to Philadelphia, and also what he needs from her. Their daughter Eliza's health, progress and education is detailed throughout, as is the well-being and goings-on of Philadelphia's extended family and of her servants left back in India. There are also the doings of their various Anglo-Indian friends and the broad EIC community; some still in India and some returned to England. Though his letters are not particularly gossipy, he can be quite acerbic at times about some of these friends and acquaintances.

Of course, there is the continuous undercurrent of references to Warren Hastings; a person integral to their lives, who seems to have disappointed Hancock, but fulfils his obligations to Philadelphia. In the letters of the couple's parallel lives they both write of their living arrangements, and what they are doing in their daily lives. Conditions in India are occasionally referred to by Hancock, as is the political situation with the EIC and the influence that might be brought to bear on it. Finally, the health of Hancock and Philadelphia and even of Eliza is dealt with continuously throughout the letters; but then most personal letters do habitually cover that ground.

When the *Lioness* returned to England in good time on 30 July 1770, she carried her massive cargo of highly valued goods from the East and the EIC's official correspondence, as well as letters to Philadelphia, a quilt, shifts and a cask of Constantia wine from the Cape. Captain Larkins would no doubt have seen them safely despatched to her in Bolton Street.

At the time of her father's departure for India, Eliza was coming up to her seventh birthday and already well into her education. There is a pleasing emphasis in her father's letters on the need for Eliza to receive as good an education for young girls of her time and class as was possible.

In the December of 1768, Hastings, the Woodmans and Hastings' aunt Elizabeth, Philadelphia and Eliza would have taken part in the usual joint birthday celebrations following Hancock's departure, at either Hastings' aunt's Kensington home or at the Woodman's in Cleveland Row. As Hastings' prestigious appointment in Madras was now known, the gathered family and close friends would have had even more reason to celebrate the occasion.

By the time Hancock records his first letter to Philadelphia in his letter book, they have already been apart for over a year. The letter he is replying to is her seventh, dated 20 March 1769, the day Hastings sailed for India.

In her letters to her husband, Philadelphia seeks to comfort and cheer him, though, now a year since his departure, Hancock is already sounding gloomy about his prospects. The plan was that he would spend three years in India to restore his fortune and return to his wife and daughter, but already that looks doubtful, as he states: 'It affords me Comfort that Betsy remembers me, Poor Child! She will find many three Years pass before she will see me again, if ever she may'.[7]

For Philadelphia, her financial situation would have been her greatest concern, for there is a brief, curt even, but revealing sentence four paragraphs into Hancock's letter that elucidates Philadelphia's situation back in England in that first year after her husband leaves: 'Mr Hastings was very kind in leaving you Money. I am greatly in his Debt'.[8]

Whatever money Hancock had left her with when he sailed for India in the previous December must have run out. Hancock perhaps assumed Uncle Francis held sufficient for Philadelphia for the time being. Later we know Philadelphia approached her uncle for funds to support her, but Hancock is reluctant for her to do that. He appears to have no idea how much is owed to him on Francis Austen's account.

Hancock's terse response to her news that she has had to take money from Hastings shows it is clearly a subject he does not wish to dwell on. Embarrassed no doubt that his wife was reduced to this, nevertheless he does not imply any objection to it. It is not a loan. Hastings gives her money even while he himself has had to borrow money. But Hastings is going out to the position of deputy governor of Madras with a salary and allowances of £2,400 a year and opportunities of making much more through trade and other perks and opportunities. Hastings' situation could not be in greater contrast to Hancock's. He tells Philadelphia in the same letter when she enquires about their funds that:

> The Balance you mention in our favour has been all paid away and was not nearly Sufficient to Discharge our Debts... [And] I must acquaint you that I am greatly disappointed in my expectations of remitting you money from this Place: everyone expected that the Government would grant Bills at a reasonable rate. But they have determined to grant none payable in less than two Years.

Unfortunately Hancock has arrived back in Bengal at a time when the EIC is experiencing financial troubles and trying to address some of them. One difficulty for the Company had arisen from the way it dealt with bills of exchange from its servants in India. The simplest way servants could remit the wealth acquired in India was to submit it in India to the Company in local currency, often as credit, which the Company would accept and then issue a bill of exchange. The bill would be presented to the Company in England which would pay it in pounds. In 1768 and 1769, just when Philadelphia saw her husband depart for Calcutta to restore their financial fortunes, the EIC set limits on how much could be remitted by Company servants on the submission of bills of exchange in Bengal. Hancock's timing could not have been worse.

The other main way of remitting money was through buying diamonds. London banks like Goslings commonly dealt with requests by letter from clients in India who had shipped diamonds to them, for the bank to sell the diamonds and put the money raised into their personal accounts. Hancock in a later letter writes of sending Philadelphia diamonds, but doubts their value will hold up very well when sold in London or in Amsterdam. Diamonds also had to be conveyed by a reliable third party. There is more bad news for Philadelphia in her husband's letter as he tells her that he has been unable to obtain the all-important dustuck, which he needs to trade profitably.

A 'dustuck' was the customs permit granted by the EIC that meant goods could be traded in Bengal without tax or duty being paid to the Nawab. Those who could trade with a dustuck gained a substantial financial advantage over those who did not have one. Without a dustuck, Hancock was going to have great trouble making the kind of money as a merchant that he had envisaged when he set out. The gloomy news he delivered to his wife was:

> From Mr Sumner's recommendation I expected the advantage of a Dustuck ... Unfortunately for me the *Lioness* brought positive orders that no man should on any Consideration be indulged with a Dustuck except those who were of the Rank of Factors.[9]

Mr Sumner was William Brightwell Sumner, a senior EIC member of council who made his fortune in India but had fallen out with Clive, and by the time of Hancock's return, was back in England enjoying the fruits of his fortune, namely the magnificent Hatchlands estate in Surrey. He was well known to the Hancocks and Philadelphia's husband must have carried his recommendation to Governor Verelst in Calcutta who had just replaced Clive.

Familiar as Philadelphia was with how things were done in India, this news about the dustuck must have been as equally worrying as the problem with remitting money. But there was worse to follow. The husband who had resigned his position as a surgeon with the EIC over eight years ago was now forced to take up his profession again, much against his inclination. He writes:

> On this occasion General Smith (who has been very much my Friend) proposed to me the taking of an office to entitle me to a Dustuck: the only one which could be thought of was that of a Surgeon extraordinary to the Garrison.[10]

'General Smith' was General Richard Smith, an archetypal EIC self-made man who we shall hear more of later. He was known as the 'nabob of nabobs'. Philadelphia would have read this with some dread for her husband. He was now 46, not a young age for a man of the eighteenth century. Furthermore, she knew how much he disliked his profession: its arduous and inherently dangerous nature, its exposure to disease, death and people's torment. It was not an older man's game. She would have also known of its impact on his pride. While it was a respectable, if not highly regarded profession, he had left it behind and had lived the life of a gentleman for many years. Now he had been forced back into it.

Hancock had presumed that the position of Surgeon Extraordinary to the garrison in Fort William would be tokenistic; allowing the dustuck and requiring little surgical practice but that was not the case, he tells her glumly in his letter, while including a copy of his appointment to present to the directors of the EIC to obtain the dustuck:

> It was intended to be a Sinecure, but it Subjects me to attend whenever I am called upon which happens too frequently... You know how much I hate the Practice of Physick, yet I am obliged to take it up again: nothing could have induced me to do so but the Hopes of thereby providing for my family.[11]

But that family is far away, and it must have been discomforting for Philadelphia now to know that he was going through all the difficulties of a surgeon's duties out in Calcutta without the comfort and cheer that his wife and daughter could have given him.

In her latest letter Philadelphia has told him of visits with/to/from her Freeman cousins; the unmarried ones, Molly (whom Hancock likes) and Stella (whom Hancock dislikes), who live nearby in Westminster, and their married sister Catherine-Margaretta Stanhope, married to Charles Stanhope since 1746 and who is likely now to be living in Yateley in Hampshire.

The news of these well-heeled family connections Philadelphia passes on to her husband is an attempt to keep him cheerful and connected too. It has the desired effect of his requesting Philadelphia to give them his good wishes. Philadelphia has raised in her letter to her husband, her plan to take Eliza to live in France. This idea about living in France had been mentioned back in 1761 in a letter from Major John Carnac to Margaret Clive. Eliza is just 7-and-a-half now and Hancock does not treat it too seriously. It has been a long-held and somewhat unusual idea for an Englishwoman of Philadelphia's class and status to take up. She must see a benefit for Eliza to live in France.

Her husband's letters reveal that Philadelphia was not only concerned with matters of family and home but also took an active interest in issues beyond the domestic; especially those relevant to India. Her husband passes on to her information about the politics of India and the EIC, and her interest in anything to do with Warren Hastings clearly extended to her friend's political progress. And when Hancock tells her in his letter to ensure she visits the wife of the returning 'nabob', General Richard Smith, he is engaging Philadelphia in the politics of the EIC and assumes she is familiar with how it operates:

> The General promised his Interest to support me: pray if you can, visit his Lady to congratulate Her on his Arrival. The Omission might be of bad Consequence to me as He will be a Man of great Power, you perfectly know his vanity and my Necessities.[12]

There is always an element of material transaction (literally) in these letters between husband and wife. The provision of fabric for clothes and household decorations and necessities is mentioned in most letters, indicating Philadelphia's access to cash at this time was limited. She, in turn, has enough money or credit to send him items he requests or she thinks he might need. Packets going between them include, on her side, Holland gin, books, tragedies and newspapers. The gin and newspapers were welcome but not so the books and plays. Fabric made up in the form of twenty-five shifts, the loose undergarments worn by women, for her and twenty for Eliza have been sent to her via Captain Larkins.

In December of 1769 at the time her husband writes, Philadelphia is spending her second Christmas in England without him, and her first without Hastings. He arrived in Madras in August, and by the New Year of 1770 is settled in as deputy governor in Fort St George 'in an exorbitantly rented house'.[13] His reputation for his mildness of temper, diligence and integrity had preceded him to Madras, though he was still a Bengal man, and therefore something of an outsider amongst the old 'Madrassers' as they were called. There were pressures and demands in the position, but he got on well with the governor of the Madras Presidency, Josias Du Pré. But he was something of a different man from the one Philadelphia farewelled in London that previous March, for on board his ship, on the long passage out, he had fallen in love with a beautiful fellow passenger, the 22-year-old, Stuttgart-born, of Huguenot descent, Anna-Maria Chapuset, now Baroness von Imhoff, who was travelling in the cabin below him with her husband and one small son.

Hastings' feelings for Philadelphia had no doubt been fondly held, bolstered by trust and obligation and, many years before may have been passionate as well, but for the 36-year-old Hastings, this lady was 'the real thing'. She was strikingly beautiful, according to all sources, with a 'cultivated mind, a lively wit, a keen intelligence, and a gay and vivacious disposition'.[14]

If Philadelphia had indeed ever entertained wishful thoughts of a future with Hastings, the advent of Anna-Maria Chapuset, whom Hastings always anglicised to 'Marian', put an end to that. The exceptionally passionate, almost desperate letters he wrote to Marian when they were apart, show Hastings' character in an extraordinary light and are a testament to him as a man of intense feeling. Here is an extract of one of many letters to his 'Dearest Marian' after she had left India to return to England in 1784, prior to his return:

> Oh God what a change was effected in the state of my existence within the Compass of a few minutes and what were my Reflexions as I passed from the ship to my Pinnace! My imagination presented you before me as I held you in my arms but a few moments past... I still felt the moisture of your sweet lips and the warm pressure of your last embrace and my heart told me I had lost you forever.[15]

Hastings is writing this at the age of 52 to the woman he has been with now for fourteen years! It has the intensity of young, new, sexual love! If indeed he had even briefly felt this way for the married Philadelphia back in Calcutta when he was 28, it is not unsurprising that she succumbed, and the noted 'extraordinary familiarity' grew between them.

For the baroness and for Hastings apparently, having a husband, in situ, as it were, was no object to the progress of the affair. It was perhaps a European tolerance of such matters that prevailed. After all, while her husband was a well-born German, with good connections, he was hard-up and travelling out as an EIC army cadet, but hoping to get by on his talents as a painter of portrait miniatures. By contrast, Hastings was now the second in charge of the Madras Presidency and where they were headed, a man of significance. Why would the baroness not find his enthusiasm for her hard to resist? The husband perhaps saw the potential in it too. She spoke little English, but Hastings could speak French, and French proved to be the language of *amour* for them.

The official version of how the affair started is that Hastings became ill on board after leaving the Cape and the baroness took on the role of nurse to him. The long hours alone with him in his cabin apparently led to ministrations of a non-nursing nature and Hastings, 'was not firm enough to hold out against the strong temptation'.[16] A Jezebel clearly, in the eyes of Hastings' nineteenth-century biographer, the Reverend Gleig, but as pointed out earlier, it was not the first time Hastings had found solace from a married woman. Even his first wife Mary, the wife of a friend John Buchanan, had only been widowed a matter of weeks before they married, and there was also mention of an earlier liaison on board the *Duke of Grafton* with a 'Mrs Thompson', going out to join her husband, an officer of the EIC Marines, who had 'caught his eye'.[17] Whatever that means.

By the time the ship arrived in Madras at the end of August, Hastings was in perfect health and the relationship firmly established. It was clearly some kind of *menage a trois*: a complacent husband, prepared to accept the situation, and perhaps profit from it. And for the British expatriate society? Almost no one blinked an eye, even though it would be seven years before Marian and the baron were divorced and she and Hastings married. Some criticism of Marian's status came after the baron departed India when Hastings was governor of Bengal from the wife of the chief justice, Mary Impey, mentioned earlier. The situation probably genuinely shocked the young Englishwoman, unused to the mores of British society in Calcutta which Hancock described at the time as being debauched. It was said by someone, rather unkindly that Lady Impey: 'made a show of being shocked by the barely concealed liaison between the governor and Marian. We are told 'she looked very coldly on her till she married Hastings'.[18]

What did Philadelphia know of this liaison with the Baroness von Imhoff, and when did she hear of it? In the package of letters from her husband, dated 23 November 1769, a letter from Hastings to Philadelphia is included, having been written in September very shortly after his arrival in Madras. In Hastings' letter to Hancock he tells him 'I have written to Mrs Hancock to inform her of my arrival'.[19] It is unlikely Hastings would have said anything about Marian in that letter. If she hears about Marian early on, it is going to be from a third party and that would have taken some time to reach London. Would Hancock have heard about Hastings and the von Imhoffs then? If he has, he does not say anything to Philadelphia about them at that time.

Hastings is in regular contact with John Woodman, his brother-in-law, attorney and London agent primarily for personal financial matters. He is doing so well that in early 1770, well within a year of his arrival in Madras, he is able to send £4,000 in bills to Woodman to pay back the money he had borrowed from William Summer before he left London.

In a letter Philadelphia writes to her husband in December of 1769 she has told him that she and Eliza have been unwell, but had tried to be out of London and in the country during the summer months. It is something she wishes to do regularly and of which her husband approves. She reveals she is feeling somewhat low about their prospects, and on 17 January 1770, Hancock responds by telling her, more hopefully than is his usual style:

> I must [insist] on your laying aside all Melancholy Reflections; these are what keep you so thin. Remember that a small Space of Time may make a great Alteration for the better with us & and that Circumstances are every Day improving.[20]

By the time of his writing this letter to his wife, she has already written at least sixteen letters to her husband since his departure. A letter written by Philadelphia in February of one year, could be received as late as April of the next year, responded to seven months later and received by her at least six months into the next year. Over two years could have passed between the letter sent and the response received. She could not be waiting to have her husband's opinion before she could act on some matter. This demanded of Philadelphia an independence of action about her life and her future, which apart from the financial fragility of her position, was liberating for her, to a degree.

In March of 1770 Hancock sends a package home with a Captain Newland and suggests Philadelphia use any influence she has with the EIC in London to recommend Captain Newland for the charge of one of their ships. There is an assumption that Philadelphia may have influence with the EIC, and one wonders if Hastings' appointment in Madras in some way extended that influence.

Throughout 1769 and into 1770 Philadelphia held out hopes for her husband to gain substantial advancement through a further EIC appointment. In her letters, she suggests she could assist him in obtaining some such appointment. How would such influence for a woman like Philadelphia work? We know that Clive had helped Hancock to gain his surgeon's position in Calcutta back in 1759, when times were difficult for them after being driven out of Fort St David by the French, but Philadelphia's friendship with Margaret Clive had been cut short at Clive's insistence. Since Clive's return in July 1767, there is unlikely to have been any appeals through the Clive channel. It is interesting though, that a number of years later, in January 1773 Philadelphia writes to Hancock telling him that she has received a request for assistance from Margaret's cousin, Jane/Jenny (née Kelsall), once Latham and now married to Clive's secretary, Henry Strachey and living closely with the Clives wherever they are, frequently in Berkeley Square, just around the corner from Philadelphia in Bolton Street.

Hancock writes in response on 7 November 1773:

> You ought not to have hesitated to tell Mrs Strachey that her behaviour to you while in India, which plainly proved her contempt of you, gave her no right to expect any favour from you.[21]

Clive was still alive then, and still influential with the EIC directors, but one can speculate Jenny Strachey took it that Philadelphia had some influence in India through Hastings. Jenny's 17-year-old son Henry Latham by her first marriage, had petitioned the Court of Directors of the EIC in 1772 for an appointment in Bengal as a writer. In his petition he cites the outstanding service of his long-dead father, Thomas Latham, as commander of the ship the *Tyger* and its action in the taking of Chandernagore, the headquarters of the French East India Company in 1757. The young Henry Latham was employed by the EIC in Bengal in 1773. It looks very much as though Jenny approached Philadelphia seeking a recommendtion for her son through Hastings or even Hancock. It is not clear if the request was followed up, but Philadelphia did send on to Hancock in January and March of 1773, letters of introduction for someone.[22]

Money and love: such strong themes throughout the eighteenth-century world of Jane Austen's fictional characters, also loomed large in the reality of Philadelphia's life. Philadelphia has been anxious about money throughout 1769 and 1770 and worries that she is unable to reduce her expenses to less than £600 a year. It is a substantial sum of money to live on in that age, in her circumstances, even in expensive London. Thirty years later, in 1795, when Jane Austen begins to write *Sense and Sensibility* she has the widowed Mrs Dashwood and her three daughters reduced to living on an inadequate £500 a year. Fanny Price's mother, in *Mansfield Park* has 'a competence' of over £400 on which her large family is expected to live.

For Philadelphia, £600 was less than half what the family had been living on in the four years previously and Hancock's expenses in Calcutta are high, as he makes the point to his wife:

> A very Paltry House costs me £450 per Annum. My servants one hundred and Sixty, my House Charges in Proportion thou' I have never yet had one Person to eat with me; added to which I am obliged to keep a Carriage... Indeed my expences [sic] are large, but it is impossible to retrench them.[23]

Hancock is now relying on Hastings in Madras to procure bills that can be paid to Francis Austen back in England, but Hancock writes to Philadelphia that Hastings has informed him that he cannot obtain 'Money remitted by bills on the Company and that diamonds are so dear that I must be a loser by purchasing them... I have wrote him [Hastings] at all events to send home a thousand pounds'.[24]

Throughout 1770, Philadelphia continues her hopeful wait on her husband's improved financial circumstances. She must be forced to accumulate a degree of debt for her everyday circumstances, and when money arrives it would have soon been spoken for. Philadelphia has to approach her uncle and tells Hancock that she had considered drawing out more than the amount of money she strictly needed at that time. That has worried him, as he is in debt to Francis Austen and is always anxious not to upset him. He chides Philadelphia stating that 'Mr Austen would certainly have taken it ill that you should have drawn more money out of his hands at a time than you wanted'.[25]

Philadelphia is, like many eighteenth-century women, trapped in a financial cage controlled by her male relatives: fathers, husbands, uncles and brothers. Francis Austen comes out of this as a somewhat intimidating figure, holding the purse strings for both Philadelphia and her brother George, to whom, as was the nature of things, he is more generous, purchasing him the Deane living and when he dies in 1791 at the great age of 92, leaving George £500 in his will, while Philadelphia has 'been entirely forgot'.[26] Though it would seem Francis did not discriminate when it came to his beneficence to his male relatives, as all his nephews, not just George, received £500.

Continuing anxious about her expenses, in mid-1770 Philadelphia writes a number of times to Hancock about how she might go about reducing them, or for him to set a specific limit on them. His replies are generous and intended to reassure. And again, a few months later, he writes, indicating an openness and tolerance in their marriage:

> I am a little surprized at your proposal that I should limit your Expenses; did I ever accuse you of Extravagance? You perfectly knew the Situation of my Affairs. I have never been deceived in them since our first connection. Who at such a distance can foresee Contingencies? Live comfortably and make yourself easy.[27]

Philadelphia's plan is to spend more time in the country, liking the idea of country life, in theory at least. Many of her relatives live out of London, and perhaps she thinks it might be a saving. Her brother George comes up from Hampshire to stay with her in Bolton Street for a few weeks at the beginning of May 1770 and there may have been quite the family reunion because when George returns to the Steventon Rectory in Hampshire he takes his sister-in-law Mrs Susannah Walter and her daughter Phylly with him.

George had suggested by letter when he first arrived at Philadelphia's that Mrs Walter and Phylly should come up to London from Tonbridge and go back to Steventon with him. Women travellers were often dependent on a male relative to accompany them on coach journeys, to provide 'protection' and defray costs. For Eliza, it must have been one of the many occasions in their childhood when the two young cousins, both turning 9 that year, spent time together, cementing a friendship that continued into adult life, despite very different personalities and ways of life. As an only child, Eliza particularly valued the friendship. Later, Philadelphia joins her other sister-in-law Cassandra Austen in going back up to Steventon from London. Mrs Austen had come down to assist in the birth of her sister Jane Cooper's first child. She arrives late for the birth, which was premature, but Deirdre Le Faye suggests Philadelphia was probably in attendance to assist.[28]

After their visit to Steventon, Philadelphia, Eliza, and their servants Clarinda and a male servant Peter, who may or may not have come from India but we hear almost nothing of him, leave at the beginning of August 1770 for a rented country cottage in Surrey. Philadelphia's reliance on the health, energy and fidelity of her husband, the affection of her friend Hastings and Uncle Francis's financial probity makes for a fragile basis of financial security for her as Hancock's stay in India stretches into its third year. The promise of a three-year stay to turn his fortunes around and return to England is beginning to seem a remote prospect now.

Chapter 11

'Grass Widow' in London
1770–1772

> *I have written to Mrs Hancock to inform her of my arrival.*
> Letter from Hastings to Hancock,
> September 1769

APART FROM THE REGULAR letters from her husband and from Hastings, Philadelphia also has a network of London connections through Hastings' Woodman relatives, acquaintances in India House, and people she knows coming and going from India to England to help sustain her. Hancock too has heard from Hastings since his arrival and in his letter of 27 December 1769 tells Philadelphia that Hastings 'is perfectly well thou' much harassed with Business of the most disagreeable sort,... and fears that he and Hastings 'shall never live together in India; unless Mr Hastings is removed to Bengal'.[1] Most reports, however of this period in Hastings' life show it to have been a happy time for him, with 'Governor and Council on best of terms ...[and] Du Pré in particular showed real appreciation of his junior's talents'.[2]

During this time, correspondence between the three of them, Hastings, Hancock and Philadelphia, is frequent, though Hastings' correspondence with Hancock is fraught. He writes twenty-one letters to Hancock from Madras between February and December 1770, urging Hancock to sort out the mess that their business partnership is now in and trying to get a proper report from him about the state of the accounts for their trading partnership. Hancock seems incapable of giving him that information. Hancock appears quite hopeless and in a bad way in all this as Hastings begs him over and over again to respond. Hastings writes: 'For God's sake exert yourself & if fortune should desert you do not desert yourself' and urging him to come down to Madras and he will give him 'every assistance in my power'.[3] By 9 July 1770 Hastings is asking Hancock 'what in the name of God is become of it [i.e. their trading partnership]'?[4] Hancock just seems too ill or too depressed to do anything despite Hastings' exhortations, though Hastings spares Philadelphia the true situation of her husband in the only surviving letter to her, written in 1772 when he minimises Hancock's problems as 'difficulties'.

One can only speculate on what Philadelphia may have written to Hastings about during this time. She would have likely told him about Eliza's progress and well-being, her living circumstances, and shared her anxieties about her husband's situation and their financial problems, as well as thanking him for gifts and news of common friendships, especially his sister's family, the Woodmans. In a letter from Hastings to Hancock at this time Hastings refers to hearing from Philadelphia and that he is 'Happy to find they were both well, & Bessy improving very fast'.[5]

His sister Anne Woodman, gave birth to her second child, a daughter, in mid-1770, which would have been of mutual interest to Philadelphia and Hastings. Perhaps she also gave him news of Clarinda, whom Hastings knew well and she probably also ventured to reveal to him more personal feelings, as she did later in the one surviving letter to him written in 1780.

Often in company with the letters, a ready supply of goods continues to be dispatched from India to Philadelphia by her husband, as well as from Hastings. The last of Hancock's letters of 1769 refers to a package of the famous Attar of Roses perfume he sends and asks her to pass on her old stock to her Payne and Freeman cousins. Fresh supplies of this perfume are sent frequently to Philadelphia. A fondness for the classic fragrance of India was one of many material aspects of her Indian life which Philadelphia brought back with her and continued to enjoy. These Indian commodities and luxuries included foods, fabrics and jewels. They must have made her seem rather exotic to her Austen relatives, with her beautiful traditionally dressed south Indian servant Clarinda and the waft of Attar of Roses invigorating the more subdued lavender-scented rooms of a country parsonage. Attar of Roses (which Hancock spells 'Ottar') is one of the oldest of perfumes made in India, and much favoured by the Moghul emperors, who encouraged its production. The emperors, their queens and harems used it lavishly. In Philadelphia's time it was difficult and expensive to obtain in England and to maintain its quality. Hancock gives her instructions about the quality of the Attar, who to share her old stock with, how to store it and to preserve it from the cold. He also tells her that his:

> Intention is to send you some exceedingly fine and you shall give what you now have (being grown old) to Mrs Payne and Miss Molly Freeman in my Name. I have sent a small parcel

to Mrs Cockell, it is of an inferior sort therefore Never Shew Yours to her.[6]

Philadelphia has sent her husband a 'picture' of their 9-year-old daughter Eliza, as a keepsake and to show how she has grown and changed in the eighteen months since he left. It was drawn in pastels or crayon, and mostly made of hair, probably using Eliza's own hair. A portrait done in hair appears an unconventional choice, though 'hair art' first became popular in England in the seventeenth century. It is said that it is a particularly intimate medium, with one writer calling it 'an ode to the person's essence'.[7] The artists were usually anonymous women. Philadelphia may have thought a portrait done using Eliza's hair might have provided an especially close and meaningful connection with his daughter for Hancock.

Unfortunately, the expense and effort undertaken by Philadelphia to have it done and sent out to her husband did not have a great outcome. Hancock hates the depiction of Eliza, thinks it is very poorly done and it does not survive the Indian climate. He writes mercilessly to Philadelphia on receipt of it on 13 March of 1771:

> I have received Betsy's Picture – Why should I who hitherto never had hid any Sentiments from you, hide them now? In looking at it I was greatly disappointed indeed. I will tell you its faults – the Drawing is so very bad that the Face is broader than the Breast and the Head bigger than the Upper part of the Body; the Face is also very full and the Features are those of a child not more than four Years old.[8]

Tellingly, Hancock says he intends to send the picture to Hastings to get his opinion. Three years later Hancock spares Philadelphia nothing by writing to say the picture is ruined with, 'the Crayons having mouldered into Dust ... & it is unnecessary to say this was a Great Disappointment to me'.[9]

Hancock often says how much he wants 'the best' for Eliza, as no doubt her mother also wants, but trying to survive a kind of widowhood, with the persistent fear of impoverishment, she must have felt she could only afford to have a less expensive and more personal portrait done. Hancock is angry with her failure in this matter, as he is often in other matters concerning Philadelphia's competence. And there is more 'picture' trouble too for her.

Hancock had taken back to India with him a miniature of Philadelphia set into a ring. It was done in London before he returned in December of 1768 by the renowned miniaturist John Smart. Sadly, that miniature of Philadelphia was deteriorating in the Calcutta climate and Hancock had to send it back to England for Philadelphia to see if it is:

Possible for Mr Smart to prevent your picture in the Ring, which
I sent home, from spoiling in India? If he could do it at any
Expense I should be glad to have the Ring sent to me'.[10]

It arrived safely back to Philadelphia in London but to Hancock's chagrin she ignored his instructions, and later he takes her to task, accusing her of disregarding his request. There could have been many reasons why her husband's wishes were not carried out. Possibly it was too expensive or not possible to have whatever work was required and Philadelphia took the decision to hold onto the miniature ring and preserve it. It does not appear to be a very practical object to be wearing out and about in India on a surgeon's rounds. It did survive and was left to his daughter in his will, and is today owned by the Jane Austen's House Museum, with diamond-studded surround, but now mounted on a pin. Upon Eliza's death it was probably passed on to Jane Austen by Eliza's then husband and Jane's brother Henry Austen. It was the most personal and intimate of possessions Eliza retained of her mother and would indicate the closeness Eliza felt to Jane. The miniature most likely came into Jane's sister Cassandra's possession after Jane's death. In her will Cassandra gave it back to Henry, now 'mounted as a brooch'.[11] Upon Henry's death in 1850, it was left to Henry's much younger second wife, Eleanor (née Jackson) and was retained within the family until it finally found its place in the museum dedicated to Jane.

On the family side of Philadelphia's life in these years between 1770 and 1773, she is preoccupied with the care and education of her daughter. Still called by the diminutive Betsy or Bessy, Eliza turns 9 in December of 1770 and there was the usual Hastings/Eliza birthday celebrations between the Woodman family, Hastings' Aunt Elizabeth and Philadelphia and her daughter. Philadelphia includes in her packets to Hancock an occasional letter from Eliza to her father, though their frequency seems to tail off as the years of separation mount. On 29 March 1773, Hancock writes despondently to Philadelphia complaining that:

> Betsy has written me but one Letter this Year; she must have forgotten me further than that by your reminding her of me...I should be glad to receive yearly a Letter from her, to know what improvement she may make in her Writing.[12]

In the first letter she sent to her father she had told him she had a new little Fox Dog and her cat had kittens. Clarinda features regularly in Eliza's news to her father, telling him of an amusing dream Clarinda had. In his replies Hancock often sends his love to Clarinda and asks after her. Most of all, Hancock is keen on news of his daughter's education. He wants Eliza to write well and in a clear hand, to learn the harpsichord and the guitar to a high standard but is also particular in wanting her to master 'Arithmetic'. Philadelphia keeps him informed, to a degree, of Eliza's achievements. He writes on 28 August of 1771:

> The improvement of Betsy gives me great pleasure... I must request you would get for Her the best Writing Master to be procured by Money and that she as soon as possible may begin to learn Arithmetic. Her other Accomplishments will be Ornaments to her, but these are most absolutely necessary.[13]

Anxious about an impoverished future for his daughter, Hancock is trying to prepare Eliza to be able to earn a living, with his emphasis on the practicalities of writing and arithmetic, but it was Philadelphia who saw to it that Eliza was not only accomplished, but lively, engaging, warm and kind.

Hancock makes a point of including Hastings in his observations and concerns regarding Eliza's education. Hancock thinks she might need an education better suited to a more prosaic life and having to work for her living. He consults Hastings, no doubt pinning his hopes on his coming to the party for Eliza. In a letter dated 17 January 1770 Hancock tells Philadelphia that Hastings is 'Resolved that the same plan of education as we formerly agreed on shall be pursued. In this resolution I am confirmed by Mr Hastings to whom I wrote on the subject'.[14]

Hastings had written reassuringly to Hancock in November of 1769 that:

> Her [Eliza's] own Natural Understanding & gentle Disposition improved by the Precepts of such a Mother as few Children are blest with will fit her Mind to be satisfied with any Lot that she may meet with & to become it. But God forbid she should be disqualified for a better Way of Life because it is Possible she may not have a Fortune equal to it ... but if I live & meet with the success which I have a Right to hope for, she shall not be under the Necessity of marrying a Tradesman, or any Man for her support. I would not say thus much, but that I wish in every respect to dispel your Apprehensions.[15]

This is a strong statement of his commitment to support Eliza's financial future and his esteem for Philadelphia, though he is a little reluctant to 'say thus much'. So Eliza's education proceeds apace. Dancing masters are employed and Mr Berg continues her harpsichord lessons. Finally, she even has someone coming to teach her arithmetic, and there are riding lessons. Her father tells her to 'beg she [Philadelphia] will purchase for you the best little horse she can buy'.[16] Philadelphia does her best with this request, though it must have been a sizable expense, but in the end a horse was purchased, and at some time in late 1772 Philadelphia has written to Hancock confirming Eliza has a horse.

Regular riding was considered a healthy pursuit for women in the eighteenth century. In *Mansfield Park*, Fanny Price's daily riding of 'the old grey pony' was seen as conducive to her health, and when the old pony died in the spring when she was about 15:

> she was in danger of feeling the loss in her health as well as her affections, for ... no measures were taken for mounting her again, 'because ... she might ride one of her cousins' horses at any time when they did not want them'.[17]

But of course her cousins always wanted to ride their horse at the most suitable times, and Fanny was left sitting at home or walking till fatigued. Her cousin Edmund saw the detriment to Fanny of the loss and swapped one of his three horses, for a more suitable one for Fanny, and she was once again free to ride at her pleasure to continue all the health benefits that riding offered. That is, until Mary Crawford turned up.

A number of scholars have seen something of Eliza in Austen's fictional creation, Mary Crawford, and the episode of the riding lessons in *Mansfield Park* and Mary Crawford's spirited approach does provide an echo of Philadelphia's daughter. Some Austen commentators even refer to 'the conventional wisdom is that Mary Crawford is based, at least partly, on Eliza Hancock de Feuillide Austen'.[18] Perhaps, but only partly, for Eliza was kind, thoughtful and generous. These were not obvious elements of Mary Crawford's character.

Eliza's horse does not last too long, as by the summer of 1774 Philadelphia has found the horse unsuitable for Betsy and given it away. Hancock is not happy, and wants her to hang the expense and buy another one but his request seems to have been ignored. So did Eliza in those years between 11 and 13 learn to sit well and ride without fear? She may have. And did the spirit of Eliza inhabit the depiction of Mary Crawford, whom Edmund Bertram, in the grip of his infatuation, allows to take over Fanny's horse? Does Mary Crawford's progress in riding capture something of Eliza's approach: 'Active and fearless, and, though rather small, strongly made, she seemed formed for a horsewoman'.[19]

It is probably fanciful to imagine that the impressionable young Jane had seen Eliza riding one of Jane's brothers' horses in just such a manner when Philadelphia, Eliza, and the infant son paid their long visit to Steventon after their return from France in the winter of 1786, as Paula Byrne so evocatively describes it:

> Eliza Hancock, now the Comtesse de Feuillide... burst into the life of the Steventon parsonage just in time for the Christmas festivities of 1786. Slight of build and extremely elegant ... She had plenty of admirers at Steventon, male and female. Jane Austen at the impressionable age of eleven, was simply enchanted by the cousin.[20]

At the time of Eliza's death in May of 1813, the mature artist Jane was writing *Mansfield Park*. Eliza must have been strongly in her mind as she wrote, and recalling the excitement of the theatricals at Steventon and perhaps too, the strong and fearless little horsewoman.

By the time Eliza has her first horse, Philadelphia has moved from Bolton Street, a little further west to Hertford Street, still in the Mayfair area, and close to the Woodman family. She informs her husband of the move in a letter sent in late 1772. The reason for the move does not seem to have been financial, as the Hertford Street house was more expensive than Bolton Street, as Hancock in one of his reprimands in a letter from India written on 29 June 1773 upbraids Philadelphia for spending 'much Time, paper, pens & ink [which] are lost on apologising for the rent. It is sufficient to me that you are satisfied with the House'.[21]

Hertford Street was a new housing development in Mayfair, on the site of the old 'St James' Fair', held from the first of May each year. By the early eighteenth century it had gained a lewd and riotous reputation and as London gentrified to the West, the old the 'May Fair' became unwanted.

A search of the Westminster rate book for 1769 shows the street had some well-to-do residents. Rents averaged around £70 a year. Hancock's name was still on the rate register in 1775, the year of his death. Included on the list of twelve rate payers in Hertford Street in 1769 were eight with titles, plus the Bishop of Salisbury. In a detailed look at the biographies of these people, researcher Sarah Murden points out a number of interesting inhabitants, including aristocrat and Royal Navy Commander Sir John Lindsay, who seems to have purchased number 11 for his new bride just after he had been appointed commander-in-chief of the navy in the East Indies.[22]

Sir John and his wife had no children, but he had already fathered a number of 'natural' children while serving in the West Indies, including Dido Elizabeth Belle. The daughter of a slave, Dido was brought up in the home of Sir John's great-uncle, Lord Mansfield, the Lord Chief Justice and reforming judge renowned for his anti-slavery judgement, who was also a friend of Hastings, as a companion to his niece. Dido Belle is uniquely preserved in a painting by Zoffany, as a lively figure, almost dancing alongside her equally young cousin.

Philadelphia remains in Hertford Street for at least three years, is visited by family and friends, and makes excursions to their country homes. But the plan to take Betsy to France remains fixed in her mind. Eliza being proficient in French was a priority of Philadelphia's, if not quite so important to her father. Although he does not disagree with the proposition of taking Eliza to France, he tends to make fun of it. He writes flippantly about Philadelphia's idea of giving Eliza a French companion and says 'I can have no objection to it, till the Child may be old enough to imbibe the Spirit of Intrigue, without which no French Woman ever existed'.[23]

Money worries continue to plague Philadelphia and while Hancock's long letter in January and February of the New Year of 1771 had been hopeful of their fortunes improving, nothing much comes to pass. He chides Philadelphia for writing to him about her feeling dejected. To cheer herself up she has decided that country life would suit her better than life in town, and so she chooses Byfleet in Surrey, not far from the Brooklands home of Philadelphia's wealthy Payne cousins.

Margaret Clive had mentioned back in 1766 in a letter to John Carnac that their friend Philadelphia and her husband were intending to move to the country; a move that did not happen at that time. In her idea of country life in England, Philadelphia has chosen to rent a 'cottage', as Mrs Austen refers to it in her letter to their mutual sister-in-law Mrs Walter, rather than a house. Philadelphia may have been influenced by the emerging idea in the second-half of the eighteenth century of the cottage as a newly-built small comfortable house, exemplifying new ideas of landscape architecture which embraced 'buildings in rustic style resembling cottages', rather than the pre-existing notion of a cottage as a dwelling 'synonymous with poverty and misery'.[24]

One country cottage depicted in Austen is Barton Cottage, in *Sense and* Sensibility, the home of the newly-widowed Mrs Dashwood. It may have been more like Philadelphia's riverside Byfleet cottage. The house was modest and the rent so cheap that it seems an excellent choice for the tightly-straitened widow and her daughters. It is new and Austen gives an unusually detailed description of the cottage, by way of mocking the current eighteenth-century craze for the rustically dilapidated cottage of the fashionably picturesque landscape:

> As a house, Barton Cottage, though small, was comfortable and compact; but as a cottage it was defective, for the building was regular, the roof was tiled, the window shutters were not painted green, nor were the walls covered with honeysuckles.[25]

Unfortunately for Philadelphia, her choice of country habitation was not so well situated, for the closeness of the River Wye proved problematic and the ideal of country life for her was short-lived. When winter came, the flooding and damp forced her to retreat to London. And although her husband was concerned that Eliza's absence from London might impede her education, he was sympathetic to Philadelphia when she wrote to him of her forced abandonment of Byfleet. From then on Philadelphia seems content to spend time out of London during the summer as a guest of various family members and friends.

Steventon rectory is the most frequently visited place during this time, including a number of visits to assist Mrs Austen in her numerous confinements. She is probably at Steventon in the summer of 1771, when Henry, the fourth son of George and his wife Cassandra is born, as a letter from Hancock acknowledges the visit and her account of the well-being of her family there. Hancock, however, does not approve of George's burgeoning flock of children. Four children in six years is not that unusual in those times, but all the Austen children surviving infancy was something of a rarity. They all grew into healthy adulthood and all except Jane into old age. Hancock's primary concern here is for his brother-in-law's financial situation, in having to provide for a family, already of four sons, on a very modest clergyman's stipend. Hancock found money increasingly difficult to make, and had only one child to support, but George Austen was clever, careful and resourceful. He also had some luck. Indeed it is something of a miracle that he managed to educate and set up all his sons to lives of success. It was something beyond Hancock, who is now desperately trying to trade his way into some fortune.

Hancock had gone into a new partnership with another merchant Benjamin Lacam, whose house he is now sharing on the river in Garden Reach. It sounded a profitable association and Hancock was able to put up money for the venture. Their intention was to provide chunam used in the government buildings in the expanding Calcutta settlement. Chunam was a sea-shell based lime extracted from low-lying sea areas, which when mixed with water and other ingredients such as sand and egg shells, made the incredibly brilliant white plaster walls which could be polished to look like marble, and were such an exceptional feature of the houses of Madras and Calcutta.

The source of the lime was to be found in the area of The Sunderbunds, the huge expanse of mangrove forest and swamp covering the Ganges delta, as it fanned out into the Bay of Bengal. In order to set up and supervise the operation, Hancock and Lacam travelled to the Sunderbunds and on his safe return Hancock sent a vivid description of this extraordinary place to Philadelphia:

> all entirely covered with jungles so thick that you cannot see ten
> feet into them, except in some few places where the salt-makers

Portrait Miniature of Philadelphia Hancock by John Smart
The miniature portrait of Philadelphia aged 38 was originally set as a ring for her husband Tysoe Saul Hancock to take with him when he returned to India in 1768. (Photo by Luke Shears, courtesy of Jane Austen's House, Chawton)

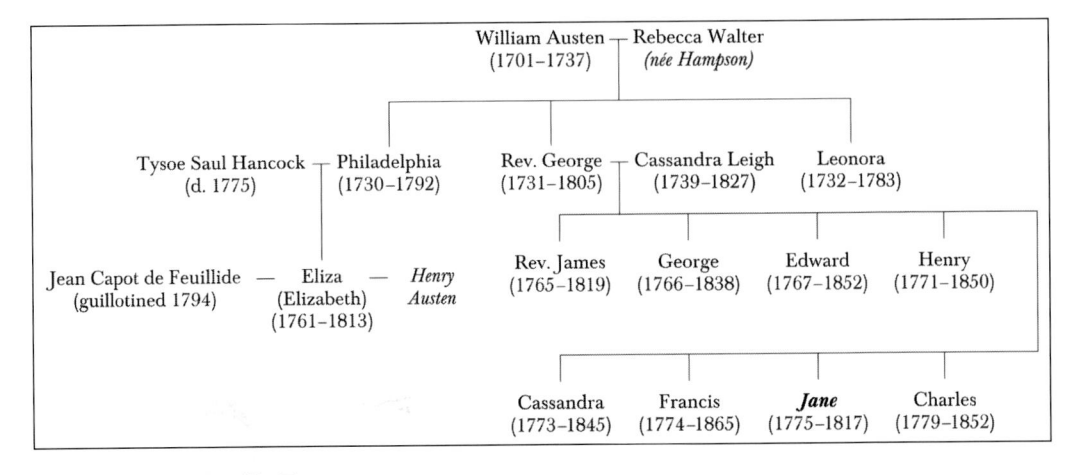

```
                    William Austen ── Rebecca Walter
                      (1701–1737)      (née Hampson)
       ┌──────────────────┬──────────────────┐
Tysoe Saul Hancock ── Philadelphia    Rev. George ── Cassandra Leigh    Leonora
     (d. 1775)        (1730–1792)    (1731–1805)    (1739–1827)      (1732–1783)

Jean Capot de Feuillide ── Eliza ── Henry    Rev. James   George      Edward      Henry
   (guillotined 1794)   (Elizabeth)  Austen  (1765–1819) (1766–1838) (1767–1852) (1771–1850)
                        (1761–1813)

                                    Cassandra    Francis      *Jane*      Charles
                                   (1773–1845)  (1774–1865)  (1775–1817) (1779–1852)
```

Austen Family Tree
This family tree omits Philadelphia's mother Rebecca's brother Sir George Hampson and her three younger sisters: Elizabeth Cure, Catherine Margaret Freeman and Jane Payne, and Rebecca's son from her first marriage, William-Hampson Walter. All were significant connections of Philadelphia's. (GL Archive/Alamy Stock Photo)

'Morning', 1738, artist J. Mollison
The satiric depiction of mid-eighteenth century Covent Garden market early in the morning emphasises the disreputable aspects of the area where Philadelphia became a milliner's apprentice in 1745. (Heritage Image Partnership/Alamy Stock Photo)

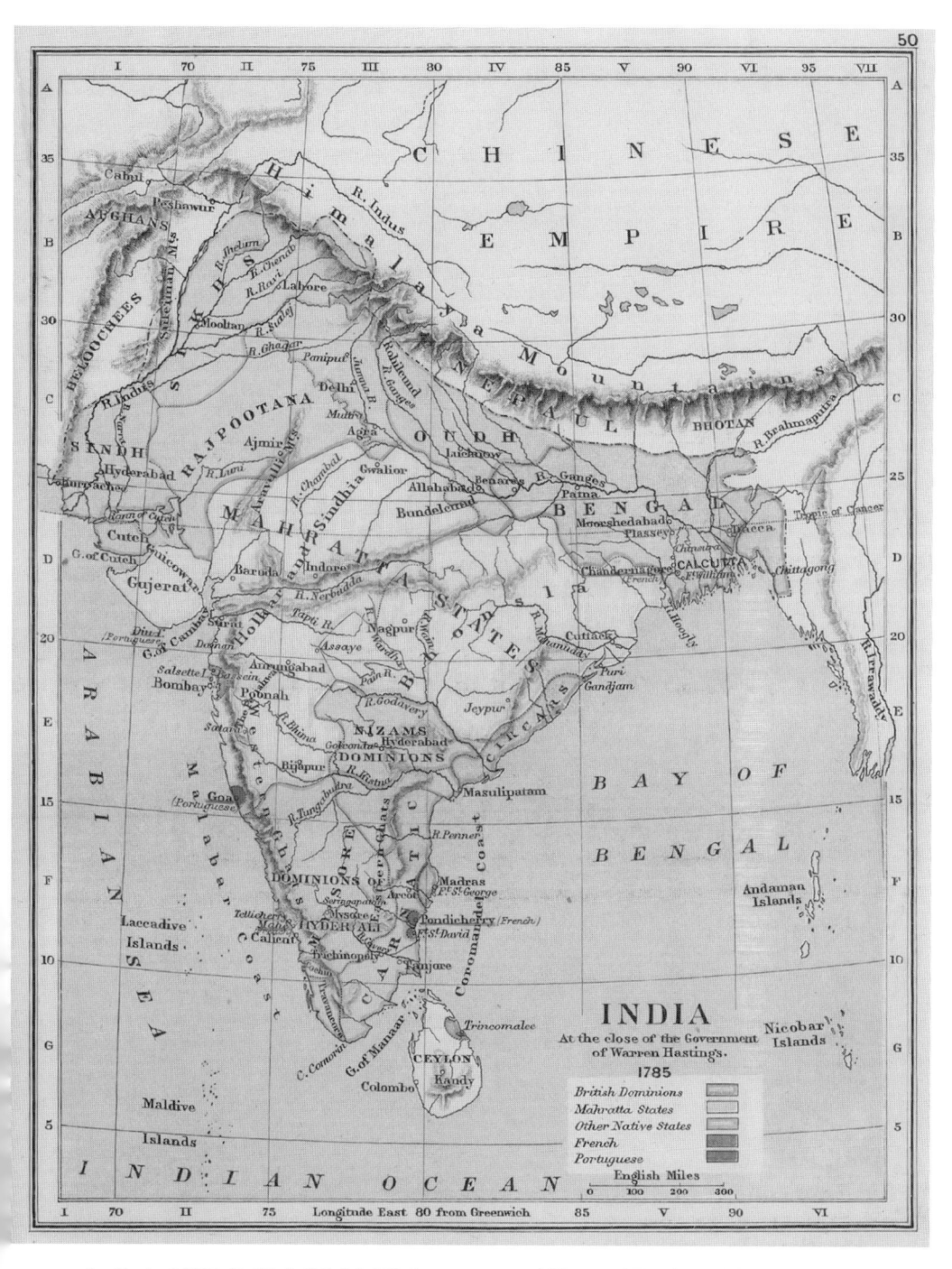

India in 1785: British (Pink). Mahratta states. Warren Hastings, 1907 old map
India as Warren Hastings left it in 1785, with the East India Company control of Bengal dominant, and far to the south, the settlement of Fort St David where Philadelphia was headed in 1752. (Antiqua Print Gallery/Alamy Stock Photo)

Margaret Maskelyne, Lady Clive
The portrait miniature of Margaret Clive in 1770 in London by John Smart, must be quite like the 16-year-old Margaret Maskelyne who travelled out to India with Philadelphia on the EIC ship the *Bombay Castle* in 1752. (Danvis Collection/Alamy Stock Photo)

Robert Clive, Lord Clive
Philadelphia's young shipboard companion Margaret Maskelyne married Robert Clive in 1753, shortly after arriving in Madras. Clive referred to his 'long Friendship' with Philadelphia's husband, Surgeon Hancock after he treated the wounds Clive suffered at the battle of Samiaveram. (Duncan 1890/iStock)

Fort St David, Madras. Painted c. 1765
The Madras stronghold of the EIC where Philadelphia arrived in August 1752 to marry Surgeon Hancock. In the foreground is an EIC ship riding at anchor with the 'fort' protecting the people and property of the company in the background. (Album/British Library/Alamy Stock Photo)

East India Company's factory at Kasimbazaar
Philadelphia met the young factory chief, Warren Hastings at Kasimbazaar, Bengal in 1759 when her husband was transferred there after the fall of Fort St David to the French. (Eraza Collection/Alamy Stock Photo)

Sir Elijah and Lady Impey and their Three Children (oil on canvas), Johann Zoffany (1733–1810)
This depiction of the life of the Supreme Court judge's family suggests an ideal of how such affluent members of the EIC ruling class lived in Calcutta in the late eighteenth century. (Photo © Christie's Images / Bridgeman Images)

Chait Singh the Raja of Benares rendering homage to Warren Hastings Governor General of Bengal

Hastings is depicted in this nineteenth-century engraving riding in a palanquin, its curtains drawn back. A favoured mode of travel for company servants in India. (Duncan 1890/iStock photo)

View of Warren Hastings' House at Alipore, William Hodges, 1744–1797

In 1763, the Nawab of Bengal, Mir Jaffir, gave his lands and buildings at Alipore, just outside Calcutta, to Hastings in gratitude for the Nawab's reinstatement. The house with its gardens became a favourite place of retreat for Hastings. (Penta Springs Limited / Alamy Stock Photo)

Tysoe Saul Hancock and his wife Philadelphia (née Austen) with their daughter Eliza and the Indian servant Clarinda, 1765–1767 by Joshua Reynolds
The family portrait was painted upon their return from India, and hung in Philadelphia and Eliza's various London houses alongside the Reynolds portrait of Warren Hastings. (Staatliche Museen zu Berlin, Gemäldegalerie / Dietmar Gunne; Public Domain Mark 1.0)

Warren Hastings by Sir Joshua Reynolds
Painted between 1766 and 1767, Hastings left the portrait in London when he returned to India in 1769, probably as a gift to Philadelphia. (© National Portrait Gallery, London)

Engraving of Steventon Rectory, birthplace of Jane Austen
The Hampshire home of Philadelphia's brother George and his family provided a warm refuge for Philadelphia and her daughter Eliza. (Heritage Image Partnership Ltd./Alamy Stock Photo)

Hanover Square, (1750)
The fashionable heart of London's Mayfair near where Philadelphia lived when her husband returned to India, with the church of St George's in the distance, centre. (RockingStock/iStock)

Portrait of Jane Austen
Engraving made from her sister Cassandra's less than flattering sketch. The 16-year-old Jane based the character of Camilla Wynne, in *Catharine, or The Bower*, on the life of 'Aunt Phila'. (Campwillowlate/iStock)

Portrait of Philadelphia's daughter Eliza de Feuillide (1761–1813)
This portrait of Philadelphia's only child is based on a miniature of the exquisitely coiffured Eliza done in Paris around the time of her marriage in 1782. Arriving back in England in 1786, after seven years in France, Eliza captivated her Austen cousins. (Photo 12/ Alamy Stock Photo)

Queen Marie Antoinette
The French queen's elaborate dress shows many of the features of Eliza's close-up description of the queen in a letter to cousin Phylly Walter. (Photo 12/ Alamy Stock Photo)

French Dragoon Soldier, Eighteenth Century of the King's Regiment
Eliza married Comte Jean-François Capot de Feuillide, a Captain of Dragoons of the Queen's Regiment in Paris in 1782. Philadelphia was happy with the match, though her English family not so. For Eliza, her husband gave her 'rank and title & a numerous & brilliant acquaintance'. (Duncan1890/iStock)

Fashionable Society promenading on the ramparts of Paris
Philadelphia's East India Company connections in Paris gave mother and daughter an entry into its highest levels of society, where Eliza was known to belong to '*la famille du fameux lord Hastings*'. (Florilegius/ Alamy Stock Photo)

A post-chaise entering a walled compound and passing between a band and a donkey train. After a watercolour by A. Heins
Philadelphia and Eliza set off in spring 1784 on the long journey from Paris to Guyenne, deep in the south-west of France to join Eliza's husband and his family there. (Classic Image/Alamy Stock Photo)

English gentry gathering on the Pantiles, Tunbridge Wells 1746 with the author Samuel Richardson
Back in England in 1786 for two years, and then permanently in 1789 on the eve of the French Revolution, Philadelphia and Eliza spent many months staying in the favoured Spa town. (Lakeview Image/Alamy Stock Photo)

An engraving of Margate, Kent, UK from a book printed in 1806
Following the latest craze for sea-bathing as a health treatment, Philadelphia and Eliza spent the winter of 1790–1791 in Margate, seeking a cure for Eliza's disabled son and perhaps also for Philadelphia. (Classic Image/Alamy Stock Photo)

The grave of Philadelphia, her daughter Eliza and grandson Hastings de Feuillide as it is today in the churchyard of St John-at-Hampstead, Hampstead, London
Philadelphia died of breast cancer on 26 February 1792 and was buried in the churchyard of St John-at-Hampstead, where the burial of her beloved daughter and grandson followed. The metal plaque was erected by the London branch of the Jane Austen Society reproducing in full the original dedication. (Author's Collection)

have cleared the ground for the space of fifty or a hundred yards... The only animals are the rhinoceros, tygers [sic] of a very large size, deer and wild hogs. The rivers abound with fish. In the Sunderbunds are neither houses nor huts [sic] therefore the people who are employed in making salt or chunam are obliged before sunset to remove in their boats from the shore into the middle of the rivers; where they are not perfectly safe, for the tygers [sic] sometimes swim off and take then out of their boats. We have unfortunately lost eight men by these terrible beasts.[26]

While he writes colourfully of his Sunderbunds exploits, which may have made exciting reading back in London, though pity the dreadful plight of the workers, for her husband to have missed being taken by a Bengal tiger must have been a relief to Philadelphia. For Hancock, being a merchant meant much harder work than sitting in a warehouse counting out his money. Arduous travel, lack of capital and frequent sickness be-devilled his efforts and his share in the partnership. The contract for chunam foundered. Hastings, as was the case on more than one occasion, came to the rescue of his friend by lending Lacam the money to buy out Hancock's share.[27] Hancock had promoted the chunam venture's financial potential to Philadelphia and then kept quiet about its demise, for he writes a letter to her at the end of 1773 expressing his impatience at Philadelphia's requesting more than once for information on how the chunam project was progressing. He has been reluctant to reply to her with the depressing facts that he had lost money on the venture.

Hancock's trading efforts never secured him the financial gain he sought. He may have always been living above his means, even when he and Philadelphia had been together in Calcutta, for when he first arrived back in Calcutta from London in the summer of 1769, it is claimed that Hancock 'had evidently left debts behind him in India, for he was arrested, though ill at the time, at the suit of a man to whom he refers as 'that dirty fellow Drake'.[28] Was this the 'Drake', governor of Calcutta, who abandoned his post and made his escape by water from the besieged Fort William back in 1757 to leave a small detachment of troops and Company servants to defend what ultimately became known as 'The Black Hole'?

Working as a surgeon was never a sufficient financial option for Hancock. So while trade, business ventures and lucrative EIC contracts were for others the way to fortune, Hancock never seemed to have the acumen, luck or even the contacts, despite his closeness to Hastings, to make the fortune he pursued. In his own words, Hancock sums up his situation: 'How little industry and application can avail when Fortune, or whatever you please to call it, is against a man'.[29] Meanwhile, back in England Philadelphia kept herself busy making waistcoats for her husband.

Chapter 12

Philadelphia, Her Husband and 'The Waistcoat Wars'
1772–1774

In a former letter I mentioned to you the fate of the Waistcoat you sent; I am greatly obliged to you for your Intention in Working another but... if there be the least finery in it, I shall never put it on.
Letter from Hancock to Philadelphia,
23 September 1772

PHILADELPHIA'S MILLINERY APPRENTICESHIP gave her more needlework skills than making hats. As indicated previously, in the eighteenth century the craft included the making of many articles of apparel and accessories, including waistcoats. While women like Jane Austen and her sister Cassandra made shirts and simple undergarments for themselves and their brothers, to make a waistcoat would have been beyond their level of skill, but not for Philadelphia. The elaborate full-fronted waistcoat, often decoratively embroidered and made of fine linen, cotton or silk such as worn by Hastings in his portrait by Sir Joshua Reynolds was the *de rigueur* item of eighteenth-century gentlemen's apparel. Perhaps for Philadelphia access to the fabulous fabrics available in India would have given her ample opportunities to exercise her seamstress skills for her husband's waistcoats. She probably continued to make his waistcoats when they returned to England and in her 'semi-widowhood' in London, kept up making them. Hancock often sent back fine fabrics such as dimity (light-weight fine cotton), muslin (very finely-woven cotton), Malda silks (from West Bengal) and palampores (exquisitely patterned hand-painted and dyed cotton bed covers) to his wife to make up into various garments and for use as household items.[1]

She makes her husband an embroidered waistcoat in the latter part of 1770 and sends it out to Calcutta from Captain Bromfield on the EIC ship *Asia*. The

Asia sails for India on 15 January 1771 but there is some mishap on board and Hancock writes to Philadelphia that: 'The waistcoat and everything sent by Captain Bromfield was lost in the *Asia*'.[2] He does not want her to make another, in fact he specifically requests that she does not make another one. He says that while he appreciates something made for him by her own hand, he does not want a fancy waistcoat. He writes:

> The value to me would only have been that it was worked by you for I am too old to wear any finery, and therefor [sic] request you will never undertake anything of the like kind again.[3]

Philadelphia probably received this letter early in 1772, but at the time was out of town, as indicated in correspondence by Woodman to Hastings. As well as the waistcoat, Hancock again raises the matter of George Austen's numerous offspring when Philadelphia writes to her husband telling him she is staying down in Steventon to assist Mrs Austen's lying-in for the birth of their fifth child, and first daughter, Cassandra. Philadelphia also reassures her husband that when she is back in London she will definitely obtain tutors for writing and arithmetic.

For Philadelphia, accomplishments may have been more of a priority for her daughter's marriageable future and they went beyond the '3 Rs' type of schooling. Eliza was to have musical tuition, dancing lessons, a horse with a riding instructor, French lessons, a new harpsichord, guitar lessons and now a writing master and an 'accomptant'. This would have been quite an expense for Philadelphia to provide, and she may have had her own priorities for her daughter to consider.

While we know how much Jane Austen, and Eliza also, delighted in dancing for its own sake, dancing instruction was seen as important for girls in their preparation for marriage, in order to display a 'young woman's body and bearing at social occasions to attract a suitor'.[4] Dancing masters and mistresses held classes and private lessons in their own establishments and also gave balls for their pupils to display their prowess. In the second half of the eighteenth century dancing instruction became very popular, with the dances on offer influenced by the latest in French fashion. Keen proponents took themselves off to Paris to learn the latest steps to pass on to their eager pupils. The dancing teacher also coached pupils in etiquette and deportment.

On her twelfth birthday in December 1773, John Woodman and his family visit Philadelphia's home for Eliza's birthday party. The next year, on her thirteenth birthday, in 1774, Woodman, in a letter to Hastings tells him that 'they had their usual party with the Hancocks on Betsy's birthday, and there was a ball given for the young people'.[5] The 'young people' included their son

Tommy. It indicates the growing maturity of Eliza, enjoying a ball, albeit a small one. In many of Austen's novels there are small impromptu dances put on in private houses, with the instrument being a pianoforte or harpsichord, but 'ball' implies something better prepared.

While Philadelphia takes to heart Hancock's wishes for their daughter, there is little hope on which to cling for a future together with her husband. Her life now is pinned on Eliza's prospects and Hastings' continued friendship. The bringing up of Eliza is really entirely in her own hands.

In his letters, Hancock often mentions family events among Philadelphia's Hampshire relatives and also her Freeman cousins, of whom Philadelphia has informed him. Early in their correspondence, Hancock tends to reply to Philadelphia's letters in groups, some of which could arrive within four to six months, and others which could take up to a year or even longer. His letter of reply is sometimes left open and added to after weeks, even months. This is often the case when he has been ill.

Philadelphia has given an account of the death of the husband of the only married female Freeman cousin, the youngest, Catherine Margaretta. She was married very young to Charles Stanhope of Westminster, and they had one child, a son. Hancock knew this family well enough to have strong opinions about them and to correspond with the eldest, Mary (Molly). There is a surviving letter in the letter book to Molly, who has enclosed with her letter to him a pair of garters she made as a gift for him. In his reply, Hancock, the miserable, decrepit, suffering husband plays quite a different role as a bit of a Falstaffian gallant. He writes:

> Your favour [letter] dated March 28th 1771 was not delivered to me till the 30th of last December. I was then at Dinner with two young Ladies who sometimes honour me with their agreeable Company – Opening the Paquet in great Haste, unluckily the garters fell out, the Ladies snatched them up immediately, declared they were sent me by some Lady who granted me as the only favour I delivered [deserved] the honor of being hanged in her Garters. They laid violent hands on me and declared they would suspend me to the Tester of my own Bed. I believe they would have executed their Thanks [Threats] had I not been rescued by some of my elder Guests, who thought it better to eat a few more Suppers with me than to see me hanged in jest and dye in earnest.[6]

This is either an exaggerated account of an actual incident or all just a joke. It contrasts with his account of his life to Philadelphia where he eats a paltry bowl of curry and rice once a day and never has any company, let alone 'two young

Ladies'. It does provide another side to Hancock. He had obviously enjoyed the circle of Philadelphia's relatives he had joined on his return to England.

He likes Molly, and regarding Catherine Margaretta, the youngest of the three female Freeman cousins, he is cheered to hear she is widowed. He writes to Philadelphia, telling her:

> On Mrs. Stanhope's account the News of her Husband's Death gives me Pleasure; she has had so Much of Matrimony that I imagine she will be cautious of trusting her Neck in the Noose again; if you should see her present my Respects and good wishes to her...[7]

It is difficult to know what marriage trials Catherine Margaretta had suffered at the hands of her first husband, but it did not prevent her from 'trusting her neck to the noose again'. Charles Stanhope died in late 1770 and in 1772 his widow marries again, this time to the Reverend John Price Jones, who from 1756 to 1767 had been the vicar of Yateley. Hancock seems to know all about the Reverend Jones, as when Philadelphia tells him of the marriage he writes on 23 September 1772 on receipt of the news: 'Surely you forgot I had lived at Yateley when you imagined that I should be much surprized to hear Mrs Stanhope was become Mrs Jones. I heartily wish her happy'.[8]

A widow marrying shortly after her husband's death is not that unusual, but the fact that it is the former vicar of Yateley, seems to be the matter of interest. Catherine Margaretta had been only 16 when she married Charles Stanhope, and from Hancock's comment, the marriage sounds as if it had not been a happy one. Catherine Margaretta Stanhope seems to have got to know the Reverend Price-Jones during his time at Yateley when her Hampson cousin Frances was married to the owner of the Yateley manor. Catherine Margaretta may also have lived at Yateley.

Philadelphia's cousin's one child, Philip Dormer Stanhope, turned 17 in the year his father died and was a scholar at Eton on his way to King's College Cambridge.[9] He did not graduate from Cambridge and seems to have been sent down because of some indiscretion. Stanhope was not without education, ability and connections and we know quite a lot more about him, as in 1774, like many a difficult young man, he sets out for India with a recommendation from Philadelphia ('my near relation', as he calls her) to Hancock. Stanhope remained in India for five years and in 1784 after his return to England published his *Genuine Memoirs of Asiaticus, in a series of letters to a friend during five years residence in different parts of India, three of which were spent in the service of the Nabob of Arcot*. More of Stanhope, India and Hancock later.

Apart from the Freeman cousins on her mother's Hampson side of the family, and with whom Philadelphia may have lived when younger, she also stays close to at least one of her other Hampson cousins; those children of her mother's brother, Sir George Hampson, the fifth baronet. These Hampson cousins were: Sir George Francis, the sixth baronet and his two sisters, Jane Louisa Hampson and Frances Elizabeth Hampson.

Like the family of her Freeman cousins, and the fictionalised Bertram family of *Mansfield Park*, the Hampson family were slave owners, with extensive sugar cane plantations in Jamaica. Unlike Sir Thomas Bertram, though, Philadelphia's cousin Sir George spent a great deal of his time in Jamaica itself. Philadelphia's sister-in-law Mrs George Austen, took an interest in her husband's well-connected Hampson relatives, of whom Philadelphia kept her informed.

One of Philadelphia's Hampson cousins, Frances Elizabeth Hampson, had married Thomas Diggle, heir to the Crandall Manor of Yateley in Hampshire. Philadelphia and her husband had visited Yateley when they returned from India, as Hancock refers to his staying there a number of times in his letters. After he went back to India, Philadelphia and Eliza kept up their visits to Yateley over the next six years.

Hancock is keen that Eliza keeps in with her mother's well-off Hampson family members. As mentioned previously, he encourages Eliza in particular to maintain her connections with their Payne cousins. These were the daughters of Philadelphia's Hampson cousin George Payne. George Payne, a few years younger than Philadelphia, had a fine estate, Broadlands, in Weybridge in Surrey. He is a wealthy barrister, judge, ambassador for Morocco, and at one time keeper of the menagerie animals at the Tower of London. He is also a friend of Hastings, though how the connection was made is not clear. Visits by George Payne and his daughter to Hastings at Beaumont Lodge, in 1789, after the latter's return to England are noted in Hastings' diary.

Eliza certainly did keep up with these Payne cousins, for in 1797 in a letter to her cousin Phylly Walter she writes of going up to the spa town of Cheltenham, and bringing her cousin, the eldest 'Miss Payne', Maria, as her holiday companion. Eliza had asked Phylly to come with her but she was needed at home to help with her father, William Hampson Walter, who was in a very bad way suffering from senile dementia. Maria Payne and Eliza had enjoyed themselves, at the newly fashionable spa town, with their walks with their matching Pug dogs and meeting the Leigh relatives 'of my Aunt Austen'.[10] They attended plays and balls where the 36-year-old widow Eliza still managed to dance every dance. Eliza says in her letter that one of her:

principal inducements for coming here was the neighbourhood of my old Friends the Hastings' whom I am just returned from visiting; They have got a place called Daylesford, which is one of the most beautiful I ever saw... fitted up with a degree of Taste & Magnificence seldom to be met with.[11]

But back to the waistcoats. Out of town, Philadelphia may have been for a few days, but she writes to her husband on 11 February 1772 and tells him she is making another waistcoat. She wants her husband to look well-dressed and as the waistcoat she has already made is lost in transit, she makes another, regardless of his objections.

On receipt of her February 1772 letter, and as part of a long letter he writes on 23 September 1772, Hancock acquiesces to her making a replacement for the lost waistcoat but objects to it being in any way fancy. He writes:

> In a former letter I mentioned to you the fate of the Waistcoat you sent; I am greatly obliged to you for your Intention in Working another but give me leave to assure you that if there be the least finery in it I shall never put it on. It is fully sufficient to have been a Coxcomb in my younger years.[12]

Philadelphia, is not to be put off her determination for a finely-made embroidered waistcoat to reach her husband. She would have been working on it again anyway by the time the letter reached her. She sends another, this time via the hands of a 'Mrs Blomers' going out to India. Mrs Blomers met a nasty fate, in drowning while coming ashore after having survived the long hazardous journey out. The waistcoat was lost with her. Hancock writes to Philadelphia in January 1771:

> You will have heard before you read this of Mrs Blomers having been drowned in going ashore. Are you convinced that Fate ordains I shall never receive any of your waistcoats? I earnestly request you will not make another for me.[13]

Once again, undaunted, Philadelphia is busily working away on the third waistcoat and tells her husband so, for in June he writes in a mildly threatening way that:

> If I should receive the third Waistcoat I will, after thanking you most heartily for your intention, return it. I should be the most ridiculous Animal upon Earth could I put any finery upon such a Carcase as mine worn out with age and diseases.[14]

When the third waistcoat is finished, Philadelphia sends it via the trusty hands of 'Mrs Ironside', the wife of Colonel Gilbert Ironside, an old colleague of Hastings who was now Hastings' military secretary. Hancock writes to Philadelphia, grudgingly accepting it upon its arrival, though complaining that he is too old and ill to ever wear it. But she had won that particular small domestic battle.

Times, for the Hancocks have been looking up somewhat with the news of Warren Hastings' Calcutta appointment. As the governor of Bengal, he will have primacy over all the presidencies of the East India Company in India, effectively 'governor general'. But to Philadelphia, Hancock writes gloomily about Hastings' return to Calcutta, even though he did have expectations of profiting by Hastings' appointment, perhaps with a secretarial position for him. But that was not to be. He tells his wife that because of the many difficult circumstances in Bengal, for Hastings the appointment he fears 'will Prove to him a Crown of Thorns'.[15]

Hastings' advancement came about because of a new direction decided upon in the Leadenhall Street headquarters of the East India Company. With the loss of the ship *Aurora* in early 1770, carrying Henry Vansittart as the new governor of Bengal, there was a hiatus in the appointment of a replacement governor. In the face of the appalling famine in Bengal, threats from warfare and panic over the impact on the value of the Company's stock, the directors held-off choosing a replacement, as Feiling writes, 'For another year the British in India were left in suspense while the India House rocked in panic and faction... [but eventually took-up] Clive's recommendation for... Hastings as Governor'.[16]

The notice of his appointment officially reached Madras in December of 1771, but Philadelphia knew of it earlier. The word must have spread from Leadenhall Street through Philadelphia's India House connections, such as Francis Sykes, (who was instrumental in getting the vote for Hastings) at the time the official decision on Hastings' appointment was made, for Mrs George Austen writes from Steventon to her sister-in-law Mrs Walter in Tonbridge on 21 July 1771:

> Sister Hancock sends us word she has had letters by these last ships from Mr Hancock & Mr Hastings, with good accounts of their health and well-being; you rejoice I am certain that the latter is appointed Governor of Bengal. What a comfort as well as of what real Consequence will he be to our good brother Hancock.[17]

The family clearly had high hopes for the Hastings connection to improve Hancock's lot. Philadelphia may have thought there could be an advantageous appointment for her husband too now under the Hastings regime, as she had previously hoped for under the doomed governorship of Henry Vansittart. Hancock was not confident that her expectations could be met, and his gloomy view of EIC politics probably meant he did not expect too much benefit for him from Hastings' new position. He had earlier written of her hopes with 'Mr Van's' appointment in 17 January 1770:

> I do not expect the appointment you solicit for me. Mr Van has too much occasion to strengthen his own interest for him to run the risque of disobliging numbers as he must do by endeavouring to carry such a point. You know Mr Sulivan [sic] [the EIC's most powerful director] opposed it when proposed many years ago by both Mr Van and his Lordship [Clive]. May your hopes not be disappointed.[18]

The future of their daughter now becomes an issue between the couple. An alternative proposition for Eliza's future, other than for her mother to take her to live in France, comes to Philadelphia with the appointment of Hastings as governor of Bengal. Could it be that Hastings' appointment has prompted Philadelphia's thought to reunite the family in Bengal when Eliza begins to approach an age when marriage would be contemplated? The letter to Hancock from Philadelphia suggesting such was probably written near the date of Eliza's tenth birthday on 21 December 1771.

Philadelphia senses that Eliza's prospects of a good marriage in England are not favourable, made obvious to her with her humiliating rejection by Margaret Clive, dear friend from her India days and godmother to Eliza, at the censorious behest of Clive a few years earlier. The stories questioning Eliza's parentage could get around via certain EIC circles in London, especially so with Hastings' rise in India. John Carnac, now a brigadier general, who initially relayed the rumour to Margaret Clive back in 1761 that Hastings was purported to be the father of Philadelphia's child, was, by 1772 living in opulence at Cams Hall, a magnificent estate in Hampshire. Would he have been a possible future source of gossip? While he probably now had no further interest in Philadelphia, we know from his earlier correspondence that Carnac liked a good gossip. So Philadelphia must have thought that rumours might surface when the time for Eliza's marriage came.

As yet, there is no definite prospect that Eliza will have any kind of fortune to go with the determined acquisition of every accomplishment that debt could acquire. Marriage settlements required a degree of legalistic detail too and even perhaps an investigation of the putative bride's background. Would Philadelphia want that for Eliza? It seems to me that with Hastings now in

Calcutta as governor, and Hancock adamant that his returning to England after a three-year stay in India re-building his fortune is now out of the question, Philadelphia thinks that good fortune could more likely come to the Hancock family over there in Calcutta. She could see the benefit to Eliza of the Hastings connection in Calcutta, and for herself the reunion with her husband as well as her 'dear and ever-valued friend' now the governor.

When she wrote the letter in December of 1771 proposing that in a few years' time she and Eliza go out to India to join her husband, she may or may not have known about Hastings' mistress, the Baroness von Imhoff. Hancock had yet to apprise her of it, as his letter about the baroness being Hastings' 'principal favourite among the ladies' (as though he kept a harem) was not written until 19 April 1772. Philadelphia would have received that letter perhaps in September or October of 1772. Hancock was a worldly man and must have known of it before though, for Hastings had written to Hancock asking him to find a house for the husband, Baron von Imhoff, now on leave from the army, when he came up from Madras to Calcutta 'to practise one of the liberal arts; in September of 1770 leaving his wife behind in Madras, 'living in Mr Hastings' house at the Mount'.[19] When Hastings had requested Hancock to find a house in Calcutta for the baron, in a letter dated 24 June 1770, he has not even been a year in Madras with the von Imhoffs. Hastings' first letter is followed by a second a month later where he disarmingly calls von Imhoff 'a shipmate of mine'.[20]

From Philadelphia's point of view, the three years of agreed separation had passed. She may not have wished to continue this 'grass' widowhood indefinitely. She has undertaken the trip out and back before and is prepared to do it again. There does not seem to be anything particularly outrageous in the suggestion of Philadelphia and her daughter going out to Calcutta in the future. The point Philadelphia makes is that Eliza's education and acquisition of accomplishments will be more or less complete by the time she is twelve; such progress she has made. Once out of childhood and their education complete, EIC children frequently came back out to India; the boys to go into service with the Company, the girls to marry. A number within the Hancocks's own circle did it. Hancock at a later date writes in a particularly, even for him, uncomplimentary way of 'Miss Vansittart', who had recently arrived back in September of 1773.

That young woman was Emelia Vansittart three years older than Eliza and one of the Vansittart children whose company Hastings' Calcutta circle enjoyed in those days in the early 1760s. Emelia Vansittart, with her mother now widowed, her uncle a close friend of Hastings, her brother also in Calcutta, like other young women we have encountered in Philadelphia's story, coming back out to India as a very young woman indeed, at 15, with close family connections there, in order to marry. And why not?

Emelia had been born in India, her father had been governor of Calcutta, her aunt, Anne Vansittart had married the former governor of Madras, Robert Palk, and her mother, Amelia Morse, had been born in Madras, daughter of another governor of Madras, Nicholas Morse. Emelia's grandfather had recently died in Madras, leaving a small legacy to his grandchildren, including Emelia. Her grandmother, Jane Morse, was still alive. So the very well connected Emelia had taken the risk of the long and dangerous voyage out.

Emelia married Edward Parry in 1774, related to a merchant family, who had come out to Bengal as a young writer around 1766. After his return to England he ultimately became a director of the EIC from 1797 and chairman for a period of time. So clearly there were advantageous marriages to be made for well-connected, even if very young, women. So there was nothing exceptional for Philadelphia's wanting to bring Eliza back to India, but Hancock is quite vehement in his opposition. He writes at length on 23 September 1772 to delineate all his objections.[21]

His first is that while she may be very accomplished, she will be too young to have any judgement and likely therefore to have her head turned by some man and be swept away by 'very Romantick' ideas of happiness which might lead to her being sadly disappointed and embittered for the rest of her days. As far as he is concerned Calcutta is now full of 'coxcombs... with very good persons & no other recommendation'. He points out how Philadelphia in particular knows just 'how impossible it is for a young girl to avoid being attached to a young handsome man whose address is agreeable to her'. Why does her husband refer so particularly to Philadelphia as knowing so well of such an attraction? Is it just general life experience? Or did Philadelphia in her past as 'a young girl' find herself irresistibly 'attached to a young handsome man whose address is agreeable to her'. Whatever personal experience of Philadelphia's he may be referring to, Hancock continues to push the point by painting a picture of Calcutta now as a sewer of depravity, where 'Debauchery under the polite name of gallantry is the reigning vice of the settlement'. He has no idea of anyone there being a suitable future husband for their daughter.

Beyond these objections, Hancock now stresses to Philadelphia the dangers of the voyage out resulting in the possible death of Philadelphia during the journey. Then, of course he brings in the prospect of his demise. It is a more likely possibility.

> It is very probable from my many dangerous ailments, to which the Climate is most unfriendly, that I may not live to receive you. Paint to yourself the distresses you must suffer in a Place where you are now a Perfect Stranger.[22]

Is it in fact true to say that Philadelphia would be 'a perfect stranger' in Calcutta? Not quite. There is her friend Hastings now the governor. There are still people there her husband mentions in his letters, including Mrs Bowers, who always asks after Eliza and sends her gifts. There are Vansittart family members and others unnamed who send Philadelphia reports of her husband's health. Hancock is exaggerating the difficulties that might arise, but he is adamant that they must not come out. In his letters to Philadelphia, often full of instructions of what she is to do or occasionally not to do, he never really takes a strong-handed dictatorial-style-husband stance. He most often is happy to leave matters at such a distance to Philadelphia's judgement. But as to her plan to return to India with Betsy, he enforces the obedience to a husband. Ultimately he has the say, and Philadelphia is obliged to acquiesce:

> I am certain that no Argument can ever induce me to give my consent to the Introduction of my Daughter to so lewd a place as Bengal now is, were all other Objections removed.[23]

So while Hancock is in happy agreement for Philadelphia to take Eliza to live in France, where they know almost no one and where the moral climate might be just as relaxed as he now he says it is in Calcutta, and where he has no influence whatsoever, yet under no circumstances are they to join him in Bengal!

Hancock's bachelor-like state seems to suit him best. He does not want Philadelphia there and he most certainly does not want Eliza there. No financial objections are made by Hancock concerning his family's joining him in Calcutta. He has most likely settled into his life there and the arrival of his family would have upset that. Overall in these last years of his life he often complains of suffering ill-health and his letters show an increasing irritability and fractiousness. Nothing much seems to give him pleasure and sadly, the arrival of his wife and daughter would not be a source of joy to him.

Then there is the Hastings situation. Hancock had written to Philadelphia about Hastings and his baroness a few months earlier, on 23 April 1772. He pointedly says that 'every thing [sic] relative to Mr Hastings is greatly interesting to you [Philadelphia]', as he recounts to her the situation of Hastings and Baroness von Imhoff. The Baroness, came up to Calcutta in the October of 1771, almost a year after her husband's move from Madras to Bengal. Hastings is yet to arrive. Hancock says in his letter to Philadelphia that, while the von Imhoffs 'do not make a part of Mr Hastings' Family, ... are often at his private Parties'. In fact the von Imhoffs were 'lodged for the time being' at Hastings' country house in Alipore.[24]

Philadelphia would not have received this letter informing her of Marian and Hastings till after she had written to her husband about her possible return with Eliza. Would it have been awkward for Philadelphia now that Hastings had become connected to another married woman? Had some closeness continued between Philadelphia and Hastings in London? It would be a closeness that could not now be continued on the same basis in Calcutta. As far as can be established, Philadelphia previously had not seemed to have had a rival for his affections since the death of his first wife. But all the implications in Hancock's letter make it clear, the situation between Philadelphia and Hastings must now be on a very different footing.

Hastings has said in his letter to Philadelphia upon leaving Madras, in the January of 1772, that he wants to bring his business partnership with Hancock to a conclusion, and perhaps other matters between them likewise.

Hancock writes another letter to Philadelphia in December 1772, this time in the form of an introduction to Philadelphia, recommending the von Imhoffs's 6-year-old son, Charles, travelling back to England. Hancock requests she give him every assistance she can. Her husband must remain on the best of terms with Hastings, one assumes. He writes:

> The young Gentleman who will deliver this to you is the son of Mr. and Mrs. Imhoff whom I mentioned to you in a former Letter. Your taking great notice of him and doing Him any good offices will be very grateful to Mr. Hastings who patronises Him, on which account I so strongly recommend Him to your notice as we cannot do too much to oblige that Gentleman who has been so good a friend to us.[25]

Baron von Imhoff is going back to England with his son, leaving his wife behind, as Hancock's next brief note to Philadelphia on 27 February 1773 makes clear. It seems that his few words say it all. Hancock is obliging Hastings as regards easing Marian's husband's and son's return to England.

Hancock's refusal to allow Philadelphia to join him in Calcutta could also be partly to spare any hopes Philadelphia may have had for Eliza's advancement through Hastings' position. He is now building a new family with 'Mrs. Imhoff'.

So while Philadelphia could not defy or overlook her husband's injunction, there may well be other considerations he does not wish to reveal as to why he does not want his family there. His health is also a valid concern. Perhaps it requires so much expense, so many arrangements and the re-organisation of his life in Calcutta that he does not feel up to it. He is respectful of Philadelphia's feelings in not spelling too much out. But it is clear, going out again to India is out of the question. So to France for Eliza it will eventually be

Chapter 13

Warren Hastings Makes a Gift
1772–1774

What I am going to tell you will I am sure make you very happy. A few days ago Mr Hastings under the polite term of making his goddaughter a present made over to me a Respondentia bond for 40,000 rupees.
Letter from Hancock to Philadelphia,
11 December 1772

MEETING THAT YOUNG EIC factor in Kasimbazaar back in 1759 had been a pivotal point in the lives of Philadelphia and her husband. The close relationship, business and personal that had been struck back then had continued beyond their journey back to England and years of living in London in close contact, and now Hastings was in Calcutta, presiding over the whole of the EIC's operations in India. Hancock had hopes this would be to his benefit. In the end though, despite Hancock's not achieving any position under Hastings' governorship, Hastings made good whatever agreement there was between them to relieve Hancock about his wife and daughter's financial future.

For Philadelphia to have Hastings located near her husband and in the highest-ranked position in the EIC in India must have relieved some of her worries. Hancock, however, soon becomes acutely aware that he has no real influence with Hastings. In reply to a recommendation from Philadelphia he tells her that:

> The Governor some months since on an application I made answered me 'As to my Friends I shall be glad to serve them, but as to my Friends' Friends I neither can nor will serve them.' Think you that after this rebuff I can ever ask again.[1]

Hancock was not without pride and sensitivity, and despite his wife's wishes for some advancement under Hastings, it was not to be. He attempted to obtain a number of appointments with Hastings, including to become Hastings' private secretary 'on account of our long intimacy and my education'.[2] Hancock's hopes seem misplaced, as it went to a much younger and very able man who had served Hastings in Madras. After the trouble Hastings had trying to get Hancock to respond to his request for information on their trading joint business when Hastings first returned from England, it was clear to him that Hancock was simply not competent enough.

Connections were everything in India, but Hastings' appointments were too important for him to trust to his old but ailing friend. Hancock shows his character by admitting that the 'young man was very worthy, and better qualified for the post than himself'.[3] In a characteristically comment to Philadelphia he refers to himself, in an allusion to Swift, as having 'made interest to be a Lord's Chaplain but was obliged to be contented with being his Lordship's Postillion [sic]'.[4] But Hastings found other ways to support him, putting Hancock in charge of some of his finances, and giving him a contract for the supply of bullocks and building products. But Hancock failed to make any real fortune from his many years in India.

Hastings, on the other hand, was very successful. While he is guarded in his letter to Philadelphia on his departure from Madras about the state of his finances, it is clear he sees a fortunate future:

> I have the satisfaction to inform you that my fortune is not worse than it was when I came here; I am not certain it is better. The best part of it is gone to Bengal, where I hope it has been employed to good account. My going there shall be attended with one useful effect, for I am determined on bringing our concerns to some sort of conclusion. I shall not have the difficulties which Mr Hancock had to encounter, nor he neither perhaps now.[5]

Hastings is resolved on finalising the partnership arrangement and it should be to her satisfaction. Perhaps the phrase 'our concerns' also implies some personal relationship being concluded. Back in 1769, shortly after arriving in Madras, in response to Hancock's fears for Eliza's future, Hastings had promised him that he would do what he can, when he can, to ensure Eliza's future financial security: He wrote then:

> But God forbid she should be disqualified for a better Way of Life because it is Possible she may not have a Fortune to equal it... I cannot say all I will upon this Subject... but if I live & meet with the success which I have a Right to for, she shall not be under the Necessity of marrying a Tradesman, or any Man for her Support.

I would not say thus much, but that I wish in every respect to dispell your Apprehensions.[6]

In December of 1772, nine months after Hastings arrives in Calcutta, he makes good this promise. Hancock writes on 11 December 1772 to Philadelphia:

What I am going to tell you will I am sure make you very happy. A few days ago Mr Hastings under the polite term of making his goddaughter a present made over to me a Respondentia bond for 40,000 rupees to be paid in China. I have given directions for the amount, which will be about £5,000 to be immediately remitted home to my attorneys.[7]

In Hancock's letter to Philadelphia on the subject of Hastings' 'present', Hancock uses the phrase, 'polite term', indicating a euphemism. He has used it in the 22 September 1772 letter to Philadelphia concerning the moral values of Calcutta where, 'Debauchery under the polite name of gallantry is the reigning vice of the settlement'. It is substantial sum of money, equating to around £5,000, and Hancock knows it is much more than merely 'a present'. Philadelphia's idea of bringing Eliza out to Bengal may have indeed helped to precipitate the gift to Eliza that would relieve Hancock's anxiety about what his daughter's future might be, and Hastings doing what he sees necessary for Philadelphia as he plans for his future with Marian von Imhoff.

Philadelphia may have actually heard of the 'present' first from Hastings, as he writes to her a month earlier on the 11 November 1772, though the letter's content is not copied to Hastings' letter file. The day before Hancock writes to her of the 'present', Hastings writes again to Philadelphia, as recorded in his file as 'one concerning China Bills per Packet, the other by Mr Anderson advising of ye Cabinet'.[8] The 'China Bills' reference suggests the money, and the other some piece of furniture he has sent Philadelphia. Invested in South Sea Annuities, the £5,000 would bring an income of £300 a year. The modern equivalent buying power is over £58,000 a year to live on.[9]

Respondentia bonds, are loans against the value of a ship's cargo. In this case the cargo going to China would almost certainly be opium. Opium was the currency of East India trade with China to pay for the vast quantity of tea now demanded by the English at home. Of concern to Hancock was the need for the source of the money for Eliza to remain highly confidential. He warned Philadelphia 'not to acquaint even the dearest friend you have with this circumstance'.

Clearly he is concerned that as few people as possible are to know that Hastings has provided this money, though there is correspondence between Philadelphia and Henry Savage an EIC Director about the money. No doubt when Philadelphia receives the letters from Hastings and her husband about the money, she is, as her husband says, 'made very happy'. Some future financial security can be looked forward to, but her anxiety about how she is to continue to live precariously in London and meet the expenses of Eliza's education are not entirely over. But, one assumes, credit with promise of payment can keep you going.

In a letter of 3 September 1773 in response to one from her asking for money to be sent, Hancock reminds her that: 'Remittances from India are now becoming difficult Transactions to be managed' and he does not consider Philadelphia capable of 'managing such complicated affairs' and tells her he wishes she had devoted herself in her earlier years less to 'dissipations' and more to 'acquiring the necessary and most useful knowledge of accounts'.[10] One assumes he uses 'dissipations' in its early eighteenth-century sense of squandering one's efforts on frivolous or amusing activities, rather than the later sense of 'vicious indulgence in pleasure'.[11] It has been over five years since he has seen his wife, and trying to make enough money in India to ensure she and Eliza live comfortably in London, he seems very weary of it all. He tells her in the same letter that he does 'not mention this to excuse my not sending you money as you desire; for I will do in this as I have ever done since our Connection and comply with your request'.

Philadelphia still remains entirely dependent on the largesse of her long-gone husband and the probity of her uncle for her maintenance. It is still a fraught position, as Hancock tells her on 7 November 1773 that he is 'Perfectly resolved to take my affairs out of your Uncle's Hands by the next dispatch; it would be cruelty to you not to do it, for by his Management I may be a fourth time ruined.[12] Presumably, when they had to flee Fort St David when it fell to the French in 1758 he was ruined then. By the time he had to depart England for India in 1768, Hancock must have felt himself 'ruined' then again. Nothing much has worked out for him in India but Hancock makes the most desperate and dramatic vow to Philadelphia on 16 January 1774 that:

> While I can crawl on the face of the earth, I will do my utmost to make you easy when it shall have pleased Providence to release you from the Remembrance of an old Wretch.[13]

Marriage probably did not bring the satisfaction to Hancock that he might have envisaged when he first made the 'connection', as he calls it, with the niece of his attorney, Francis Austen, in Cuddalore twenty-two years earlier. Children had eluded them for many years, and he gained substantial responsibilities by marriage that had to be honoured, and which he did, but they proved burdensome for him.

Even though from the time of her husband's vociferous rebuff to her idea of joining him in Calcutta, Philadelphia probably did not totally 'give up on him', she must have felt the relationship not easy to maintain. Attempting to keep her husband cheerful from such a distance was trying and his letters contained little joy for Philadelphia. When she wrote to him in the spring of 1773 telling him she has recently met with a lady returning from Calcutta to London who brought good news of her husband's health and well-being, he replies churlishly:

> Who the Lady from India is I cannot guess: I am not acquainted with more than five or six, and these I very seldom see; I never breakfast, dine or sup from home; I never go to any publick or private Diversion: therefore how and by what means this Lady should be so well acquainted with the State of my health I know not: it would be fortunate for you were it in the state she is pleased to represent it.[14]

His letters, when they reach Philadelphia showed her he was alive and gave her that comfort, but little else. She must have expressed some of this dissatisfaction with his way of responding to her letters, as when he writes in August of 1774 he says that he had 'recently received six letters from her, and intended to answer every paragraph of each, but as she apparently does not want to receive very long letters from him, he will not bother'.[15]

Despite the declining satisfaction they gained from their correspondence, Philadelphia assiduously kept up with hers and Hancock responded when he had something to impart and his health allowed it. Tellingly, a number of his letters break off saying he is too unwell to continue at that point. He mentions frequent bouts of illness in his letters to Philadelphia throughout 1773 and into 1774 and his correspondence becomes quite brief. It must be obvious to Philadelphia that her distant husband's health is failing, and she is powerless to do anything helpful about it.

Her life in London, though financially precarious, is comfortable. She is established in new and fashionable Hertford Street, Mayfair, close to Hastings' sister's family, in a house of her own choosing, though it may have been a little expensive, and is occupied with the education and upbringing of a dear only daughter, managing her household and her modest number of servants. Life for Philadelphia now was very different from when she had lived in India with her husband, yet the experience of those years in India, however, and the period of her 'grass widowhood' in London, during his absence, has marked her out differently from most of the other women in her extended family.

Her sister Leonora, single and dependent, had remained in the city household of Stephen Austen, their bookseller uncle. While both uncle and aunt were now dead, Leonora remained in the home of John Hinton, their aunt's second husband who had taken over Stephen Austen's bookselling business.

Then there was Philadelphia's sister-in-law, Cassandra Austen absorbed in her busy life as a country vicar's wife, running an increasing household on a modest parson's income, as well as keeping her poultry and a milking herd. She wrote about her country pursuits in a letter to their mutual sister-in-law Susannah Walter the previous year, inviting her and her daughter Phylly to come up to Steventon:

> I have got a nice dairy fitted up, and am now worth a Bull & Six Cows, and you would laugh to see them; for they are not much bigger than Jack-asses – and here I have got Jackies [long-eared rabbits] & Ducks & Chickens for Phylly's amusement.[16]

Cassandra Austen and her husband George now have a sixth child on the way. George has been given a second living, the adjoining parish of Deane, purchased by his uncle in March of 1773. George employs a curate for the everyday tasks of the parish and attempts to let the rectory. The Deane living was a welcome addition to the Austen's income, but it was not much. In improving his income and achieving a good education for his sons at minimal expense, George Austen was not only clever but also entrepreneurial, supplementing his income by boarding and teaching the young sons of friends along with his own sons.

Cassandra Austen was now responsible for maintaining a large household with live-in pupils and five children and all done with minimal domestic help. George Austen would have been able to afford few servants, and was fortunate in having an energetic and capable wife.

Philadelphia's city life must have seemed serene by comparison to Mrs George Austen's country life. But even though Philadelphia did not have the responsibilities of the kind of household her sister-in-law had, she still had plenty to occupy her. The education and refinement of Eliza was foremost. Providing the best possible future for Eliza was Philadelphia's great purpose in life. The idea, long-nurtured by Philadelphia, to take Eliza to France made the acquisition of the language an imperative now. In the spring of 1774 Philadelphia writes to her husband telling him she wants to speed up the progress of the 12-year-old Eliza's French by obtaining a French companion for her. This she may well have done, for three years later when they do leave England to live in France, Philadelphia must have felt sufficiently confident of Eliza's command of the language.

In the wider world, Philadelphia also maintained her India House connections and was sought out to provide recommendations for positions in India, via her husband, and receiving in turn, recommendations to her from her husband for people returning to London from India. Philadelphia was kind and obliging and happy to meet the requests. Among his recommendations, as mentioned previously, Hancock gives a letter of introduction to Baron von Imhoff. Would that have been an awkward encounter for Philadelphia?

The baron returned to London in 1773, leaving his wife behind in Calcutta under Hastings' 'protection', though 'it was given about that he would be returning to India'.[17] The baron also presented himself to John Woodman, who arranges to pay the baron £1,000 in two instalments, on Hastings' behalf. It was most likely to go towards the process of the baron obtaining a divorce from his wife through the German courts on the grounds of incompatibility.[18] The baron's artistic gifts had been put to work on a painting of Hastings, which he presented to Mrs Woodman. They did things differently then.

As Hastings' star rises, the approaches to Philadelphia for influence and recommendations rise too. As noted earlier, Margaret Clive's cousin Jenny Strachey presents herself to Philadelphia for some 'favor' [sic] for her son going out to India. Would such a recommendation to Hastings have been successful? Already Philadelphia has sent a recommendation for a 'Dr Brinkley' for Hancock to pass on to Hastings which her husband says is a waste of time. But Philadelphia, we know, is not easily dissuaded. The recommendations continue until they appear to become such a problem for Hancock that in November 1773 he writes a formal letter to Philadelphia which she is to show to anyone approaching her for an introduction 'refusing to accept such requests'.[19]

This deterrent may have arrived too late for Philadelphia to implement, or she chose not to employ it, for in August of 1774, with Philadelphia clearly still keeping up with her various Freeman cousins, Hancock has received a letter from her recommending her Freeman cousin, Catherine Margaretta's son, Philip Dormer Stanhope, for Hancock to receive the 21-year-old in Bengal and give him all the assistance he can. It is an offer her husband really cannot refuse, though it makes his heart sink. He writes to Philadelphia:

> It gives me, I own, infinite Pain to have [Stanhope] recommended to me in the Manner He is. Represent to yourself that I have lived many Months without entertaining any Company that I have confined my diet to one dish a day...
>
> *Now* I must keep a Table, which the least Recollection will remind you cannot be done but at a very great Expence.[20]

As the problematic son of one of his wife's well-to-do Freeman cousins, with whom Philadelphia most likely grew up, and whom Hancock got to know during his return to England, he feels he must oblige and will look after the young man. And he certainly does that, for in the young Stanhope's racy account of his five years in India, *Genuine Memoirs of Asiaticus* ... Under the nom de plume 'Asiaticus' published after his return to England in 1784, we have a number of mentions of Hancock and what he does for Stanhope.[21]

The two accounts of Stanhope's time in India, the published *Genuine Memoirs* and Hancock's letters to Philadelphia, share some common ground, but from very different points of view. Their two perspectives both substantiate each's account and provide an amusing contrast: one the long-suffering, and now quite ill, Hancock's trials with the devil-may-care young relative of Philadelphia, and Asiaticus's published version of his action-packed life in India. It is worth looking at this lively story of a young man's progress in India in more detail.

The pseudonymous Asiaticus's *Genuine Memoirs,* which includes a fawning dedication to Hastings, is written as a series of letters to a friend back in England. In Asiaticus's version, Stanhope left England after being sent down from Cambridge and is summoned by his father to depart to India. His account of the journey out is a mixture of arrogance, artifice and fact. The style is in the manner of a disdainful young rake, but with echoes of everyone else's account of the journey, especially regarding the other passengers:

> My fellow passengers...form a group altogether entertaining enough... They consist of two young ladies who go out under the immediate protection of the Captain in hopes that some wealthy Nabob may be attracted by the power of those charms... a young Hibernian who finds it necessary to travel... and a Captain in the Bengal artillery.[22]

When Asiaticus arrives in Bengal in September of 1774 and anchors in Culpee, he is helped by 'my friend Hancock' who has sent a 'Budgeroe' to take him up to Calcutta.[23] Asiaticus takes the assistance in easy fashion, whereas Hancock complains to Philadelphia that he has 'paid more than £20 for a Budgerow to collect him [Stanhope] from Idgelli'.[24] On 20 February 1775, in response to Philadelphia's enquiries about her young cousin, Hancock writes that Stanhope has now gone to Madras, but that:

> a few days after his arrival here, [in Calcutta] he was seized by a most severe obstruction of his liver: as he was your relation I would not trust my own skill but put him under the care of Dr Campbell to whom I paid twenty guineas for his attendance.[25]

Asiaticus has nothing but glowing praise for the kindness and generosity of his friend Hancock, whose 'lady is my near relative', and says that he 'went out particularly recommended to Mr Hancock... whom I formerly knew in England':

> I want words to express my gratitude for the favours with which this gentleman has loaded me. He has given me an apartment in his house... granted me an unlimited order for money on his Sarcar or cash-bearer ... [and his] general knowledge of mankind renders him a most agreeable companion, and who though upwards of fifty years of age still retains all the fire and pleasantry of youth'.[26]

Asiaticus tells a similar tale to Hancock's when relating the illness which overtook him soon after his arrival in Calcutta. Asiaticus tells his friend what the cause was, which Hancock spares Philadelphia in his account as a 'disorder from certain acts of intemperance... contrary to the advice of Mr Hancock'.[27]

Hancock does not however spare Philadelphia his withering assessment of Stanhope's character; all of which rings true to Asiaticus's account. Hancock sums him up as 'like his mother, very satirical & censorious, ridicules his mother, uncle, aunts & everybody but Mr Jones, [his stepfather] proud of his education & consequently overbearing in company'.[28]

It was a trial and an expense for the quite ill, by this time, Hancock to have his wife's reprobate young cousin under his roof. The arrogance and inflated sense of his own superiority and entitlement which Hancock describes, permeates every page of Asiaticus's *Genuine Memoirs*.

Keen to get rid of Stanhope, Hancock does introduce him to Hastings. Asiaticus paints Hastings as a paragon of the virtues and also claims that 'Mr. Hancock... has been for many years on terms of the most intimate friendship with him, and to whose recommendation he never fails of paying immediate attention'.[29]

Asiaticus's account also echoes the desperate effort of Hancock to be rid of him.

> Mr. Hancock advises me to return to Madras, where the recommendations of Mr. Hastings to the governor of Fort St. George cannot fail of procuring me a commission and where I may gather perhaps a greater quantity of military Laurels than of sterling gold.[30]

Hancock writes to Philadelphia on 20 February 1775 and confirms her cousin's departure from Calcutta to Madras, telling her that 'Mr. Stanhope... has written to me but once since he went to Madras & was then in daily expectation of getting a Commission'.[31]

Hancock hopes Stanhope is off his hands. But not quite, for in a letter to Philadelphia in May of 1775 Hancock tells her that her young cousin has returned, caused trouble and but is now gone again to Madras. In Asiaticus's account he also tells of how he does not make Madras at his first attempt. Hancock's letter to Philadelphia does not divulge the reason for Stanhope's return to Calcutta but in Asiaticus' *Genuine Memoirs*, he becomes stranded at sea on his way to Madras and faces many hardships which force his return to Calcutta.

Asiaticus describes the joy upon his return of the friends in Calcutta, who had 'supposed us buried in the ocean, and now received us as men risen from the grave'.

> My obligations to Mr. Hancock on this occasion are beyond the power of words to express... He now welcomed my return to life and liberty with tears of sincere affection. The governor-general too... congratulated me on my deliverance, and renewed his offer of recommendations to Madras.[32]

While Hancock does not mention any of the perils Asiaticus claims he endured, in his 20 May 1775 letter to Philadelphia, he does say of his return:

> Stanhope has been again in Calcutta; his impudent Quarrel [sic] on board the Ship has rendered him liable to two Duels. He owes me two thousand Rupees; I could not see him in Danger of a Gaol without relieving Him. He is returned to Madras but I fear he will never be prudent.[33]

Hancock is now finally rid of his wife's young cousin.

Philadelphia has assiduously maintained her correspondence with her husband throughout the whole period of his absence in India; it is coming up to six years now they have been separated. Apart from being her financial lifeline, as her daughter's father, she wishes to keep Eliza in his mind and heart through her letters; even when he writes bitterly of how the portrait of Betsy Philadelphia sent to him many years before is now 'moulded into Dust'. She writes to her husband in the late summer of 1774 that she is looking at ways to economise, but Hancock hates to hear it, reminding him as it does of his failure to reap the financial rewards his return to India had promised and his lack of influence with Hastings. He writes bitterly:

> I have confined my Diet to one Dish a Day & that generally Salt Fish or Curry & Rice, that I eat neither Breakfast or Supper: & all this I may save a little for you... The failure of my Contract and

the Accidents which have happened to a Ship I this year lose forty thousand rupees... You will be convinced how little Influence I have with the Governor; indeed I have not the hundredth Part of what his Head-Bearer enjoys.[34]

Philadelphia has also told him she has a 'Scheme for a Carriage', of which he approves, but he writes feelingly on 6 December 1774 that, 'Some of your economical Expressions hurt me much; they teach me that I ought in future to be silent on the subject of my Health & Circumstances'.[35] The generally miserable tone of her husband's letters must have been difficult for Philadelphia to deal with, though Hancock acknowledges he has received twenty letters from her 'in the last few months'.[36]

Philadelphia must still have continued her correspondence with Hastings, and we know he also wrote to her. John Woodman writes to Hastings in early 1775 of the frequency with which they see Philadelphia, their family visits and of the usual parties they hold together in December 1774 to celebrate the birthdays of Hastings and Eliza. She has turned 13 and is entering a critical time in a young woman's life. Woodman in his Christmas Day letter approvingly writes to Hastings that 'Mrs & Miss Hancock are very well, whom we have often the pleasure of seeing'.[37]

Chapter 14

The Death of Mr Hancock
1775–1776

The death of Mr. Hancock has deprived me of a sincere friend and generous benefactor, I believe no man ever lived more generally beloved, or died more universally regretted.

         Asiaticus, aka Philip Dormer Stanhope,
            The Genuine Memoirs of Asiaticus

THE YEAR 1775 opened in much the same way for Philadelphia as had her previous six years of 'grass' widowhood' in London: keeping in touch with her extended family, maintaining her London household in a fashionable part of town in the best style she can afford, with her maid servant Clarinda by her side, educating Eliza and writing anxiously to her husband in Calcutta and keeping up with Hastings, his family and her EIC connections. But of course no connection with Margaret Clive, whose husband had taken his own life in November 1774. One wonders what Philadelphia's reaction to that news would have been? Could she have wished to now reach out again to the devastated Margaret? Probably not.

  However, it will soon be the end of this particular era in Philadelphia's life. Her husband's letters are less frequent, he occasionally mentions being unwell, yet seems to have kept to his undertaking made in his letter of December 1774 that he would keep silent on his health.

  Philadelphia had already told him previously that she did not wish to have long letters from him anymore. His letters must give her little comfort, or she is distressed by his news always being so negative, or perhaps too, she wants to spare him the trouble of feeling he has to return letters in kind to her. She knows he is not well, and burdened by efforts to make money, while she has the health and time, and probably plenty of cheery news and gossip to pass on. The tenuous thread of their connection from London to Calcutta is never broken, but it has become very thin and perhaps she sees little point to it all. She has a husband she will never see again and a daughter who must barely remember him. It must be painful to think too much on it.

The best that Eliza has managed in communicating with her father are 'two little letters' he receives in March of 1775. Philip Stanhope reappears in Hancock's correspondence as part of an unusual story he tells Eliza:

Calcutta 26th March 1775

My dear Child

I have received your two little letters; greatly pleased that you seem to be at the time of writing them in health and good spirits... As your horse did not suit you, I have desired your Mamma to buy you another, not only to please you but for the sake of your health & because I think your good behaviour deserves encouragement.

The Governor, your godfather, desired me to send a very fine white Persian cat of mine to you as a present from him, which I would have done with pleasure but your cousin Stanhope having quarrelled with a gentleman who lived at a house next to mine & that cat having straied [sic] into his house, the gentleman or some of his people shot her-I suppose to be revenged on Mr Stanhope. If I should be so fortunate as to procure another I will send it next year.

May God bless you and make you good when you will be happy & make happy.[1]

Three months prior to this letter to Eliza, on 9 December 1774, Hancock made his will. He is no fool, and has shown himself always to be a realist. Dogged by bad luck and wanting the ruthless financial acumen other EIC servants used to their advantage to acquire fortunes in India, Hancock knows that he has very little to leave his wife and daughter. As a medical man, he may also think he has not much time left to him.

A last will and testament usually reflects the conventions of its period and the personality of its author. This is so with Tysoe Saul Hancock: the eldest son of a Kent clergyman, now a merchant of Calcutta and former East India Company surgeon. Hancock's will begins with a standard but simplified oath typical of the time: 'In the Name of God, Amen, I Tysoe Saul Hancock in the Kingdom of Bengal Merchant, being of sound mind and memory do make this my last Will and Testament'.[2] He makes no further religious exhortations. He is not much of a believer; in fact there is little evidence of much Christian fervour in the EIC India of the eighteenth century. Perhaps surrounded as they were by

The Death of Mr Hancock: 1775–1776

the fervid and colourful spectacles of the faiths of India, the British truly saw the tepid devotions of the Church of England revealing what it really was: more a social emollient than a sustaining system of belief.

Hancock's will reflects the kind, loyal, yet pragmatic man who maintains his responsibilities to his family. He leaves all that he has to his 'beloved wife Philadelphia Hancock', with a small bequest to his 'beloved daughter Elizabeth Hancock', and an annuity of £30 a year to his only sister, 'Olivia Hancock of Canterbury', if his estate has sufficient funds to support such a legacy. Realist to the end, if his estate is not at least worth £11,000, which is what he must have optimistically calculated his assets in India and England to be, then the annuity to Olivia would be 'null and void' and he could 'only recommend her to such assistance as my wife and daughter can afford'. Philadelphia did try to keep that commitment to Olivia Lightfoot, as she was known.

His immediate legacy to Eliza was the 'miniature picture of her mother painted by Smart and set in a ring with diamonds round it which I request she will never part with as I intend it to remind her of her virtue as well as of her person'. This is the ring miniature Hancock took with him to India in the autumn of 1768. He had sent the ring back to England for Philadelphia to have it restored and returned to him, saying in a letter to Philadelphia written on 3 March 1771 that he 'should be glad to have the Ring sent to me as all hopes of my returning to England are at an End'.[3] Philadelphia never does send the ring back.

There were three witnesses to Hancock's will: Thomas Ashburner, a member of an old EIC connected family and who was at that time sharing Hancock's house, William Larkins, the accountant general to the EIC in Bengal, son of Hancock's old friend Captain Larkins, who was very close to Hastings and instrumental to all his financial dealings, and an Archibald Roberton. The executors were Hastings, described as 'my generous patron Warren Hastings Esq the present Governor General of Fort William in Bengal' and 'Edward Baber Esq now of Cossimbazar', an able servant of the EIC, well-known and respected by Hancock, and good friend of Hastings. Both Larkins and Baber gave evidence for Hastings many years later at his impeachment trial before parliament. With Larkins as a witness and Baber as a fellow executor, both men of acknowledged integrity and very close to Hastings, he must have been aware of the poor state of both the health and the finances of his old friend. It had always been difficult to find out from Francis Austen exactly how his financial affairs stood in England and from Hastings' letters to Hancock, he was not at all a good financial manager. He also held other people's money to invest on their behalf, which at this point was more likely to be a debt on his estate than a profit to the lenders. Such debts later become a great concern of Philadelphia's. Hastings would have seen the urgent need to do more for the financial future of Philadelphia and her daughter.

Hastings was renowned for his generosity, even to those with far less call on his patronage than the Hancock family. He soon doubled the amount he had previously committed to settle in trust on Philadelphia and her daughter. This was on top of the various amounts he had been able to pass on to Philadelphia in the six years since he'd left London. An extensive correspondence (though almost none survive) had been kept between them throughout that time, and Philadelphia's intimate connection in London with his closest family, the Woodmans, had also been maintained, despite his being no longer in business with Hancock and his passionate attachment to the Baroness von Imhoff. It is not easy to say whether all the money he arranged for Philadelphia to receive in those years was from his own sources or on Hancock's account. It seems to have been a mix of both.

On 1 March 1775, three months after Hancock's will was prepared, Hastings makes out an indenture increasing his gift to Philadelphia and Eliza to £10,000. Three weeks later he writes to John Woodman's firm, 'instructing them to pay £10,000 to John Woodman and Rev G.A. Austen either in cash or stock to that amount'.[4] Hancock writes to Philadelphia on 25 March 1775 to tell her the news. He points out to her that he has given John Woodman and her brother George as trustees to receive this money and invest it on her behalf, though it would be some time before Philadelphia could take control of her own finances.

Hancock writes that the interest on the money should provide an income sufficient for Philadelphia to live on and 'a large fortune to Betsy after your death'. Well, perhaps not a 'large fortune' but enough to allow Philadelphia an income of around £600 a year and handsome enough dowry to attract a suitable husband for her daughter. In *Pride and Prejudice*, Miss King's 'sudden acquisition of ten thousand pounds' was more than sufficient for Wickham to drop Elizabeth Bennet and make 'himself agreeable' to Miss King.[5]

The tone of her husband's letter is low key and transactional; it does not express much joy at such good fortune for them. It may carry a sense of Hancock's shame that his life has come to this, while bringing the relief that his wife and daughter are provided for after his death. If indeed Philadelphia had 'abandoned' herself to Hastings, as Clive put it, in those now far off days, the affair may have been in some way sanctioned by her husband, and this is the payoff. Hancock has shown himself to be a proud and dignified man and his dependence now on Hastings to fund his wife and daughter's future does not fit the sense of his own honour that he probably holds. But he has always been a pragmatic man, and tells Philadelphia the brutal facts of his current state of health:

> As you and the child are now provided for, I may venture to tell you that I am not well enough to write a long letter, but should our

patron send a boat with more letters to overtake the ship, I will write again tomorrow, if I be able.

Give my love & blessing to Betsy & remember me to Clarinda.

I am, my dear Phila
Your most affectionate[6]

There is a long pause now in his letter book; either because he was not well enough to write to Philadelphia or had not the strength or need to keep a copy. His next recorded letter is written in late May 1775 where he writes of Stanhope's return and departure from Calcutta for Madras. There are just two more brief letters recorded to Philadelphia from her husband between May and August 1775.

As 1775 draws on, Hancock appears to be in a steep decline. A short letter on 22 May passes on to Philadelphia that their old friend Mrs Bowers, has just called on him to say that she has sent to England via a Mrs Geary, a gift for Eliza of 'four Strings of Pearls and a Philagree Blotter sewed on a Bag'. Mrs Bowers must have been keeping an eye on her failing old friend. In the letter Hancock shows he keeps his droll sense of humour at least, as he says: 'This Mrs Geary kept an House of Entertainment at Madras (I do not mean an House of ill Fame)'.[7]

Hancock's mention of Stanhope in one of his last letters, indicates that by mid-1775 Philip Stanhope seems at last gone for good to Madras. In Asiaticus's account the young hero arrives back in Madras with smug hope in his heart: 'My own situation begins already to afford me the most flattering prospect'.[8] He lands on his feet in Madras, staying with Mr Adams 'Master Intendent at Fort St George... [where] under the friendly roof of Mr Adams I enjoy all the luxuries of life in a most unlimited degree'. Stanhope seems to personify the type of eighteenth-century privileged young man who believes he is entitled to whatever he wants. It is the familiar eldest son in Jane Austen's work: Henry Crawford, Tom Bertram, John Dashwood and Robert Ferrars, to name a few. The world owes them everything.

Stanhope gains a cavalry position in the Nawab of Arcot's army, but in May 1776 he is recalled to Madras where he hears of Hancock's death. Asiaticus pays tribute to Philadelphia's husband.

> I have sustained a loss which requires all my philosophy to support, -and the death of Mr. Hancock has deprived me of a sincere friend and generous benefactor, I believe no man ever lived more generally beloved, or died more universally regretted... and I pay but a just tribute to his memory, when I say that in unaffected charity and real integrity of heart he was not inferior to Mr. Hastings.[9]

The news of her husband's death takes seven months to reach Philadelphia. His letters written in May would have reached her around October 1775, perhaps, and then one more, brief letter is recorded in his letter book in August. It is an important recommendation to Philadelphia of a young Mr Elliot. Hancock writes:

> Calcutta August 5 1775
>
> Dear Phila,
> Mr Elliot, who is Sir Gilbert Elliot's son will deliver this to you. Your judgement will readily point out to you that he is a very fine young gentleman: as he can give you a perfect Account of the Disputes in Bengal, I will not write on so disagreeable a subject.
> Pray treat the Gentleman with the greatest Civility; He is best Friend of our great Friend.[10]

Hastings is indeed a great man now and his task as EIC ruler over all of the Company presidencies in India is a demanding and fractious one. At the time Hancock writes his letter recommending 'Mr Elliot', Hastings is embroiled in an ongoing war with the Marathas in the west of India as well as the trial and execution of the West Bengal tax collector, Maharaja Nandakumar, a long-time enemy of Hastings who had brought bribery charges against Hastings. Both these disputes cast long shadows into Hastings' future. Hastings had sent young Alexander Elliot back to London with documents to assist his defence of the matter.

Tysoe Saul Hancock died in Calcutta on 5 November 1775 and was buried in the South Park Cemetery, just a little distant from the main British settlement. With the destruction of the old St Anne's Church, in Calcutta back in 1756 there had been no obvious burial ground for the British in Calcutta and it had been decided, probably by Clive, that a cemetery, not associated with any religious place of worship, be established in Chowringhee near enough to the town to walk to.

> The funeral procession would then proceed down Chowringhee... before turning sharply left along Burying Ground Road. The cortege, lit by torches of oil-soaked rags on poles, usually made its melancholy journey at night. It was thought too demoralising for the British residents to see their fellow countrymen and women borne with distressing frequency to their last resting places.[11]

A handsome chest tomb encloses the resting place of Hancock, with a markedly simple inscription, both still evident today. 'HERE Lieth the BODY of TYSOE

SAUL HANCOCK Esq who died the 5 NOV 1775 AGED 64 YEARS.[12] Not an inexpensive monument, but the age given was twelve years older than he actually was.

Back in England unaware of his death, it looks as though Philadelphia was short of money, as her brother George's account at Hoare's bank shows he paid her £50 in January of 1776. Two months earlier, the Austens had been expecting the birth of their seventh child. They had thought it was due in November, but November came and went. A miscalculation by the couple apparently. George passed on the good news to his Walter sister-in-law, writing on 17 December 1775 that 'last night the time came, and without a great deal of warning, everything was soon happily over'.[13]

The event was the birth of their second daughter, Jane Austen, with a fortuitously quick and easy passage into the world. There would be one more child for Cassandra Austen and then she would be over child-bearing. She survived all eight births and all her children reached adulthood. At the time of Jane's birth George was 44 and Cassandra 37. There has been speculation that Philadelphia was there at Steventon to assist her sister-in-law for the birth of Jane, as she had done earlier with some other births. But while it may have been the original intention, it seems unlikely that Philadelphia was there that cold December evening, as the birth was well overdue and in a letter to Hastings from John Woodman, written on 15 December, he tells Hastings that the Woodmans, along with the Hancocks and other friends, will be going to the home of Hastings' aunt Elizabeth in Kensington on 17 December to celebrate their usual party for his birthday.

Hastings' Letter of Advice instructing John Woodman to pay £10,000 for Philadelphia in trust in the names of Woodman and her brother George is received in London in late January 1776.[14] From India, Hastings sends 'two pipes of Madeira' to John Woodman, with half of it to go to Philadelphia.

The new baby Jane had been baptised by her father, privately at Steventon on the day of her birth. Then at Easter when the weather was far more clement, she was publicly christened. Did Philadelphia and Eliza go down to the Steventon Rectory to visit for the occasion? They may have, to join in the family celebration and it would also have been an opportunity to discuss the Hastings gift with her brother, a trustee. It was a very significant financial transaction, and even though at that point neither knew that Hancock was dead, Philadelphia was going to have to manage the money herself to some degree. She would open an account with one of the established banks in the City, Hoare & Co. in Fleet Street, whose customers were drawn from the upper classes and with whom her brother banked.[15]

While her husband mouldered in his grave in the burial ground at Chowringhee, unknown as yet to her, Philadelphia in London began to see the monetary promise of Hastings bear fruit. In May 1776 her trustees purchase £6,000 worth of Old South Sea Annuities for her at the cost of £5,145.[16] With their new baby Jane weaned and out to the foster care of a local village family for the next eighteen months, Mr and Mrs Austen are free to come to London for George to attend to his responsibilities as Philadelphia's trustee, and must decide to make a short holiday of it, staying with Philadelphia and Eliza in Hertford Street, and perhaps bringing one or two of their older boys. By now there were seven young Austens, from ages 10 to 6 months. Hancock had earlier pointed out to Philadelphia that, 'You must get your brother to come to town, & with Mr Woodman to sign the Deed taking care that the proper seals be affixed at or before signing', and that 'It ought not to occasion any expense to your brother therefore you must repay what his journey to London may cost'.[17]

Thus the Austen's were in London staying with Philadelphia on Friday, 7 June that summer, when Philadelphia's mail from India comes in and there is a letter from Calcutta from Mary Bowers telling her the news of her husband's death.[18]

It had been eight years since Philadelphia had last seen him. His physical presence had been long lost to her, but they had kept their marriage alive through those years in tangible and intangible ways: letters, gifts, messages through intermediaries and private thoughts. She must have often talked of him with Eliza, family, friends and common Indian connections. She kept in touch with his family, and the handsome Reynolds family portrait on her dining room wall kept his image alive too. The receipts of money and gifts from him and his strenuous efforts to make a fortune sufficient for her and Eliza to live on were proofs positive of his love and loyalty to her. It must have been a devotion harshly tested at times. The thought of his dying alone and far from her may have preyed on her, as would have the thought that he had been dead for months and she did not know.

John and Anne Woodman were also with Philadelphia when the letter from Mrs Bowers arrived, probably Woodman had brought the mail from India via the official EIC packet with him on that day. We know these details because Woodman writes to Hastings four days later telling him that Philadelphia had received the news of Hancock's death and that 'her brother and sister Austen were there to help comfort her, as well as the Woodmans themselves'.[19] Just a few days later Philadelphia receives a letter from Hastings telling her of Hancock's death and also some bad news about her husband's finances. He has left many debts.

Philadelphia has just turned 46 and is now truly a widow. The death of her husband has brought sorrow and some anxiety about the debts he has left; but she has had her financial future secured by Warren Hastings, and in a sense she has gained a freedom of action she has never had before. Many of the constraints that bound her as a single, penniless, orphaned young woman and as the dutiful wife of a rather dull and absent husband are gone. That free spirit we glimpsed earlier of the young Philadelphia sitting on the verandah of the Clive Garden House in Calcutta 'thrusting mangoes down her throat', perhaps emerges again. If they had money, widows could be much freer women in the eighteenth century: free of child-bearing, free to manage their own money and free to make their own life choices. Where would that freedom take Philadelphia?

In the wider world in that June of 1776, the Americans were challenging British colonial power, and France and Britain were again about to plunge into war and play out their conflicts in India. In France proper 'the spirit of the age was not to be denied [and] Through chinks and crannies in the rotted structure of the old regime, reform irresistibly continued to find its way'.[20]

While in the quiet domestic world, a widow in London mourned her husband and the Duke of Saxony's courts 'granted the prayer of Baron von Imhoff, as 'an abandoned conjugal mate' for the dissolution of his marriage'.[21] Warren Hastings would be free to marry his 'beloved Marian'. More than one line was being firmly drawn through Philadelphia's life.

Chapter 15

Off to Europe
1776–1780

> *Ten thousand pounds, including the late legacies was all that remained for his widow and daughters.*
>
> *Sense and Sensibility,* p.6

IN THE EIGHTEENTH CENTURY, even men of fame and fortune whose lives were documented extensively, have blank spaces that biographers struggle to fill. Warren Hastings' biographer, Keith Feiling, points out in regards to his subject's life from 1760 to 1764 that: 'We know little of his personal life at this stage'.[1] Feiling carries on nevertheless to make the effort. For the life of an undocumented eighteenth-century woman like Philadelphia, it is always a struggle, as it is most often a life explored through others. Such it has been for the past eight years through her husband's preserved letter book. His letters to her have provided us with glimpses of Philadelphia's progress, but now that reveal is closed and we are left with scant documentation until her daughter Eliza's letters, dated from May 1780 when she was 18, allow us to follow Philadelphia's life more closely once more. She begins to make choices and seek out imperatives about how to live that are to a degree against the conventions of her gender, class and time.

Although her husband had died seven months before she knew of it, we can assume on hearing the news Philadelphia went into a period of formal mourning, as well as a time of personal grief and anxiety about the future. Throughout the rest of 1776 and into 1777, Philadelphia's trustees move to shore up her finances by investing another tranche of the money from Hastings to add to the £6,000 of South Sea Annuities they had purchased in May. Firstly, they buy £1,642 worth of consuls, and then another £3,785 worth. Consols, like Old South Sea Annuities, were an investment in government debt, not unlike bonds today, but they had no particular term to run before being cashed in.

Consols would pay 3.5 per cent in perpetuity. Consols, short for 'consolidated annuities', were established earlier in the century as a way of the government controlling and reducing the costs of its national debt. Old South Sea Annuities were also now at this time, long after the infamous fraud of the 'South Sea Bubble', a safe investment in a stock that was also a vehicle for government debt. Philadelphia would receive dividends from these investments, paid half-yearly, of £90 from the South Sea Annuities, £51 from one consols purchase and £82 from the other. At this point in mid-July 1776 she will have a reliable annual income of £440.

Her trustees have now invested all of Hastings' £10,000 gift to Philadelphia and Eliza. The shock of her husband's death would have made her consider her future and shortly after the news of his death she seeks solace with her brother's family in the quiet of the Hampshire country side. In late October 1776 John Woodman writes to Hastings and includes a letter to him from Philadelphia.[2] Woodman comments that her letter was written some time ago and that he has not seen her recently because she has been spending time down in Steventon with her brother. Though the Steventon rectory was so full of children it must have been hectic, Philadelphia would have made herself useful no doubt to her sister-in-law and while Eliza's Austen cousins were all younger than her, she probably enjoyed their company as they did hers. The eldest, James was 12 and still at home, along with Edward, 9, Henry was just 5, Cassandra, 3, and Francis, 2. Baby Jane, not yet 1, was still in the village being cared for by a local family.

Did Philadelphia discuss with her brother her plan now to move to France to live? We know from later exchanges between Woodman and George Austen that he did not really approve of this adventurous step, but something was driving Philadelphia along this course, because by April of the next year, her plans were well advanced.

Philadelphia had returned to London by late November 1776 and she is mentioned in letters to Hastings by both John Woodman and George Vansittart, Hastings' closest friend and his latest emissary sent to London to represent him to East India House. Woodman tells Hastings that Philadelphia and Eliza are both well and George Vansittart tells Hastings that he has 'called on' Philadelphia in London, saw both her and Eliza and passed on the letter and 'little parcel' to her from Hastings.[3] That 'little parcel' in the hands of a most trusted friend could well have been diamonds. Vansittart comments to Hastings that: 'they are both well but I did not think Mrs Hancock looked very stout'.[4] Always very slim, perhaps Philadelphia was showing some strain on her health at this difficult time. Vansittart's letter was written on 17 December 1776, perhaps he had joined the usual birthday celebrations. Eliza would be turning 15 on the twenty-first of the month; a young lady now.

Hastings' earlier news that at the time of Hancock's death, that he had 'many debts' must have chilled Philadelphia. We can't know how much Hancock owed but his will stipulated that all of his debts were to be paid, and his executors had a responsibility to carry this out. We know who some of these creditors were. Two of them were women, known to Philadelphia and in difficult situations themselves.

The first creditor we hear of is Louisa Forde, mentioned in Woodman's November 1776 letter to Hastings. Woodman writes that Louisa's mother Margaret is very anxious about her daughter's fortune left in the hands of Hancock. Margaret Forde was the widow of Colonel Francis Forde, known as Clive's right-hand man. In 1767, Colonel Forde went back to his estate in Ireland but took the call in 1770 to serve again in India as one of the three EIC 'Supervisors' who were to go out to Bengal under the leadership of Henry Vansittart to reform the administration there. Their ship the *Aurora* disappeared after leaving the Cape in late December of that year.

Mrs Forde was a good friend of both Margaret Clive's and Philadelphia's and were close enough for Philadelphia to have been Louisa's godmother. Louisa was the little 4-year-old girl for whom Margaret Clive had spent her time on the return voyage from India in 1760 making frocks. It is not clear when Mrs Forde invested funds with Hancock on her daughter Louisa's behalf, but she had learnt of Hancock's death and was pursuing the funds through his estate. There was little prospect of regaining it, for as late as 1780 Philadelphia is still concerned about the fate of Mrs Forde's investment, as she writes later to Hastings regarding Mrs Forde, who she states:

> Continues to write to me and distresses me beyond measure on Account of Louisa's Fortune which was in Mr Hancock's Hands. I know not what to answer her & have vainly waited to receive some Account from you. I shall be happy to hear it will not all be lost.[5]

Philadelphia is also concerned about another creditor, a Mrs Ellinor Davis. In 1760 Ellinor Davis seems to have been a young woman either separated from her husband or widowed, and living in Calcutta. It is noted in the Hastings papers lodged in the British Library that 'Mrs Ellinor Davis lends 5000 rupees to T.S. Hancock for him to invest on her behalf'.[6]

Hastings and Hancock continue to have some responsibility for Mrs Davis' financial affairs for in 1765, Ellinor Davis, still in India, makes them 'her attorneys to manage her 1760 investment of 5000 rupees'.[7] Nine years later in 1774, following their return to Calcutta, Hastings and Hancock are suing a fellow executor for the estate of young James Lyon, concerning a debt on Lyon's estate 'for payment of outstanding money and interest, amounting to

Off to Europe: 1776–1780

more than 82000 rupees' on behalf of Mrs Ellinor Davis'.[8] Single women could readily be exploited financially and like Anne Elliot's old school friend, the crippled and poor Mrs Smith in *Persuasion*, were dependent on men to act in their financial interest for them.

So when Philadelphia's husband dies the following year, it seems Mrs Davis has not recovered her money, for in 1780 Philadelphia reveals to Hastings that 'Mrs Davis is returned from America a Widdow [sic] with two Children in great Distress. Is there anything for her?'[9] It is a worry to Philadelphia but she does not, one senses, feel any responsibility herself for these debts, but anxious and ashamed for her husband, nevertheless. One final mention of Ellinor Davis comes in the form of a diary entry for Hastings, who in March of 1781 in response to Philadelphia's plea, one assumes, notes 'to Eleanor Davis a gift being in extreme want of 9 guineas'.[10] That should have kept the wolf from the door for a few months.

Philadelphia, despite her husband's pressing creditors, is financially quite well provided for in comparison to the hapless Louisa Forde and Ellinor Davis and prepares to leave London, and put her life in England well behind and take Eliza, along with Clarinda (who is also owed money from Hancock's estate) to live on the Continent. The idea was conceived many years before.

Philadelphia's determination to take Eliza to France indicates that French society held a particular attraction for her, and reveals she was less bound to the strictures of contemporary English society than might have appeared. In France, Philadelphia could see a better chance for her daughter to marry well away from the innuendo of London gossip as regards Eliza's connection to Hastings. Indeed, there is evidence that what might have been kept very quiet in England could in France be allowed to be known to their advantage.

In France, Warren Hastings was referred to as 'Lord Hastings' and 'fameux' as the 'gouverneur de l'Indie' in a French reference acknowledging Eliza's particular connection to him: *'Il epousa une Anglaise, Miss Hanckock, qui didsit-on, appartenait a la famille du fameux lord Hastings, ancien gouvernour de l'Inde. Elle etait, disait-il toujours, immensement riche*, in a twentieth-century article written by a French scholar researching Eliza's future husband's estate in the Barbotan area of south-west France.[11]

While there is no evidence that Philadelphia had ever been to France, or that she spoke French, she had already spent eleven formative years away from England in the exotic and challenging environment of India, which meant the country of her birth may not have held strong sentimental bonds for her. Starting out again in a foreign land may not have been especially daunting for a woman who'd made the journey to India young, alone and single.

As an escapee from the French assault and capture of Cuddalore and Fort St David in 1758, one might think Philadelphia would hold anti-French sentiment, but it appears not. The Seven Years' War between France and Britain was concluded with the Treaty of Paris in 1763, which heralded a substantial period of peace between the two countries after many years of conflict. But even when they were at war with the French, British visitors to France appeared to have been quite welcome. Mid-eighteenth-century France, under the fifty-nine-year reign of Louis XV, the great-grandson of the 'Sun King' Louis XIV, may have struggled politically and economically but it still held its appeal as Europe's great centre of art, culture and fashion.

Philadelphia's principle motive in taking Eliza to live in France and build a new life there cannot just have been based on financial considerations, as suggested in Deirdre Le Faye's account:

> She [Philadelphia] knew that such an income [£600 per annum from interest] would be inadequate for life in London, and so decided to move to the Continent, where the cost of living was much cheaper; this would also fulfil her husband's wish that Betsy acquire some French culture.[12]

Philadelphia's husband's early letters reveal that the removal of Eliza to France was a long-held 'sentiment' of Philadelphia's, mentioned in John Carnac's correspondence with Margaret Clive as early as a few months after Eliza's birth. When Philadelphia made the move in 1777, she was at last financially settled in a way she had never been before. Her primary motive must have been to ensure a good marriageable future for her daughter.

As 1777 progressed, Philadelphia was preparing to leave: arranging her finances, ending the lease on her Hertford Street house, making farewell visits to her family, packing-up, storing, or selling some of her possessions. She now opened her own bank account, with Hoare & Co. This private bank, gracefully located in a fine Regency building is still there today and has an excellent archivist who allows one to peruse Philadelphia's ledger displaying her credit and debit columns of amounts large and small, throughout the five and a half years she held her account there. Following the money is a useful way of tracking Philadelphia's 'doings' in those first five years of living on the Continent. Amounts given here are usually rounded down to pounds.

Philadelphia's account is opened on the 9 April 1777 with a deposit from John Woodman of £3,438. This was money additional to and separate from Hastings' trust gift. It was most likely from the sale of the rough diamonds Woodman had written about to Hastings in the March. Deirdre Le Faye notes: '*London*: John Woodman writes to Warren Hastings, giving the price which he has been able to get for rough diamonds sold on Mrs PH's behalf – net total is 3939.3s.6d.'.[13] These rough diamonds may have been from Hancock's remaining assets in India, but as his debts there seemed substantial, more likely they were a gift from Hastings. Diamonds had to be sent through a reliable third party, and likely were in 'the little parcel' Vansittart handed over to Philadelphia back in December.

That opening deposit for Philadelphia was followed by the first withdrawal two days later of £2,699 for the purchase of consuls 'for benefit of daughter'.[14] Following that withdrawal, she drew for herself £100, 'To receipt', on the 16th of the month and then another £200 eight days later. How satisfying it must have been to no longer have to wait in hope of receiving something from her husband or her uncle.

Her dividends begin to flow into her account now, starting with the £90 in May from the £6,000 worth of Old South Sea Annuities. Her brother George is struggling to maintain an income sufficient for his growing family, and Philadelphia lends him a little over £384 in May. But there was an expectation he would repay her, for one year later on 1 May 1778 George pays £17.19 to Philadelphia, and follows with similar repayment amounts more or less regularly once a year for the period Philadelphia maintains her account with Hoare & Co.

There was one further major deposit made into Philadelphia's account on the 5 November 1777, an amount of £4,800 'By Bill India Co.'. Another substantial amount coming to Philadelphia from India, perhaps from Hancock's estate, perhaps from Hastings, perhaps a combination. It is not clear except that it was money paid through an East India Company bill and was extra to the Hastings £10,000 held in trust. The total amount was used to buy more consuls a week later. Her total investments in consuls and South Sea Annuities amounted to over £19,000, producing an annual income over £600. While making such calculations can be difficult, in terms of a purchasing power calculation it would be equivalent to an annual income of £83,250 today.[15]

By May 1777, Philadelphia's plans to move to the Continent are well advanced, for her bank ledger shows on the 29 May she makes the first of many regular monthly payments of £50 to 'Madame Nettine'. The ledger entry refers to Madame Louise Nettine, a Brussels banker, who took over the most important bank in the country that was then known as the Austrian Netherlands, from her husband after his death in 1749. Hoare's used Madame Nettine's bank for other local clients travelling to Brussels, and the £50 a month was probably what Philadelphia envisaged was a suitable amount for her to live on in Europe. She seemed to manage her money quite well, despite what her husband had to say on the topic from time to time in his letters to her. Those transfers to the Nettine bank in Brussels continued till July 1798.

Before Philadelphia set out for Europe she visited her family to make her farewells, including to her half-brother's family in Tonbridge. Eliza mentions in a later letter from Paris to her cousin Phylly about a visit to Tonbridge that she and her mother made, where Phylly's youngest brother James Walter, who would have been 17, is very taken by the charms of his 15-year-old cousin. In the letter, Eliza writes of James, now at Cambridge:

> I suppose he is much grown since I saw him... I fancy we are both a little altered since the time when he made verses on me in which he compared me to Venus & I know not what other divinity, & played off fireworks in the cellar in honour of my charm. This happened as you may recollect in a visit I made to Tonbridge some years ago.[16]

And what of Philadelphia's sister Leonora, still living in London in Paternoster Row in the household of John Hinton, the bookseller who had married her aunt, the widow of her uncle, Stephen Austen, who herself had died a few years prior? Mr Hinton had married again but remained kind to 'poor' Leonora, as Hancock described her. Philadelphia made some financial arrangement for the provision of Leonora before she left, as when John Hinton died in 1781, a few months later his widow married another bookseller, Stephen Austen Cumberlege, who was in partnership with Hinton and Leonora remained with the Cumberlege family from 1778. In June of that year Philadelphia arranges with her bank to make regular annual payments to 'Cumberledge' [sic]. These annual payments continue, along with £10 to Stephen Cumberlege from George Austen each July, until Leonora's death in February of 1783. She was buried at St Mary's Church Islington.

A farewell visit to Steventon was most likely made, but there is no record of it. There may have been no particular intention of permanently living in France when Philadelphia, Clarinda and Eliza set out, in the summer of 1777. She may have thought of it as some kind of modest version of the 'Grand Tour' for Eliza. Was it to be a form of 'finishing school' for Eliza, giving her that 'French polish' of language, manners, fashion and style that would ornament her already established accomplishments and improve her chances of marrying well? The reliable income from her investments allowed Philadelphia to give this gift to Eliza; and there was clearly nothing Philadelphia would not do for her daughter's happiness; though ultimately that happiness proved elusive. Was the original intention to leave England forever? Probably not. In the first extant letter of Eliza to her cousin Phylly, Eliza writes in Paris, in 1780:

> You are very good in saying you wish for my return to England... As to my settling abroad, it is not at all likely, although not absolutely impossible as it is a thing that at this moment entirely depends on myself... I think like you that there are many worthy

persons among my own countrymen, but I think likewise that worth is confined to no country or nation & equally found in Germany, Flanders or France.[17]

It may be assumed from Eliza's reference to 'Germany and Flanders' that Philadelphia had taken her and Clarinda to these countries before coming to France. Philadelphia's initial destination was Brussels; much more of a lesser European light than Paris, but a good starting-off point for a tour of Europe. Brussels was still essentially, in the second half of the eighteenth century a small medieval-style city. It was also French speaking and there was a good connection by boat from Dover to Ostend on the coast. Society would have been less demanding, and as a provincial outpost of the Austrian Empire, might have been a more comfortable alternative to Paris.

Another reason for Brussels rather than Paris being their first stop may have been less of a personal choice but of necessity. The American War of Independence, which erupted in the summer of 1776, caused France and Britain to once again become enemies. The easy route from Dover to Calais by regular packet boat appears to have been disrupted. Safe passage, free from attack could not could not be guaranteed.

From the 'To Receipt' payments of £300 in cash to herself in April and the gift to her brother on 13 May, there were no further payments from her account, except for the monthly £50 transfers to 'Madame Nettine' until December when the first of a regular 5 guineas was paid to Mrs E. Hinchliffe. As the payments to Brussels started at the end of May, it is unlikely Philadelphia would have continued to stay in London for very long after she began sending the money, so we can assume her departure came in June.

These payments made from her account, amounting to £600 a year were only a little less than her annual income from investments; they are sufficient for Philadelphia to live on without dipping into her capital. At the end of 1777, she had received £8,574 into her account and paid out £8,561, mostly into investment. A slim margin of credit difference. But of those receipts she invested £7,469 in consuls to improve her income.

Setting off by private carriage, post-chaise, or stage coach, the trip from London to Dover for the Ostend 'packet' would have taken more than a single day. If it were by post-chaise (the favoured private transport if you didn't have your own carriage or had the use of someone else's) there was room for two in the carriage and a 'dicky seat' at the back for a servant. The poste-chaise was lighter and faster than older style coaches. Instead of a coachman sitting up on the coach, a 'post-boy', who was usually not a young boy at all, rode one of the horses. Or perhaps they went by stage-coach, or a 'Flying Coach', which sounds terrifying!

Travelling in Europe with only her daughter and Clarinda was a challenge, but one Philadelphia seems happy to meet. The journey from Ostend to Brussels was about 70 miles, so unlikely to be done in a single day. Perhaps they went by way of Bruges and Ghent, both formerly great medieval cities but Brussels was their destination and Philadelphia probably arrived with her two charges, safely into Brussels while summer nights were still long.

The most exclusive and modern area of Brussels at that time was the Royal Quarter where the aristocracy and wealthy bourgeoisie lived. At the time of Philadelphia's arrival the area's conversion from the site of the old-burnt-out palace to a great square surrounded by brand new neo-classical buildings would have been still under construction. Did they find accommodation near that area? In Brussels as in Paris at that time, well-to-do people were not averse to letting rooms in their spacious houses to English visitors with the right credentials. What connections did she have in Brussels? It is unlikely that an unaccompanied woman like Philadelphia, would have just turned up in Brussels, 'on spec' as it were. Perhaps her main connection was through the Nettine bank.

Philadelphia presented her journey to Europe as 'travels', rather than a permanent move. When her banker, Henry Hoare Jr writes to her in June of 1778, replying to a letter from her regarding money transfers to Paris, he refers to her as a traveller. So the travellers have settled in Brussels for at least a year, with their intention to move on in mid-1778, as Philadelphia has written to Hoare's bank. We do not have her letter but Mr Henry Hoare Junior writes:

> I am very sorry I was not at home when your Letter came, as it has occasion'd a Delay, in the answering, which I hope however will not be attended with any Inconvenience to you, as you do not propose to Leave Bruselles till the End of this Month. As Sir Robert Herries's Notes are very convenient to Travellers who are moving about, I have sent you four of them to the Amount of £200, & I have likewise sent you a Letter of Credit on Sir John Lambert at Paris for £200 more, which I hope you will approve of.[18]

Philadelphia did not go straight to Paris, and may have gone to Germany at this time, as mentioned by Eliza in a letter to Phylly. The last £50 payment to Madame Nettine's bank in Brussels from Philadelphia's account is made in July of 1778. When John Woodman writes to Hastings in mid-June 1778 he mentions that 'Mrs Hancock is yet there' [in Brussels] as he clearly thinks Hastings wants to know about Philadelphia's travels, and passes on other communication that says that Philadelphia and her daughter are both in good health.

Off to Europe: 1776–1780

In Brussels they would have enjoyed a similar life to what they had lived in London, with introductions opening up a more limited circle, and without any family, but clearly an opportunity for Eliza to blossom in that society and to further develop her fluency in French and other accomplishments. Eliza had been secured from the handicap of a lack of fortune by Hastings' gift, but for Eliza to come out into society and for her fortune of £10,000 to be known by a suitor, its source would also be need to be revealed. The connection to the family of 'Lord Hastings' as one French commentator puts it, would, one assumes, be more tolerated in Europe than in London.

Did Philadelphia secure invitations to morning visits, balls, dances, dinner parties for herself and Eliza in this cultivated city? It seems likely. There was a British diplomatic mission in Brussels and there was strong British trade in products like Belgium carpets. As a province of the Austrian Empire, Belgium was ruled at this time, fairly benignly by the Austrian Empress Maria Theresa. Although Belgium was fiercely Catholic, Philadelphia must have felt comfortable enough living amongst people of that religious faith.

After a year in Brussels the little party seem set to move. Hoare's bank withdraws the £200 worth of Herries & Co. notes suggested and sends them to Philadelphia in Brussels in early June 1778. The cash for travelling would be needed. Philadelphia keeps up her London correspondence with Hastings' sister Anne Woodman and her friend Elizabeth Hinchliffe, also known to the Woodmans, for Woodman in the same letter to Hastings where he assures them both Philadelphia and Eliza are well, obtains the information from 'the Miss Hinchliffes [who] drank tea with us yesterday [and] said they had a letter from Brussels this week'. As mentioned previously, Elizabeth and Martha Hinchliffe lived in Mayfair, nearby to both the Woodmans and Philadelphia's house in Hertford Street. When writing to cousin Phylly to direct her future letters to Eliza in France via Miss Hinchliffe's Hanover Square address, Eliza describes Elizabeth Hinchliffe as 'an intimate friend of Mama's [who] has frequent opportunities of sending to France & will not fail forwarding your Letter to me'.[19]

After her final £50 payment to the Nettine bank in Brussels on 8 July 1778, her next withdrawal is to 'D. Danoot' on 5 September 1778 for the sum of £200. Philadelphia needs cash for the next part of her journey, wherever that is to, and this time she uses Daniel Danoot, another prominent Brussels banker of considerable wealth and a great art collector. She uses Danoot's bank again in early March 1779. Winter travelling was difficult along the icy muddy roads of anywhere in northern Europe and was to be avoided unless absolutely necessary. Philadelphia seems to have taken her English banker's advice to use the convenience of Sir Robert Herries's notes when she is on the move.

Sir Robert Herries was a Scottish-born banker credited for coming up with the circulating note, a form of early travellers' cheque. The £400 sent to Danoot's bank was three-quarters of her annual income and must have carried her through her travels from Brussels from mid-1778. She seems to have been back to Brussels by the spring of 1779, and preparing for her move to Paris. Her money (as a letter of credit) is now transferred to Sir John Lambert, Hoare's bank's connection, or 'correspondent' as they were called at the time, in Paris. She also draws two lots of £100 worth of Herries's notes; one in May and one in August. The little party seems to have set off for Paris to arrive in the French capital in the early autumn. Still a reasonable season for travelling.

By October 1779, the travellers are in Paris, with Philadelphia drawing down the first £40 from her credit there with Lambert. Sir John Lambert III was a member of a prominent Protestant banking family who had lived in England as exiled Huguenots but who had been forced from England and returned to France for their involvement in the 'South Sea Bubble' scandal. At the time of Philadelphia's arrival in Paris, the banking Lamberts were very well established there on the Rue de Richelieu and continued their strong connection to England. Sir John and his family offered much more than merely banking services to visitors from Britain and were known to provide assistance with accommodation and introductions to the better-off visitors to Paris.

Her long-standing connections with some significant figures associated with the East India Company, not least of whom would have been Hastings, must have provided her with other introductions. In the blog by Bodleian archivist, Mike Williams posted on 24 October 2017, he identifies one of these connections as Captain Thomas Pattle, a colourful character who had left England and his family to live in Paris in his final years, following a long shipping career with the EIC. His town house was in Place Royale. Pattle also had a country house in Argenteuil.[20] Philadelphia was moving in circles in Paris with EIC connections.

Philadelphia continues to draw money in regular amounts via Lambert's more or less monthly throughout the rest of 1779, so we can assume they are still in Paris. She also draws two lots of £100 Herries's Notes in January and February of 1780, undoubtedly to meet unforeseen additional expenses. For all is not well in her small household. Clarinda has become very ill. On the 3 March 1780 Philadelphia writes to Hastings. It is the only letter of many that she had written over the years of their friendship that has been preserved in the Hastings Papers in the British Library.[21]

The letter opens with Philadelphia apologising for writing to Hastings. It has been almost five years since her husband died, Hastings has now been governor general of Bengal for eight years, and married to Marian for three. He is clearly a busy, preoccupied man. Philadelphia has still been writing to him, though it seems it has been some time since he returned the favour. But he is the executor of her husband's estate and her reason for writing is to ask about the progress in finalising the estate. Hancock's will was not probated until November of the next year.

She opens formally and with her apology:

> Dear Sir, After a silence of so many years on your part nothing shd have prevailed on me to have troubled you with another Letter but my earnest desire to have some information concerning Mr Hancock's affairs, and to whom can I apply but you?[22]

There is something rather sad about the phrase 'a silence of so many years on your part', but she cannot, however, help herself become more personal:

> Let me therefore conjure you by your Friendship for his memory and by those uncommon marks you have given of it to his Family not to refuse me this request the last perhaps I shall ever make you.[23]

Philadelphia pleads for information from Hastings about how 'far his Creditors are satisfied or likely to be so'. She is clearly distressed by the imprecations coming from at least two people mentioned above, Margaret Forde on behalf of her daughter Louisa and Mrs Ellinor Davis. Perhaps escaping such embarrassment might have also contributed to her wish to quit England at least for a few years. The £1,500 Tysoe loaned his brother Colbron, seems unlikely to be ever repaid and Philadelphia thinks her uncle Francis is holding about £2,000 of Hancock's money and asks Hastings to look into that. Her acute embarrassment is summed up when she says:

> I have met with many mortifying and disagreeable Events in my Life but none that has given such lasting affliction as the reflection that many worthy persons may be sufferers by the confidence they have unfortunately placed in the person whose name I bear.[24]

Not that Philadelphia blames Hancock, as she says, he was the most principled of men, but yet one of those people 'born to be unfortunate'. And then there is Clarinda. She too placed her savings into Hancock's hands; what of them? Philadelphia encloses in her letter Clarinda's 'demand' and then goes on to tell Hastings of what has happened to Clarinda.

Lovely Clarinda with her dark be-jewelled skin and glistening black hair sits at the centre of the Reynolds's portrait of the Hancock family, done when hopes must have been high. In Hancock's letters to Eliza from India he almost always mentions Clarinda in some way. In a letter to his daughter dated 20 December

1770, he writes: 'Remember me kindly to Clarinda, tell her that Mrs Bowers always inquires after her: I told her Clarinda's dream on which she laughed very heartily'.[25] Indian servants who returned to England with their masters and mistresses did not survive so well in the climate and circumstances of the alien land. But not Clarinda it seems.

In the group portrait Clarinda appears dressed in traditional South Indian attire. She looks robust in the painting, but now, fifteen years later, her life is under threat in Paris. Philadelphia tells Hastings of Clarinda's plight:

> It is now more than five months that she has been quite helpless and that from so small a beginning as a whitlow on her left thumb which notwithstanding all possible assistance and after six operations performed threatened the loss of her Hand & even her life & and before these wounds were healed the humour conveyed itself to her right shoulder where she has already had three severe operations performed and threatened with a fourth without some extraordinary change in her favour. She has been attended by three Surgeons, one of them the first in Paris, and a Physician; the latter still attends her and one of the Surgeons Dresses her Arm twice a Day – God knows how it will end, though I am assured her life and the use of her Hands are at present in no danger.[26]

Philadelphia also tells Hastings of the very high expenses involved but, 'of that I shan't complain if the poor faithful creature is restored to me'. The business matters relating to Hancock's estate concluded, Philadelphia can't help but relate more personal concerns. Again she begins in an apologetic tone but soon we see a quite intense intimate note captured:

> I once thought to have confined this Letter to Business but knowing your Heart as I know it and being convinced that in spite of appearances it is not changed for your Friends, I cannot refuse you the satisfaction of knowing my Daughter, the only thing I take Comfort in, is in perfect Health, and joins me in every good wish for your Happiness – you may be surrounded by those who are happy in frequent opportunities of shewing their attachment to you, but I will venture to say not one among them who can boast a more steady and unshaken Friendship for you than that which for so many years has animated and will ever continue to animate the Breast of
>
> Dear Sir Your obliged friend Phila: Hancock.[27]

She cannot resist claiming a special place in Hastings' heart for herself and her daughter. We only know of one specific outcome of this letter, and that was a payment made from Hastings' personal account to the Mrs Davis mentioned above. But the conclusion of the letter shows the strength with which Philadelphia holds her connection to Hastings, as it does the dedication to her daughter. Eliza is almost a sacred charge; but it is what drives Philadelphia through trying times. She adds a postscript to the letter two weeks later saying Clarinda is much improved.

Philadelphia remains in Paris with Clarinda and Eliza for another two months, waiting for Clarinda to be 'out of danger & ... able to quit her chamber'. John Woodman writes to Hastings in April 1780 with news of Philadelphia that 'Mrs. & Miss Hancock are at this time in Paris the young Lady is almost as tall as her Mother'.[28] It is not clear who the source of information is concerning Eliza, but probably comes from Philadelphia herself in a letter to the Woodmans, or her friends the Misses Hinchliffes. The Woodmans continued in correspondence with her; Mrs Anne Woodman with family news and John Woodman on business matters. Eliza is now a young woman of 18 and mother and daughter would have made an elegant and well-connected pair.

Philadelphia leaves Paris to spend the summer in the country in early May. From this date we have the first of Eliza's letters, many of them fortuitously kept, preserved and handed down in the family of Philadelphia's half-brother William Hampson Walter's descendants, and published in full in Deirdre Le Faye's book, *Jane Austen's Outlandish Cousin: The Life and Letters of Eliza de Feuillide* (2002). These are letters to her cousin Phylly Walter, the same age as Eliza, named after her aunt and living with her parents in various parts of Kent over the next twenty or so years. Not all of the letters have been kept, and there are gaps, but they do give us a sense and some details of what Philadelphia was up to in France and then back and forth to England in these last years of the ancient regime.

Philadelphia has just had her fiftieth birthday in the May of 1780, when the first of the extant letters of her daughter is written to Cousin Phylly. There is no mention of any birthday celebrations for her mother, but then most women don't celebrate turning 50!

Chapter 16

Philadelphia and Eliza's Friend The Comtesse de Tournon
1780–1782

The house we are in belongs to an acquaintance of the Lady [The comtesse de Tournon] ... one of my best friends.
Letter from Eliza to her cousin Phylly
from France, 27 June 1780

PHILADELPHIA HAD ALWAYS been drawn to the idea of living in the countryside and as soon as Clarinda is well enough to travel, the party leave for a house in the village of Combs-la-Ville, just outside Paris, and while Clarinda is much better she is 'still entirely helpless'.[1]

Before leaving Paris, Philadelphia and Eliza go to Versailles to see 'their Majesties & all the royal family dine & sup'.[2] Eliza's close-up description of Marie Antoinette might give the impression that the two women were moving in the highest ranks of society, but observing the royal family dining at the '*grand couvert*' was available to any well-dressed person with connections who, with a crowd of fellow visitors at Versailles, were ushered past the royal diners through a fenced-off area. But it must have been a special moment for Philadelphia, to bring her beautiful young daughter into such an exulted milieu; even if they were 'in the back row' of the spectators, as it were. Eliza's description of the queen impressed her country cousin. No details of her dress are spared:

> The Queen is a very fine woman, She has a most beautiful complexion, & is indeed exceedingly handsome ...; She was most elegantly dressed, she had on a corset & Petticoat of pale green Lutestring, covered with a transparent silver gauze, The petticoat & sleeves puckered & confined in different places

with large bunches of roses an amazing large bouquet of White Lilac, The same flower, together with gauze Feathers, ribbon & diamonds intermixed with her hair.[3]

In contemporary images of Marie Antoinette, many features of Eliza's description of the 28-year-old queen's dress are captured: the elaborate hair decorations, the corset and the petticoat 'puckered and confined in different places with large bunches of roses'. Eliza's interest in fashion seems to have been shared by her cousin Phylly, who had little opportunity to experience such extravagances of dress first hand in rural Kent, and she tells Eliza that she enjoyed her descriptions of Versailles.

By the end of June 1780 Philadelphia has settled into the house in Combs-la-Ville, for the summer. Combs-la-Ville was then a small town situated 20 miles south-east of Paris, not far from Fontainebleau. The house, Eliza first tells her cousin Phylly, belongs to 'a Lady' and later to 'an acquaintance' of the Comtesse de Tournon, whom Eliza describes as 'one of my best friends'. Was the Comtesse an important connection for Philadelphia and her daughter into a certain level of French society, as well as a possible Parisian link to an EIC acquaintance of Philadelphia's? Did she provide the introduction to the gentleman who ultimately became Eliza's husband? It seems likely that the Comtesse is that connection.

Eliza calls her friend by the name the lady wished to be known by at this point in her life, but history knows her as Rose-Marie-Hélène de Tournon, Vicomtesse du Barry, and Marquise de Claveyson. She had a sadly short but colourful life. She is four years older than Eliza, and mother and daughter were most likely to have been introduced to her in Paris in 1779.

In a book written about the comtesse, published in 1892, called *La Vtesse Adolphe, RoseMarie-Hélène de Tournon, et Les Barry*, the author, Marius Tallon has gathered information about her life and in particular her connection with the du Barry family.[4] The comtesse came from one of the oldest noble houses of France. Noble her family certainly was, however not wealthy. She was married to the Vicomte Adolphe du Barry, the 24-year-old son of Jean-Baptiste, Comte du Barry, known as *Le Roué*, a notorious figure associated with the court of Louis XV, who had arranged for his young mistress, an exceptionally beautiful young woman, called Jeanne Becu, to come to the attention of the king, and become his favourite mistress. Jeanne was married to *Le Roué*'s brother Comte Guillaume du Barry to become Comtesse Madame du Barry in order to become the king's official mistress.[5] Spurned by Marie Antoinette and the aristocratic women of the court, Madame du Barry looked to cultivate other women as her Versailles companions, as well as to favour her du Barry connections and it seems her interest extended to seeking a wife for

Jean-Baptiste du Barry's son the Vicomte Adolphe and the choice ultimately fell on Rose-Marie-Hélène de Tournon. She was only 16 when she was married to the vicomte for the financial advantage of her family, and told her father later that he had 'sacrificed' her. Rose-Marie-Hélène is said to have been one of Louis V's 'little mistresses'.[6] Sacrificed indeed.

When the king, Louis XV died suddenly, all the du Barrys were exiled from Versailles, including Rose-Marie-Hélène and her husband. The vicomte was an inveterate gambler and took up with an equally enthusiastic gambler, an Irishman, called Count James Louis Rice, and the trio became inseparable. Rumours arise as to Count Rice's relationship with the vicomtesse. Deeply unhappy, she leaves her husband, but is persuaded by his father, *Le Roué*, to return to him and even more generous assistance is provided to the de Tournons with her brother, Paul-François de Tournon being bought a commission as a captain of Dragoons. In 1778, the couple leave Paris and with Rose-Marie-Hélène's young sister Sophie and Count Rice, first go to Spa in Belgium and then to Bath. The reason for Bath is because her husband is bent on revenging his gambling losses to (in translation) 'a certain Smith, an Indian general, a strong player, who had won [from] the viscount a lot of money'.[7]

General Smith we have encountered before. This is the Brigadier General Richard Smith, an EIC military officer who had taken over from Robert Clive as head of the East India Company's army in Bengal in 1767, and whom Hancock referred to in a letter upon his return to Calcutta as being very helpful to him in securing a position by which he could benefit. Hancock wrote to Philadelphia that 'General Smith (who has been very much my Friend) proposed to me the taking of an office to entitle me to a Dustuck'.[8] Later in December of 1768, when General Smith retires from the EIC and returns to England with a great fortune, Hancock writes to Philadelphia telling her to be certain to call on General Smith's wife:

> The General promised his Interest to support me: pray if you can, visit his Lady to congratulate Her on his Arrival. The Omission might be of bad Consequence to me as He will be a Man of great Power, you perfectly know his vanity and my Necessities.[9]

Smith was known as the archetypal 'nabob'; those men of humble birth who had served the EIC in India and returned to England with wealth and influence. While they purchased great country estates and seats in parliament, they may not have always endeared themselves to the established arbiters of wealth, taste and power.[10] General Smith was known for his generosity and achieved a degree of notoriety for how he spent his money. In 1776 he was tried, fined £1,500 and given six months imprisonment for bribing his way into parliament.

In the years following his release from prison, he spent some time in France, and there encountered the vicomte at the gambling tables of Paris, and perhaps Spa also. Vicomte Adolphe was very bitter at his losses to General Smith. The young Frenchman, one assumes, no match for a man like the general.

The cicomte, his wife and her sister and his great friend Count Rice arrive in Bath in the late summer of 1778 and set up together in a house in the fashionable Royal Crescent. But the good mood soon deteriorated, for on 17 November 1778 at their house, Count Rice and Vicomte Adolphe had an argument that developed into a challenge to a duel from the vicomte to his long-time friend. There are a variety of sources and accounts of this famous duel and its aftermath, the death of the vicomte. The sources include the count's evidence at his trial and acquittal for manslaughter at the Taunton Lent Assizes in 1779. It was a great *cause celebre* at the time.

In London, where the news of this duel had reached the populace, the Vicomtesse du Barry found (in translation):

> A considerable number of lords and ladies, who hardly knew Madame du Barry, came to offer her their services and... hastened to her help, among others, General Smith... whom she accepted, to settle her affairs.[11]

General Smith helps Rose-Marie-Hélène to settle the debts of the vicomte in Bath and gives her £400 to get her and her sister back to France. No actual reason was ever given for the cause of the argument, perhaps debt, or perhaps an affair between the count and the unhappy vicomtesse.

Back in France within a few weeks of the duel, the vicomtesse makes extraordinary efforts to distance herself from her husband's family, freeing herself from the hated du Barry name, while obtaining her rightful inheritance as the vicomte's widow. She uses her now considerable wealth to buy estates in Corsica, which by some legal process she is able to make the 'county' of Tournon and therefore entitled to be called the Comtesse de Tournon, which is how she is known by Eliza. Later, in 1782 she also marries a cousin, Jean-Baptiste de Tournon, Marquis de Claveyson and thus legally and officially became the Marquise de Claveyson. She kept the du Barry fortune but got rid of the name, and was once again acceptable at court. Time caught up with Rose-Marie-Hélène, though, for within a year of her marriage, she died.

Did Philadelphia know about the scandal of the duel in Bath the year before? And what about the connection with General Richard Smith? Did he provide the introduction? Her life in India had very much taken Philadelphia into 'the world'; a world where duels and scandals were not that uncommon. A year later, in August of 1780, Hastings himself fights a duel with Philip Francis, his arch rival on the Calcutta Council of Bengal, and no real scandal or social exclusion surrounded it. Did she know the Comtesse de Tournon was the niece of Madame du Barry, the old king's last *maitresse en-titre*, now living again on her estate at Louvecienne near Versailles, with her lover the Duc de Brissac? Most likely.

Philadelphia herself knew of scandal and its implications. She withdrew Eliza from England before scandal's clutches could possibly grasp her and ruin her chances of a good marriage. Besides, the Comtesse de Tournon clearly had valuable contacts in Paris, which Philadelphia was happy to use, as we see in her taking the house at Combs-la-Ville, arranged through the comtesse. Did the comtesse also help facilitate the marriage of Philadelphia's daughter? It seems quite possible.

It is not yet known which regiment her brother, the Vicomte de Tournon was attached to but it could well have been one of the regiments at Versailles. He may have been a brother officer of Jean-François Capot de Feuillide, who was at this time still a captain of Dragoons in the Queen's Regiment. The comtesse may have been the link between Philadelphia and her daughter and the 29-year-old soldier who was said to be the *'le plus beau des officiers de l'armee francaise'*.

Philadelphia and Eliza's sojourn at Combs-la-Ville lasted the summer of 1780, in their 'pretty place', enjoying walking and rambling in the evenings in 'the large Garden and plantation belonging to the House', and reading, playing music and doing their needlework together. Philadelphia would have taken delight in her daughter's musical accomplishments, with Eliza now having added the harp to her harpsichord. She lets Phylly know that the harp is 'at present the fashionable instrument'.[12]

One cannot help reflecting on the echoes here of Eliza in Mary Crawford, in *Mansfield Park*, seated prettily at her harp near the rectory window and beguiling a passing Edmund Bertram. For mother and daughter it seems a rather quiet life, compared to the bustle of Paris. Eliza mentions only a few visitors from Paris coming to see them from time to time. Who might these visitors be? Does the surgeon still call to treat Clarinda? Did the comtesse introduce possible suitors to Eliza? Eliza represents herself to her cousin Phylly in her letter of June 1780, as being so: 'I have friends here who are so good as to desire to keep me with them, & who therefore do everything in their power to prevail on me to accept offers which would attach me to this country'.[13] While she maintains a joking tone and trivialises any serious talk of marriage, this topic seems close to Eliza's mind, and must have been also to Philadelphia's. Clearly the comtesse was a valuable connection for a mother to have when seeking an appropriate marriage.

This is the circle in Paris into which Philadelphia has been introduced. Thus far we know of her connections to Captain Thomas Pattle, ex-EIC ship's captain and merchant mentioned earlier, living with most likely his mistress, Madam de Villette in an exclusive part of Paris, and known for enjoying the high life; the Vicomtesse du Barry (a *petite maitresse* of Louis XV and in flight from a disastrous *cause celebre* in England in the fatal outcome of a duel between her husband and perhaps her lover) who is now known as the Comtesse de Tournon, and is the niece by marriage to the late king's *maitresse-en-titre* Madame du Barry; General Richard Smith, known as the 'nabob of nabobs', maker of a great fortune in India and notorious gambler who has come to the rescue of the victomesse following the death of her husband.

Mother and daughter are back in Paris from Combs-la-Ville, in the winter of 1780–81, but we do not know where they were living. But Clarinda seems to be no longer with them, no further mention of her can be found, and she must have never recovered from what was initially an infection of a fingernail that spread unrelentingly. Sadly, no record of Clarinda's death or burial has been found, but she does live on magnificently in the Reynolds portrait, an important member of Philadelphia's family. She must have been with Philadelphia for at least twenty years and was possibly in her forties when she died.

For Philadelphia, now with Clarinda gone, her husband dead, her friend Margaret Clive estranged from her, there remains Warren Hastings as her strongest India connection. He had married the Baroness von Imhoff in Calcutta as soon as the news of her divorce came through, in August of 1777, at the time Philadelphia was leaving for Europe. The correspondence between Philadelphia and Hastings has fallen away in the years since, but the personal tone of her letter to him, in February 1780, sharing her distress over Clarinda's illness suggests warm feelings still remain on her side. As she wrote about the money still owing the ailing Clarinda from Hancock's estate, she probably later wrote to Hastings, as Hancock's executor, telling him of Clarinda's death. But there is no existing evidence of her further correspondence with him from France, though information on her and Eliza is regularly sent to Hastings by John Woodman.

Finding a more permanent home in Paris in the winter of 1780–81 would have been a priority for Philadelphia as well as seeking a new maidservant. In her letter of 27 June 1780 Eliza tells her cousin Phylly to write to her care of Sir John Lambert's, viz *'A Mademoiselle Hancock de soin de Chevalier Lambert a Paris'*.[14] Between 7 November and 23 December of 1780 Philadelphia draws £200 from her Hoare & Co. bank account, which looks a little more than usual for a two month period, so there may have been extra expenses re-establishing herself in Paris and also costs associated with Clarinda's final illness and death.

English visitors to Paris with the financial means to do so would obtain furnished rooms in one of the large houses in a fashionable area. The faubourg Saint-Germain and the area around the Palais Royal were two such areas, and the convent where Eliza's friend, the Comtesse de Tournon's sister lived, mentioned in a letter from Eliza to Phylly, was in the faubourg Saint-Germain, so perhaps they lived in one of the houses there. Philadelphia's £600 plus per year would have gone further in Paris than London, so they could have lived quite well. Finding a servant to replace Clarinda would have been more of a challenge, but after being in Europe for four years, Eliza's French is clearly fluent and Philadelphia's no doubt improved. Eliza refers to her 'miss Rosalie' in a much later letter to Phylly in 1788 and when Philadelphia seeks to return to England in 1789 for initially a brief visit, she writes to John Woodman that they just have 'our maid Rosalie' who is with them.[15]

From Eliza's letters we get the impression that both she and Philadelphia enjoy their life in Paris, with Philadelphia living a far less quiet life than the one Margaret Clive depicted in London with Hancock. Eliza describes lots of social life out and about in Paris, and later in England, when Philadelphia and Eliza entertain Phylly in Tunbridge Wells and London, Philadelphia gives her niece the time of her life; determined to make her stay with them as active and interesting as possible. This seems more like the old Philadelphia we recognise from Margaret Clive's description of their Calcutta days, lively and vivacious but also kind and caring. Her husband seems to have been the one who dragged down her spirits, was often unwell and averse to socialising. Philadelphia certainly seems to have been freer in France at this time perhaps than ever before in her life.

The major event of 1781 for both Philadelphia and Eliza, was Eliza's marriage. The search for a suitable husband for Eliza may have been underway for some time. In her letter to her cousin back in June 1780, Eliza had told Phylly that she might 'introduce un cousin francais' to her one day.[16]

When Eliza, some months after her marriage, tells Phylly Walter that she is perfectly satisfied with the marriage, Eliza comments on how her decision was made. It was, she says:

> the effect of a mature deliberation, & ... a step I took much less from my own judgement than that of those whose councils & opinions I am the most bound to follow, I trust I shall never have any reason to repent it; on the contrary... I must esteem myself the most fortunate of my sex.[17]

The primary one of those 'councils and opinions' would have been Philadelphia's, but there had been no rush to marry, and Philadelphia's marked fondness for her daughter meant she would have made the best choice available, within the limitations of nationality, class, wealth and religion. Eliza was English, middle-class, had a modest fortune and was Protestant. She was fairly well-educated, fluent in French, accomplished, lively and very pretty. In December 1780 she had turned 19, and opportunities were now presenting themselves. The candidate who gained Eliza's hand was Jean-François Capot de Feuillide, known as Comte de Feuillide, 30 years old, a captain of the Queen's Regiment of Dragoons and from Guyenne in the south-west of France. They became engaged in the summer of 1781.[18]

In the pamphlet by Abbe Michel Devert on the history of the marshlands of Gabarret and Barbotan, near Agen on the Garonne river there is much about Eliza's new husband and his life and family[19]. According to Abbe Devert's research, Jean-François was born in Nerac, a substantial medieval town in Guyenne, in the south-west of France. The south-west area was one of the centres of Protestantism in France, and Nerac was briefly the court of Henri IV of France, the Protestant Henri of Navarre. The region suffered during the sixteenth-century Wars of Religion between Catholics and Protestants. After being sacked, Nerac fell into insignificance for the next century but by the eighteenth century was once more a thriving agricultural centre.[20] The Capot de Feuillide family had a modest beginning with an ancestor, Jehan Capot being the porter at the castle of Nerac in 1610, and they gradually rose in wealth and prestige from that time.

The father of Jean-François, Sir François de Capot-Feuillide was a lawyer who held important positions in Nerac and its administrative district. Devert's research indicates he was lawyer in the *Parlement,* a royal judge of Moncrabeau and deputy for the king's prosecutor in Albret, and became in 1757, mayor *'perpetuel'* of Nerac.[21] Jean-François's mother was Anne-Esther Bartouilh, daughter of a consul (government official) of Nerac and he had two sisters and a younger brother, who later became a doctor. So in terms of class, there was little social difference between the couple with Jean-François's family fitting the description of middle level bourgeois: urban, property owning, a degree of affluence and with influence and prestige within their community, but not 'noble'.[22]

Eliza's family was also typically of the English 'middling sort', with the exception that she was known to have belonged to the family of the famous Lord Hastings, former governor of India. She was, the comte maintained, 'immensely rich' '*qui didsit-on, appartenait a la famille du fameux lord Hastings, ancien gouvernour de l'Inde. Elle etait, disait-il toujours, immensement riche'.*[23] This account by Devert has no source for Jean-François representation of Eliza as being very rich, and it was perhaps more an assumption based on her family connection to the legendary wealth of the English 'nabobs'. Hastings had significant wealth and had made a generous 'present' to Philadelphia and Eliza, but he was far from being immensely rich, let alone Eliza, and it is doubtful that Philadelphia would have presented Eliza's position for anything more than it was. It would have suited the comte's purposes to allow this to be generally thought. Being part of the famous East India Company's governor's family naturally presumed a greater wealth on her part than was in truth the case.

Capot de Feuillide's military record shows that in 1779 he had been in the Queen's Dragoons for ten years. He had joined in the ranks in 1769 and rose to the equivalent of corporal, then sergeant and had become a captain in 1778, in command of a company of the Queen's Dragoons.[24] He was most likely stationed near Versailles or Paris when he was introduced to Eliza. While officers were supposed to be of noble birth, there was a way for a commoner through his own merit rather than birth to achieve high rank and become what was known as an *officier de fortune*. It seems Jean-François was not alone in styling himself 'comte', as officers at Versailles who were not noble often took the title of comte. Achieving, proving and maintaining one's nobility was a complex matter in the France of the ancient regime, and there could be an acceptance of it, in a general way, by simply being in the role and looking the part in a position that was reserved for a noble. This would seem to be Jean-François' situation. His family had been 'on the way up' for a number of generations, so this was the next step. From Philadelphia's point of view, there would be no requirement to prove his four generations of nobility. Let us then call him 'comte' and join that acceptance, as Philadelphia, Eliza and the rest of the family did. When Hastings refers in his diary to Eliza he usually calls her 'Mme' but at least once as 'ye Countess'.[25]

When the comte's father died in 1779, Jean-François, the oldest son, inherited property in Nerac, and would no longer, as was the custom, be still under the control of his father. As the head of his family, Jean-François would have been in a position to marry whoever he chose. He had been made a captain the year before with an annual pay of 3,500 livres. A thousand livres at that time was equivalent to around £41.[26] So his salary was adequate. An officer would have to have had the permission of his commanding officer to marry and a future wife to be approved had to have an income of at least 1,200 livres. A single officer lived in barracks but as a married man he would have to maintain his own household. Eliza was clearly suitable on the financial front, and probably came with the promise of more; for the comte had grand schemes.

By August of 1781, Philadelphia has written to John Woodman and to her brother George, of the engagement of Eliza to Jean-François. She is very happy with the prospective bridegroom and sees her future in France with her daughter. Woodman writes to Hastings on 7 August 1781 and tells him that 'Eliza Hancock is now engaged to a French officer ... Revd GA is much concerned at the thought of his sister and niece leaving England permanently and probably changing their religion'.[27]

The letter states:

> Mrs & Miss Hancock are yet in France & likely to continue there the young Lady being on the point of Marriage with a French Officer which Mrs Hancock writes is of good family with expectation of good Fortune, but at present of little. Her Letter was to Mr Austen & Self on the Subject and she seems inclined to give them up the Sum which was settled on her for Life, and wants the Money transferred into the French Funds which we have thought prudent for her sake to decline and Mr Austen is much concerned at the connection which he sais [sic] is giving up all their friends their Country, and he fears their Religion.[28]

While Philadelphia may be happy, others in England are not. For George Austen it is the issue of Philadelphia and her daughter becoming Catholic and their sojourn in France becoming permanent. He also fears for Philadelphia being entirely dependent on her daughter's husband in the future if she hands over her money to them. As she is now to live in her son-in-law's household, Philadelphia must think it is appropriate for Eliza to have the money, which is ultimately to be hers, now, rather than to wait till after Philadelphia's death.

Eliza's nationality does not seem to be any barrier to her marriage, from the comte's point of view. In a later letter to cousin Phylly, Eliza claims that her husband 'has the greatest desire to see England & even to make it his residence for part of the year'.[29] As she speaks fluent French, is dressed in the latest French fashion, she is about as French as an English woman of the time could be. And of religion? It is more complicated, one expects. In a letter cousin Phylly writes to her clergyman brother James in 1787 after her visit with Philadelphia and Eliza to Tunbridge Wells she reports of Eliza that, 'her religion is not changed'.[30]

If we assume the comte was Catholic, as required for his military position, he seems to have had far from particularly strong religious views, and may have even been secretly Protestant, coming from a strongly Protestant area of France. Otherwise it is difficult to explain his affection for England, the acceptance of his wife's not becoming a Catholic, and of his son and heir being born in England and later baptised into the Church of England. Eliza writes to Phylly in May of 1786, five years into their marriage, of her pregnancy (she has had at least one miscarriage previously) and says: 'should a son be in *store* for M. de Feuillide, he greatly wishes him to be a native of England, for he pays me the compliment of being very partial to my country'.[31]

Perhaps there is more truth to George Austen's concern for Philadelphia's financial security, though Hastings' money is for Philadelphia to use the interest from for life and to preserve the capital for Eliza. Was she really wanting to change this? Philadelphia does have a considerable sum of her own money, and is prepared to use that as Eliza's dowry and later loans 15,000 livres (£6,500) to her son-in-law.[32]

Woodman writes again to Hastings in December to say that Eliza is now married to the comte and refers to Philadelphia as being entirely satisfied by the marriage, 'the Gentleman having great connections and expectations'.[33] He also reports Uncle Francis's disapproval. I doubt Philadelphia was much concerned by that. Once more, Philadelphia is taking something of a risk, this time with Eliza's marriage, but she seems confident and hopeful. The young man seems more than suitable and Eliza is happy with the arrangement. Jean-François assures Eliza that she may be 'certain of never being separated from my dear Mama whose presence enhances every other blessing I enjoy'.[34] The love Eliza had for her mother seems never to have been supplanted by anyone else.

Exactly where and when Philadelphia saw her daughter married is not clear, but most likely in Paris, between September and early December of 1781, probably not in a Catholic church because Eliza was Protestant, but by 'the increasingly common practice of contracting a marriage merely before a notary and witnesses'.[35] There seems to have been no other family present on either side except Philadelphia, as Eliza says she had not met her husband's family till much later. For Philadelphia, her life, always closely bound to her daughter since her birth, became even more so. From now on where Eliza's life took her, Philadelphia followed; her presence in Eliza's life is essential to her daughter's continued happiness, even if she now has a handsome French husband.

Chapter 17

A Daughter Married
1782–1784

Mrs Hancock... is in France, where I believe she intends to end her Days, having married her Daughter there to a Gentleman of that Country... entirely to her satisfaction, the Gentleman having great connections, and expectations.

Letter from John Woodman to Warren
Hastings, December 1781

THE NEW YEAR of 1782 opens with Philadelphia living with Eliza and Jean-François in a house in Paris. Where exactly is not known. It sounds to be a different place to where she and Philadelphia had been living. Eliza describes their house in the first letter she writes to her cousin after her marriage, as being in 'an elegant and convenient house here [in Paris] in an airy situation with a large garden', which supplies them 'with a vast quantity of flowers, Peaches, Melons etc.' but which Eliza considers too small for them.[1] Jean-François remains in some way in the service of the Queen's Dragoons for many years, until 1788 when he was *'reforme le 1ˢᵗ mai 1788'*, that is, either invalided, dismissed or put on half pay.[2] He is most likely on half pay, as Eliza expresses her concern that he might be called-up in August of 1788 and 'borne arms against his fellow Countrymen'.[3]

The December 1781 letter from Hastings to Philadelphia which was sent on to her after being received by John Woodman by the hand of Hastings' newly arrived agent of influence in London, Major John Scott, shows they were still in touch. He had not forgotten her. Woodman had passed on the news to Hastings of the disapproval of Eliza's marriage by George Austen and Uncle Francis, but there is no evidence Hastings disapproved of his god-daughter's marriage. If Philadelphia was satisfied with the match, then that would be enough for Hastings. Who was he to mind a foreign marriage?

Woodman's letter to Hastings had also referred to the awkward situation of Philadelphia's brother-in-law, Colbron Hancock, the Charing Cross glassmaker, who has now gone bankrupt, with the £1,500 loan from Hancock unlikely to be recovered. Woodman tells Hastings that Hancock's will is now to be administered to recover at least some of the debt, which he hopes can go to 'Miss Louisa the daughter of the late colonel Forde in part of the £1,500 of hers which was in Mr Hancock's hands at the time of his death'.[4] Philadelphia would have been relieved to hear of that particular mortification being resolved.

Now living with her newly married daughter and son-in-law, Philadelphia would join in that winter season in Paris. For Eliza, the new bride, it was a social whirl. Eliza tells cousin Phylly that she has 'danced more this winter than in all the rest of my life'.[5] Mother and daughter appear to relish being well-connected to fashionable Paris. We can assume Philadelphia went with Eliza to most of the events described in her letters. Eliza tells her cousin that marriage to Jean-François has now given her 'the advantages of rank and title & a numerous & brilliant acquaintance'.[6] Even allowing for some gilding of the lily on Eliza's part, Philadelphia should be proud of what she has achieved for her daughter.

They attend spectacular celebrations surrounding the birth of the Dauphin, the second child and first son of Marie Antoinette and Louis XVI. It was a short and painful young life, but his birth was celebrated 'with illuminations, fireworks, balls etc.' including a ball at court which Eliza attended and describes it as having 'magnificence beyond conception'.[7] Eliza gives her eyewitness account:

> The ball was given in a most noble salon, adorned with paintings, sculpture, gilding etc. etc. Eight thousand lights disposed in the most beautiful forms shewed to advantage the richest & most elegant dresses, the most beautiful women, & the noblest Assembly perhaps anywhere to behold; nothing but gold silver & diamonds & jewels of all kinds were to be seen on every side ... In short altogether it was the finest sight I ever beheld.[8]

They spent most of their time in the city and when they needed country air, they travelled just outside Paris where they were welcome guests at the houses of accommodating friends. There is no plan yet for them to travel south to the comte's estate near Nerac where his mother, unmarried sister and younger brother live, but Philadelphia's son-in-law has now gained sufficient status and favour within the court, not to mention access to some of Eliza's fortune, to look to his future beyond the army. Philadelphia has assured her family and Hastings that she is happy with Eliza's husband and shows she is keen to support the couple financially, though Woodman implies that de Feuillide is a

A Daughter Married: 1782–1784

fortune-hunter, and it is true that Jean-François certainly has grand plans which will require a great deal of money.

His great scheme is to acquire a large area of swampland belonging to the crown, near the estate he has just inherited from his recently deceased father, to enclose and improve. The area is called '*Le Marais de Gabarret et de Barbotan*'. He is looking to take advantage of the enthusiasm then current in France, as in England, for enclosure and improvement.

While it is not emphasised, all the fictional large landowners in Jane Austen's novels, Mr Knightley, Mr Darcy, Sir Thomas Bertram and Mr Rushworth had properties, which no doubt had benefited from the enclosure and improvement of common land, which began in the seventeenth century and reached its peak in the eighteenth. Jane Austen's father George was a signatory for a land enclosure in his Hampshire parish in the 1770s. Swamps and fens were an early target, seen to be unproductive, because no crops could be grown or animals grazed on them, and unhealthy because of the idea that diseases were caused by the miasma given into the air from such areas. And while the large swamp, fens and wetlands of Gabarret and Barbotan on the edge of Armagnac had been common-land used by local people for marine harvesting, the king encouraged the owners of such land to drain and improve it for occupation and cultivation. If they did so, they were exempt from paying tax.[9] It would be a scheme for Eliza's husband to make him a significant landowner in his part of France and create significant wealth for his family and his descendants.

Within a few months of their marriage, the comte had the ownership of the lands of the Marais, amounting to 5,000 arpents (4,224 acres) transferred to him under the conditions laid down by the king's commissioners. They were: that he paid a small royalty in grain each year, had a plan and report by qualified engineers for the draining of the swamps drawn up, and to drain and clear the lands for cultivation. In October of 1782 the officials of the region approved the plans and the agreement was confirmed by the king and his council.[10] Despite opposition from the local people who had used the swamps for their livelihood for centuries, and from landowners who considered their rights were being trespassed upon, a third decree of the king, in August of 1783 confirmed all the previous decrees.[11] The comte, however, was already confidently proceeding with his works by the end of 1782.

It seems an enormous and expensive undertaking, and one wonders did Jean-François really know what he was getting into. What experience did he have of such projects? Known for his good looks and elegance of manners and person, he must have been relying on the expertise of others. From the start he seems to have over-reached himself. Did he hope Eliza had access to enormous sums of money via her connection to Hastings? Did he think the great debts he would acquire would be able to be paid in the end? Perhaps. But history caught up with Jean-François in a way no one could have predicted, as the fashionable and rich of Versailles and Paris danced away these years, with Philadelphia joining in from the sidelines, enjoying the glow of 'rank and title... & brilliant acquaintance' that now surrounded her daughter.

Becoming a grandmother for Philadelphia, and for Jean-François becoming a father, must have been in their thoughts by the end of the first year of the marriage. Perhaps Eliza hints at a pregnancy in her letter to her cousin in March of 1782 when she writes of her health being 'not strong'. As Eliza seems always to have been in the best of health, perhaps she had a particular reason for their spending the summer quietly. If she was indeed pregnant, she must have miscarried.

As to Philadelphia's financial position in 1782, she draws £200 in Herries notes in the January from her account with Hoare's and another £51 in June. Her expenses are moderate, with small amounts to her friend and 'postmistress' Miss Hinchliffe. Philadelphia also continues her financial support of her sister Leonora by paying the Cumberleges for her keep. She receives into her account her consuls and South Seas dividends, as well as George Austen's repayments, until she closes her account with Hoare & Co. in November 1782, after transferring £105 to her new bank, Gurnell, Hoare & Harmon. They have no association with Hoare & Co., but are known as a bank with foreign connections, and it may have been easier for her to access her funds from France with Gurnell, Hoare & Harmon. At present I have been unable to access any records for Philadelphia's account. While she was not able to touch the capital held in trust from Hastings, she would have had access to her own capital, which amounted to around £9,400 in consuls. It was £6,500 of this money she would soon use to advance a loan to her son-in-law to keep him going with his grand scheme.

There is a sense that by 1783, having been gone from England for six years and her daughter married to a French citizen, Philadelphia has indeed chosen to remain in France until she 'end[s] her Days' as Woodman puts it to Hastings. But Eliza holds out to her cousin Phylly the promise of their return to England. Britain and France are once again at peace. While being at war did not seem to worry the English in Paris at all, there is a sense of relief in Eliza's letter to her cousin when she states that: 'The peace has at last taken place, little to the Satisfaction of the political world but much to mine ... [and] this Event likewise affords me the greatest pleasure as it will hasten my return to my native country'.[12] Philadelphia would have shared her daughter's enthusiasm for peace and the possibility of a visit to England to see her family again.

The new year of 1783 brought the news of the death of Philadelphia's sister Leonora, who was buried at St Mary's Church Islington in London on the 4 February 1783.[13] 'Poor Leonora', as Hancock referred to her, appears to have been not as clever, accomplished or as adventurous as her older sister. She was 50 years old and had remained single.

Throughout her time abroad, Philadelphia has kept in touch with her brother George and his family in Steventon. By 1783 the youngest, Charles, is now 4 and the eldest, James, has gained his BA from St John's College Oxford. George, the disabled second-born son who was the godson of Philadelphia's husband, remains apart from the family, now living in the Hampshire village of Monk Sherborne, along with his similarly disabled uncle Thomas Leigh, with a family called Culham. Henry and Francis are still at home being tutored by their father, Edward is spending more and more time with the rich relatives, the Knights, and about to be officially adopted and become their heir, while little Jane, just 7, is sent off to boarding school, of sorts, in Oxford with her sister Cassandra and their cousin Jane Cooper.

It must have seemed like a good idea at the time, though Jane was very young, with the house bursting at the seams with boys and the Austens must have felt they had the money to afford it. It seems to have been a matter of wherever Cassandra went, Jane insisted she follow. It was a disaster, however, when the school moved to Southampton in the summer and all three girls caught typhoid and came close to death. They were rescued by Mrs Austen's sister Mrs Cooper, early enough to save the girls, but it proved fatal for Aunt Jane Cooper, who died of the disease after they returned home.[14] In France, Philadelphia hears of the family tragedy from both her niece Phylly and the Austens. Eliza tells Phylly of how 'the melancholy news of the death of the valuable Mrs Cooper' had upset them.[15] Philadelphia had written to George and Cassandra Austen in Steventon in sympathy and anxious for assurances as to how Mrs Austen was taking the death of her sister. She was assured that all the Steventon family were well.

But all may not be well with Philadelphia's health. She had always been thin, but occasionally she has been described as particularly so. Eliza mentions in her letter to Phylly of May 1783 that 'Mamma has I thank God had much better health this year than last, she is however very thin & that sometimes makes me uneasy'.[16] So we find that Philadelphia health has been poor throughout 1782. Eliza understates her anxiety to her cousin, but her fear for her mother is patent. 'Her presence', she states feelingly, 'is one of the greatest & enhances every other blessing I enjoy'.[17] Clearly, Eliza's husband occupies a different space in her heart from the irreplaceable Philadelphia. Perhaps her ill health had made her more concerned to transfer her funds to France and ensure Eliza benefited. Both women would like to see their home country again, but that is not to happen soon, for in early 1784 they are to move far south, to Eliza's husband's expanded estate in Guyenne, to meet for the first time his family. Philadelphia and Eliza would remain there for the next two years.

The winter of 1783–84 had been a particularly cold one in Paris, with Eliza saying she could not ever remember being so cold, with the streets 'almost impracticable from the snow & ice with which they were filled'.[18] Philadelphia must have nostalgically remembered those balmy Calcutta evenings as they 'froze by the fireside' of their house. The open fireplaces of their Paris home offered none of the warmth they experienced from the great tile stoves installed in the houses and apartments when they had wintered in Germany and Flanders. Eliza writes that they 'froze by the fireside & never did I so much regret the Stoves of Germany & Flanders'.[19] Philadelphia and her daughter perhaps viewed the prospect of the sunnier southern climes with relish. Thin and not as well as she would have wished, Philadelphia must have looked forward to that change, though the life ahead would once again be very different and no doubt have its own challenges.

It would have been imperative for Philadelphia's son-in-law to go back to Guyenne to re-establish himself there, institute the program of works and arrange accommodation for his family. By mid-1783 most obstacles to his great scheme were overcome and with assurance of ownership of at least one major section confirmed, he enclosed it in September 1783.[20] Taking possession of almost 2,000 acres of his granted lands, he then began draining them.

Jean-François must have been already down in Guyenne for some time when Eliza writes in her May 1784 letter to Phylly that she and Philadelphia are setting out for the south before the end of the month.[21] Eliza thinks Phylly will be shocked by the fact that mother and daughter are eagerly looking forward to the prospect of the journey of 'six hundred and fifty miles from Paris' to Guyenne. Eliza has a good share of the wanderlust of her mother it seems, for she tells Phylly that:

> A less frequent Traveller than myself would shrink at the thoughts of such an undertaking, but it occasions me none but agreeable Sensations. I have my share of the <u>wandering spirit</u> our Countrymen are generally possessed with which together being so early accustomed to a <u>vagabond</u> Life makes me seldom regret a change of scene.[22]

Now that to me sounds like Philadelphia's daughter; unfazed by a long journey, a new life in an unknown place with unknown people. Philadelphia probably shared Eliza's excitement and was willing to follow wherever her daughter's life now took her. She had once again lost agency in the determinants of her life, but, confident of her daughter's love for her, seems happily to concede it, and although Philadelphia and Eliza are always welcome wherever they go, and while Eliza tells Phylly that 'the Comte's mother ... who is far advanced in Years [has] the greatest desire to see me.'[23] I wonder how *les dames* of Guyenne welcomed these English ladies into their family.

Chapter 18

Off to Guyenne
1784–1786

This excursion I tell you so coolly of removes me only about Six hundred & fifty miles from Paris. A less frequent Traveller than myself would shrink at the thoughts of such an undertaking, but it occasions me none but agreeable sensations.

Letter from Eliza to her cousin Phylly,
May 1784

THE JOURNEY TO Guyenne, part of the old kingdom of Aquitaine, deep in the south-west of France, in the spring of 1784 would have taken Philadelphia and Eliza many days. Some of their possessions may have been sent before, and mother and daughter and a servant or two, set out at the end of May, travelling perhaps in a post-chaise.

They would have left Paris on the old route south, towards Toulouse, much the same route as the *Route nationale* 20 follows today, going from Paris to Orléans first, then on through Vierzon and Châteauroux to Limoges. The first 'stage', as each section of the trip was called, took them from the *Porte d'Orleans* in Paris on the ancient road between the two major medieval cities of France, Paris and Orleans, through the king's domain.

As coaches at that time did not do much over 5 miles an hour, even on good roads, and with that first stage of Paris to Orleans being 65 miles, it was a full day's journey, the first of many, but perhaps they lingered and rested for a few days in one of the major towns further south. Roads leading directly out of Paris had been improving in the second half of the eighteenth century, but as they travelled further south, the going would have been far less predictable. Staying at inns on the way would have been a familiar experience for the two women, 'accustomed to a vagabond Life', as Eliza tells Phylly, and seeing new parts of France would have interested them too. From the ancient city of Orleans they would have crossed the Loire and on, lumbering through heavily timbered country on towards Limoges at the foot of the *Massif Centrale*, the vast highland region of mountains and plateaux in the centre of the south of France.

Limoges was an ancient town, which had regained its prosperity in the eighteenth century with the development of its fine porcelain industry. If Philadelphia and Eliza did rest for a few days there, they would have had to wait for the arrival of a different coach to take them away from the main route down to Toulouse to take a more direct road, south-west through Perigeaux, Bergerac and Vileneuve-sur-Lot to Agen on the Garonne, just 40 miles from their final destination.

A great journey, over many days, but successful, though Philadelphia must have been very weary when they arrived at Agen, to be met, hopefully, by Jean-François, now well advanced with his great project. A large house for his family was part of his construction plans, along with a house for his brother and other accommodation for workers and outbuildings, but it would take a few more years before *Le Château Marais* would be completed. On their arrival, Philadelphia and her daughter lived with Jean-François and his mother and sister in the rented *Château de Jourdan*, a short distance from the Barbotan marshes and in the small village of Sainte-Meille. It was a change from the life of bustling Paris, and while Philadelphia had implied a preference for a quiet country life from time to time, this isolated village was probably not what she had in mind as a permanent home. But she had thrown in her lot with Eliza and her husband and this was where she would live for the next two years.

It may be called a 'château' but from a twentieth-century photograph, *Le Château Jourdan* looks more like a substantial house, an attractive house in fact, with outbuildings and gardens and must have been able to accommodate a family that included four adult women. It still exists today and a perusal of an aerial view shows it close to but separate from the village and the area very agricultural still. Philadelphia and Eliza got on with their lives much as before, with some local society. It may have been dull for them, and if Eliza was unhappy, though she never admits as such to her cousin, that must have been distressing for Philadelphia.

Jean-François's drainage works proper had begun early 1784, judging by Eliza's letter to Phylly on 25 July 1785 from the Château, and sounds as though everything has not gone quite as smoothly, domestically for them, as she hints that she has had a miscarriage, and that her husband has been unwell with a fever for quite some time, as had many in the family. She tells Phylly that her mother-in-law died suddenly in June of that year. Philadelphia and Eliza escaped the illness, however. So far the comte's scheme is prospering, with the drainage completed and the planting and harvesting of crops on the fertile drained land well underway. Eliza expresses some pride in her husband's success and high standing in the community; though Eliza somewhat 'lays it on, one suspects in her letter to Phylly:

> Very considerable and expensive Works carried on for eighteen Months past, have entirely drained this large extent of Ground... I have the Pleasure of seeing My Husband looked upon as the Benefactor of a whole Province, from the Salubrity of its Air has acquired from being freed from the pernicious exhalations of such an extent of stagnant Water, very advantageously replaced by a fertile plain.[1]

Yet while there was some opposition and sense that such a scheme could not be practical, there is support for Eliza's claims for her husband in a report (enquiring into Jean-François's improvements) for the success of what the count had achieved, if not the complete admiration of the populous. The report stated that he had indeed fertilised a land deemed useless and pestilent, set up families living and working there in comfort and had delivered clean air to the surrounding drained land.[2]

Eliza, by Philadelphia's example, knows what is required of a wife and attempts to take an interest in the agricultural pursuits, but you can tell her heart is not really in it. She writes in her same letter to Phylly that:

> The unusual want of Rain which you assure me has been complained of in England has not been less sensibly felt on the Continent... for thus far self-interest brings me acquainted with farming concerns, which otherwise I confess I might chance never to trouble my Head about.[3]

While loyalty to her husband and some interest in the financial importance of a good harvest might drive Eliza's interest in 'farming concerns', Philadelphia had at this point a great deal of 'self interest' in the success of her son-in-law's venture having now having invested most of her remaining capital in it.

Was Philadelphia foolish in this, or was it integral to her commitment to Eliza's future? Philadelphia could not access the £10,000 Hastings had given in trust in the hands of her brother and John Woodman, the income from which could now be assigned to Eliza, but she had access to the other money she had acquired after her husband's death: £8,238 in total and placed in investments. When Philadelphia closed her Hoare's account and opened one with Gurnell, Hoare & Harmon a year after Eliza's marriage, she must have wished to do whatever she could to continue supporting Eliza.

The loan could been seen as an investment, bringing a return, hopefully, though Woodman had expressed the unkind view to Hastings back in December of 1782, along with news of their marriage, that the count and Eliza are 'desirous of draining the Mother of every Shilling she has'.[4] It is doubtful Hastings cared much about what Philadelphia and Eliza chose to do with the money. His later actions indicated that it was entirely a matter for them. Besides, he had some very worrying concerns of his own to occupy him.

By the time of Eliza's letter to Phylly in July 1785, Hastings has returned to England; his time as governor of Bengal and the supreme servant of all the EIC presidencies in India is over. He is not that old, 52, but he must have felt his age, after a further seventeen years of taxing service at the helm for the Company in India. His wife, Marian had gone back to England the year before, and, desperately missing her, he began to keep a personal diary from then on. He is no Pepys, and it is more like an appointment book, but it provides us with a reference point for how he and Philadelphia kept in touch over the period from 1786 till 1792. The entries regarding Philadelphia are brief, but telling, and show that their friendship continued over the years.

He arrived in Plymouth on 13 June 1785 and the news of his return quickly reached Philadelphia in Guyenne. Eliza does not doubt that cousin Phylly too has heard the news of his return; it would be public knowledge, but it is implied that they have had private conveyance of it, perhaps through Philadelphia's correspondence with the Woodmans. Eliza enthuses over her famous godfather to cousin Phylly:

> The Public News must long ere this acquainted you with Mr Hastings' arrival in England, a circumstance which gives great Satisfaction to his Friends, that is to say a very extensive circle for who that is neither blinded by interest nor biased by Party can possibly refuse Esteem & Admiration to a Character too much the ornament of the present Age not to be consigned in the Records of succeeding ones.[5]

On his return, 'the ornament of the present Age' is reunited with his adored wife, his family and old India friends. He is welcomed home by the great and the good. He reports to India House, has an audience with the king, 'who was graciousness itself. ... Ten days were spent in ceremony, welcome and reunions'.[6] But the peace of mind assured by such a welcome would soon be disrupted, as his enemies continued to plot, and within a fortnight of Hastings' return, Edmund Burke, renowned writer, polemicist, orator, Whig politician and member of the House of Commons gives notice in the House 'that he would move resolutions regarding "a gentleman just returned from India".'[7] Burke's 'resolutions' would be the first salvo by Hastings' enemies to bring him down. It would prove a long and difficult period of ten years for Hastings, leading to a trial before the House that dragged on for years, before ultimate acquittal of the maliciously-brought charges. He would be denied for many years, the honours and peace of mind many felt he deserved.

Hastings rented a house in St James's and attempted to buy back the Hastings family estate of Daylesford in Worcestershire, staying with Philadelphia's sister-in-law Cassandra's Leigh family in the adjoining village of Adlestrop; old friends of Hastings' since childhood, where he nostalgically rides over the grounds of Daylesford.[8] Philadelphia must have heard of his return from many sources, perhaps even from him. It may have stirred in her a powerful wish to return to England; and that return in fact would come quite soon and for reasons, which on the surface, seem unusual.

By mid-1785, Jean-François has spent a huge amount of money already, in so deep no doubt there is no turning back, and continues to proceed, as he must in order to turn a profit and keep to his royal agreement. Philadelphia's money must have been a help. Fifteen thousand livres were owing to her in a statement submitted by the comte to the authorities in pursuit of an extension of time to pay his creditors in 1788.[9] By then he had used all of his fortune, part of his wife's and he has many creditors, including 15,000 livres from 'Mademoiselle Hincock [sic], his mother-in-law'.[10] Records show that by 1788 he had spent 400,000 livres on the works, but time and the rush of history would soon overtake Jean-François and his great scheme.

In the summer of 1785, however, there would be a diversion for Philadelphia and Eliza, with a stay at the newly fashionable watering hole of Bagnères at the foot of the French Pyrenees. Philadelphia and Eliza over the years, like many of those better-off in the eighteenth century, loved a spa.

While Eliza tells Phylly the reason is in order for Monsieur de Feuillide to take the waters to help him recover from the Fevers which had kept him unwell for some time, it is clear that she is feeling 'a Gloom' as she tells Phylly. She sounds as if she is full of grief from one or more miscarriages. She has been married now for almost three years, is a healthy young woman but has not yet had a living child. She must be feeling the pressure to provide the heir, and Philadelphia would be all sympathy and concern for her. She describes her feelings to Phylly in stronger than usual terms:

> A change of Scene I think is indispensable for us all, & I can alone dispel the Gloom the Mind contracts from such repeated strokes as I have had to acquaint You with of late, but let me not admit the acknowledgements I owe You for the kind concern You express for the melancholy event my last informed you of & which has caused me too much real Grief.[11]

They spend two months at Bagnères, August and September, which Eliza likens to Bath and Tunbridge Wells, and where there are many English tourists. Once again they are able to make elite connections, as Eliza writes to Phylly of the highlight of their trip being with charming English society. Eliza cannot resist some name-dropping, telling Phylly that they met up with Lord Chesterfield, the British ambassador to Madrid and his lady. Deirdre Le Faye points out the Lord Chesterfield Philadelphia and Eliza meet was a somewhat errant ambassador who in the three years of his appointment to Spain never in fact crossed the border into that country.[12]

It must have been heartening for Philadelphia to see Eliza so well and enjoying herself, but things are not quite so positive for her. While Eliza describes herself to Phylly as being 'perfectly restored in Health & good Looks' in a long letter to cousin Phylly written on 26 January 1786 after their return to *Le Château de Jourdan*, she mentions in a 'by-the-by' manner at the end of her letter that 'Mamma ... has been some-what indisposed of late but is now perfectly recovered and sends a thousand Loves and compliments to yourself & Family... [and] the Compliments of the Season'.[13]

Two significant future events are mentioned in this letter. The first is that Philadelphia and Eliza are intending to be back in England in June, but not with Eliza's husband. He is to remain in Guyenne, it seems. They have made their mind up some time ago, but now there is a complication in that Eliza is now around three months pregnant. The sojourn in Bagnères seems to have been beneficial to the couple and Eliza's baby will be due in July. She reveals she is in two minds now about 'undertaking so long a journey in a situation so unfit for travelling'.[14] Eliza suggests her reluctance is not shared by her husband who, 'should a son be in store for M. de Feuillide he greatly wishes him to be a native of England for he pays me the Compliment of being very partial to my Country'.[15]

It seems such an odd position for the Frenchman to take in relation to his son, whom one would assume would be heir to his estates, to not be French born. Is it the Protestantism perhaps? When the child is born, he is baptised in England into the Church of England. Are there tensions in the family? It may be that the lease of *Le Château de Jourdan* is coming to an end and the new house near the Marais is not yet completed. Philadelphia would be even more eager than Eliza to return, one expects. And perhaps money comes into it, in the mind of the comte, with Hastings and his assumed Indian fortune, now returned to England.

In the previous spring in 1785 Philadelphia had missed the opportunity of being visited by her relatives, the wealthy Mr and Mrs Knight, of Godmersham in Kent, who had taken as their adopted son and heir, her nephew Edward Austen. The Knights had left England in September 1784 with a substantial party, for a tour of the Continent. They winter in Nice and planned to travel via Agen. Mrs Knight writes from France on 2 and 10 April 1785 to her sister-in-law in England of how they have written to Philadelphia at *Le Château de Jourdan* with:

> the design of visiting them in our return, & desiring an answer to meet [Mr Knight] at Toulouse or Montaubon, but at neither of those places did he find any; I make no doubt but she has written, but perhaps her letter is sent on to Bordeaux.[16]

It was indeed sent on to Bordeaux with Philadelphia extending a warm invitation to the Knights to visit. Mrs Knight is effusive in her description of Philadelphia whom she describes so: 'It is impossible for anything to be civiler than her letters, or the messages she has sent from her Son & Daughter respecting our visit to them', but the chance to see some family from England does not eventuate for Philadelphia, for when Mr and Mrs Knight arrive in Agen, they find the village of Sainte-Meille is 'forty miles off & a cross road, [Mr Knight] did not think it worthwhile to go; he therefore wrote a letter of excuse to Mrs Hancock'.[17] A disappointment probably for Philadelphia. In her letter to the Knights she has told them she plans to visit England the next spring, but Mrs Knight is doubtful the visit will happen as in her letter to her sister-in-law she has written that 'the Comte is engaged in the cultivation of a vast tract of Land I shou'd imagine their coming must be uncertain'. So the plan to return may have originally included the comte.

Come the end of May 1786 and Philadelphia and the very pregnant Eliza are preparing to leave for England. In her letter to Phylly of 26 May 1786, on the eve of their departure, Eliza expresses some anxiety about the journey ahead while heavily pregnant and the separation from her husband at such a time. Philadelphia and her daughter prepare to set out at the end of May and in doing so will miss yet another 'projected' visit by a relative to Guyenne.

James Austen plans a visit to his aunt and cousin. He seems to have had plenty of time on his hands with short terms at Oxford and long vacations at Steventon. In late 1785 he tells Philadelphia and Eliza of his plan to come to Guyenne to visit them there in the coming spring and stay for some months. It may have been something of a Grand Tour on the cheap. Eliza had long been a favourite and perhaps it was thought he could also be of some use to the comte. Philadelphia and Eliza have already advanced their plans to travel to England at the end of May, but James still sets out for Guyenne, but now it is in the autumn and he spends many months there with the comte, not returning till late in 1787.

Philadelphia intends to stay in Paris for a short time to see friends and to be in London by the end of June with time in hand to prepare for Eliza's expected July confinement. It may be cutting it a little fine. Philadelphia would have also been concerned for her daughter's condition but, like Eliza, excited at the prospect of being back with family and friends again. Jean-François obviously has full confidence in Philadelphia's capability of handling any situations arising. So once again mother and daughter set off through the centre of France to arrive in Paris in early June.

We know they are definitely in Paris on 17 June for they are at a dinner party at Mr Pattle's house in the Place Royale attended by the anonymous English Grand Tourist who has noted in his diary entry for 17 June 1786, the following:

> Saturday 17th
> *... Nous avons aujourdhui dine chez Monsr. Pattle ou il se trouvait le Doct. Geary, deux Anglais, Made Hancock anglaise & sa fille[,] un Curé[,] Mde Villette & Monsr. Pattle qui se trouvait bien indispose, mais il nous a reçu avec beaucoup d'honnetété & nous a conté beaucoup d'Histoires – Mde Hancock en des Indes & connait tres bien Mons Sumner, Mde Yorke, la famille Birch &ca. Le Doctr ma dit que sa fille etait de Monsr Hastings. ...*[18]
> [We dined today at Mr Pattle's, where were Doctor Geary, two Englishwomen, Madame Hancock and her daughter, a Curé, Madame Villette and Mr Pattle, whom we found was very unwell, but he received us with great sincerity, and recounted to us numerous stories. Madame Hancock was in the Indies, and knew well Mr Sumner, Madame Yorke, the Birch family etc. The Doctor told me that her daughter was Mr Hastings' ...]

Philadelphia and Eliza are most likely staying at Mr Pattle's house in the Place Royale. Captain Thomas Pattle, now 76 and not in good health is well-known to Hastings. His young unknown visitor, who makes the note about Philadelphia and Eliza's presence at a dinner Mr Pattle holds on 17 June 1786, also knows Hastings as it is also pointed out in Mike Williams's blog that:

> The student assigned to work on this diary discovered that the author had visited Mr Pattle on 13 June. His house was in Place Royale, and the author delivered to him 'our letters and parcels', one of which was from Mr Hastings, thanking Mr Pattle for his offer of his services 'on the trial'.[19]

Preparing to defend himself before the bar of the House of Commons and stave off impeachment, Hastings was drawing on many old India friends and supporters with knowledge and experience of his actions in India for assistance in putting together his speech. Both Captain Thomas Pattle and his son Thomas

J. Pattle served the EIC in Hastings' time there and it appears typical of Captain Pattle's generous nature to offer his support to Hastings. The Pattle family were famous for their wealth and hospitality. Captain Pattle's wife had died in 1770, and after a period of time he had moved, without his family, from London to live in great style in Paris. As Eliza is so advanced in her pregnancy, it seems likely they were house guests, than guests invited just for the dinner; though they might have been because of the diarist's close connection with Hastings. The conversation with the young man, rich with Indian associations and fresh with news of Hastings must have been an exceptionally pleasing part of Philadelphia's stay in Paris.

Philadelphia has not seen Hastings since he left England in March 1769, and now Hastings is back in England, with his wife, in a townhouse in St James' and has just purchased Beaumont Lodge, near Windsor, in Berkshire, a county much favoured by returned EIC servants who had made their mark and their fortune. Philadelphia's plan was, after a short stay at a hotel in London they would, if Eliza's condition allowed it, go down to Steventon. As it turned out their visit to Steventon was much delayed, as, setting out for England soon after the Pattle dinner party, they are delayed in Calais when Eliza goes into labour. It seems likely the birth was significantly premature.

It would have been a scramble to find accommodation and support for the birth, though Philadelphia's previous experience assisting in confinements would have made her a calm and reassuring presence for Eliza. Her 'beloved Mama' would have been exactly the person Eliza would have wanted to see her through. And while finding suitable accommodation in Calais for the birth and lying-in would have taxed Philadelphia's resources, Eliza's title and fluent French must have eased their way with an apartment in a private home, or rooms in a hotel providing most of what was needed, and a midwife or even a doctor could have assisted.

On the 25 June, Eliza is safely delivered of a baby boy. Her husband had his heir. Like her mother, Eliza would have only the one child; but he would have a very different life from Eliza's, though she gave him every loving devotion. The baby would be named Hastings François Louis Henri Eugene Capot de Feuillide, though it would be another year before that name was officially bestowed on him. It is a name with a significant nod to Eliza's godfather, but in the list of names, which includes his father's first name as well as the names of kings of France, there is not even a hint in the direction of Tysoe Saul Hancock in the baby's fine title.

In his diary entry on the day of the baby's christening in London, almost exactly one year later, on the 1 June 1787, Hastings notes that Eliza's baby was 'born [left blank] June 1786'.[20] The baptismal register of St George's Hanover Square gives the birth place and date as 'Calais on 25 June 1786'.[21] Hastings appears to have attended the christening and writes in his diary, 'Xd. The Csse de Feuillide's Child – Hastings'.[22] More on that later.

Delayed in Calais while mother and baby recover their strength and take the customary three weeks of lying-in, they then must have set out to cross to Dover by 20 July. They arrive back in London almost two months after leaving Guyenne, and a little less than nine years since they left for the Continent. It may have been a moving moment for Philadelphia who would have felt a sense that she had achieved what she had set out to do.

The original plan was to stay just a few days in London, and then if Eliza's condition allowed it, to take Eliza straight down to Steventon. Was the intention for Eliza to have the baby there? In those planned days in London, Philadelphia must have hoped to see Hastings again in particular. After the birth of the baby in Calais, she would have written to her family and the Woodmans about Eliza's situation, requiring a change of plans and a delay in their return. A hotel has been booked, Lothian's Hotel, in Albemarle Street in familiar Mayfair.

Hastings calls on her on what looks to be the very day of her arrival at Lothian's Hotel. He notes in his diary for Monday, 24 July 1786, 'Mrs Hancock & her Daughter arrived at Lothian's Hotel – Evg. Visd. them'.[23] He had last seen them when Eliza was only 7 and now she is a woman of 24, married, a comtesse and the mother of a month-old baby boy. He seems to have been keen to see them, for the next day he brings his wife to meet them and arranges for Philadelphia and her daughter and baby to come and stay with them in the new house he has purchased, Beaumont Lodge in Windsor. His diary notes: 'Mrs H. w. me visd. Mrs Hk. & ye Csse de Feuillide, & eng. Ym to BL on Tuesday next'.[24] He must consider Lothian's Hotel as not suitable for them for a longer stay. Philadelphia and her daughter are important to him, and while he may not say such in any recorded way, his actions consistently show it to be so.

Philadelphia's family and friends took Eliza's status as a comtesse seriously. They accepted it and often referred to her using the title, as she did when referring to herself. The trappings of a certain style of living were provided by the limited, but adequate financial resources she and Philadelphia had been provided with. Still, living in London in Lothian's Hotel with a young baby, albeit with servants, would have been awkward and expensive. How long had they intended to stay in England? It must have been for at least until the comte's new house, *Le Château Marais* was completed and set up for them.

Nevertheless, even with a new baby, they seem to have got out and about in London, catching up with old friends. Hastings always kept a London base, first in St James', then in Wimpole Street and later in Park Lane. It was critical that during the period of impeachment and subsequent trial that he stay close to the centre of things. He was at this time assembling the evidence for his defence and trying to keep track of what his enemies were going to use against him. But it seems the political mood of the time was very much against him. A scapegoat for the East India Company's actions in India was being sought. Hastings was not the only one being pursued, but with Clive long dead, he was by far the most prominent of Company servants who could be called to answer the complaints. And while Hastings had expected to be criticised on his return, he had thought it would be a passing threat and that with a strong vindication by him, on the ground, in person, it would subside in due time and he would be recognised for his achievements. But it did not happen that way.

Three months before, on 1 May 1786, Hastings had appeared before the bar of the House of Commons to present a detailed response to the charges threatening him with impeachment. It was a lengthy and detailed defence of his actions in India, and one which he thought would bring an end to the matter. Detailed and lengthy it might have been, so lengthy that he could not read it all himself and had to get others to take over. It went on into the next evening. He felt buoyed by what he had presented, but a month later in June, one of the charges was voted on by the House of Commons in favour of impeachment. Hastings and his supporters were shocked. But as a later biographer pointed out:

> If he could have realised it, his defence at the bar had not only bored the House to extinction, but had done him positive harm. It had been thought arrogant, seemed almost to convict him of holding oriental despotic notions of government.[25]

Quickly following that blow was the death of his aunt, Elizabeth Hastings around the time of Philadelphia's arrival back in London. The aunt had been like a mother to both Hastings and his sister Anne. He notes in his diary that he 'visited my aunt ... who scarcely knew me'.[26] His aunt died that night. Both Hastings and his sister named their daughters Elizabeth, after their aunt and in her will, leaves her household furniture, silver and plate to Hastings, along with £1,000, while giving her house and land in Ewell, Surrey to Anne Woodman.[27]

Philadelphia knew the elderly Miss Hastings well, as visits to her home in Kensington to join the Woodmans to celebrate the birthdays of both Hastings and Eliza in December had been a regular feature of Philadelphia's London life between 1764 and 1777. Elizabeth Hastings was Hastings' father's unmarried sister who had cared for her motherless nephew in his grandfather's house in Churchill, Gloucestershire and had moved to London to live with Howard Hastings, the uncle who became Hastings' guardian. Hastings' sister Anne had also lived with her aunt in Kensington before Anne married John Woodman. Philadelphia would have shared Hastings' sorrow at the loss of his aunt. His biographer called Elizabeth Hastings 'one who had loved him longest'.[28]

Hastings' self-belief no doubt propelled him to carry on his life as best he could while the threat of a trial before the House hung over him. He seemed eager to help Philadelphia and Eliza and to show them his new house. On 4 August, Philadelphia, Eliza and the baby planned to head off early to Beaumont Lodge, a journey of about 25 miles. They experienced some delay, as when Hastings went to meet them in his phaeton at Hounslow, where the post-chaise horses would have been baited, about 10 miles from Windsor, he found he had missed them, as they had been delayed by Eliza's 'indisposition'. Happily they arrived at Beaumont Lodge 'about 1'.[29] While the splendid porticoed house that stands there today is not the house that Hastings purchased, his home when Philadelphia and Eliza arrived would still have been impressive. Berkshire was the much favoured county for the returning, well financed Company men (the 'nabobs') to buy their landed estates that gave them entry into the status which their wealth entitled them to, in eighteenth-century terms.

When the author Fanny Burney, a novelist much admired by the young Jane Austen, visited Beaumont Lodge around this time, she reported that Mrs Hastings had made her stay very pleasant. In a letter of May 1786, she describes Hastings' wife as: 'lively, obliging, and entertaining'.[30]

Philadelphia must have been made welcome too by Marian. What did Mrs Hastings know of her husband's long-standing friendship and support of Philadelphia and Eliza? Speculation might lead us to think that she knew as much as Hastings was prepared to share with her; and that was probably a great deal. Hastings' letters to his 'beloved Marian' reveal a man strongly bound in intimacy with his wife and she herself faced difficulties, as a divorced woman, being accepted in London society, though she was happily received by the queen, to some raised eyebrows, courtesy of Marian's patron Madame Schwellenberg, the queen's mistress of the robes and confidante. Marian's first husband, Baron von Imhoff knew Madame Schwellenberg sufficiently for her to have assisted him in gaining his military cadetship with the EIC. We know perhaps more about Madame Schwellenberg than she would have wished, as Fanny Burney, who had served as second mistress of the robes for Queen Charlotte from 1786 to 1791, wrote scathingly of Madame Schwellenberg in her (Burney's) diaries.

Philadelphia stayed for three weeks at Beaumont Lodge, with help for Eliza to care for the new baby, and opportunities to meet old India friends among the 'Berkshire nabobs'. Both Hastings and Marian were noted as kind and generous to their friends and guests. Hastings notes in his diary that Philadelphia left on 25 August: 'Mrs. Hancock & her Dr left Us'.[31] They may have gone back to London, but they did not yet take a more permanent residence at this stage, and they had a number of good friends to help them, it seems.

Among them were Sir William and Lady Burrell in Harley Street, off Cavendish Square east of Mayfair in the Marylebone area. We know from later correspondence that Eliza was a good friend of Lady Sophia Burrell, née Raymond. Later, during her years in England, Eliza stayed extensively with Sophia Burrell in her country house, the Deepdene, near Dorking in Surrey. Sophia was eight years older than Eliza and was already married to her older second cousin William Burrell when mother and daughter left England in 1777. Sophia's very wealthy father, Sir Charles Raymond was a principal managing owner of EIC ships from the 1750s to his retirement in 1777.[32] He was well-known to Hastings and probably a friendship with the Burrells had formed through that connection. Philadelphia's friend and helpful 'post mistress', Elizabeth Hinchliffe was living in Woodstock Street Mayfair, also nearby. From a later letter of her niece Phylly, it is clear that Philadelphia also kept up with her family in London, as Phylly mentions seeing both Hampson and Freeman relatives when she stays in London in April of 1788. Phylly's letter also reveals that Philadelphia and Eliza are frequently in the company of Mr and Mrs Hastings, as Phylly tells her brother when she stays with Philadelphia, that she had seen the Hastings very often and exceedingly admired Mrs Hastings.[33]

In October Philadelphia and Eliza were staying with the Woodmans in their country house in Ewell in Surrey, and may have been there for some time, for on 26 October Hastings records in his diary that he 'rode ye Arab to Ewell. Mrs Hs. [Hastings] folld. in ye Phaeton, passed 4 Days w. Mr & Mrs Woodman, Mrs Hancock & her Dr'.[34]

By the end of November, however, Philadelphia has taken up more permanent accommodation for herself and her daughter by renting a house in Orchard Street, Marylebone, opposite Portman Square. It was a similar newly developed fashionable area to where she had been living in London before she went to France. It was a few blocks away from Harley Street where the Burrells lived, and Hastings' townhouse in Wimpole Street. There is no hurrying back to France now in mind.

Hastings calls on Philadelphia in the evening when he is in London on 28 November: '… Evg. Called on Mrs Hancock'.[35] He is back again a week later on 7 December with a birthday gift for Eliza. His diary notes: '… called in Orchard Street w. Prest. to my Goddau.- deposd. W. Mrs Hk'.[36] On both these occasions Eliza appears not to be at home. Philadelphia may have been giving Eliza opportunities to be out and about while she helped to watched over the baby. Hastings fairly regularly calls on Philadelphia during these months in London. They appear to have unselfconsciously enjoyed a tete a tete together. There may be passion only for his wife, but Hastings' and Philadelphia's affection, albeit evidenced by little more than these meagre diary entries, seem to have endured. Hastings was loyal to his old friends, and sought out their company, but his family was scant, and there may have been some sort of comfort in Philadelphia's home when he was in town, from the distressing swirl of accusations and public humiliations that surrounded him. An echo of Philadelphia's letter sent, hesitatingly, to him from Paris in 1780 also rings true in these circumstances. She had written then that:

> you may be surrounded by those who are happy in frequently shewing their attachment to you, but I will venture to say not one among them who can boast a more disinterested steady and unshaken friendship for you than that which for so many years animated and will ever continue to animate the Breast of
> Dear Sir, your obliged Friend, Phila: Hancock.[37]

Philadelphia and Eliza are off to Steventon for Christmas, on the 21 December, just in time for Eliza's twenty-fifth birthday on 21 December, and with a gift for Philadelphia's niece, Jane, who had just celebrated her eleventh birthday on 16 December. It was an eagerly awaited event for the Austens of Steventon.

Chapter 19

Return to England
1786–1788

We are now happy in the company of our Sister Hancock Madame de Feuillide & the little Boy... They all look & seem to be remarkably well... I don't think your Aunt [Philadelphia] at all alter'd in any respect.
Mrs George Austen to her niece Phylly
Walter, 31 December 1788

ALMOST A DECADE HAD passed since Philadelphia left England, and her daughter was now a married woman with a small child, but seems to have retained her youthful beauty and vivacity, and Philadelphia, in Mrs Austen's words, is 'unchanged'. The interesting aunt, the delightful, elegant cousin who is now a French countess and a chubby, pretty baby are more than welcome additions to the rectory. While George Austen's pupils have gone home for the Christmas holidays, his daughters have now returned, for good, from the Abbey School in Reading, where both Cassandra and her sister Jane had been boarders. Henry, now 15, is still at home, but soon to go up to Oxford.

From this time on, Henry seems to become a favourite with Philadelphia and Eliza. He may have from this time developed an infatuation with his sparkling young relative, though she is married and ten years his senior. It was an attachment that persisted. One of Jane Austen's earliest stories in her *Juvenilia*, usually dated from between 1787 and 1789 is the tale of *Henry and Eliza*, with the character of Eliza 'when she grew up was the delight of all who knew her'.[1] Henry Austen is accepted as the brother closest to his sister Jane, and a particular favourite of his father. Henry was tall, handsome, engaging and spirited. There is a family tradition about Henry that has him as:

> The handsomest of his family, and in the opinion of his own
> Father, also the most talented ... [and] for the most part greatly

> admired... From the Austen side Henry seems to have inherited also the same strain of impetuosity that had manifested itself in his aunt Mrs Hancock.[2]

Philadelphia's so-called 'impetuosity' stems from a conservative interpretation by subsequent family historians of a life forged by less conventional decisions, though the young Henry Austen did seem to have something in common with Philadelphia; a taste for a more interesting life perhaps? He certainly didn't initially follow the conventional path of his father and older brother into the clergy. There are hints from time to time in the Austen family stories that Philadelphia was seen as foolish and reckless. Deirdre Le Faye suggest some of this attitude in describing her as 'impulsive'.[3]

Amongst the other Austens also at home that Christmas is the youngest, Charles but not Edward who has taken off on a splendid Grand Tour of Europe that lasts almost four years, while his brother, James, the eldest Austen, has made do with his trip to Guyenne. Francis is there too, on holidays from the Royal Naval Academy in Portsmouth. Also coming to stay are the two Cooper cousins, whose mother Jane, Mrs Austen's sister, had died three years before. It is quite a full house, but a very happy one, as Mrs Austen tells Phylly, pointedly indicating what she is missing.

> I wish my <u>third niece</u> could be here also; but indeed, I begin to suspect your Mother never intends to gratify that wish. You might as well be in Jamaica keeping your Brother's house, for anything that we see of you or are like to see.[4]

In her letter on 31 December 1786, Mrs Austen gives small vignettes of her sister-in-law Philadelphia, her niece Eliza and baby Hastings. She tells Phylly that 'they all look and seem to be remarkably well, the little Boy grows very fat, he is very fair & very pretty'. She pays Philadelphia the compliment of telling her younger namesake that 'I don't think your Aunt at all alter'd in any respect'. Mrs Austen may have thought the years in France and Eliza's marriage to the comte might have given Philadelphia some foreign notions, but the nine year's absence seem to have had little impact on Philadelphia's looks or conduct. Eliza and her mother once again have added an exotic touch to the Steventon home, first it had been of India, now it was of France. This was literally so, as a book in the young Jane Austen's possession with her name written on the fly-leaves was 'twelve little volumes of Arnaud Berquin's *L'Ami des Enfants*', assumed to have been brought by Philadelphia and Eliza as a gift to Jane for her birthday when they arrived.[5]

Here Jane most likely met for the first time since very early childhood, the elegant and kindly aunt who had travelled to India to marry, and the pretty, talented cousin who had been to Versailles and married a French count. Jane had obviously often heard about them and perhaps had read their letters. Now here they were, staying for a whole month. Any girl would have been impressed, let alone the keen-eyed Jane. The Austens' had 'borrowed a Piano-Forte, and she [Eliza] plays to us every day'.[6] There is to be a dance in the parlour, with the Austen sons also very much enjoying the company of their cousin Eliza, whom Mrs Austen now describes as 'quite lively', in comparison to the younger Eliza whom she considered shy and reserved. The term 'grave' was used by Mrs Austen. It seems it was not long after their visit that a piano was acquired for the Austen home and Jane had lessons for the next decade at least, and continued to play regularly throughout her life.[7] Was this visit by her cousin her inspiration? Certainly, young women playing the pianoforte feature frequently in her works and their performances carry a surprising variety of narrative functions, from Elizabeth Bennet unknowingly bewitching Darcy who positions himself to gain the best view of her playing the piano forte, to the expression of Anne Elliot's joylessness and lost 'bloom' by her merely playing the instrument so others can take their lively pleasures.

It must have been gratifying for Philadelphia to have spent that month with her brother, and no doubt assuaged his fears about her life in France. The Hastings' money was still held in trust and provided an income sufficient for her and Eliza, and Eliza had not adopted the Catholic faith. But at six months was all well with that beautiful baby boy? Were there questions arising about his development? Were there worrying signs that an experienced mother like Cassandra Austen noticed?

Certainly the family would have discussed the impeachment threatening Hastings. It was the *'cause celebre'* of the age. The Austens were staunch supporters of the former governor general by virtue of their numerous connections to him thorough Philadelphia, the Leigh family and the tragic circumstances of his son's death in George Austen's care. Hastings' attempts to buy back his family's estate in Daylesford took him up to visit Mrs Austen's cousin, the Rev. Thomas Leigh of Adlestrop, Hastings' childhood friend, within a few months of arriving back in England to gain his assistance in negotiating the purchase of 'the advowson of Daylesford' as a step in the process.[8]

February 1787 was the critical month when 'impeachment was now taken as a certainty' for Hastings, with Prime Minister Pitt convinced that 'Hastings must be "at least charged" however unpopular it might be with his [Tory] party' [and by April] 'the only doubts were the choice of articles, and the date of the trial'.[9] Impeachment, or trial by the parliament of a high public office holder for crimes or misdemeanours, is a rare procedure and its use against Hastings for when he was the head of the EIC in India was an appalling situation for him. He had many supporters both inside and outside of the Houses of Parliament, but not enough to save him from going to trial. In May the articles of impeachment were approved and he was arrested on 21 May 1787 and appeared at the bar of the House of Lords as his biographer Feiling describes:

> There he endured what he described as the single thing he felt in this 'base treatment', the ceremonial of kneeling, 'a punishment not only before conviction, but before the accusations'. But his appearance, the Archbishop of Canterbury thought was 'proper, neither daunted nor insolent'. Anyhow, he spent two days of June at Ascot races.[10]

Back in London in their Orchard Street home at the beginning of February 1787, and keeping a close eye on the baby, Philadelphia may have kept to a quieter regimen allowing Eliza the freedom to enjoy some of the diversions of the London 'Season'.

In the late eighteenth century, 'The Season' was the period of London-based entertainments for the social elites who removed from their country estates for the parliamentary session which ran from November till May. The court at St James' Palace played its part in these social events by holding court presentations. Eliza seems to have the right connections to attend, for she tells Phylly in early April that she has just been to St James' and complains about having to wear the required full court dress, characterised by an enormous hooped skirt. Eliza, a young woman who had been to balls at Versailles and seen Marie Antoinette at close quarters, may have been less impressed by the court of George III and Queen Charlotte, but it does indicate the level of society into which Philadelphia's daughter, the comtesse, was accepted.

Perhaps Eliza was out and about with her friends the Burrells. She still loved dancing and going to Almack's which was the place to be for the most fashionable balls held during 'The Season'. Almack's Assembly Rooms had been opened since 1765 in St James' where 'for a subscription fee of 10 guineas, the fashionable men and women of London could attend a weekly Wednesday night ball with supper during the three months that comprised the London social season'.[11]

In late April of 1787, Philadelphia has Henry Austen staying for a short visit, prior to his going up to Oxford for the start of Trinity term. Eliza has had to put off cousin Phylly, whose intended visit clashes with Henry's. Eliza's baby is coming up to his first birthday on 25 June and on 1 June 1787 he is baptised at the fashionable church of St George's Hanover Square. Hastings notes the christening in his diary and that he is given the name Hastings. Can we assume he and Marian attended the christening? Hastings may well have been one of the child's godparents. Eliza has told Phylly that while 'my little Boy ... is in perfect health [he] has got no teeth yet, which somewhat mortifies his two Mammas'.[12] The word 'mortifies' seems a strong term to use and for Eliza to mention the baby's lack of teeth indicates that she and Philadelphia, his 'two Mammas' as she touchingly puts it, are concerned. Philadelphia's little grandson may not be developing as expected, but nevertheless much loved by his mother and his grandmother, who, by Eliza's account continues to take much of the responsibility for him.

On 7 July Hastings' diary notes that he visits Philadelphia after 'Horse sat to Mr Stubbs', presumably for the portrait of Hastings on his Arabian mare by George Townley Stubbs. At the end of August, Hastings and his wife set off for two months touring in the north, as far as Edinburgh and visiting old India friends. Hastings returned to his St James' Place townhouse in the middle of October to refine his defence before parliament on 28 November.

Philadelphia with Eliza too, left town in early September to stay in the still fashionable spa town of Tunbridge Wells, in Kent, just a few miles from Philadelphia's home town of Tonbridge. The Walter family were now living in the village of Seal, near Sevenoaks in Kent, where Philadelphia's uncle, Francis Austen, now 89, still held sway in the Red House. The area was redolent of connections for Philadelphia.

After they settle into Tunbridge Wells, Philadelphia and Eliza come up to the Walter home in Seal, in their fine coach and four with Eliza's coronet emblazoned on its doors, to see the family and to take Phylly back with them to 'The Wells', as it was called, locally. After ten years of letters, Phylly meets Eliza and her aunt in person once more. Nothing shows their lifestyle more clearly than Phylly's description of her 'wild' ten days in Tunbridge Wells with the Hancocks. She writes to her brother after her return home to Seal on 19 September 1787, her adventure still fresh in her mind:

> I had spent ten days with them at the Wells ... and lived a gayer life than ever before experienced, engagements for every hour.... We all left Seal at 5 o'clock on the 6th inst. ... got to the Wells and went directly to the Rooms, for the benefit of two celebrated Italian singers: after which they had done singing some gentlemen proposed dancing which was readily agreed to and we kept it up till past twelve o'clock.
>
> On Friday morning the Comtesse and I hunted all the Milliners' shops for hats ... I danced almost all the Evening and kept it up till past two o'clock ... Saturday morning went to see a horse race rode by Lord Sackville & Mr Cumberland ... In the evening to the

play. ... Sunday morning went to chapel, then took an airing, paid several visits by leaving cards; in the evening drank tea at the Rooms. Monday by myself to Frant; my aunt fetched me home and we all went to the play ... Tuesday my aunt and I went to the Rocks and rambled there; in the evening to the ball.[13]

On the Friday before her departure, the Hancocks take Phylly to dine at Major Yorke's, where there was a large party.

Major Martin Yorke, who had been an officer in the East India Company's army under Clive was an old friend of Philadelphia and her husband. When Yorke returned to England in 1772 he purchased a mansion, 'Bishop's Down Grove' in Tunbridge Wells. Like many old India hands, he was renowned for his generosity and affability, entertaining in the usual grand style, characteristic of the returned 'nabobs'. A sister, Miss Yorke is mentioned in one of Mr Hancock's letters to Philadelphia, dated 31 January 1772, where he writes that 'Miss Yorke is arrived and tells me that she has seen you & Betsy'.[14] Invitations to dine with Indian friends and connections always formed an important part of Philadelphia's social life. On the Saturday Philadelphia had taken Phylly to dine with their cousin Motley Austen, Uncle Francis's eldest son and heir, in his house at Lamberhurst, also in Tunbridge Wells. It does sound as though visiting and dining with friends and family, going to plays and dances and attending assembly rooms were very much Philadelphia and Eliza's style of life and town life seemed to suit them best.

Phylly gives another insight into Philadelphia's character and values when she says that neither Eliza nor Philadelphia ever gamble at cards, and she praises Philadelphia to her clergyman brother James Walter, who had lit fireworks in the basement for Eliza, so smitten with her when they visited just before Philadelphia left for the Continent in 1777. Perhaps Phylly expected some quite different, worldly kind of woman in her aunt. She writes:

> You will expect my opinion of my friends. To begin with my Aunt, I do not know a fault she has – so strictly just and honourable in all her dealings, so kind and obliging to all her friends and acquaintance, so religious in all her actions, in short I do not know a person that has more the appearance of perfection.[15]

But there is an edge to her assessment of Eliza whom she says 'has many aimiable qualities, such as the highest duty and respect for her mother' and esteems her husband, never gets into any kind of debt and shows Phylly great 'partiality'. But in her letter to her brother, Phylly calls Eliza's life 'dissipated'. 'Dissipated' means the coach, the balls, the plays, the shopping, the clothes, the visiting, the wit, the beauty, the title and the handsome 'aristocratic' husband, one assumes. All things denied to Phylly, stuck in Seal with the aged parents. Later, Phylly has some mean things to say about Eliza, but mere envy may be the core of it all, for Eliza's life, after all, had more than its share of difficulties not experienced by Phylly.

From Tunbridge Wells, Philadelphia and Eliza are soon off to Brighton, then an emerging fashionable resort for the new health craze of sea-bathing. They are keen to take Phylly to Brighton, and also urge her to come to Steventon for Christmas and take part in the Austen family plays in 'my uncle's barn which is fitting up quite like a theatre and where all the young folks are to take their part'.[16] But the country-cousin is not keen and fears that she has neither the courage nor the desire to act a part. Not unlike Fanny Price in *Mansfield Park* when faced with the same prospect. In the end, Phylly says that Philadelphia and Eliza reconciled her to their lifestyle, but it is really not her metier. Phylly's letter to her brother James ends with the news that Philadelphia and Eliza and the little boy intend to return to France in the spring of 1788.

By October, Philadelphia and Eliza are back in London in their house in Orchard Street. Little Hastings de Feuillide is now developing teeth but his teeth are a continuing problem. Eliza is perhaps hiding some of the truth as to what is plaguing the little boy. When her letter was written to Phylly from Orchard Street in mid-November of 1787, the baby is now 17 months old. He should be toddling around, beginning to speak, but that cannot be the case. The truth that their precious child is not as he should be must be an agony for his mother and 'Grand Mamma', though they continue to devote themselves to him. And while their own private tragedy is unfolding, Philadelphia's 'sincere & faithful friend' undergoes his humiliation before the bar of the House of Lords. His trial is to begin in February of the New Year of 1788, and becomes the greatest spectacle in town. It is the show that everyone who is anyone must get a ticket to see.

But family life goes on for Philadelphia, Eliza and little Hastings that December and with their maid, Rosalie, who has probably been with them since before they returned from France, they go down to Steventon again on 17 December for the Austen Christmas festivities. This year they will include productions of *The Wonder: A Woman Keeps a Secret*, a saucy early eighteenth-century comedy by the woman playwright, Susannah Centlivre, where Eliza plays the part of the lively heroine, Donna Violante, and *The Chances* an adaption by David Garrick of a racy comedy originally written by Beaumont and Fletcher. Paula Byrne suggests that in this play Eliza most likely 'played the role of the "low-born" Constantia, a favourite of the great comic actress Mrs Jordon.'[17] James Austen is now back from France with news no doubt to share of the progress of the works in Marais, and especially of the house Eliza's husband is completing for the return of his family. We have no communication currently available between Eliza and her husband, though Deirdre Le Faye states that some of Eliza letters to Guyenne survived amongst papers placed in the presbytery of the church of Casaubon, a town near Nerac, by a local historian, Chanoine Ducroc. A later attempt to uncover them was unsuccessful.[18] How much did Eliza tell her husband of little Hastings' difficulties? She may have tried to keep the picture rosy, and certainly in her other letters she tries to maintain the positives about her son.

The family tradition tends to portray Philadelphia as an over-indulgent mother to Eliza, but while this might be somewhat true (deep love can be like that), she obviously enjoyed seeing her lively daughter's gift for taking and giving pleasure and would have enjoyed her performances. Eliza says the gathering at Steventon it is going to be 'a most brilliant party & a great deal of Amusement, the House full of Company & frequent Balls'.[19] The place must have positively sizzled, with both James and Henry much taken with their cousin. The situation of the racy plays, the cousins taking parts and the implied romantic attractions and rivalries begs to be compared with the theatricals so pivotal to the plot of *Mansfield Park*. One cannot help but see the eagle-eyed young Jane, now 12 years old taking in all the bustle and sparkle and tension of the play rehearsals, preparations and performances. It must have been an exciting time for her and became ultimately grist to the mill of her novelist's mind when twenty-five years later, as Eliza, now sister-in-law as well as cousin, endures her 'long and dreadful illness', Jane is already well into writing *Mansfield Park*.[20]

But soon the 'brilliant party' is over, the pupils with their much needed fees must return to the rectory and Philadelphia and Eliza, go back to Orchard Street at the end of January, with the promise of a visit from Phylly in the April. The plan to return to France in the spring is altered to a later return in the summer with Henry Austen accompanying them. Perhaps the house in the Marais is not ready. By 1788 the comte has achieved much of his grand scheme, but the financial cost has been massive. He claims to have drained the swamp, created a substantial canal, planted the land, put up fourteen buildings, including *Le Château Marais* and a house for his brother. He also has twenty-four pair of oxen, had excellent harvests and has eliminated the pestilence caused by the swamps.[21] He is now being pressured by his creditors and has used up all of his fortune, some of his wife's fortune and has borrowed money from creditors who have begun seizing his property. He appeals to the government to give him time to pay. On 31 October 1788, the steward from Bordeaux orders an enquiry in consideration of de Feuillide's appeal.

It is hard to say for whom the new year of 1788 would be the most stressful, Hastings or the comte. Hastings' trial began on 13 February in the House of

Lords which had been turned into 'a vast improvised theatre... [where] he sat, cynosure of the British political world... A solitary and almost emaciated figure in a plain poppy-coloured suit'.[22] Fanny Burney thought he looked 'pale, ill and altered', while another thought he looked 'bold, determined and indignant'.[23] He sat that first year of the trial for thirty-two days, but refused to succumb to misery, continued to live his life as he wished, and endured the trial as something that would eventually pass. He notes in his diary that on 1 April he 'Went in a P. Ch. To Town' with a list of people he called on, including 'Mrs Hk'.[24]

In April of 1788 the disabilities being suffered by little Hastings would have become more apparent, but Philadelphia and Eliza were also not daunted and were set to return to France in the summer. Phylly stayed with them in Orchard Street in early April as planned and again writes to her brother James on the details of her stay, but as Deirdre Le Faye points out that this letter of Phylly's 'was heavily edited prior to its publication' by R.A. Austen-Leigh in the *Austen Papers*, and, as the originals appear to no longer exist, it may be a conflation of a number of letters. We have again, however a taste of their London life from Phylly's perspective. By 23 April, Phylly has already spent two weeks in town. She is particularly aggrieved by the practice of spending their mornings 'in ridiculous sort of calls from one door to another without ever being let in'.[25] Ridiculous as the practice might be to Phylly, the making of morning calls and leaving a visiting card was an essential part of the etiquette of the fashionable upper-class life which Philadelphia now found herself to be in. They walk in Kensington Gardens, see the Hastings couple often, go to the opera and sit in Mrs Hastings' box, have tea with them at St James' Place, go to the trial and see the Hampson and Freeman cousins.

They take Phylly back home to Seal, stay again in Tunbridge Wells and go to Ramsgate, a former seaside fishing village (a la Sanditon) now becoming a place popular with the fashionable for restorative treatments. It is the first of many visits to such places for the health benefits they hope will be brought to little Hastings. By the time of their return to London in July 1788, the reality of the little boy's situation is obvious. He is now having convulsions. What Phylly writes to her brother about the 2-year-old is heart-breaking but appears precise and correct.

> Seal, 23rd July 1788 – Madame de F. and my aunt are returned to London. Poor little Hastings has had another fit; we all fear very much his faculties are hurt; many people say he has the appearance of a weak head; that his eyes are particular that is very certain; our fears are of his being like poor George Austen. He has every symptom of good health, but cannot yet use his feet in the least, nor yet talk, tho' he makes a great noise continually.[26]

While the return to France is delayed from the original plan of leaving London in the spring, preparations are underway for what seems a permanent move to the new house in Guyenne on the reclaimed land of the drained Barbotan marshes. While the work has been completed, de Feuillide's financial situation appears ruinous. Nevertheless, with the promise of their own brand new home, Eliza and Philadelphia purchase furniture and fittings to be sent to France, but with some anxiety about the journey with little Hastings to meet his father for the first time. They intend to leave in September. Henry was to have gone with them to France, but now will not be able to accompany them after all as a vacancy for a fellowship at St John's College Oxford had come up which he was obliged to take. Phylly tells her brother James that the disappointment over this 'was particularly harped upon on both sides'.[27]

There are farewell visits to be made and in mid-August George Austen and his wife and daughters visit Philadelphia in Orchard Street, dining with her on their way home from an excursion down to Kent to pay their respects to old Francis Austen. It seems to have been Jane's first visit to London and to observe something of where her aunt and cousin lived in their fashionable quarter of the city. Eliza tells Phylly that the Austens found she and her mother surrounded in what Eliza called a 'hurry & worry... with [a] plague & fatigue of mind and Body which ever attend such a removal as ours'.[28] In *Sense and Sensibility* there is an echo of the portrayal of Philadelphia in the character of Mrs Jennings, the comfortably-off widow who is free to live her life as she wishes and who resides, like Philadelphia, in a house in the fashionable West End of London. Among the farewell visits Philadelphia makes with her daughter is a trip out to Windsor to see the Hastings couple at Beaumont Lodge, where they stayed for one night, as Hastings records in his diary, and then up to Oxford where they are squired around the colleges by James and Henry Austen. Eliza cannot help but tell Phylly how impressed she is by Henry, now looking even taller and very fashionably got up.

Their return to France is imminent and Philadelphia has expressed her intention to spend the next three years in France. While they seem all set to go, will the brewing social and political discontent in France overturn their plans? Philadelphia and Eliza are aware of what Eliza calls the 'troubles in France' which have been underway since the early spring. The alarm at the news of these uprisings has reached even the quiet corners of the home-counties, as Phylly wonders if the disorder is going to prevent Philadelphia and her daughter returning to France. Eliza assures her that she understands that the situation is quieter and won't prevent their departure. In spite of her usual sunny take on difficulties, there must have been a background of concern. The 'troubles' are personal for Philadelphia and Eliza, for if the severe disturbances had grown, Jean-François, 'would have been cal [led up] & it would have been a very unpleasant kind of Duty because he must have borne arms against his own Countrymen'.[29] In the very difficult financial situation he was now in, such disruption may have made his position worse. Furthermore that year's harvest was a bad one over many parts of France, including Guyenne.

A familiar journey for Philadelphia, down the Dover Road and aboard a Channel packet for the unpredictable crossing. Eliza's bright and spirited nature leads her to present even grave difficulties in the best light, but the reality must undoubtedly be borne, that the son and heir she brings to her husband may be a disappointment or worse. The security Philadelphia had constructed for her daughter could well be undone. Things have not worked out for the comte in the way they all must have hoped.

Chapter 20

Paris, Revolution and Return to England
1788–1791

When I left England I flattered myself I should see it again in about three years, I may possibly enjoy that pleasure much sooner.
　　　　　　　　　Letter from Philadelphia to John Woodman,
　　　　　　　　　　　　　　　　　　　　February 1789

THE AUTUMN OF 1788 was not the most propitious time for Philadelphia to be returning to France. In the spring and summer the *noblesse* had joined forces with the lawyers and magistrates. The *parlementaires,* who had seen their courts closed down by the Crown and were themselves sent out of Paris into exile in the provinces.[1] Riots in support of the *parlements* and their urging of provincial self-government spread widely throughout the provincial capitals. Even in Pau in Gascony there were significant disturbances in May and June of 1788. The king's army was called out to quell the rioters. The riot on 7 June 1788 in Grenoble, known as the 'Day of the Tiles', when the rioters broke tiles off the roofs of houses and pelted them at the soldiers below, was a flagrant denunciation of the King's rule and defiance of a weak army. Historians mark it as the true beginning of the French Revolution.

By the time our travellers arrive in Paris in mid-September, the rioting has died down, with a promise from the king that a meeting of the Estates General, the Monarch's consultative assembly drawn from the three classes of French society (the aristocracy, the clergy and the common people), would be held in May of 1789. The Estates General had not been called for over 170 years. Around the time of Philadelphia's and Eliza's arrival in Paris, 'the *parlement* of Paris made its triumphal re-entry into Paris, amid the plaudits of the crowd, the ringing of bells, and firing of cannon'.[2] If they were there, they must have heard that.

All we have of this brief return to France are two letters written from Paris. One is a rare letter from Philadelphia, this time to John Woodman, on 5 February 1789 and the other is from Eliza to Phylly, a few days later. The news is that Philadelphia and Eliza have not gone down to Guyenne and remain in Paris, and that the Comte has come up from his estate in the south to join them there. Philadelphia tells Woodman that she will be coming back to London much sooner than anticipated. She will be there in June for about a one month to 'transact some affairs'.[3] Philadelphia says she has already written to her brother George explaining the circumstances of their delay in going down to Guyenne.

Eliza does not mention in her letter to Phylly that she is returning to London, but Philadelphia makes it clear to Woodman that 'should Mons. de Feuillide join his Regiment about that time my Daughter will certainly accompany me'.[4] The reason given by Eliza for staying in Paris and not going to Guyenne is because her husband had informed her 'that a malignant fever raged at the Marais and... he did not think it safe I should come there and preferred joining me in Paris'.[5]

When Jean-François does join them in Paris, he is still unwell, for Philadelphia tells Woodman that 'the Ct. de Feuillide has an intermitting Fever which he [brought] from the Country hanging about him for some time'.[6]

The reasons for not going down to her husband's estate may be more complicated than her explanation to Phylly. The comte we know is now deeply in debt and struggling to hold off his creditors. When he joins them in Paris, in the autumn of 1788, seeing his wife and mother-in-law again after two years and his infant son for the first time, he is still waiting to hear from the authorities in Bordeaux whether he has been granted the desperately needed time to prevent his creditors laying further claim to his lands and buildings in the Marais and his estate in Gers inherited from his father.[7] With the threat of eviction from the Marais hanging over him, the comte, one assumes, is not in a position to install his family in the newly-completed house.

On 23 January 1789, the Intendent of Bordeaux (the authority to whom de Feuillide had appealed) requests further details of his capacity to furnish the debt if the delay is granted.[8] This brings us to Philadelphia's letter to Woodman on 5 February 1789 asking that she take up the offer made before they left England to stay at the Woodman's London house, if they should ever need to. She asks would he 'infinitely oblige me by giving me an apartment in it during my stay which will not exceed a Month & perhaps not three Weeks'.[9]

Philadelphia does not tell Woodman, too much about 'the affairs' she is coming to London to 'transact' but they are concerned with the money in trust and relate to the financial needs of her son-in-law. Is M. de Feuillide wanting documentation regarding Hastings' trust money to verify the means Philadelphia's son-in-law has to pay off his debts? He has already borrowed

£6,500 of Philadelphia's own capital, and now he may want either access to the trust money, or documentation proving his access to it. The financial security Philadelphia had acquired, mostly from Hastings' generosity, is evaporating, and there is a hint of desperation in her return to England. As well, there is the worrying agitation in Paris and in the south, which must be obvious to anyone living there. Perhaps too there are tensions in her daughter's marriage that prey upon her mind. We have no record of how Jean-François took the now obvious disabilities of his only child, but we can guess he may have been disappointed.

In Philadelphia's letter to Woodman there is a modest, even humble tone that might appear somewhat cringing to a modern reader, but she shows a strength of character in doing what has to be done. It cannot have been easy to be forced to go back to England under these circumstances. We know the anguish and mortification she felt over the messy financial affairs of her husband when he died. Mounting and unpaid debts, bankruptcy, debtors' prison even, were not matters to be easily accommodated by the 'middling sort' of Austens such as Philadelphia and George. Despite what her husband might have said about her being not very competent with money Philadelphia showed herself to be quite sensible about it.

The appeal for extra time to meet his debts was ultimately granted to de Feuillide and he returns to Guyenne and takes up residence in his newly-built house, *Le Château Marais*, in Gabarret with his mother and sister. The house still stands today, as do at least some of the other buildings which are these days rented out as holiday lets. While it is more of a house than what one would think of as a 'chateau', the comte seems to have lived there for a few years in some style, including, perhaps with some of Eliza's furniture and furnishings, for when his property was confiscated in 1793 the furniture sold for almost 3,000 livres. One comment made about the *Le Château Marais* of this time was that it attracted a brilliant society with the ladies (Jean-François' sisters?) travelling in grand carriages to the nearby castle of Seailles.[10]

In April 1789, the elections to the Estates General were concluded, but when the first session was called on 4 May, the Third Estate was not admitted with the clergy and the nobles but had to wait outside in the rain while the privileged were seated. It was not a good beginning for the men of the provinces, mostly lawyers, professional men and men of finance, commerce and industry who felt they represented the 'real' France, to be treated with such disdain. Historians have tracked a complex and often disconnected series of actions and events by many players over that period from early May to July that quickly brought massive changes to the absolutism of the monarchy and authoritarian fabric of French society. Disturbances at this time were described as 'endemic' throughout France, with the king's authority so weakened as to be unable to control a distressed people and 'Paris itself was becoming ungovernable'[11] The protests and demonstrations that broke out on 24 April 1789 in the St. Antoine district of Paris showed that Paris was becoming an increasingly dangerous place.

June 1789 goes by without Philadelphia and Eliza able to set off for London. Despite the increasing unrest in France, Jean-François was not called up. At this point the improved land provided considerable revenue, and perhaps without the Revolution he might have been able to manage his debts, persevere and ultimately prosper. But his efforts gradually became less successful and the disgruntled local community saw even less reason to approve of him.[12]

In Paris, the disturbances in the populace and the worsening political situation culminated in the storming of the Bastille on 14 July 1789, but by now Philadelphia and her daughter, little Hastings and their maid Rosalie were back in London. Hastings notes in his diary on 7 July 1789 from London that 'Mrs Hk. and Mme de Feuillide arrived from France'.[13] We can assume Mr Woodman was generous in his hospitality and Philadelphia was staying in the Woodman's house in Cleveland Row, around the corner from Hastings' London town house in St James' Place Westminster.

There is scant evidence of how Philadelphia and Eliza spent those next eighteen months from July 1789 to early 1791. Staying initially at the Woodman's house in Cleveland Row, it quickly becomes clear that Philadelphia is keen to consult Hastings as to how the money in trust, worth £11,000 stands in relation to the availability of the interest and capital for her son-in-law. The relevant documentation is made available to Hastings and his diary notes that on 31 July 1789 he 'called on Mrs Hancock: Mr Cruse Her C. [*Counsel*] of Opn. yet [that] the trustees cannot safely sell out, or transfer ye £11000 Stock'.[14] On 2 August Hastings notes, 'Returned Mme F's papers. Her husband can have no Claim but to the Intt. of ye 11000 till the Death of Mrs H., his wife, and Children, & therefore cannot alienate it'.[15]

So Jean-François has a claim on the interest but not on the capital of the trust money, while Philadelphia, and Eliza and her son are all still alive. Eliza's husband most likely considered all of Eliza's money as his own, but the trust held and even if Philadelphia had been prepared to give him access to it, most likely to prove to the Intendent of Bordeaux that the comte had the means to clear some of his most pressing debts, it was not to be permitted. While the disturbances in France swung into the full revolution of history, Philadelphia must have been wondering how she and her daughter could best proceed with their lives. Was return to France a likely option and also under what circumstances might Eliza and her husband be reunited? A marriage of long separation between husband and wife seemed also to be Philadelphia's daughter's fate.

In her letter to Woodman Philadelphia had indicated that she would not be needing to stay at Cleveland Row for much more than three weeks, but now it seems there would be no brief stay in England. A quick return to Paris seems out of the question. The swiftness of the takeover of Paris by mobs was surprising, and by October, thousands of Parisians had marched on Versailles with the royal family soon surrendering to the will of the new order.

> A triumphal procession set out on the muddy march back to Paris – National Guard armed and royal bodyguards disarmed, wagons laden with corn and flour lumbering, market men and women straggling along, Regiment of Flanders and Swiss Guard, La Fayette riding alongside the carriage bearing the royal family, also beside them the heads of two of the Royal Guard on pikes.[16]

While Philadelphia had secured the information regarding the trust that she had come to London to seek, clearly it was not the time to think of returning to Paris. Philadelphia shares much of the responsibility for the care of her grandson, who turned three in June of 1789. At years' end, Philadelphia and Eliza, with no permanent home as yet, may have gone down to Steventon to stay with George and his family.

In France the year that followed, after a better harvest, was a quieter one, even though there was some scattering of unrest. Eliza must have felt it safe for her to return to Paris to see her husband. Hastings notes in his diary that on 24 February 1790 he 'took leave of Mme. Fde. going this morning to Paris'.[17] He notes Eliza's return three months later on 25 May: 'Mme de Feuillide arrd. this morning'.[18] These two entries imply that Philadelphia did not go to France with Eliza this time and the child stayed behind too.

Eliza most likely was reunited with her husband and an arrangement made for his subsequent visit to England. In a letter to Phylly, written the following 7 January 1791 from Margate, Eliza refers to 'M. de Feuillide had given me hopes of his return to England this Winter'.[19] Cobban calls that period in France 'A cloud cuckoo-land of political ideals [where] the revolutionaries dwelt... and the king's government continued its decline into ever-increasing impotence'.[20]

Eliza's husband may have felt safe enough from any repercussions of the local peasantry who had lost the rights to the common land with his enclosures, attempts to seize his property by his creditors, or a recall to the king's army, to join his wife and mother-in-law later. Eliza's return to England in May is celebrated in a poem dedicated to her by her friend Lady Sophia Burrell, which Deirdre Le Faye reproduces in full. It refers to Eliza as a 'friend so lov'd so long deplor'd, /Welcome again to Britain's shore' and later 'We will enjoy the sweets of spring'.[21]

After Eliza's return from France at the end of May, Philadelphia and Eliza spent much of the rest of 1790 away from London. They may have been waiting for more permanent accommodation becoming available in London or they still may have been considering a return to France. Among places popular with Philadelphia were Tunbridge Wells, where their friends Lady Rous and her daughter Louisa had a house, and as the fashion for sea-bathing as a cure-all grew, Brighton and Margate.

Hastings had sold Beaumont Lodge and had purchased the lease on a house in Park Lane, into which he moved in November 1789 and which became his London residence for the next eight years.[22] Philadelphia and Eliza headed off for Margate with little Hastings for an extended stay that took them through Christmas of 1790 to the end of February 1791. While the idea of wintering on the Kent coast had not initially been the plan, the benefits to the little boy's health and 'the inconvenience of removing so numerous a family' made them remain in Margate for quite a few months.[23]

So it is back to that peripatetic life for Philadelphia; no settled home once again. Margate had taken advantage of what has been called 'the cult of cold water and of sea-bathing' with even the 'royal stamp of approval [placed] on the idea of sea-bathing' when George III recuperated at Weymouth in 1789.[24] So while Philadelphia and Eliza were right up there with the fashion, it also shows some desperation about the health of the little boy. Being 'dipped' into the freezing waters was not for fun. The health-promoting benefits of the shock from the cold plunge was supposed 'to strengthen the 'fibres'.[25] While the primary attraction was supposed to be for the health-giving properties of sea water, the new seaside resorts, like the older spa towns, catered for the entertainment of the well-to-do patrons, with the new Theatre Royal opening in Margate in 1787. However, Eliza bemoans to Phylly the lack in January of 'any Rooms Balls or Plays and hardly any agreeables in Margate' at that time of year.[26] But 'Grandmamma' Philadelphia has been occupied with teaching 4-and-a-half-year-old Hastings 'his letters', in which Eliza tells Phylly she has succeeded.[27] Philadelphia has been in correspondence with the family at Steventon and she and Eliza also had a visit from Edward Austen, back from his Grand Tour at last.

While her husband had told Eliza he intended to return to England that winter, she tells Phylly that the situation in France now means he cannot 'quit the Continent at this Juncture'.[28] Philadelphia's son-in-law has closely aligned himself with the Royalists and emigres. If known on his return to Gabarret, surely that would have singled him out as even more of a target for local revolutionaries. He was certainly back in Gabarret in 1791 and living in the *Le Château Marais,* for in August 1791 a farmer had provided the comte with grain between September 1790 and August 1791 and owes him money.[29] But the way of life of the *'seigneur'* of *Le Château Marais* of Gabarret is beginning to look very problematic indeed.

Chapter 21

Final Days
1791–1792

Notwithstanding all her Sufferings however her Spirits continue surprisingly good, and she appears (I say appears for perhaps she only seems thus in order to keep up my spirits) convinced that time & patience will accomplish her Cure.

Letter from Eliza to Phylly Walter,
23 December 1791

PHILADELPHIA RETURNS TO London from Margate with Eliza at the end of February 1791 and at last she has a permanent home, once again in Orchard Street, Marylebone. She has been assisted in this by Warren Hastings. A note in his diary for 7 February 1791, states that he 'Pd. into Harman & Co's 500£ Acct. Mrs Hancock'.[1] Philadelphia may have written to him out of some desperation. Hastings looks to have provided her with the means to lease the Orchard Street house. It is a substantial gift; a generous gift. That year Hastings does not spend much time in London. His house in Daylesford is nearing completion and his trial sits for only seven days. The prosecution's case concluded mid-year and on 3 June 1791 he gives a speech to open the defence's case, where he defends his twelve years of governorship in Bengal.

A few weeks later he moved into his new house at Daylesford, built of finest Cotswold stone with the interior resembling 'a museum with its picture room, its Indian treasures, its library of rare volumes... [and the house] notable for its modern conveniences almost unheard of at the time.[2] Hastings spent most of the rest of that year up in Daylesford and during his few visits to London to his Park Lane house when his trial required it, he visited Philadelphia from time to time, as his diary notes.

While Orchard Street was where Philadelphia had lived in her previous return to England, it may not have been the same house. She would have been relieved to settle back into a more permanent home again because, although

Eliza in January had told Phylly that her mother was 'in good health [and] indeed She has not for some time experienced any complaint except a slight attack of the Rhumatism [sic]', Philadelphia is in fact already suffering from breast cancer. At the time of a visit by her niece Phylly to Orchard Street in April 1791, just a little more than a month after their return from Margate, Philadelphia is ill with a painful 'swelling and hardness' in her breast.[3]

Philadelphia must have already been very unwell at that time, for when Eliza writes to her cousin after Phylly's return to Kent, Eliza is very open about her mother's illness and also gripped by a terrible fear. While Eliza detects 'some change for the better' since Phylly's visit, and of Philadelphia's 'Breast I trust is in a more promising state than when You quitted Town', and that she has great hopes 'I shall have the unspeakable happiness of seeing my beloved parent restored to health', there is an underlying current of doubt in the likelihood of Philadelphia's recovery.[4] Eliza's words are laced with fear. She 'hopes', 'ventures', 'thinks' and shares her heartbreaking fears with Phylly:

> You who know of what importance this event [Philadelphia's recovery] is to My peace of mind must also be convinced of the trembling anxiety with which I await it indeed what I have suffered for this last month beggars all description and has convinced me that thou' I had met with trouble before, they were all trifles compared to this last heavy affliction.[5]

And so throughout the rest of 1791 the relentless progress of the cancer takes over Philadelphia's and Eliza's lives, with Eliza's letters to Phylly tracking its passage and capturing more of the spirit of the character of Philadelphia than it has been possible to see before. In the first publication of much of Eliza's correspondence in the *Austen Papers*, the sections of Eliza's letters dealing with Philadelphia's illness were left out with the comment 'writes about her mother'. We have to be grateful to Deirdre Le Faye's work in publishing all of Eliza's remaining letters to Phylly in full to give the detail of the last year of Philadelphia's life.

Here in her letters to Phylly, in the six months from 23 June to 23 December 1791, Eliza has the time and indeed the need to pour out her feelings about her mother, and in doing so shows the love and empathy Philadelphia and her daughter share. Each one tries to spare the other anguish. Philadelphia plays down her suffering and Eliza keeps up a brave face for her mother. Since the first serious symptoms took hold, Philadelphia has consulted a woman, a 'Doctress', Eliza calls her, and has put herself under her care. The Doctress 'continues to give us the most flattering hopes of a perfect cure'.[6] Even Eliza doesn't really believe this. She tells Phylly she has given up what she calls 'the gay World' and spends all her time with her mother, hoping to divert and amuse her in order to keep her in better spirits. This, she tells Phylly, gives her 'infinitely more satisfaction' than anything else she could be doing.

No woman in England at that time could legally practise in any of the medical occupations: neither physician, surgeon nor apothecary. However some trades were in fact taken up by women on the death of their husbands, so it could be the case that some women had acquired the skills of the apothecary and practised them 'undercover' as it were. There were a number of prosecutions of women carrying out medical procedures illegally, usually brought to light by disgruntled patients. There were, however, numerous 'wise women', midwives and nurses who practised healing arts. The reality in eighteenth-century England was that medical practitioners were able to offer so little in the way of a cure for terrible diseases like breast cancer that these 'Doctresses' may have been no more quacks and charlatans than many of their legalised male colleagues. A physician had to have only a degree from a university, but not necessarily a medical one, in order to hang up his shingle.

Surgeons concentrated on the external body and surgical removal of the lump in Philadelphia's breast was an option, but a fearsome one. How successful might that be and who would be prepared to undergo it? Philadelphia was the wife of a surgeon and may have known more than most of its horrors.

By the end of the century, though, such operations, while not common, were becoming more accepted, horrific as the notion of non-anaesthetised surgery is to us, and were moreover survivable.[7] It was a demanding operation which women initially avoided at all costs. Frequently, they were only prepared to resort to it when all other remedies had failed. It was often then too late, and reputable surgeons would not operate. Edinburgh surgeon, James Latta published a treatise in three volumes entitled *A Practical System of Surgery*, where he details procedures and presents case studies on all the various aspects of what seem today gruesome practices. Latta insisted that advanced breast cancer cases should not be operated on.

> The patient's health and strength being already too much impaired by the long continuance of the disease, she must undoubtedly be very little able to bear the additional pain and weakness of one of the most formidable operations which can be performed on the human body.[8]

The author Fanny Burney gives a strikingly explicit account of the mastectomy she underwent in her apartment in Paris in September 1811. It was written some six months after the operation as a letter to her sister Esther. Fanny Burney 'seems to have feared the operation more than the cancer'.[9] When the dreadful day came, she waited in her apartment, after ensuring her husband and son were absent, for the carriages with the surgeon and his entourage to arrive. Five doctors and two assistants, all male, all dressed in black, entered her room.[10] She was given a wine cordial by the physician. When required to lie down on an old mattress which had been brought in and to remove her robe, she is almost overcome by the violation and humiliation of the process itself, never mind the impending agony, but she prepares herself to go through the terror of it all 'in order to save her life'.[11]

Philadelphia's cancer seems to have come on quickly and worsened rapidly. It is also possible that Philadelphia may have kept the breast lump to herself for quite a long time; it was a common reaction, then and now. Whatever the treatment options may have been available, there is no mention in Eliza's correspondence of any consideration of a mastectomy for her mother.

Breast cancer was very well known in the eighteenth century as essentially an incurable disease, but many authors did write about it with passion and bemoaned 'the lack of means to help their suffering patients'.[12] Treatments often began with harmless and relatively simple directions: to eat a special diet, to rest and avoid strenuous exercise. It was also considered necessary for the patient 'to remain in a calm and trouble-free state' and avoid any situations of anxiety, grief or mental anguish. And as for rest, Eliza in her letters, talks of Philadelphia's 'Spirits continue good' and while forbidden any 'violent exercise; is 'allowed to take a little Air once a Day'.[13] Other treatments were bleeding, cupping and of course sea-bathing.

Medical people of the time, while they could not cure breast cancer were often dedicated to 'relieve the symptoms of cancer, pain and ulcerations especially'.[14] Philadelphia and Eliza also persisted in seeking treatment throughout the whole course of the illness. Medicines were also an essential part of the treatment; some of which 'well proven useful and helpful by generations before, new substances promoted by the chemists and the occasional sensational novelty promising to perform miracles'.[15] It does not sound that much different to what happens today. And then there were the external applications.

> Plaster and poultices were used throughout the long century to treat the tumour from the outside. Applying pressure on the tumour with linen compresses was frequently proposed. One plaster ... was made with two spoonfuls of alum and honey mixed with half a spoonful of oatmeal. Sir Kenelm Digby [seventeenth century diplomat, privateer, and founder of the Royal Society] proposed treating breast cancer with a cataplasm made of 'an old mellow Pippin, a late sweet apple, filled with hog's grease and roasted. This was tried by Mr Bressieurs on Mrs Brent's cancerous breast and proved good in softening the tumour.'[16]

Philadelphia may have gained relief from some such treatments, for Eliza tells Phylly in her June letter that her mother has been recently in less pain than previously. She says that Philadelphia 'declares that the Pain She at one time suffered is greatly abated since She has made use of the remedy on which our Hopes are now Founded'.[17]

At the time of Eliza's June letter to Phylly, Philadelphia has only very recently allowed her family in the Steventon rectory to know about her illness. Eliza has written to George Austen. She tells Phylly that 'The family at Steventon were perfectly unacquainted with the present state of things, till the receipt of a letter which I wrote my Aunt last Saturday'.[18] It seems typical of Philadelphia not to wish to worry her brother and his family unnecessarily, but clearly her condition is such that they need to know. Edward Austen, had called in to see them at Orchard Street the previous Sunday. He had last seen them when they were staying in Margate. Edward did not know about Philadelphia's illness. He is clearly shocked by Philadelphia's condition. Eliza puts it more mildly to Phylly: 'he was much surprized at finding we had so much cause for anxiety'.[19]

On 21 June, a few days before Philadelphia is visited by her nephew, Uncle Francis Austen dies, at 93. Older than the century itself, and outliving all his siblings, he had risen to considerable wealth and prominence in his community and was the initial lynchpin in securing George Austen's future. In his will, he had left Philadelphia's brother £500. As mentioned earlier, there was nothing left to Philadelphia, whose droll comment, as reported by Eliza, was that she was not surprised that her uncle left her [Philadelphia] nothing, 'as he had given a widowed niece, Mrs Fermor, who had kept house for him since his second wife died eleven years before, a mere 100 guineas'.[20] This comment by Philadelphia seems to capture something of her character despite her being dreadfully ill.

The summer days of 1791 go by, with Philadelphia continuing unwell and Eliza doing all she can to divert her mother and assist in her care. Advanced breast cancer tumours can break through the skin, ulcerating and oozing odorous and offensive matter. One can imagine how distressing, painful and acutely embarrassing such suffering would have been for Philadelphia. Visitors are few and stays are brief, but Eliza has sought other medical advice and assistance.

On 1 August 1791, Eliza writes to her cousin and apologises for the delay in replying to a letter from Phylly. She has so little time for anything except trying to comfort Philadelphia. She is, she explains to Phylly,

> My Dear Mother's constant Companion, and using my utmost endeavours to amuse and divert her Thoughts, so that there

are few moments in the Day which I can devote to any other employment, and besides I really at intervals have been prey to such racking anxiety.[21]

Nevertheless, Eliza tries to reassure Phylly that she 'flatters' herself that her mother is better, but still in a great deal of pain. The 'Doctress' may have persuaded Philadelphia that a cure can be accomplished with time and patience, or at least that is what Philadelphia tells Eliza. At this point Eliza gives an assessment of her mother's character which is both generous and has the ring of truth.

> Her Courage and resignation under all the pain, inconvenience and confinement which She suffers is wonderful and a fresh proof of the happy disposition and excellent way of thinking which all who know her must long since have been convinced She was endowed with.[22]

Long ago Philadelphia's husband had acknowledged that she 'was not of a Melancholy disposition' and she seems able to summon some of that positive spirit in these worst of times. As someone who had enjoyed being out and about, remaining cooped up in London in the summer seems a particular trial for Philadelphia, who had always professed a love of the countryside. Eliza says that her 'Mother laments much being detained in London which You know is her Aversion and sorry I am for her sake that there appears no probability of a removal being practicable for some time to come'.[23]

So they remain in the house through the September where Philadelphia's health continues to decline. Hastings must have known for some time now of Philadelphia's illness, for when he visits her on 23 September he notes in his diary that he 'found her poorly, but hoping'.[24] It seems to sum up the situation Eliza has described to Phylly. Philadelphia now is confined to her bedchamber and sees almost no one, though Edward Austen has called again and she has been visited by her half-brother William Hampson Walter, whom she particularly wished to see. Eliza allowed him to sit with Philadelphia for a few minutes, but other visitors cannot be allowed, Eliza tells Phylly in a letter to her on 13 October. In a letter to her brother James a few weeks earlier, on 4 September 1791 Phylly tells James she has just heard from Eliza and passes on the news of the situation between mother and daughter:

> Eliza is compleatly [sic] miserable and has the hard task of being forced to appear cheerful when her heart is ready to burst with grief & vexation. My aunt privately exprest [sic] to me how much

she felt for her, & that she endeavoured to stifle her pains to avoid her of the concern of seeing her mother's suffering.[25]

Through that summer of 1791 and into the autumn, while Eliza sits by Philadelphia's bedside, Eliza's husband is in *Le Château Marais*, attempting to resolve his debts and manage his new estates amidst the turmoil of the revolution. In August, Eliza has had a letter telling her that he hopes to join her in London in September, and if so, and Philadelphia's health allows it, they plan to go to Bath. But the disorder that is rife throughout France will interrupt his plans.

Jean-François did not join Eliza in London in September 1791, but sometime after August, de Feuillide fled his estate in Guyenne after his property came under attack and had necessitated his keeping guards, one of whom was shot and killed while taking the air.[26] His 'flight' meant that under laws passed by the new Legislative Assembly, if he left France he would be considered an émigré and subject to confiscation of his property and citizenship.

So Eliza continues alone to care for Philadelphia as her condition worsens as the autumn days of 1791 draw in. On 13 October, Eliza gives a detailed account of Philadelphia's state of being in a letter to Phylly. She now has a surgeon, a Mr Rooss looking after her and some aspects of her condition have improved. Philadelphia is now able to eat something, has less pain, free from fever and able to leave her bedchamber for a few hours each day. But it is a wicked suffering. Phylly wants to visit, but Eliza is quite emphatic in telling her that: 'Your Aunt [Philadelphia] is not able to see anyone but myself, and I endeavour as much as I cannot to let her feel the want of any other nurse'.[27] On 5 October, Hastings notes in his diary that he has received a letter from Eliza saying that Philadelphia has been very ill since he last saw her on 27 September.[28]

By mid-November Philadelphia's illness has so far progressed, that she suffers a number of near-fatal collapses, and then somehow recovers. Philadelphia has been on Laudanum (a tincture of opium and alcohol) to ease her pain and help her to sleep, but is now able to come off it. Eliza calls Philadelphia 'the dear Sufferer'. She is by her illness almost reduced to being just her suffering. She has been suffering pain from this cancerous tumour now since early in the year; the tumour itself is now breaking down and Eliza wonders if this is a good thing or a bad thing. It is a bad thing. How much longer can Philadelphia continue?

Knowing that the only release from her appalling suffering would be her death, and that could not now be far off, Philadelphia makes her will on 14 December 1791. Her executors and trustees are the same as her husband's, Warren Hastings and Edward Baber. The strong India links hold to the end.

Final Days: 1791–1792

Edward Baber, friend of Hancock, guardian of the young Eliza, and great friend of Hastings, now lives nearby in Park Street.[29] The will is drawn up and witnessed by her solicitor Edward Holden Pott of 9 Grays Inn, and another gentleman, Mr Timothy William Bruce, a neighbour, called in for the occasion, for his address was 29 Orchard Street Portman Square.

Her will shows most of her own capital was on loan to her son-in-law and her bequests were entirely dependent on that £6,500 being repaid. It shows Philadelphia's consideration for others, that in her will she requested that her executors not force Jean-François into honouring the debt.[30] Eliza was her principal heir but she made a number of bequests. One was of £1,000 to Louisa Forde, her goddaughter, with the bequest being Philadelphia's attempt to make up for Louisa's lost fortune with Hancock. Another annuity was provided for Hancock's widowed sister, Olivia Lightfoot, as Hancock had wished for in his will. She also left money to provide an annuity for her grandson, Hastings de Feuillide. But all of these were dependent on the £6,500 being recovered. It never happened.

As Christmas nears, Eliza writes the last letter to her cousin that gives an account of Philadelphia's condition. While there seems to be no visit from her brother George, her half-brother, William Hampson Walter, Phylly's father, has visited Orchard Street a number of times in the past few months. On 23 December, Eliza tells Phylly that 'Your Good Father who kindly called on us some days since has undoubtedly told You how he found my Dear Mother'.[31] This attention from her older half-brother, and what must have been his anxious concern for his sister, born to his widowed mother when he was 9 years old, to have made these visits from Kent to London, points up the continuing importance of the parentless Philadelphia for what family she had. George or Edward Austen may well have come to see Philadelphia in those last months, as Eliza mentions that she has 'visits of those friends whom kind solicitude brings'.[32] But there is no evidence of the favourite nephew Henry Austen, visiting Orchard Street at this time. Indeed, 'some Coolness... [had] taken place between H. and [Eliza]' at some time after Eliza's return from France in 1789 and persisted throughout the time of Philadelphia's illness and death.[33] Shortly after Philadelphia's death, the coolness between them 'ceased'. Eliza reveals that Phylly knows about this 'Coolness', but no further explanation is revealed. It is possible that the young man wanted more from his married cousin than she was prepared to give.

There is one particular friend, however, who continues to call on Orchard Street, even as Philadelphia seems incapable of seeing anyone. Warren Hastings notes in his diary of 20 January 1792 that he 'Called on Mme de Fde. whose Mother had been attacked by symptoms of imminent danger'.[34] He may or may not at that time have seen Philadelphia for the last time. Their friendship had lasted for thirty-three years. The least you can say is that it was a special friendship between a man and a woman, and that Hastings showed a loyalty to Philadelphia to the very end of her life. It was in his character to be loyal; he was said to have never forgotten a friend, and it appears to be also an important aspect of Philadelphia's character. Had they once been lovers? It is most likely. Was Eliza his only surviving child? Most likely also. The truth of Eliza's paternity is beyond discovery. But ultimately it does not matter. What has mattered is the enduring strength of Philadelphia's and Hastings' connection.

In those last few weeks of her life, it is conjectured that Eliza may have taken Philadelphia up to Hampstead. Did somehow Philadelphia's pain-wracked and emaciated body take this short journey from Marylebone up to what was then still something of a health resort? This is evidenced by her being buried in the churchyard of St John-at-Hampstead on 6 March 1792. The date of her death is given by Deirdre Le Faye, based on the Pedigree of R.A. Austen-Leigh as 26 February 1792. There is no information on her funeral, but as Hastings and Edward Baber went to Eliza's on 7 March, the day after Philadelphia's burial, and opened her will, it suggests they may have assisted in arranging and attending the funeral on Eliza's behalf. Had her husband arrived from France to see her through her mothers' last days? It seems not, as Hastings only mentions in his diary that the will was opened in front of 'Mme. Fde.' as witness. There is no mention of Jean-François yet having arrived in London but he could have been there or very soon after, for, after obtaining leave of absence from the army, he joins Eliza for the few months following Philadelphia's death, and prior to the beginning of June, Eliza suffers a miscarriage. She tells Phylly in her letter of 3 June that she suffered 'an accident' in April, followed by a nasty fever and then chicken pox, so the comte must have been in London early enough to have made Eliza evidently pregnant by April. Eliza is now quite unwell. The agonising year watching her mother die had taken its toll.

The executors acted swiftly and probate was declared the next day. In Philadelphia's last year of her life she had suffered a great deal, but Eliza always reports that Philadelphia kept her spirits up. Did she think of her life? Did she remember herself as a young girl without a mother or a father, moving from one relative to another and feeling she never belonged, yet was treated with kindness? What about her years in the milliners; hard work but perhaps some fun living in Covent Garden with her fellow apprentices? Did she recall the people she had known? The days out to India on board the *Bombay Castle* with the other young women, like her, taking a chance on life? The kind and loyal husband she had now long out-lived, she would recall of course. What about her time in Calcutta in the governor's house with her friend Margaret Clive? That would be both a sweet and a bitter memory, and then on joining her husband in Kasimbazaar, she encounters Warren Hastings, her 'ever dear and

Final Days: 1791–1792

faithful friend', destined to become one of the exceptional figures of his age. The years in London, trying to hold it all together and maintain the standard of life she had set herself to hold onto with the haphazard remittances from India; she would recall those days and their constant financial anxieties and all the letters she wrote to her husband and to Hastings over those years; what did they say? And her daughter, her precious daughter, her great comfort from the day Eliza was born to the very end of her life; she had taken Eliza away from any malicious gossip that might have surfaced in London, to France and achieved what seemed a good marriage for her. She had become a countess with a handsome and well-connected husband, and a fine income courtesy of Hastings. And then the dear little grandson, whose life had soon became a source of sorrow and worry for them both.

She would have also thought of her family in Steventon; her brother George and all his fine brood of children. And Jane she had liked, and Jane who was particularly fond of her daughter. Perhaps I could be allowed to imagine that many of these memories came to her consciousness as she slipped away from life.

On the substantial ledger stone in the churchyard of St John-at-Hampstead, in Hampstead, London, which she shares with her grandson and her daughter, Philadelphia was described thus:

> Wife of Tysoe Saul Hancock Whose Moral excellence united the practice of every Christian virtue. She bore with pious resignation the severest trials of a tedious and painful malady and expired on the 26 Feby 1792 aged 61.

The engraving on the ledger stone has long since deteriorated to be unreadable, but a copy was found by Deirdre Le Faye who persuaded the Jane Austen Society in 1982 to have an abbreviated version re-engraved at the top of the ledger stone. That too now is barely legible. In 2015, the London Branch of the Jane Austen Society installed a metal plate in front of the ledger stone that bears the full inscription.

Eliza appears to have been quite unwell in those months after her mother's death. Her husband, whom she most likely never sees again, soon returns to France to face a most uncertain future; a future that has him guillotined two years later. Eliza must feel quite alone in the world. However, in the summer a few months after her mother's death, Eliza goes down to Steventon and stays for the rest of the year with the Austen family. Here she sought love and restoration, and found the likeness of her uncle to her mother a source of both comfort and grief. She got to know and very much like the 16-year-old Jane even more. As Eliza describes it, 'My Heart gives the preference to Jane, whose kind partiality to me, indeed requires a return of the same nature'.[35]

In the summer of that same year, Jane writes up her story *Catharine, or The Bower*, with the dedication to her sister Cassandra dated August 1792. Her recently deceased aunt and the visit by Eliza must have put Philadelphia's story very much in the mind of the young Jane, because she tells of the fate of Cecilia Wynn, which has been described as a 'bleak, frank summary of her late aunt's experience'.[36] She writes of Cecilia 'being obliged to accept the offer of one of her cousins to equip her for the East Indies'. It is referred to twice, and is placed at the centre of a lengthy argument between two of the young women, Catharine, who is outraged by the idea of 'a Girl of Genius and Feeling to be sent in quest of a husband in Bengal' as opposed to Camilla who says that Cecilia 'is not the first girl who has gone to the East Indies for a husband, and I declare I should think it very good fun if I were as poor'.[37] Tomalin calls this taking of the specific experience of Philadelphia and using it as 'a real argument... a unique moment in Austen's writing'.[38]

We know that Philadelphia's story is much more than the 'obliged' marriage. But Jane Austen, even at that young age, pinned down the pivotal experience of her real aunt's life, and it was that experience which enabled Philadelphia to break away from the predictable penniless orphan's path and find a way to live a life that was uniquely hers.

THE END

Endnotes

Introduction

1. Jane Austen, *Catharine, or the Bower*, in *Sanditon, Lady Susan, & The History of England &c. The Juvenilia and Shorter Works of Jane Austen* (London: Macmillan's Collector's Library, 2016), p. 217.
2. John C. Leffel, 'Conjugal Excursions, at Home and Abroad, in Jane Austen's "Juvenilia" and *Sanditon* (1807)', in *Jane Austen's Geographies* ed. by Robert Clarke (New York: Routledge, 2017) Ch. 2, p. 7 of 48, [e-book].
3. Claire Tomalin, *Jane Austen: A Life*, revised edn. (London: Penguin Books, 2000), p. 19.
4. Jane Austen, *Emma* ed. by Fiona Stafford (London: Penguin Books, 1996), p. 151.
5. Ibid., p. 154.
6. J. E. Austen-Leigh, *A Memoir of Jane Austen, and Other Family Recollections*, ed. by Kathryn Sutherland (Oxford: Oxford World Classics, 2002), p. 273.
7. Jane Austen, *Persuasion* ed. by Gillian Beer (London: Penguin Books, 1998), p. 220.
8. Ibid., p. 218.
9. Warren Hastings, letter to Philadelphia Hancock, 31 January 1772, repr. in Deirdre Le Faye, *Jane Austen's 'Outlandish Cousin': The Life and Letters of Eliza de Feuillide* (London: The British Library, 2002), p. 30.

Chapter 1

1. Deirdre Le Faye, *A Chronology of Jane Austen and her Family, 1600*. 2000 revised edition (Cambridge: Cambridge University Press, 2013), p. 12.
2. Mark Ballard, 'Tales of Inheritance in West Kent', in *Jane Austen's Geographies* ed. by Robert Clarke (New York: Routledge), 2017, Ch. 4. pp. 1-51, [e-book].

3. Ibid.
4. W. Austen-Leigh and R.A. Austen-Leigh, *Jane Austen: A Family Record* revised and enlarged by Deirdre Le Faye (New York: Konecky & Konecky in association with The British Library, 1989), p. 3.
5. Le Faye, *Chronology*, p. 11.
6. Ballard, Ch. 4.
7. David Nokes, *Jane Austen: A Life* (New York: Farrar Strauss & Giroux, London, 1997), p. 9.
8. Geoffrey Beard and Christopher Gilbert, eds. *Dictionary of English Furniture Makers 1660-1840* (Leeds, 1986), *British History Online* <http://www.british-history.ac.uk/no-series/dict-english-furniture-makers> [22 November 2023].
9. Deirdre Le Faye, ed. *Jane Austen's Letters*, (London: The Folio Society, 2003), p. 206.
10. University College London, Centre for the Study of Legacies of British Slavery, 'John Cope Freeman, Profile & Legacies Summary 1726-1788' <https://www.ucl.ac.uk/lbs/person/view/2146634480#> [22 November 2023].
11. Letter repr. in Richard Arthur Austen-Leigh, *Austen Papers, 1704-1856* (London: Privately pub., 1942), p. 57.
12. Jane Austen, *Mansfield Park*, ed. by Kathryn Sutherland (London: Penguin Books, 1996), p. 16.
13. Gary Kelly, 'Education and accomplishments', *Jane Austen in Context*, ed. by Janet Todd (Cambridge: Cambridge University Press, 2005), p. 256.
14. Jane Austen, *Pride and Prejudice*, ed. by Vivien Jones (London: Penguin Books, 2015), p. 38.
15. Ibid., p. 39.
16. Kelly, p. 258.

Chapter 2

1. Ballard Ch. 4, p. 11 of 51.
2. *Emma*, p. 154.
3. Tomalin, p. 15.
4. Le Faye, *Letters*, p. 183.
5. Tomalin, p. 15.
6. Ibid.
7. Amy Louise Erickson, 'Clockmakers, Milliners and Mistresses: Women Trading in the City of London Companies 1700-1750' <https://www.campop.geog.cam.ac.uk/research/occupations/outputs/preliminary/paper16.pdfErickson> [Accessed 20 February 2022].
8. Ibid., p. 18.
9. Ibid., p. 11.

10. 'Milliners', in *ENCYCLOpedia.com* [n.d.] <https://www.encyclopedia.com/fashion/encyclopedias-almanacs-transcripts-and-maps/milliners> [24 November 2023].
11. Erickson, p. 16.
12. Le Faye, *JAOC*, p. 12.
13. Letter repr. in Le Faye, *JAOC*, p. 42.

Chapter 3

1. De Courcy, *The Fishing Fleet: Husband Hunting in the Raj* (London: Phoenix, 2012), p. 14.
2. W. and R.A., Austen-Leigh, *A Family Record*, p. 4.
3. G.H. Tucker, *A Goodly Heritage, A History of Jane Austen's family* (Manchester: Carcenet New Press, 1983), p. 38.
4. De Courcy, p. 2.
5. BL Mss Eur G37/29/4ff. 55-58.
6. BL Mss Eur G/37/29/4ff. 61-62.
7. Le Faye, *Letters*, p. 332.
8. *Pride and Prejudice*, p. 123.
9. *The Watsons*, p. 353.
10. Eliza Fay, *Original Letters from India (1779-1815)*, ed. by E.M. Forster (London: The Hogarth Press, 1986), p. 128.
11. Fay, p. 229.
12. Ibid.
13. Ibid., p. 231.
14. Ibid.
15. Ibid.
16. Mark Bence-Jones, *Clive of India* (London: Constable), 1974, p. 34.
17. Ibid.
18. William Hickey, *Memoirs of William Hickey*, quoted in Katie Hickman, *She-Merchants, Buccaneers & Gentlewomen: British Women in India* (London: Virago, 2019), p. 47.
19. *Catharine, or the Bower*, pp. 204-205
20. Mrs Cassandra Austen, letter to Mrs Susannah Walter, repr. in Le Faye, *JAOC*, p. 25.

Chapter 4

1. *Catherine, or the Bower*, p. 217.
2. Ibid., pp. 215-217.

3. Brian Southern, 'Professions', in *Jane Austen in Context* ed. Janet Todd (Cambridge: Cambridge University Press, 2005), p. 366.
4. John Venn and Venn, D.J., 'Thomas Saul Hancock vicar of Hollingborne', *Alumni Cantabriginensis*, Biographical List of All Known Students, Graduates and Holders of Office at the University of Cambridge from the Earliest Times to 1900 (Cambridge at the University Press, 1922). <https://archive.org/details/alumnicantabrigipt1vol1univiala/page/n5/mode/2up> [23 November 2023], p. 298.
5. Le Faye, *Chronology*, p. 15.
6. Clifford Norton Morgan, 'Surgery and Surgeons in Eighteenth Century London', Thomas Vicary Lecture delivered at the Royal College of Surgeons of England on 26 October 1967, <https://www.ncbi.nlm.nih.gov/pmc/articles/PMC2312162/?> [15 November 2023].
7. Ibid.
8. John Wiltshire, 'Medicine, Illness and Disease', in *Jane Austen in Context* ed. by Janet Todd (Cambridge: Cambridge University Press, 2005).
9. Dirom Grey Crawford, *A History of the Indian Medical Service, 1600-1913*, London School of Hygiene and Tropical Medicine, London, 1914, <http://archive.org/details/b21352148>, [15 November 2023], p. 169.
10. Letter repr. in Richard Arthur Austen-Leigh, *Austen Papers, 1704-1856*, (London: Privately published, 1942), p. 40.
11. Letter repr. in Le Faye, JAOC, p. 19.
12. Edward Ives, *From England To India in the Year 1754 and an Historical Narrative of the Operation of the Squadron and Army in India, Under the Command of Vice Admiral Watson and Colonel Clive, in the Years 1755, 1756, 1757, including a Correspondence Between the Admiral and the Nabob Serajab Dowlab* (Edward and Charles Dilly, 1773) <https://archive.org/details/in.ernet.dli.2015.502897/page/n31/mode/2up> [12 March 2020].
13. Margaret Macmillan, *Women of the Raj: The Mothers, Wives and Daughters of the British Empire in India* (London: Thames & Hudson, 2018), p. 41.
14. Ives, p. 21.
15. Ibid., p. 19.
16. Bence-Jones, p. 175.
17. 'Lady Impey's Bird Picture', *Eastern Art Online*, Ashmolean Museum, Yoursef Jameel Centre for Islamic and Asian Art <http://jameelcentre.ashmolean.org/collection/6980/10198> [16 November 2023].
18. Ives, p. 21.
19. Letter repr. in *Austen Papers*, p. 48.
20. Fay, p. 157.
21. Letter repr. in *Austen Papers*, p. 73.
22. Bence-Jones, p. 68.

Chapter 5

1. Bence-Jones, p. 86.
2. Ives, p. 21.
3. Bence-Jones, p. 86.
4. Charlotte Mitchell and Gwendolen Mitchell, 'The identity of the sitters in Joshua Reynold's group portrait in the Gemäldegalerie, Berlin', *The Burlington Magazine,* April 2018, No 1381, Vol 160, pp 292-298.
5. William Dalrymple, *The Anarchy: The Relentless Rise of the East India Company* (London: Bloomsbury, 2019), pp. 106-7.
6. Bence-Jones, p. 92.
7. Ibid., p. 86.
8. Keith Feiling, *Warren Hastings* (London: Macmillan, 1974), p. 61.
9. Fay, p. 189.
10. Le Faye, *JAOC*, p. 17.
11. Fay, p. 197.
12. Dalrymple, p. 109.
13. Feiling, p. 18.
14. Ibid., p. 23.
15. Letter repr. in *Austen Papers,* p. 226.
16. Feiling, p. 25.
17. Bence-Jones, p. 155.
18. Dirom Grey Crawford, *A History of the Indian Medical Service, 1600-1913* London: London School of Hygiene and Tropical Medicine (London: Thacker, 1914) <http://archive.org/details/b21352148. [15 November 2023].
19. Letter of 3 March 1780, repr. in Le Faye, *JAOC*, pp. 42-44.
20. Dalrymple, p. 111.
21. Bence-Jones, p. 176.
22. Ibid., p. 178.
23. Ibid.
24. Mitchell and Mitchell, p. 294.
25. Bence-Jones, p. 191.
26. Feiling, p. 18.
27. Ibid., p. 27.

Chapter 6

1. Sydney C. Grier, 'A Friend of Warren Hastings' in *Blackwood's Edinburgh Magazine*, April 1904 (Edinburgh: W. Blackwood) <https://archive.org/

details/blackwoodsmagazi175edinuoft/page/514/mode/2up> [18 October 2023], p. 476.
2. Feiling, p. 18.
3. Ibid., pp. 22-23.
4. Bence-Jones, p. 177.
5. Letter repr. in *Austen Papers*, p. 58.
6. Ibid., pp. 59-60.
7. Feiling, p. 40.
8. G. R. Gleig, *Memoirs of the Life of Warren Hastings, first Governor-General of Bengal* (London: Bentley, 1841) <http://www.columbia.edu/itc/mealac/pritchett/00generallinks/macaulay/hastings/txt_complete.html#03> [22 November 2023], p. 229.
9. Ibid., p. 231.
10. Feiling, p. 17.
11. Cited in Mitchell and Mitchell, p. 294.
12. Macmillan, pp. 54-55.
13. Letter repr. in *Austen Papers*, p. 65.
14. Bence-Jones, p. 186.
15. Fay, p. 212.
16. Feiling, p. 28.
17. Letter repr. in *Austen Papers*, pp. 48-49.
18. Le Faye, *JAOC*, pp. 16-17.
19. Feiling, pp. 39-40.
20. Ibid.
21. Fay, p. 239.
22. Le Faye, *Chronology*, p. 25.
23. G. H. Tucker, *A Goodly Heritage, a history of Jane Austen's family* (Manchester: Carcenet New Press, 1983), pp. 28-29.
24. Le Faye, *Chronology*, p. 26.
25. Ibid.
26. Feiling, p. 39.
27. Tomalin, p. 11.
28. Patrick Turnbull, *Warren Hastings* (London: New English Library, 1975), p. 44.
29. Feiling, p. 39.
30. Mitchell and Mitchell, p. 294.
31. BL Mss Eur F 128/13.
32. Robert Clive letter to Warren Hastings, 14 August 1759, BL, MS Add.29131, fols.84–85, in Mitchell and Mitchell, p. 294.
33. BL Mss Eur F128/13.
34. Feiling, p. 41.

35. Mitchell and Mitchell, p. 294.
36. BL Mss Eur G 37/29/4. Ff. 21-22.

Chapter 7

1. Le Faye, *Chronology*, p. 24.
2. MS Eur G37/29/5 ff.1-2.
3. Eyre Chatterton, *A History of the Church of England in India Since the Early Days of the East India Company* (London: SPCK, 1924) <http://anglicanhistory.org/india/chatterton1924/05.html> [accessed 3 December 2023] Ch. V.
4. Le Faye, *JAOC*, p. 18.
5. Letter repr. in Le Faye, *Letters*, p. 221.
6. Le Faye, *JAOC*. p. 25.
7. Rozina Vizram, *Ayahs, Lascars and Princes: The story of Indians in Britain 1700-1947* (Oxford: Routledge, 2015), pp. 11-13.
8. Bence-Jones, p. 200.
9. BL Mss Eur F128/13.
10. Kathleen Blechynden, *Calcutta: Past and Present* (London: W. Thacker & Co., 1905) <https://en.wikisource.org/wiki/Calcutta:_Past_and_Present/Chapter_5> [accessed 3 December 2023], Ch. 5, p. 92.
11. Dalrymple, p. 168.
12. Feiling, p. 49.
13. Dalrymple, p. 177.
14. Feiling, p. 50.
15. Bence-Jones, p. 208.
16. Feiling, p. 51.

Chapter 8

1. Bence-Jones, p. 208.
2. Fay, p. 211.
3. Feiling, p. 310.
4. Letter repr. in *Austen Papers*, p. 43.
5. Ibid., p. 48.
6. Letter repr. in Le Faye, *JAOC*, p. 19.
7. *Persuasion*, p. 93.
8. Ibid., pp. 94-5.
9. Feiling, p. 310.

10. Ibid., p. 61.
11. Bence-Jones, p. 209.
12. Sheila Johnson Kindred, *Jane Austen's Transatlantic Sister: The Life and Letters of Fanny Palmer Austen* (Montreal & Kingston: McGill-Queen's University Press, 2017), p. 98.
13. Ibid.
14. Dennis Kincaid, *British Social Life in India, 1608-1937* (Newton Abbot: Readers Union, 1974), p. 85.

Chapter 9

1. Turnbull, p. 44.
2. Ibid., p. 45.
3. Mitchell and Mitchell, p. 296.
4. Ibid., p. 295.
5. Bence-Jones, p. 191.
6. Ibid., p. 190.
7. Mitchell and Mitchell, p. 295.
8. Ibid.
9. Ibid.
10. Bence-Jones, p. 220.
11. Ibid.
12. Mitchell & Mitchell, p. 295.
13. Ibid., p. 296.
14. Letter repr. in *Austen Papers*, p. 74.
15. W. and R.A. Austen-Leigh, *A Family Record*, p. 28.
16. Feiling, p. 55.
17. National Portrait Gallery, London, 'Mid-Georgian Portraits Catalogue', Warren Hastings by Sir Joshua Reynolds < https://www.npg.org.uk/collections/search/portraitExtended/mw02979/Warren-Hastings?> [accessed 27 November 2023].
18. Mitchell and Mitchell, p. 298.
19. Ibid., p. 297.
20. Hancock letter to Philadelphia, 23 November 1769, repr. in *Austen Papers*, p. 40.
21. University College London, Centre for the Study of Legacies of British Slavery, 'Stella Frances Allan (née Freeman)' Profile and Legacies Summary, <https://www.ucl.ac.uk/lbs/person/view/-1855725876,> [accessed 23 November 2023].
22. Le Faye, *JAOC*, p. 19.
23. Le Faye, *Chronology*, p. 31.
24. Ibid.

25. Feiling, p. 55.
26. Ibid., p. 56.
27. Ibid.
28. P.J. Marshall, 'The Personal Fortune of Warren Hastings', *The Economic History Review,* New Series, Vol. 17, No. 2 (1964), pp. 284-300, p. 285.
29. Barclay's Bank Group Archives, Goslings bank account ledger for Tysoe Saul Hancock from 23 March 1768 to 11 October 1768, ledgers 039, 041, folios 396, 380.
30. Hancock letter to Philadelphia, 29 June 1773, repr. in *Austen Papers*, p. 71.
31. 'George Berg (1730-1775)', *HH music publishers* <https://www.editionhh.co.uk/ab_G_Berg.htm> [accessed 20 November 2023].

Chapter 10

1. Letter repr. in *Austen Papers*, p. 41.
2. Turnbull, p. 47.
3. Feiling, p. 57.
4. Ibid., p. 61.
5. Virginia Blain, Patricia Clements and Isobel Grundy, *The Feminist Companion to Literature in English* (London: Batsford, 1990), p. 462.
6. Letter of 17 January 1770, repr. in *Austen Papers*, p. 46.
7. Letter of 23 November 1769, repr. in *Austen Papers, p. 39.*
8. Ibid.
9. Ibid.
10. Ibid., p. 41.
11. Ibid.
12. Ibid.
13. Feiling, p. 64.
14. Turnbull, p. 5.
15. Sydney C. Grier, *The Letters of Warren Hastings to his Wife* (Edinburgh: W. Blackwood & Sons, 1905), pp. 236-7.
16. Gleig, *Memoirs of the Life of Warren Hastings*, in Patrick Turnbull, p. 49.
17. Feiling, p. 62.
18. Turnbull, p. 51.
19. Le Faye, *Chronology*, p. 40.
20. Letter repr. in *Austen Papers*, 43.
21. Letter repr. in *Austen Papers*, p. 74.
22. Le Faye, *Chronology*, pp. 56-57.
23. Hancock letter of 17 January 1770, repr. in *Austen Papers*, p. 43.
24. Ibid., p. 46.

25. Letter of 7 September 1770, repr. in *Austen Papers*, p. 52.
26. Eliza de Feuillide letter to Phylly Walter, 1 August 1791, repr. in Le Faye, *JAOC*, p. 102.
27. Letter of 28 August 1771, repr. in *Austen Papers*, p. 56.
28. Le Faye, *Chronology*, p. 44.

Chapter 11

1. Letter repr. in *Austen Papers*, p. 41.
2. Turnbull, p. 55.
3. Warren Hastings letter to Hancock, 5 November 1769, BL. Mss 29, 125-54.
4. BL Mss 29, 125-54.
5. Le Faye, *Chronology*, p. 41.
6. Letter of 27 December 1769, repr. in *Austen Papers*, p. 42.
7. Allison Meier, 'The Curious Victorian Tradition of Making Art from Human Hair,' Feb 14, 2018, *Artsy Vanguard* < https://www.artsy.net/article/artsy-editorial-curious-victorian-tradition-making-art-human-hair> [accessed 20 November 2023].
8. Letter repr. in *Austen Papers*, pp. 53-54.
9. Letter of 6 December 1774, repr. in *Austen Papers* p. 77.
10. Letter of 13 March, 1771, repr. in *Austen Papers*, p. 54.
11. Le Faye, *Chronology*, p. 663.
12. Letter repr. in *Austen Papers*, p. 70.
13. Letter, repr. in *Austen Papers*, p. 56.
14. Letter repr. in *Austen Papers*, p. 44.
15. Warren Hastings letter to Hancock, 5 November 1769, repr. in Le Faye, *JAOC*, p. 23.
16. Hancock letter to Eliza, 21 November 1771, repr. in *Austen Papers*, p. 57.
17. *Mansfield Park*, p. 34.
18. Nigro & Phillips, 'Jane Austen, Madame de Stael and the Seductiveness of Conversation', *Persuasions on-line*, Vol. 33, No. 1, (Winter 2012) <https://jasna.org/persuasions/on-line/vol33no1/nigro-phillips.html> [accessed 3 December 2023].
19. *Mansfield Park*, p. 63.
20. Paula Byrne, *The Real Jane Austen: A Life in Small Things* (London: Harper Press, 2013), p. 40.
21. Letter repr. in *Austen Papers*, p. 71.
22. Sarah Murdan, 'Who lived in these houses on Hartford Street Mayfair?', *All Things Georgian*, 26 February 2020 <www.georgian.press.com> [accessed 14 November 2023].

23. Hancock letter to Philadelphia, 26 August 1774, repr. in *Austen Papers*, p. 76.
24. J. Crowley, 'In Happier Mansions, Warm, and Dry: The Invention of the Cottage as the Comfortable Anglo-American House'.1997, *Winterthur Portfolio*, 32(2/3), 169-188 <http://www.jstor.org/stable/1215171> [accessed 15 November 2023], p. 170.
25. Jane Austen, *Sense and Sensibility*, ed. by Ros Ballaster (London: Penguin Books, 1995), p. 30.
26. Grier, 'A Friend of Warren Hastings', p. 502.
27. Ibid., p. 503.
28. Ibid., p. 501.
29. Ibid., pp. 503-4.

Chapter 12

1. W. and R.A. Austen-Leigh, *A Family Record*, p. 31.
2. Deirdre Le Faye, 'Jane Austen and her Hancock Relatives', *The Review of English Studies,* New Series, vol. 30, no. 117 (February, 1979) pp. 12-27, p. 23.
3. Ibid.
4. Kelly, p. 257.
5. Le Faye, *Chronology*, p. 63.
6. Hancock letter to 'Molly' Freeman, 29 March 1772, repr. in *Austen Papers*, p. 61.
7. Letter of 6 December 1771, repr. in *Austen Papers*, p. 58.
8. Letter, repr. in *Austen Papers,* p. 66.
9. Thomas Harwood, *Alumni Etonenses; or a Catalogue of the Provosts & Fellows of Eton College & King's College, Cambridge, from the Foundation in 1443 to the Year 1797; With an Account of their Lives & Preferments, 1797.* <https://archive.org/details/bim_eighteenth-century_alumni-etonenses-or-a-_harwood-thomas_1797> [21 November 2023], p. 349.
10. Le Faye, *JAOC*, p. 144.
11. Ibid. p. 145.
12. Letter repr. in *Austen Papers*, p. 67.
13. Le Faye, 'Jane Austen and her Hancock Relatives', p. 23.
14. Letter of 22 June 1773, repr. in *Austen Papers*, pp. 70-1.
15. Letter of 6 December 1771, repr. in *Austen Papers*, p.58.
16. Feiling, pp. 75-6.
17. Le Faye, *JAOC*, p. 28.
18. Letter repr. in *Austen Papers*, p. 45.
19. Letter repr. in *Austen Papers*, p. 64.

20. Warren Hastings letter to Hancock, 19 July 1770, BL MSS Add, 29,125.
21. Letter repr. in *Austen Papers*, pp. 64-7
22. Ibid.
23. Ibid.
24. Feiling, p. 79.
25. Letter of 11 December 1772, repr. in *Austen Papers*, p. 69.

Chapter 13

1. Letter of 3 December 1773, repr. in *Austen Papers*, p. 74.
2. Grier, 'A Friend of Warren Hastings', p. 501.
3. Ibid.
4. Letter of 26 August 1774, repr. in *Austen Papers*, p. 77.
5. Letter of 31 January 1772, repr. in *Austen Papers*, p. 59.
6. Letter of 5 November 1769, *JAOC*, p. 23.
7. Letter repr. in *Austen Papers*, p. 68.
8. Deirdre Le Faye, *Chronology*, p. 55.
9. Eric W. Nye, 'Pounds Sterling to Dollars: Historical Conversion of Currency'. <https://www.uwyo.edu/numimage/currency.htm> [2 September 2020].
10. Letter repr. in *Austen Papers*, p. 73.
11. C.T. Onions, ed. *The Shorter Oxford English Dictionary*, 3rd edition (Oxford: Oxford University Press, 1973), vol. 1, p. 578.
12. Letter repr. in *Austen Papers*, p. 74.
13. Letter repr. in *Austen Papers*, p. 75.
14. Letter of 3 September 1773, repr. in *Austen Papers*, p. 73.
15. Le Faye, *Chronology*, p. 62.
16. Mrs Cassandra Austen letter to William-Hampson Walter and family, June 1773, quoted in Austen-Leigh, *A Family Record*, p. 23.
17. Feiling, p. 88.
18. Ibid., p. 89.
19. Le Faye, *Chronology*, p. 60.
20. Letter of 26 August 1774, repr. in *Austen Papers*, p. 76.
21. Philip Dormer Stanhope, *Genuine memoirs of Asiaticus, in a series of letters to a friend, during five years residence in different parts of India*, 1784 <https://archive.org/details/bim_eighteenth-century_genuine-memoirs-of-asiat_stanhope-philip-dormer_1784> [accessed 31 December 2020].
22. Ibid., p. 13.
23. Ibid., p. 14.
24. Letter of 26 August 1774, repr. in *Austen Papers*, p. 76.
25. Letter repr. in *Austen Papers*, p. 78.

26. Stanhope, pp. 43-5.
27. Ibid., p. 50.
28. Letter of 20 February 1775, repr. in *Austen Papers*, p. 78.
29. Stanhope, pp. 44-5.
30. Ibid., p. 52.
31. Letter repr. in *Austen Papers*, pp. 77-8.
32. Stanhope, pp. 67-8.
33. Letter repr. in *Austen Papers*, p. 80.
34. Letter of 26 August 1774, repr. in *Austen Papers*, pp. 76-7.
35. Ibid.
36. Le Faye, *Chronology*, p. 63.
37. Le Faye, *Chronology*, p. 63.

Chapter 14

1. Letter repr. in *Austen Papers*, pp. 79-80.
2. Will of Tysoe Saul Hancock, Merchant of Bengal, East Indies, 17 November 1781 PROB/11/1084/184, National Archives, Kew, <https://discovery.nationalarchives.gov.uk/details/r/D405768> [24 September 2019].
3. Letter repr. in *Austen Papers*, p. 54.
4. Le Faye, *Chronology*, p. 64.
5. *Pride and Prejudice*, p. 147.
6. Ibid.
7. Letter repr. in *Austen Papers*, p. 81.
8. Stanhope, p. 70.
9. Ibid., pp. 115-16.
10. Letter repr. in *Austen Papers*, p. 81.
11. Rosie Llewelyn Jones, 'City of the Dead: South Park Street Cemetery', *Sahapedia*, 3 February 2017 <https://www.sahapedia.org/city-of-the-dead-south-park-street-cemetery> [20 November 2023].
12. Find a Grave, Memorials, 'Tysoe Saul Hancock' <https://www.findagrave.com/memorial/69079188/tysoe-saul-hancock#> [accessed 21 December 2023].
13. W. and R. A. Austen-Leigh, *A Family Record*, p. 24.
14. Le Faye, *Chronology*, p. 66.
15. D. M. Joslin, 'London Private Bankers, 1720-1785'. *The Economic History Review*, vol. 7, no. 2, 1954, <https:www.jstor.org/stable/2591620> [27 November 2020].
16. Le Faye, *Chronology*, p. 67.
17. Letter of 25 March 1775, repr. in *Austen Papers*, p. 79.
18. Le Faye, *Chronology*, p. 67.

19. Ibid.
20. Alfred Cobban, *A History of Modern France*, Vol 1: 1715-1799, 3rd edn. (Harmondsworth: Penguin, 1963), p. 105.
21. Feiling, p. 179.

Chapter 15

1. Feiling, p. 39.
2. Le Faye, *Chronology*, p. 67.
3. Ibid., p. 68.
4. George Vansittart, letter to Warren Hastings, 17 December 1776, in Le Faye, *JAOC*, p. 39.
5. Philadelphia, letter to Hastings, 3 March 1780, repr. in *JAOC*, pp. 42-4.
6. Le Faye, *Chronology*, p. 23.
7. Ibid.
8. Ibid., p. 62.
9. Philadelphia, letter to Hastings, 3 March 1780, repr. in *JAOC*, pp. 42-4.
10. Le Faye, *Chronology*, p. 82.
11. Abbe Michel Devert, 'Le Marais de Gabarret et de Barbotan', Extrait du Bulletin de la Societe de Borda (Aire-sur-l'Adour: Castay S.A.R.L, 1970) 6.
12. Le Faye, *JAOC*, p. 40.
13. Le Faye, *Chronology*, p. 68.
14. Philadelphia's account, Hoare's ledger #100 Folio #406.
15. 'Five Ways to Compute the Relative Value of a UK Pound Amount, 1270 to Present'. MeasuringWorth, 2023 www.measuringworth.com/ukcompare/ [27 November 2023].
16. Eliza, letter to Phylly Walter, 27 March 1782, repr. in *JAOC*, p. 52-5.
17. Eliza, letter to Phylly Walter, 16 May 1780 repr. in *JOAC*, p. 45-7.
18. Henry Hoare Jnr., letter to Philadelphia, 2 June 1778, Hoare's bank Archive.
19. Eliza, letter to Phylly Walter, 7 May, 1784, repr. in *JAOC*, p. 62.
20. Williams, Mike, 'A brief encounter with Jane Austen's Aunt and Cousin in Paris 1786', 24 Oct. 2017, Archives and Manuscripts at the Bodleian Library: A Bodleian Library blog. <https://blogs.bodleian.ox.ac.uk/archivesandmanuscripts/author/webbm/> [23 November 2023].
21. Philadelphia, letter to Hastings, 3 March 1780, repr. in *JAOC*, pp. 42-4.
22. Ibid.
23. Ibid.
24. Ibid.
25. Letter repr. in *Austen Papers*, 52.
26. Philadelphia Letter to Hastings, 3 March 1780, repr. in *JAOC*, pp. 42-4.

27. Ibid.
28. Le Faye, *JAOC*, p. 44.

Chapter 16

1. Eliza, letter to Phylly Walter, 27 June 1780, repr; in *JAOC*, pp. 48-50.
2. Eliza, letter to Phylly Walter, 16 May, 1780, repr. in JAOC, pp. 45-7.
3. Ibid.
4. Marius Tallon, *La Vitesse Adolphe, Rose-Marie- Hélène de Tournon* (Ardeche: Impr. Centrale de l'Ardeche, 1892) <https://play.google.com/books/reader?id=PFvnx_j33-AC&pg=GBS.PA136&hl=en> [accessed 24 October 2021].
5. Robert Darnton, *The Forbidden Best-Sellers of Pre-Revolutionary France* (London: Harper Collins, 1996) Ch. IV, '*Anecdotes sur Mme la comtesse du Barry*', (London, 1775, probably written by Mathieu-François Pidansat de Mairobert) pp. 337- 89.
6. Minega, *Canalblog*, 'Royal Favorites 11 Louis XV of France, Hélène de Tournon, little mistress of the Beloved' <http://favoritesroyales.canalblog.com/archives/2012/07/28/24790120.html> [accessed 22 December 2023].
7. Tallon, p. 211.
8. Letter of 23 November 1769, repr. in *Austen Papers*, p. 41.
9. Ibid.
10. James M. Holzman, *The Nabobs in England: A Study of the Returned Anglo-Indian, 1760-1785* (New York: Columbia University, 1916) <https://archive.org/details/dli.ernet.16727> [accessed 21 November 2023].
11. Tallon, p. 155.
12. Eliza, letter to Phylly Walter 27 June 1780, repr. in *JAOC*, pp. 48-50.
13. Ibid.
14. Ibid.
15. Philadelphia, letter to John Woodman, 5 February 1789, repr. in *JAOC*, pp. 92-3.
16. Eliza, letter to Phylly Walter, 27 June 1780, repr. in *JAOC*, pp. 48-50.
17. Eliza, letter to Phylly Walter, 27 March 1782, repr. in *JAOC*, pp. 52-5.
18. Le Faye, *Chronology*, p. 84.
19. Abbe Michel Devert, 'Le Marais de Gabarret et de Barbotan', *Extrait du Bulletin de la Société de Borda* (Aire-sur-l'Adour: Castay S.A.R.L., 1970).
20. Sue Aran, 'What to see and do in Nerac Gascony The Gers', *The Good Life France* (n.d.) <https://thegoodlifefrance.com/what-to-see-and-do-in-nerac-gascony-the-gers/> [accessed 27 November 2023].
21. Devert, p. 6.

22. Pierre Goubert, *The Ancien Régime: French Society 1600-1750*, translated by Steve Cox (London: Phoenix, 1997), p. 233.
23. Devert, p. 6.
24. Ibid.
25. Le Faye, *Chronology*, p. 105.
26. Rodney Edvinsson, 'Historicalstatistics.org: Historical currency converter (test version 1.0)' <http://www.historicalstatistics.org/Currencyconverter.> [23 September 2022].
27. Le Faye, *Chronology*, p. 84.
28. John Woodman, letter to Warren Hastings, 7 August 1781, repr. in *JAOC*, p. 51.
29. Eliza, letter to Phylly Walter, 27 March 1782, repr. in *JAOC*, pp.52-5.
30. Phylly Walter, letter to James Walter, 19 September 1787, repr. in *JAOC*, p. 80.
31. Eliza, letter to Phylly Walter, 26 October 1792, repr. in *JAOC*, pp. 115-19.
32. Devert, p. 8.
33. John Woodman, letter to Warren Hastings, 26 December 1781, repr. in *JAOC*, pp. 51-2.
34. Eliza, letter to Phylly Walter, 27 March 1782, repr. in *JAOC*, pp. 52-5.
35. F. C. Green, *The Ancien Régime: A Manual of French Institutions and Social Classes* (Edinburgh: Edinburgh University Press, 1958), p. 51.

Chapter 17

1. Eliza, letter to Phylly Walter, 27 March, 1782, repr. in *JAOC*, p. 52-5.
2. Devert, p. 6.
3. Eliza, letter to Phylly Walter, 22 August 1788, repr. in *JAOC*, pp. 88-90.
4. Thomas Woodman, letter to Warren Hastings, 26 December 1781, *Chronology*, p. 85.
5. Eliza, letter to Phylly Walter, 27 March 1782, repr. in *JAOC*, p. 52-5.
6. Ibid.
7. Ibid.
8. Ibid.
9. Devert, p. 7.
10. Ibid., p. 8.
11. Ibid.
12. Eliza, letter to Phylly Walter, 1 May 1783, repr. in *JAOC*, pp. 56-9.
13. Le Faye, *Chronology*, p. 91.
14. Tomalin, p. 38.
15. Eliza, letter to Phylly Walter, 7 May 1784, repr. in *JAOC*, pp. 59-62.

16. Ibid.
17. Ibid.
18. Ibid.
19. Ibid.
20. Devert, p. 8.
21. Eliza, letter to Phylly Walter, 7 May 1784, repr. in *JAOC*, pp. 59-62.
22. Ibid.
23. Eliza, letter to Phylly Walter, 1 May 1783, repr. in *JAOC*, pp. 56-9.

Chapter 18

1. Letter repr. in Le Faye, *JAOC*, pp. 64-7.
2. Devert, p. 12.
3. Letter repr. in Le Faye, *JAOC*, p. 64-7.
4. John Woodman, letter to Hastings, 26 December 1781, in Le Faye, *JAOC*, pp 51-2.
5. Letter repr in Le Faye, *JAOC*, pp. 64-7.
6. Feiling, p. 332.
7. Ibid.
8. Ibid., p. 333.
9. Devert, p. 12.
10. Ibid.
11. Letter repr in Le Faye, *JAOC*, pp. 64-7.
12. Le Faye, *JAOC*, p. 70.
13. Letter repr. in Le Faye, *JAOC*, pp.68-70.
14. Ibid.
15. Ibid.
16. Letter repr. in Le Faye, *JAOC*, pp. 63-4.
17. Ibid.
18. Williams, 24th October 2017.
19. Ibid.
20. Le Faye, *Chronology*, p. 110.
21. Ibid.
22. Ibid.
23. Ibid., p. 105.
24. Ibid.
25. Feiling, p. 345.
26. Ibid., p. 344.
27. Will of Anne Hastings, National Archive PROB 11/1145/25.
28. Feiling, p. 344.

29. Le Faye, *Chronology*, p. 106.
30. Burney, Fanny, *The Project Gutenberg eBook of The Diary and Letters of Madame D'Arblay — Volume 1* 'A Visit to Warren Hastings and his Wife' < https://www.gutenberg.org/files/5826/5826-h/5826-h.htm#link2H_4_0146?> [27 November 2023].
31. Le Faye, *Chronology*, p. 106.
32. Friends of Valentines Mansion, 'Sir Charles Raymond of Valentines 1754 – 1788'<https://valentines.org.uk/charles-raymond-of-valentines-1754-1788> [27 November 2023].
33. Le Faye, *JAOC*, p. 84.
34. Le Faye, *Chronology*, p. 106.
35. Ibid., p. 107.
36. Ibid.
37. R.A. Austen-Leigh, *Austen Papers*, p. 88.

Chapter 19

1. *Henry and Eliza*, in *Sanditon, Lady Susan Etc.*, p. 57.
2. W. and R. A. Austen-Leigh, *Family Record*, p. 52.
3. Le Faye, *JAOC*, p. 25.
4. Mrs Cassandra Austen, letter to Phylly Walter, repr. in le Faye, *JAOC*, pp. 74-5.
5. Le Faye, *JAOC*, p. 75.
6. Mrs Cassandra Austen, letter to Phylly Walter, repr. in le Faye, JAOC, pp. 74-5.
7. W. and R. A. Austen-Leigh, *Family Record*, p. 55.
8. Le Faye, *Chronology*, p. 102.
9. Feiling, p. 347.
10. Ibid., p. 348.
11. David Ross, 'Almack's Assembly Rooms', *Britain Express*, 'Passionate about British History' <https://www.britainexpress.com/History/almacks.htm > [accessed 22 November 2023].
12. Eliza, letter to Phylly repr. in Le Faye, *JAOC*, pp. 76-7.
13. Phylly Walter, letter to James Walter, repr. in Le Faye, *JAOC*, pp. 79-81.
14. Letter repr. in *Austen Papers*, p. 60.
15. Phylly Walter, letter to James Walter, repr. in Le Faye, JAOC, pp. 79-81.
16. Ibid.
17. Byrne, p. 17.
18. Le Faye, *JAOC*, p. 176.
19. W. and R. A. Austen-Leigh, *Family Record*, p. 58.

20. Tomalin, p. 236.
21. Devert, p. 9-10.
22. Feiling, p. 350.
23. Ibid.
24. Le Faye, *Chronology*, p. 114.
25. Phylly Walter, letter to James Walter, 21 April, 1788, repr. in Le Faye, *JAOC*, pp. 84-5.
26. Phylly Walter letter to James Walter, repr. in Le Faye, *JAOC*, pp. 85-7.
27. Ibid.
28. Eliza, letter to Phylly Walter, 22 August 1788, repr. in Le Faye, *JAOC*, pp.88-90.
29. Ibid.

Chapter 20

1. Cobban, p. 132.
2. Ibid., p. 134.
3. Philadelphia, letter to John Woodman, repr. in Le Faye, *JAOC*, pp. 92-3.
4. Ibid.
5. Eliza, letter repr. in Le Faye, *JAOC*, pp. 93-6.
6. Ibid.
7. Devert, p. 10.
8. Ibid., p. 12.
9. Philadelphia, letter to John Woodman, Le Faye, *JAOC*, pp 92-3.
10. Devert, p. 9.
11. Cobban, pp. 147-8.
12. Devert, pp. 11-3.
13. Le Faye, *Chronology*, p. 124.
14. Ibid.
15. Ibid.
16. Cobban, p. 162.
17. Le Faye, *Chronology*, p. 128.
18. Ibid., p. 129.
19. Eliza, letter to Phylly Walter, repr. in Le Faye, *JAOC*, pp. 97-99.
20. Cobban, p. 169.
21. Le Faye, *JAOC*, pp. 99-100.
22. Feiling, p. 352.
23. Eliza, letter to Phylly Walter, repr. in Le Faye, *JAOC*, pp. 97-99.
24. Wiltshire, p. 310.
25. Ibid.

26. Eliza, letter to Phylly Walter, repr. in Le Faye, *JAOC*, pp. 97-99.
27. Ibid.
28. Ibid.
29. Devert, p. 13.

Chapter 21

1. Le Faye, *Chronology*, p. 132.
2. Turnbull, p. 218.
3. Eliza, letter to Phylly Walter, 23 June 1791, repr. in Le Faye, *JAOC*. pp. 100-1.
4. Ibid.
5. Ibid.
6. Ibid.
7. Marjo Kaartinen, *Breast Cancer in the Eighteenth Century* (London: Routledge, 2016).
8. Ibid., p. 72.
9. Ibid., p. 89.
10. Ibid., p. 92.
11. Ibid., p. 93.
12. Ibid., p. 2.
13. Eliza, letter to Phylly Walter, 23 June 1791, repr. in Le Faye, *JAOC*. pp. 100-1.
14. Kaartinen, p. 15.
15. Ibid., p.16.
16. Ibid., pp. 20-2.
17. Eliza, letter to Phylly Walter, 23 June 1791, repr. in Le Faye, *JAOC*. pp. 100-1
18. Ibid.
19. Ibid.
20. Eliza, letter to Phylly Walter, 1 August 1791, repr. in Le Faye, *JAOC*, pp. 101-2.
21. Letter repr. in Le Faye, *JAOC*, p. 101-3.
22. Ibid.
23. Ibid.
24. Le Faye, *Chronology*, p. 136.
25. Phylly Walter, letter to James Walter repr. in Le Faye, *JAOC*, p. 103.
26. Devert, p. 13.
27. Eliza, letter to Phylly Walter, 13 October 1791, repr. in Le Faye, *JAOC*, pp. 104-6.
28. Le Faye, *Chronology*, p. 136.

29. Feiling, p. 136.
30. Will of Philadelphia Hancock, The National Archives, PROB 11/12/1216/92 <https://discovery.nationalarchives.gov.uk/results/r?_dss=range&_ro=any&_p=1700&_q=Philadelphia+Hancock> [28 November 2023].
31. Eliza, letter to Phylly Walter, repr. in Le Faye, *JAOC*, pp. 109-11.
32. Ibid.
33. Eliza, letter to Phylly Walter 26 October 1792, repr. in Le Faye, *JAOC*, pp. 115-19.
34. Le Faye, *Chronology*, p. 140.
35. Eliza, letter to Phylly Walter 26 October 1792, repr. in Le Faye, *JAOC*, pp. 115-19.
36. Tomalin, p. 82.
37. *Catharine, or the Bower*, p. 218.
38. Tomalin, p. 89.

Selected Bibliography

Unpublished sources

Barclay's Bank Group Archives, Goslings bank account ledger for Tysoe Saul Hancock from 23 March 1768 to 11 October 1768, ledgers 039, 041, folios 396, 380

Clive, Margaret, letters sent and received from 1759, BL, MS Eur G37/29

Carnac, John, letters on Microfiche, BL, MS Eur F128/13 and to Margaret Clive MS Eur G37/29

Hancock, Tysoe Saul, letter book, in Hastings Papers, BL, Add MS 29/236

Hastings, Warren, letters in Hastings Papers, BL, Add MS, 29/125 to MS 41/608

__, diary in Hastings Papers, BL, Add MS 39880/ 39881/ 39882

Hoare's Bank, London, Ledger of Philadelphia Hancock's account from 9 April 1777 to 16 November 1782, ledger 100, folio 406

Le Faye, Deirdre, 'Le Faye Collection', 'Hancocks file', held by Chawton House Trust

Woodman, John, letters to Warren Hastings in Hastings Papers, BL, Add MS 29/133 folios 24-25

Published sources

Adkins, Roy and Leslie Adkins, *Jane Austen's England* (New York: Viking, 2013)

Aran, Sue, 'What to see and do in Nerac Gascony The Gers', *The Good Life France* (n.d.) <https://thegoodlifefrance.com/what-to-see-and-do-in-nerac-gascony-the-gers/> [accessed 27 November 2023]

Austen, Jane, *Sanditon, Lady Susan, & The History of England &c, The Juvenilia and Shorter Works of Jane Austen* (London: Macmillan's Collector's Library, 2016)

__, *Emma*, ed. by Fiona Stafford (London: Penguin Books, 1996)

__, *Mansfield Park*, ed. by Kathryn Sutherland (London: Penguin Books, 1996)
__, *Persuasion*, ed. by Gillian Beer (London: Penguin Books, 1998)
__, *Pride and Prejudice*, ed. by Vivien Jones (London: Penguin Books, 2015)
__, *Sense and Sensibility*, ed. by Ros Ballaster (London: Penguin Books, 1995)
Austen-Leigh, J.E., *A Memoir of Jane Austen, and Other Family Recollections*, ed. by Kathryn Sutherland (Oxford: Oxford University Press, 2002)
Austen-Leigh, Richard Arthur, *Austen Papers, 1704-1856* (London: Privately published, 1942)
Austen-Leigh, William and Richard Arthur Austen-Leigh, *Jane Austen: A Family Record,* rev. and enlarged by Deirdre Le Faye (New York: Konecky & Konecky, in association with The British Library, 1989)
Ballard, Mark, 'Tales of Inheritance in West Kent', in *Jane Austen's Geographies* ed. by Robert Clarke (New York: Routledge, 2017) Ch. 4 [e-book]
Beard, Geoffrey, and Christopher Gilbert, eds. *Dictionary of English Furniture Makers 1660-1840* (Leeds, 1986) British History Online <http://www.british-history.ac.uk/no-series/dict-english-furniture-makers> [accessed 22 November 2023]
Bence-Jones, Mark, *Clive of India* (London: Constable, 1974)
Bernstein, Jeremy, *Dawning of the Raj: the life and trials of Warren Hastings* (London: Arum Press, 2000)
Beyer, Antoine, 'la numerotation des routes francaises', 2004 <https://en.wikipedia.org/wiki/Route_nationale_20> [accessed 22 November 2023]
Blechynden, Kathleen, *Calcutta: Past and Present* (London: W. Thacker & Co., 1905) <https://en.wikisource.org/wiki/Calcutta:_Past_and_Present/Chapter_5> [accessed 3 December 2023], Ch. 5, 92
Blain, Virginia, Patricia Clements, and Isobel Grundy, *The Feminist Companion to Literature in English* (London: Bashford, 1990)
Burney, Fanny, *The Project Gutenberg eBook of The Diary and Letters of Madame D'Arblay — Volume 1* 'A Visit to Warren Hastings and his Wife' <https://www.gutenberg.org/files/5826/5826-h/5826-h.htm#link2H_4_0146?> [accessed 27 November 2023]
Byrne, Paula, *The Real Jane Austen: A Life in Small Things* (London: Harper Press, 2013)
__, 'Manners', in *Jane Austen in Context*, ed. by Janet Todd (Cambridge: Cambridge University Press, 2005), 297-305
Chatterton, Eyre, *A History of the Church of England in India Since the Early Days of the East India Company* (London: SPCK, 1924) <http://anglicanhistory.org/india/chatterton1924/05.html> [accessed 3 December 2023]
Clark, Robert, ed., *Jane Austen's Geographies* (New York: Routledge, 2018)
Cobban, Alfred, *A History of Modern France, Vol 1: 1715-1799*. 3rd edn. (Harmondsworth: Penguin, 1963)

Copeland, Edward, 'Money', in *Jane Austen in Context*, ed. by Janet Todd (Cambridge: Cambridge University Press, 2005), 317-326

Copeland, Edward and Juliet McMaster, *The Cambridge Companion to Jane Austen,* 2nd edn, (Cambridge: Cambridge University Press, 2011)

Cotton, H.E.A., *Calcutta Old and New. A Historical Handbook to the City* (Calcutta: W. Newman & Co., 1907) <https://archive.org/details/in.gov.ignca.9391/page/n3/mode/2up> [accessed 29 November 2023]

Crawford, Dirom Grey, *A History of the Indian Medical Service, 1600-1913* (London: London School of Hygiene and Tropical Medicine, 1914*)* <http://archive.org/details/b21352148> [accessed 15 November 2023]

Crowley J., 'In Happier Mansions, Warm, and Dry: The Invention of the Cottage as the Comfortable Anglo-American House', *Winterthur Portfolio*, 32(2/3) (1997) 169-188. <http://www.jstor.org/stable/1215171> [accessed 15 November 2023]

Dalrymple, William, *The Anarchy: The Relentless Rise of the East India Company* (London: Bloomsbury, 2019)

Darnton, Robert, *The Forbidden Best-Sellers of Pre-Revolutionary France* (London: Harper Collins, 1996) Ch. IV, 'Anecdotes sur Mme la comtesse du Barry' (London, 1775, probably written by Mathieu-François Pidansat de Mairobert), 337-389

De Courcy, Ann, *The Fishing Fleet: Husband Hunting in the Raj* (London: Phoenix, 2012)

Devert, Abbe Michel, 'Le Marais de Gabarret et de Barbotan', *Extrait du Bulletin de la Societe de Borda* (Aire-sur-l'Adour: Castay S.A.R.L., 1970)

Edvinsson, Rodney, 'Historicalstatistics.org: Historical currency converter (test version 1.0)'. <http://www.historicalstatistics.org/Currencyconverter.html> [accessed 23 September 2022]

ENCYCLOpedia.com,<https://www.encyclopedia.com/fashion/encyclopedias-almanacs-transcripts-and-maps/milliners> [accessed 24 November 2023]

Erickson, Amy Louise, 'Clockmakers, Milliners and Mistresses: Women Trading in the City of London Companies 1700-1750' <https://www.campop.geog.cam.ac.uk/research/occupations/outputs/preliminary/paper16.pdfErickson> [accessed 20 February 2022]

__,'Eleanor Mosley and other milliners in the City of London Companies 1700-1750', *History Workshop Journal* 71, (spring 2011), (Oxford: Oxford University Press, 2011), 147-72

'John Woodman 1724-1816', In *Epsom and Ewell History Explorer* <https://eehe.org.uk/?p=25771> [accessed 2 May 2020]

Fay, Mrs Eliza, *Original Letters from India (1779-1815)*, with Introductory and Terminal Notes by E.M. Forster (London: The Hogarth Press, 1986)

Feiling, Keith, *Warren Hastings* (London: Macmillan, 1974)

Find a Grave, Memorials, 'Tysoe Saul Hancock' <https://www.findagrave.com/memorial/69079188/tysoe-saul-hancock#> [accessed 21 December 2023].

Finn, Margo and Kate Smith, eds., *The East India Company at Home, 1757-1852* (London: University College of London Press, 2018)

Friends of Valentines Mansion, 'Sir Charles Raymond of Valentines 1754 – 1788' <https://valentines.org.uk/charles-raymond-of-valentines-1754-1788> [accessed 27 November 2023]

'George Berg (1730-1775)', *HH music publishers* <https://www.editionhh.co.uk/ab_G_Berg.htm> [accessed 20 November 2023]

Gleig, G.R., *Memoirs of the Life of Warren Hastings, First Governor-General of Bengal*, 3 vols. (London: Bentley, 1841) <https://archive.org/details/memoirsoflifeofr02gleiuoft> [22 November 2023]

Goubert, Pierre, *The Ancien Régime: French Society 1600-1750*, trans. by Steve Cox (London: Phoenix, 1997)

Green, F.C., *The Ancien Régime: A Manual of French Institutions and Social Classes* (Edinburgh: Edinburgh University Press, 1958)

Grier, Sydney C., 'A Friend of Warren Hastings', *Blackwood's Edinburgh Magazine*, April, 1904 (Edinburgh: W Blackwood, 1904) <https://archive.org/details/blackwoodsmagazi175edinuoft/page/514/mode/2up> [accessed 18 October 2020]

__, 'A God-daughter of Warren Hastings', *Temple Bar*, Jan. 1902-Dec.1905, London vol. 131, iss. 534, 562-571

__, *The Letters of Warren Hastings to his Wife* (Edinburgh: W. Blackwood and Sons, 1905)

Halperin, John, *The Life of Jane Austen* (Baltimore: Johns Hopkins University Press, 1996)

Harwood, Thomas, *Alumni Etonenses; or a Catalogue of the Provosts & Fellows of Eton College & King's College, Cambridge, from the Foundation in 1443 to the Year 1797; With an Account of their Lives & Preferments, 1797*. https://archive.org/details/bim_eighteenth-century_alumni-etonenses-or-a-_harwood-thomas_1797> [accessed 21 November 2023]

Hickman, Katie, *She-Merchants, Buccaneers & Gentlewomen: British Women in India* (London: Virago, 2019)

Holzman, James M., *The Nabobs in England: A Study of the Returned Anglo-Indian, 1760-1785*. (New York: Columbia University, 1916) <https://archive.org/details/dli.ernet.16727> [accessed 21 November 2023]

Ives, Edward, *From England To India in the Year 1754 and an Historical Narrative of the Operation of the Squadron and Army in India, Under the Command of Vice Admiral Watson and Colonel Clive, in the Years 1755, 1756, 1757, including a Correspondence Between the Admiral and the Nabob Serajab Dowlab* (Edward and Charles Dilly, London, 1773) <https://archive.org/details/in.ernet.dli.2015.502897/page/n31/mode/2up> [accessed 21 November 2023]

Jeffers, Regina, 'Fleet Prison Marriages of the 1700s'. 25 September 2020. <https://reginajeffers.blog/2020/09/23/fleet-prison-marriages-of-the-1700s/> [accessed 21 November 2023]

Johnston, Freya, *Jane Austen, Early and Late* (Princeton & Oxford: Princeton University Press, 2021)

Joslin, D.M., 'London Private Bankers, 1720-1785', *The Economic History Review*, vol. 7, no. 2, (1954), 167–186 <www.jstor.org/stable/2591620> [accessed 14 November 2023]

Kaartinen, Marjo, *Breast Cancer in the Eighteenth Century* (London: Routledge, 2016)

Kelly, Gary, 'Education and accomplishments', in *Jane Austen in Context*, ed. by Janet Todd (Cambridge: Cambridge University Press, 2005), 252-261

Kincaid, Dennis, *British Social Life in India, 1608-1937* (Newton Abbot: Readers Union: 1974)

Kindred, Sheila Johnson, *Jane Austen's Transatlantic Sister: The Life and Letters of Fanny Palmer Austen* (Montreal & Kingston: McGill-Queen's University Press, 2017)

'Lady Impey's Bird Picture', Eastern Art Online, Ashmolean Museum, Yousref Jameel Centre for Islamic and Asian Art <http://jameelcentre.ashmolean.org/collection/6980/10198> [accessed 20 November 2023]

Le Faye, Deirdre, *A Chronology of Jane Austen and her Family, 1600-2000*, rev. edn (Cambridge: Cambridge University Press, 2013)

__, 'Jane Austen and Her Hancock Relatives', *The Review of English Studies*, New Series, vol. 30, no. 117 (February, 1979) 12-27

__, *Jane Austen's 'Outlandish Cousin': The Life and Letters of Eliza de Feuillide*. London: British Library, 2002

__, ed. *Jane Austen's Letters* (London: The Folio Society, 2003)

Leffel, John C. 'Conjugal Excursions, at Home and Abroad, in Jane Austen's "Juvenilia" and *Sanditon* (1807)', in *Jane Austen's Geographies* ed. by Robert Clarke (New York: Routledge, 2017) Ch. 2, 1-48, [e-book]

Llewelyn Jones, Rosie, 'City of the Dead: South Park Street Cemetery'. 3 February 2017, Sahapedia <https://www.sahapedia.org/city-of-the-dead-south-park-street-cemetery> [accessed 20 November 2023]

Macmillan, Margaret, *Women of the Raj: The Mothers, Wives and Daughters of the British Empire in India* (London: Thames & Hudson, 2018)

Marshall, P. J., 'The Personal Fortune of Warren Hastings', *The Economic History Review*, New Series, vol. 17, no. 2, (1964), 284-300

__, ed., *Trade and Conquest: Studies on the rise of British dominance in India* (Brookfield, Vt., Variorum, 1993)

Maxwell, M., 'Protestant Marriage in Eighteenth Century France', *Social Science*, 1955, 30 (2) 89–93 <http://www.jstor.org/stable/41884368> [accessed 21 November 2023]

Selected Bibliography

Measuring Worth, 'Five Ways to Compute the Relative Value of a UK Pound Amount, 1270 to Present', 2023 <www.measuringworth.com/ukcompare/> [accessed 27 November 2023]

Meier, Allison, 'The Curious Victorian Tradition of Making Art from Human Hair,' 14 February 2018, Artsy Vanguard < https://www.artsy.net/article/artsy-editorial-curious-victorian-tradition-making-art-human-hair> [accessed 20 November 2023]

Minega, *Canalblog*, 'Royal Favorites 11 Louis XV of France, Hélène de Tournon, little mistress of the Beloved' <http://favoritesroyales.canalblog.com/archives/2012/07/28/24790120.html> [accessed 22 December 2023]

Mitchell, Charlotte & Gwendolen Mitchell, 'The Identity of the Sitters in Joshua Reynold's Group Portrait in the Gemaldegalerie, Berlin', *The Burlington Magazine*, April 2018, vol. 160, no 1381, 292-98

Morgan, C.N., 'Surgery and Surgeons in 18th-Century London', Thomas Vicary Lecture delivered at the Royal College of Surgeons of England, 26th October 1967 <https://www.ncbi.nlm.nih.gov/pmc/articles/PMC2312162/?> [accessed 15 November 2023]

Murdan, Sarah, 'Who lived in these houses in Hertford Street Mayfair?' February, 26, 2020. *All Things Georgian* <https://georgianera.wordpress.com/2020/02/26/who-lived-in-these-houses-on-hertford-street-mayfair/> [accessed 14 November, 2023]

Murphy, David, 'James Louis Count Rice', in *Dictionary of Irish Biography* <https://www.dib.ie/biography/rice-james-louis-a7655> [accessed 23 September 2022]

National Portrait Gallery London, 'Mid-Georgian Portraits Catalogue', Warren Hastings by Sir Joshua Reynolds < https://www.npg.org.uk/collections/search/portraitExtended/mw02979/Warren-Hastings?> [accessed 27 November 2023]

Nigro, Jeffrey A. and Phillips, William, 'Jane Austen, Madame de Stael and the Seductiveness of Conversation', *Persuasions on-line*, vol. 33, no.1, (winter 2012) <https://jasna.org/persuasions/on-line/vol33no1/nigro-phillips.html> [accessed 3 December 2023]

Nokes, David, *Jane Austen: A Life* (New York: Farrar Strauss & Giroux, 1997)

Nye, Eric, W., 'Pounds Sterling to Dollars: Historical Conversion of Currency' <https://www.uwyo.edu/numimage/currency.htm> [accessed 2 September 2020]

Onions, C.T., ed., *The Shorter Oxford English Dictionary*, 3rd ed. (Oxford: Oxford University Press, 1973)

Roberts, Warren, 'Nationalism and Empire', in *Jane Austen in Context*, ed. by Janet Todd, (Cambridge: Cambridge University Press, 2005), 327-336

Ross, David, 'Almack's Assembly Rooms', *Britain Express*, 'Passionate about British History' <https://www.britainexpress.com/History/almacks.htm > [accessed 22 November 2023]

Sée Henri, *Economic and Social Conditions in France during the Eighteenth Century*, trans. by Edwin H. Zeydel (Kitchener, Ontario: Batouche Books, 2004)

Southam, Brian 'Professions', in *Jane Austen in Context*, ed. by Janet Todd, (Cambridge: Cambridge University Press, 2005), 366-376

Stanhope, Philip Dormer, *Genuine Memoirs of Asiaticus, in a series of letters to a friend, during five years residence in different parts of India* (London: G. Kearsley, 1784) <https://archive.org/details/bim_eighteenth-century_genuine-memoirs-of-asiat_stanhope-philip-dormer_1784> [accessed 31 December 2020]

Tallon, Marius, *La Vitesse Adolphe, Rose-Marie-Hélène de Tournon* (Ardeche: Impr. Centrale de l'Ardeche, 1892) <https://play.google.com/books/reader?id=PFvnx_j33-AC&pg=GBS.PA136&hl=en> [accessed 24 October 2021]

The National Archives, <https://www.nationalarchives.gov.uk/> [accessed 28 November 2023]

__, Will of Tysoe Saul Hancock, PROB/11/1084/184

__, Will of Philadelphia Hancock, PROB 11/12/1216/92

__, Will of Elizabeth Hastings, PROB 11/1145/25

Tomalin, Claire, *Jane Austen, A Life,* rev. edn (London: Penguin Books, 2000)

Tucker, G.H., *A Goodly Heritage: A History of Jane Austen's Family* (Manchester: Carcenet New Press, 1983)

Turnbull, Patrick, *Warren Hastings* (London: New English Library, 1975)

University College London, 'Centre for the Study of Legacies of British Slavery' <https://www.ucl.ac.uk/lbs/> [accessed 23 November 2023]

Venn, John and Venn, J.D., *Alumni Cantabriginensis, Biographical List of All Known Students, Graduates and Holders of Office at the University of Cambridge from the Earliest Times to 1900* (Cambridge at the University Press, 1922) <https://archive.org/details/alumnicantabrigipt1vol1univiala/page/n5/mode/2up> [accessed 23 November 2023]

Vizram, Rozina, *Ayahs, Lascars and Princes: The Story of Indians in Britain 1700-1947* (Oxford: Routledge, 2015)

Williams, Mike, 'A Brief Encounter with Jane Austen's Aunt and Cousin in Paris 1786', *Archives and Manuscripts at the Bodleian Library: A Bodleian Library Blog*, (24 Oct. 2017) <https://blogs.bodleian.ox.ac.uk/archivesandmanuscripts/author/webbm/> [accessed 23 November 2023]

Wiltshire, John, 'Medicine, Illness and Disease', in *Jane Austen in Context*, edited by Janet Todd (Cambridge: Cambridge University Press, 2005), 306-316

Index

Ackell, Mrs, 14
Adams, James, merchant, 14
Adlestrop, Gloucestershire, 43, 56, 185, 197
Agen, France, 171, 182, 187
Alipore, Calcutta, 58, 66–7, 128
Almack's Assembly Rooms, 198
Attar of Roses perfume, 78, 109
Austen, Cassandra *née* Leigh:
    letter describing PH's trip across Bagshot Heath, 24
    letter re WH's appointment as G-G of Bengal, 124
    life at Steventon, 135
    marriage to George Austen, 68, 82
    opinion of Eliza, 195–7
    opinion of PH, 24, 195–6
Austen, Edward, 151, 179, 186, 196, 211, 216–17
Austen, Francis, 3, 15, 25, 199
    agent for TSH, 25, 87, 106, 133, 143, 161
    assistance to George Austen, 106, 216
    connection to PH's travel to India, 15
    death & Will, 106, 216
    disapproval of Eliza's marriage, 174
    guardianship of brother's children, 3
    law apprenticeship, 8
    wealthy marriages, 8
Austen, Rev. George, viii, 2, 82, 135, 195
    as PH's trustee, 144, 147–8
    burgeoning family, 69
    care of George Hastings, 57, 83
    career, 12, 56
    education in Tonbridge, 3, 7
    early life, 2–4
    loan from PH, 155
    marriage to Cassandra Leigh, 68
    opinion on Eliza's marriage, 173
    Oxford, 12, 53, 56
    Steventon living, 57, 91
    tutor to George Hastings, 56–7
    visits to PH in London, 148, 204
Austen, Henry Thomas, 111, 195, 202, 204
    birth, 116
    estrangement from Eliza, 219
    resemblance to PH, 196–7
    visits to PH & Eliza, 198, 204
Austen, Rev. James, 187, 201
Austen, Jane, vii, viii, 179, 202, 204, 221
    birth & baptism, 147
    birthday gift & visit from PH & Eliza, December 1786, 194, 196–7
    comment on WH concerning Eliza, 64
    Catharine or the Bower, vii, xi, 23, 59, 222
        Camilla Stanley, 26
        Catharine 'Kitty', 26
        Cecilia Wynne, vii, 23, 26, 222
        date when written, vii
        on arranged marriages, 26
        similarities to PH's life, vii, 23, 26
    Emma, viii, 28
        Colonel Campbell, ix

Harriet Smith, viii
Jane Fairfax, viii–ix, 8
Miss Bates, viii
Mr Perry, 28
on 'single women' & poverty, 17
Henry & Eliza, 195
Mansfield Park, 4, 26, 122, 168, 201–202
    echoes of PH & Eliza in, 4–5, 112–13, 168, 202
    Edmund Bertram, 4, 113, 168
    Fanny Price, vii, viii, 4, 113, 201
    Maria Bertram, 26
    Mary Crawford, 112–13, 168
    Mr Rushworth, 26
    Mrs Price, 105
    Sir Thomas Bertram, 4
Persuasion, 70, 153
    Anne Elliot, ix–x
    Captain Wentworth, 74
    Mrs Croft, 70, 74
    Mrs Smith, 152
Pride & Prejudice, 72, 144
    Charlotte Lucas, x, 17–18, 26
    Elizabeth Bennet, 5, 17
    female accomplishments, 5–6
    marriage argument, 17
    Miss Bingley, 5
    Mr Bennet, 72
    Mr Collins, 26
    Mr Darcy, 5
Sense & Sensibility, 6
    Barton Cottage, 115
    echo of PH in Mrs Jennings, vii, 204
    Mrs Dashwood, vii, x, 6, 105, 115
The Watsons, 17–18
Austen, Leonora, viii, 4, 7, 53, 82, 135, 156, 178
Austen, Philadelphia, *see* Hancock, Philadelphia
Austen, Rebecca, formerly Walter, née Hampson, 1–2
Austen, Stephen, 3, 7
Austen Susannah, *see* Kelk, Susannah, later Austen
Austen, William, surgeon, 1–3, 12
Austen-Leigh, James Edward, ix
Austen Papers, 1704–1856, x, 203, 213

Baber, Edward, 143, 218–20
Bagnères, France, 185–6
Bagshot Heath, 24
du Barry, Comte Jean-Baptiste, 'Le Roué', 165
du Barry, Vicomte Adolphe, 165, 167
du Barry, Madame, formerly Jeanne Becu, 165
Bath, Somerset, 166–7
Beaumont Lodge, Berkshire, 189–90, 204, 211
Begum Johnson, Frances Croke, 70–1
Belle, Dido Elizabeth, 114–15
Bence-Jones, Mark, 22, 51, 79–80
Benkulen, Sumatra, 19
Berg, George, musician, 90–1
Boddam, Charles, 14
Bolton Street, Mayfair, 89
Bowers, Mrs Mary, 73, 145, 148, 162
Breast cancer treatment in 18th c, 214–16
Brussels, 155, 157–9
Buchanan, Capt. John, 14, 43, 49
Buchanan, Mary, later Hastings, 14, 43, 49
Buchanan, Catherine & Elizabeth, 49, 89–90
Burney, Fanny, later Mme d'Arblay, 17
    account of mastectomy, 214–15
    and Madame Schwellenburg, 192
    Evelina, 17
    visit to Hastings & his wife, 192
Burrell, Sir William & Lady Sophia, 192–93, 198, 210
Butler, Rev. Dr, 'Padre', 55
Byfleet, Surrey, 115–16

Calais, 189–90
Calcutta siege & retaking of, 40, 45, 43
Cambridge, 27–8, 88, 121, 137, 156
Carnac, Major John, 16, 79, 125
    comments on Hancock's 'impotency', 59
    comments on PH's pregnancy, 59

Index

comments on PH & WH's
    relationship in Calcutta, 58–60, 80
  description of Elizabeth Sellen, 16
  friendship with Margaret Clive, 38–9
  letters to Margaret Clive, 16, 35,
    38–9, 58, 154
  military career, 54, 67
Carnatic Wars, 30
Château de Jourdan, 182, 186–7
Château Marais, 182, 208, 211, 218
Christ's Hospital School, London, 27
Chunam, 116–17
Clarinda, maidservant, 24, 72–3, 153,
  156, 170
  affection for in Hancock family, 64–5
  background, 64
  depiction by Sir Joshua Reynolds,
    85–6, 161
  illness in France, 161–63, 164
  presumed death in France, 169
  reference to in TSH's letters, 145, 162
Cleland, John, 9
Clive, Lady, *see* Margaret Maskelyne
Clive, Robert, 15, 22
  appointment as Deputy Governor of
    Madras in 1756, 38
  appointment as head of Calcutta
    Council, 1759, 46
  assistance given to Hancock, 40, 46,
    53, 104
  censure of PH in letter to wife, 80
  comments on PH & TSH, 46–7
  death, 141
  departure from India in 1753, 36
  departure from India in 1759, 47
  early life & family background, 36, 46
  marriage to Margaret Maskelyne, 36
  relationship with Hastings, 94
  return to India in 1765, 68
  treatment of wounds by Hancock, 30
  victories in Bengal in 1757, 41–4
  welcome to Fort St David, 38
Cockell, Mrs Elizabeth, 62, 110
Cole, Mrs Hester, milliner, 8–9, 11, 78
Combs-la-Ville, France, 164–5, 168–9
Consols, 150–1, 155, 178

Coramandel Coast, India, vii, 14, 19, 24
Covent Garden, London, 6–9, 11
Cuddalore, India, 30, 40
Cumberlege, Stephen Austen, 156, 178
Cure family, 3–4, 9

Dalrymple, William, 45
Daylesford, Gloucestershire, 185, 197, 212
Danoot, Daniel, Brussels banker, 159–60
Danvers, John & Sarah, 2
Davis, Mrs Ellinor, 152–3, 161
Devikottai, India, 29–30, 32
Dustuck, 93, 99, 166
Dutch East India Company, 43, 49

East India Company, (EIC) 'The
  Company', 12–14, 78
  Court of Directors, 13–14, 94
  factories, 25
  sending European women to India, 15
  appointment as EIC 'servant', 29
  panic & factionalism of, 124
  remittances by EIC 'servants', 98–9
  ships, 14, 18
Elliot, Mary, 14–15
Ellis, William, surgeon, 8
Erikson, Amy Louise, research on
  milliners, 9–10
Essex Street, London, 78

Famine in Bengal in 1770, 94
Fay, Mrs Eliza, 18–20, 34–5, 42, 54
  account of dinner party in
    Calcutta, 42
  conditions on board ship for
    women, 20–21
  dancing & diversions on board
    ship, 21
  husband's 'natural' child, 56
  luggage & valuables taken on board,
    19, 71
  Original Letters from India, 18
  protectress for single woman on
    ship, 20
  return to India, 20
  women & motherhood in India, 54

Feiling, Keith, 52, 55, 58
Feuillide de, Eliza, *née* Hancock, later Austen, vii, x, 163
   admiration for WH, 184
   anxiety about & description of PH in final illness, 213–14, 216–18
   birth & baptism, 62, 64
   birth of son, 189
   brief visit to Paris in 1790, 210–11
   character & personality, 170–1, 180, 196–7, 200–201
   comparison to Mary Crawford, 113–14
   connection to WH, 123, 171–2
   correspondence with Phylly Walter, 156, 163, 165, 170, 176, 179, 183–6, 213, 216–17, 219
   devotion to mother PH, 174, 179, 200, 214–18, 220
   education & accomplishments, 97, 112, 119
   fondness for cousin Jane Austen, 221
   friendship with Comtesse de Tournon, 164–5
   godparents, 62, 64
   horse riding, 113
   impact on Steventon family in 1786, 114
   letters to her father, TSH, 111
   life at Château de Jourdan, 182–3
   marriage to the Comte & married life, 168, 170, 173–4, 176, 180, 208
   move to Château de Jourdan, 180–2
   pregnancy & birth of son, 186, 190
   return to England in 1786, 190, 197
   visit to Steventon after PH's death, 221
de Feuillide, Comte Jean Francois Capot, 168
   access to trust money, 209
   background & family, 168, 171–2, 182
   debts from land works, 185, 202, 204–205, 207–209
   execution, 221
   flees estate in Guyenne, 218
   impact on of political situation in France, 204–205, 210–11, 218
   joins PH & Eliza in Paris in 1788
   marriage to Eliza, 172–73
   military record, 172
   religion, 173
   scheme of land improvement, 177, 182–3, 202
   title, 172
   visits Eliza in London, 220
de Feuillide, Hastings Francois Louis Henri Eugene:
   birth & baptism, 189, 198
   development problems, 195, 197, 199, 201–203
Fishing fleet, 13
Fleet marriages, 1, 27
Forde family, 19
   Francis Forde, Colonel, 19, 152
   Louisa Forde, 19, 152, 161, 219
   Margaret Forde, 152, 161
Fort St David, Madras Presidency, India, 14, 25
   description of settlement, 31
   Governor's Garden House, 38
   siege & capture by French, 44
France, 153
   political disturbances & revolution, 204–205, 208–10
Freeman family 4, 86, 100, 120
   Cope Freeman, 4
   Catherine Margaretta Freeman, *see* Stanhope
   John Cope Freeman, 4, 86
   Mary Clementina Freeman, 'Molly', 4, 86, 124
   Stella Frances Freeman, later Allan, 4, 86–7
Fullerton, Dr William, 46, 54
Fulta, India, 43, 49

Garden houses, 31–3
Gleig, Rev, George Robert, 52, 102
Godowns, 47
Gregg, Hilda Caroline, aka Sydney C. Grier, 14–15, 95

Index

Guyenne, France, 179–81, 186, 202, 207–208

Hampson, Sir George, Bart. MD, 2
Hampson, Frances Elizabeth, later Diggle, 122
Hancock, Colbron, 78, 91, 161, 176
Hancock, Elizabeth, née Colborne, 27
Hancock family portrait by Sir Joshua Reynolds, 85–6
Hancock, Olivia, later Lightfoot, 143, 219
Hancock, Philadelphia, née Austen, (PH):
approval of Eliza's marriage to Comte de Feuillide, 173–4
arrival in Fort St David, 19, 25, 31
assisting at Mrs Austen's confinements, 116, 119
bank account with Hoare & Co., 154, 155–7, 158–9, 178
birth & baptism, 1
birth of daughter, 62, 64
breast cancer & its treatment, 213–18
burial at St John-at-Hampstead Church, 220
challenges to her respectability, 9, 15, 59, 64
character & disposition, 15, 24, 35, 45, 66, 69, 135, 149, 180, 196, 200, 216–17
childlessness, 40, 60
closeness to WH's family, 82–4, 91, 163
correspondence with George Austen, 179
death, 220
death of TSH, 46, 148
debts on TSH's estate, 152–3, 161, 176
devotion to daughter, Eliza, 162–3, 202, 221
domestic responsibilities, 33
early life, 3
as depicted in *Catharine or the Bower*, 24, 26
education, 5–6
end of millinery apprenticeship, 11–12
escape from Fort St David, 44, 47
family visits & connections maintained, 41, 86–7, 106, 151, 179
financial investments after TSH's death, 150–1, 154–5, 178, 183
financial worries & dependence, 94–5, 105–106, 133, 208
financial assistance provided by WH, 98, 130, 132, 212
first impressions of India, 31
French companion for Eliza, 135
friendship with Margaret Clive, 38–41, 79–81
friendship with the Misses Hinchliffe, 88, 157, 159, 163
gifts from India from Hancock, 110
gifts from Hastings, 51, 151, 155
grave, 221
hopes for TSH's advancement, 125
household servants in India, 33, 65, 72–3
house in Calcutta, 55
Indian tastes acquired, 41, 78, 110
influence & recommendations with EIC, 104–105, 136
joint birthday parties for WH & Eliza with Woodman family, 91, 97, 111, 119, 140, 151
journey out to India, 18–22
knowledge of WH's relationship with 'Marian' Hastings, 103, 128–9
letter from Henry Hoare, 1778, 158
letters from WH to PH, 103
letters to John Woodman, 172–3, 206–208
letters to WH from PH, 109, 175
letters to TSH in India 1768–1776, 95, 97, 104
life in Calcutta, 54, 170, 180
life in Kasimbazaar, 47, 50–51
living with Margaret Clive in Calcutta, 1758–59, 44–6
life in Covent Garden as an apprentice milliner, 11
departure for Europe in 1777, 157–8

255

life in Fort St David, 31–7, 41
moving to & living in France, 66, 100, 115, 153–4, 160–64, 169–70, 175–6, 178
life in London after return from India, 72, 77–9, 82, 85–90, 134
limitations of biographical sources, ix
loan to son-in-law, 174, 178, 183–4, 219
marriage prospects, 15–16
marriage to TSH, 32, 59–60
meets WH in Kasimbazaar, 48
millinery apprenticeship, 7–11, 118
miniature portrait by John Smart, 25, 110, 143
move to Bolton Street, Mayfair, 89, 91
move to Château de Jourdan, 179–82
move to Hertford Street, Mayfair, 114, 172
move to Orchard Street, Marylebone in 1786 & again in 1791, 193, 212
Paris visit en route to England in 1786, 187
peripatetic life, 4, 53, 210–11
petition to EIC, 14
pregnancy, 60
proposal to return to India, 125–6, 128–9
relationship with TSH, 133–4, 141–2, 144
relationship with WH, 50–1, 58–9, 64, 66, 128–30, 144, 162–3, 193–4, 220–1
return to England from France in 1786, 185–7
return to England from France in 1789, 207, 209
return to France in 1788, 202–204, 206
journey home to England from India in 1765, 68–9, 72–5
rumours & gossip of daughter being WH's child, 59, 125, 153, 171
shipboard life, 75
social life in Fort St David, 35, 39, 42

social life in Calcutta, 63
social status in India, 32–3
surviving letter to WH, 51, 152, 160–63, 194
trust money from WH, 147, 207, 209
visits to Steventon, 194, 195–97, 201, 210
waistcoats for TSH, 118–19, 123–4
Will, 218–20
Hancock, Rev. Thomas Saul, 27
Hancock, Thomas Jnr., 28
Hancock, Thomas Snr., 27
Hancock, Tysoe Saul (TSH), 15
  attitude to surgical practice, 30
  birth & baptism, 27
  business partnership with WH, 50, 55, 57
  Calcutta appointment in 1760, 53
  career as surgeon in India, 29
  character & disposition, 27, 33, 50, 96, 120–1, 124, 134, 144
  client of Francis Austen, 25, 106
  Clive's recommendation for Calcutta appointment, 48
  complaints of ill-health, 128, 134, 144–5
  criticism of George Austen's growing family, 116
  death in India, 145–7
  debts, 117, 143
  describes Hastings appointment as G-G of Bengal, 124
  Devikottai appointment, 29
  difficulties experienced on return to India, 93–4
  early life & education, 27
  escape from Fort St David in 1758, 44, 47
  expenses for return to England, 72
  expenses in Calcutta after return, 105
  family background, 27–8
  fears his daughter will forget him, 98
  financial difficulties, 72, 89–92, 94, 98
  Fort St George appointment in 1758, 44
  godfather to George Austen Jnr., 83

Index

Goslings Bank account, 90, 94
Kasimbazaar appointment, 46
lack of 'dustuck' on return to India, 99
lack of success in India & influence with WH, 117, 130–1, 140
letter book among 'Hastings Papers', *see* Letter book of TSH from India 1769–1775
letter to Eliza re 'Persian cat' from WH, 142
letters to PH from India, 93, 96–7
marriage, 29–30, 133
on Margaret Clive's 'coolness' to PH, 81
opinion of PH's relationship with WH, 128
opinion of Philip Dormer Stanhope, 138
reappointment as EIC Surgeon in Calcutta, 176
resigns as EIC surgeon in 1760, 57
return to England, 69
return to India in 1769, 93
salary as a surgeon, 26
'secrecy' regarding WH's 'present' to Eliza, 132
skill as a surgeon, 30
surgeon's apprenticeship, 27–8
surgeon's mate appointment, 29
treatment of Robert Clive's wounds, 30
Will, 142–3, 161
Hastings & Hancock trading company, 50, 57, 60, 69, 89
Hastings, Elizabeth, 83, 191
Hastings, George, 48, 50, 55–7
Hastings, Marian, *née* Anna-Maria Chapuset, formerly Baroness von Imhoff, 11, 68, 71, 101, 128, 144, 184, 193
Hastings Papers in British Library, 95
Hastings, Warren (WH), x, 43, 152–3
  affection for Eliza, 51
  appointment as governor-general of Bengal, 124, 172
  appointment & service on Calcutta Council, 55, 58, 63, 66–8
  birth of son, 50
  character, disposition, & scholarship, 58
  conflict with Calcutta Council, 67
  connections to PH's family, 43, 49, 56–7
  death of first wife, 48–49
  Deputy-Governor of Madras, 94, 98
  diary entries on PH, 189–90, 192–3, 203–204, 209, 212, 217–19
  early life & family background & education, 45, 52, 58
  executor of TSH's Will, 143
  executor of PH's Will, 218, 220
  fame, 153, 159, 171
  financial difficulties, 89–90
  departure from India in 1765, 73
  gifts to PH, 51
  gift of money in trust to Eliza, 130, 132, 144
  godfather to Eliza, 62, 64
  house in Park Lane, 211–12
  illness in London, 90
  impeachment & trial, 184–5, 188–90, 192, 197–98, 201–203
  imprisonment in Kasimbazaar during Calcutta siege, 50
  letter to Amelia Vansittart contrasted with letter to PH, 51
  letters to TSH, 108–109, 112
  letter to TSH to seek accommodation for Baron von Imhoff in Calcutta, 116
  life in London, 1765–1770, 84
  love affair with Anna-Maria Chapuset von Imhoff, 'Marian', 101, 126, 128
  marriage to Anna-Maria Chapuset Baroness von Imhoff, 'Marian', 169
  marriage to Mary Buchanan, 43, 50
  ménage à trois in Madras 1770, 58, 103
  meeting PH in Kasimbazaar, 47

257

nature & significance of relationship with PH, x–xi, 50, 58, 101, 129
opinion on sea travel, 76
passionate nature of love for 'Marian', 102
portrait of by Reynolds, 84, 119
rescues TSH from failed chunam venture, 117
residency in Murshidabad, 48, 52–3
resignation from EIC in 1764, 68
return to India in 1770, 94, 102
return to London in 1765, 73, 75–6, 78
surviving letter to PH, p. 49, 51–2, 129, 131
Herries, Sir Robert & 'Herries Notes', 159–60
Hertford Street, Mayfair, 114–15, 134, 154
Hicks, Miss, later Lacey, 20, 56
Hickey, William, 23
Hinchliffe, Misses Martha & Elizabeth, 88, 157, 159, 178
Hinchliffe, John, Bishop of Peterborough, 88
Hinton, John, stationer & publisher, 82, 135, 156
Hoare & Co, Bank, London, 83, 147, 154–5, 158–9
Hogarth sisters, Mary & Anne, milliners, 10
Hollingbourne, Kent, 27
Holwell, John Zephaniah, 48
Hooper, George, 2–3
Hughli River, Bengal, India, 46–7

von Imhoff, Baron Karl, 102, 126, 136, 149
von Imhoff, Baroness Anna-Maria Apollonia, *née* Chapuset, *see* Hastings, Marian
Impey, Lady Mary, 33, 103
Impey, Sir Elijah, 33
Ironside, Col. Gilbert, 63, 124
Ironside, Mary, 26, 63
Ives, Edward, 31–2

Kasimbazaar, Bengal, India, 43, 46–7
Keirnander, Rev John, 41
Kelk, Susannah, later Austen, 2, 86
Kelsall, Jenny, later Latham, then Strachey, 13, 37, 39, 104–105
Knight, Mr & Mrs Thomas, of Godmershan, 186–7

Lacam, Benjamin, merchant, 116
Lambert, Sir John, Paris banker, 160, 169
Lardner, John, haberdasher, 14
Larkins, Captain, 93–4, 97
Larkins, William, accountant, 143
Latham, Capt. Thomas, 39
Le Faye, Deirdre, 154
Jane Austen's Outlandish Cousin, x, 163
view of PH's millinery apprenticeship, 11
reason why PH moved to France, 154
Liege, Samuel, surgeon, 27
Leigh family of Adlestrop, 43, 56
Le Marais de Gabarret et de Barbotan, France, 177
Letter book of TSH from India 1769–1775, 95–6, 141
admonishment of PH, 127, 133
description of visit to the Sunderbunds, 116–17
final letters, 145–6
letters to Eliza, 111
objections to PH & Eliza returning to India, 127–8
on Eliza's education & health, 97, 112
on gifts to PH, 109–10, 118
on living arrangements in Calcutta, 97, 105
on money problems, 97, 105
on PH's character & disposition, 103
on Philip Dormer Stanhope, 136–9
on the waistcoats PH makes for him, 118–19, 123
'present' to Eliza from WH, 131–2
regarding picture of Eliza, 110
regarding WH, 97, 105, 110, 131–2

Index

Lifestyle of British in 18th century India:
   children, 56
   eating & drinking, 41–2
   travel, 34–5
   afternoon rest, 42
   music & balls, 42
   effects of climate & diseases, 46
   social mores & relationships, 45–6, 51
London 'Season', 198
Louis XV, King of France, 165
Lothian's Hotel, London, 190

Macmillan, Margaret, 53
Madras Presidency, India, 25
Margate, Kent, 211
Marie Antoinette, Queen of France, 164–5, 198
Marriott, Randall, 53, 89
Maskelyne, Margaret (later Lady Clive), 13, 16, 21, 70–1, 141, 152, 154, 170
   arrival in Fort St David in 1756, 25, 38
   character & personality, 22, 39
   children, 37, 41–2, 44, 54
   ending of friendship with PH, 80–1
   enjoyment of life in India, 35
   esteem held for PH, 38–9, 79–80
   family background, 22
   godmother to Eliza, 62, 64, 79
   return to England in 1760, 19, 47, 54, 79
   friendship with PH, 16, 38–9, 41, 47, 79
   letter to John Carnac, re PH, 77, 79–81
   letters to John Carnac, 38, 45–6, 80–1
   letters re Elizabeth Sellen, 22
   marriage to Robert Clive, 36
   move to Calcutta to join Clive, 44
   opinion of PH in letter to John Carnac, 77, 79–80
   on single women going out to India, 16
   pregnancies & confinements, 37, 39, 41–2
   return to India in 1753, 36

Masulah boats, 24
Medical Register of India, 44
Medical profession in 18th C England, 27–9
Milliners, 10–11
Mir Jaffir, 43, 66
Mir Kasim, 66–7
Mitchell, Dr Charlotte & Gwendolen research on Reynolds portrait of Hancock family, 85–6
Murshidabad, India, 43, 47

Nettine. Madame Louise (Brussels banker), 155, 157–8
Nerac, France, 171
Norfolk Street, London, 78, 83

Old South Sea Annuities, 151
Orchard Street, Marylebone, 193, 198, 201–202, 219

Palanquins, 34
Pattle, Captain Thomas, 160, 168–9
   PH & Eliza's visit to home in Paris in 1786, 188–9
Payne, George 3, 86–7, 122
Payne, Maria, 3, 122
Potts, Percival, 28
Powell, Capt. Caleb, 58–9
Plassey, Battle of, victory, 42–3
Price-Jones, Rev. John, 4

Respondentia bonds, 130, 132
Reynolds, Sir Joshua:
   Hancock family portrait, 25, 84–6
   Hastings portrait, 84–6
Rice, Count James Louis, 166–7
Rosalie, maidservant, 201, 209
Roundels, 34

Sainte Meille, France, 182, 187
Sellen, Elizabeth, later Reed, 16, 26, 34
'Seven Years' War', 30, 154
Smith, General Richard, 99–100, 166–7
South Park Cemetery, Calcutta, 146

Stanhope, Catherine Margaretta *née* Freeman, later Price-Jones, 4, 86, 120–1, 136
Stanhope, Philip Dormer, 121, 136, 142, 145
   Genuine memoirs of Asiaticus, 121, 137
   assistance by TSH in India, 137–9
   adventures in India, 137–9
   praise of TSH, 138–9
   tribute to TSH on his death, 1775, 145–6
Staveley, Rev. Stanley, 30, 63, 73
Steventon Rectory, Hampshire, 91, 106, 113–14, 151, 202
St George's Hanover Square, London, 83, 189, 198
Summer, William, money lender, 90, 94, 103
Sykes, Sir Francis, 53, 56–7, 90, 124

The *Aurora*, 124, 152
The *Bombay Castle*, vii, 14, 18, 25, 36, 220
The *Duke of Grafton*, 102
The *Grosvenor*, 54
The *Larkins*, 93
The *Lioness*, 93–4, 97
The *Medway*, 73, 75–6
The *Tyger*, 39, 105
Tilden, George, attorney, 8
Tilden, Mary, 1
Tomalin, Claire, 8–9, 58
Tonbridge, Kent, xi, 1, 3
de Tournon, Rose-Marie-Hélène, Vicomtesse du Barry, later Marquise de Claveson, 164–8, 170
Tunbridge Wells, Kent, 2, 173, 186, 199, 203, 211

Vansittart family, 16
   Vansittart, Amelia, *née* Morse, 16, 51, 61
   Vansittart, Emelia, later Parry, 126–7

George Vansittart, 151
Vansittart, Henry, 16, 55, 63, 65, 67–8
   lost at sea on *The Aurora*, 124
Verelst, Henry, 93–4
Versailles, France, 154, 164, 176, 210
Vick, Robin, 8–9

Wales, Frederick Louis, Prince of, 3, 9
Walter family, 2, 87, 106
   Philadelphia Walter, 'Phylly', x, 106, 122
   admiration for WH's wife Marian, 193
   high opinion of PH, 200
   letters to brother James, 199–200, 203, 217
   opinion of Eliza, 200–201
   visits to PH & Eliza, 193, 199–200, 203, 213
   Rev, James Walter, 156, 199, 217
   Susannah Walter, née Weaver, 24, 106
   William Walter, surgeon, 2
   William-Hampson Walter, 2, 87, 122, 217, 219
Westminster School, 52, 84, 88
Woodman, Anne *née* Hastings, 83, 89, 191
Woodman, John:
   as Hastings' London agent, 103
   correspondence with Hastings re PH, 140, 151, 154, 158–9, 163, 172–6, 184
   news of death of TSH conveyed to PH, 148
   payment of £1,000 to Baron von Imhoff, on WH's behalf, 136
Woodman, Thomas 'Tommy', 83–4
Wollstonecraft, Mary, 6
Wormshill, Kent, 27

Yateley, Hampshire, 4, 121
Yorke, Major Martin, 200